Herausgegeben von / Edited by
Wolfgang Jean Stock

Mit Beiträgen von / Essays by
Friedrich Achleitner, Fabrizio Brentini, Marc Dubois,
Albert Gerhards, Winfried Nerdinger, Riitta Nikula,
Wolfgang Pehnt, Gabriele Schickel, Horst Schwebel,
Wolfgang Jean Stock

Prestel
München / Munich · Berlin · London · New York

Dieses Buch wurde angeregt von Architekt Erhard Fischer, dem ersten Vorsitzenden des Vereins Ausstellungshaus für christliche Kunst e.V., München. Der 1918 von katholischen Künstlern und Kunstfreunden gegründete Verein soll nach seiner Satzung die Kunst auf der Grundlage des christlichen Glaubens fördern. Dem Kirchenbau als Baukunst gilt seine besondere Aufmerksamkeit. Für dieses Buch hat der Verein Ausstellungshaus die Grundfinanzierung übernommen, darunter die Kosten für Recherchen, Bildbeschaffung, Archiv- und Fotorechte sowie für Redaktion und Honorare.

Konzeption, Redaktion und Texte zu den Bauten:
Wolfgang Jean Stock

This book was the idea of Erhard Fischer, architect and first chairman of the Verein Ausstellungshaus für christliche Kunst e.V., in Munich. This organisation, which was founded in 1918 by Catholic artists and patrons, is committed in its statutes to the promotion of art based on the Christian faith. Church architecture thus attracts its particular attention. The Verein Ausstellungshaus has generously financed this book, in particular the costs of research, picture fees, archive and photographic rights, as well as editing fees and royalties.

This volume was created and developed by Wolfgang Jean Stock, who also contributed the project texts.

Inhalt

Contents

Fast vier Jahrzehnte sind vergangen, seit der europäische Kirchenbau letztmals in Buchform behandelt wurde. Nach ausführlichen Recherchen hatte der amerikanische Architekt und Autor George E. Kidder Smith 1964 seinen Band *Neuer Kirchenbau in Europa* veröffentlicht. Bei diesem kritischen Überblick von christlichen Sakralbauten seit 1945 standen fachliche Gesichtspunkte der Architektur im Mittelpunkt.

Dieses Buch verfolgt einen erweiterten Ansatz. Vor allem das Zweite Vatikanische Konzil (1962–1965) hat das Verständnis vom Kirchenbau entscheidend verändert. Architekten und Gemeinden haben darauf sehr unterschiedlich reagiert. Um auch der irrigen Auffassung zu begegnen, Kirchenbau sei eine ›zweckfreie‹ Aufgabe, betont dieses Buch die Ansprüche von Theologie und Liturgie an die architektonische Lösung. Zwei einleitende Fachaufsätze erläutern deshalb das ›Kirchenbild‹ aus katholischer und protestantischer Sicht. Auf dieser Grundlage haben wir uns dafür entschieden, die Thematik des Buches auf jene europäischen Länder zu beschränken, in denen die Entwicklung des Kirchenbaus nach dem Zweiten Weltkrieg mit vergleichbarer Kontinuität verlaufen ist: Es ist der bis 1990 übliche Begriff von ›Westeuropa‹.

Die vorgestellten Bauten sind eine Auswahl aus mehreren hundert Kirchen und Kapellen, die der Herausgeber besichtigt hat. Einige Beispiele wurden aufgrund von Empfehlungen der Autoren aufgenommen. Genau 60 Bauten sind einzeln dokumentiert, weitere 85 werden im Rahmen der sieben Essays gezeigt, die wichtigen Personen und Regionen gewidmet sind. Als Datum ist das Jahr der Fertigstellung angegeben. Nicht selten standen wir vor der Qual der Wahl. Dabei haben wir uns bemüht, im Einzelfall in gerechter Weise abzuwägen. Die wesentlichen Kriterien für unsere Auswahl waren: Charakter und Qualität der Architektur (vom Städtebau bis zum Detail), ihre historische Bedeutung im nationalen oder regionalen Zusammenhang, die Bezüge zur neuen Liturgie – Kirche als stimulierender Erlebnis- und Handlungsraum.

Dieses Buch ist eine Gemeinschaftsarbeit. Besonders die Autoren der Essays haben das Projekt mit ungewöhnlichem Einsatz unterstützt. Für Hinweise oder praktische Hilfe geht ein ebenso herzlicher Dank an Kaye Geipel in Berlin, die Botschaftsräte Ritva-Liisa Elomaa und Kaj Virtarinne in Helsinki, Christiane Lange und Elfriede Strothmann in München, Ulf Grønvold in Oslo, Walter Zahner in Regensburg, Peter Blundell Jones in Sheffield sowie an Benedikt Loderer und Irma Noseda in Zürich. Ohne eine erhebliche finanzielle Förderung kann ein Buch wie dieses heutzutage nicht mehr erscheinen. Der zunehmende Aufwand bei der Bildbeschaffung wie auch bei den Kosten für Archiv- und Fotorechte macht eine normale Kalkulation unmöglich. In unserem Fall kam hinzu, dass auch viele Maßstäbe und Nordpfeile recherchiert werden mussten, da solche Angaben sogar in Fachbüchern nicht mehr selbstverständlich sind. Außerdem wurde die Mehrzahl der Pläne neu gezeichnet.

Herausgeber und Verlag danken deshalb dem Verein Ausstellungshaus für christliche Kunst e.V., München, für seinen überaus großzügigen Beitrag zu den Kosten dieser Veröffentlichung. Wir wünschen uns, das Buch möge nicht nur Architekten und Planer anregen, sondern auch alle jene, die als Auftraggeber für die Baukultur der beiden großen christlichen Kirchen verantwortlich sind.

It is almost forty years since European church building was last dealt with in book form. According to our extensive research, the American architect and author George E. Kidder Smith published his volume *The New Churches of Europe* in 1964. This critical survey of Christian religious building since 1945 focused mainly on architecture from the technical point of view.

The present book takes a broader approach. It was the Second Vatican Council (1962–65), in particular, that brought about decisive changes in our understanding of church construction. Architects and congregations reacted to this in very different ways. In order to counter the incorrect view that the building of churches is a 'pure' task, this book also emphasises the theological and liturgical demands made on any architectural solution. Two introductory essays thus elucidate the 'image of the church' from Roman Catholic and Protestant perspectives. This formed the basis for our decision to limit the book's subject-matter to those European countries in which the development of church-building following the Second World War has shown comparable continuity: in other words, we have restricted our coverage to what was generally meant by the term 'Western Europe' up until 1990.

The buildings presented here are a selection from the several hundred churches and chapels that the editor visited. A few examples were included on the basis of recommendations by the authors. Exactly 60 buildings are documented individually. A further 85 are illustrated within the framework of the seven essays devoted to important people and regions. In every case, the date cited is the year of completion. Not infrequently we were faced with the agony of choice, but we endeavoured to weigh up individual cases fairly. The basic criteria for selection were: character and quality of the architecture (from urban development down to the details), its historical importance in the national or regional context, and its references to the new liturgy — the church as a stimulating space for experience and action.

This book is a team effort. The authors of the essays, in particular, have shown uncommon commitment in their support for the project. For advice and practical assistance we must also extend heartfelt thanks to Kaye Geipel in Berlin, to the embassy officials Ritva-Liisa Elomaa and Kaj Virtarinne in Helsinki, to Christiane Lange and Elfriede Strothmann in Munich, Ulf Grønvold in Oslo, Walter Zahner in Regensburg, Peter Blundell Jones in Sheffield, and Benedikt Loderer and Irma Noseda in Zurich. It is no longer possible nowadays for a book such as this to appear without considerable financial support. The increasing expense of obtaining picture material, as well as the rising costs of archival and photographic rights, make any normal estimates impossible. In our case there was the added factor that numerous scales and compass arrows had to be researched, since such information is no longer a matter of course, even in reference books. In addition, the majority of the plans have been redrawn.

The Editor and Publishers are thus grateful to the organisation Ausstellungshaus für christliche Kunst e.V., Munich, for its very generous contribution to the costs of this publication. We hope the book will inspire not just architects and planners but also all those who, as clients, are responsible for the architectural culture of two great Christian Churches.

Wolfgang Jean Stock

Von Aalto bis Zumthor
Fünfzig Jahre europäischer Kirchenbau

Den Auftrag für einen Kirchenbau dürfe der Architekt nicht
»nach der Fachroutine« auffassen, mahnte der Münchner
Theologe Aloys Goergen am Ende der fünfziger Jahre, in genau
jener Zeit, als der europäische Sakralbau einen bis dahin noch
nicht gekannten Boom erlebte. Weil sich der Kirchenbau von
den anderen Aufgaben der Architektur grundsätzlich unterschei-
de, hänge nicht alles von den künstlerischen Fähigkeiten ab.
Vielmehr habe das Bauwerk in erster Linie den »inneren Erfor-
dernissen« zu genügen, den präzisen Ansprüchen von Theologie
und Seelsorge, »den Voraussetzungen, die sich vom Geschehen
im Kirchenraum aus ergeben«. Gerade weil Goergen als ehe-
maliger Assistent von Romano Guardini für eine grundlegende
Reform der katholischen Kirche stritt, beispielsweise schon
vor dem Zweiten Vatikanum (1962–1965) für eine neue Liturgie
eintrat, sprach er sich mit Nachdruck gegen nur »stimmungs-
volle« oder allgemein »erhebende« Räume aus. Auch der neue
Kirchenbau müsse die geistige Übereinstimmung von Aufgabe
und Lösung verkörpern.[1]

Mitteleuropa als Zentrum der Entwicklung

Damals lag der Beginn der neuen Kirchenarchitektur lediglich
eine Generation zurück, selbst heute umfasst ihre Geschichte
nicht mehr als 70 Jahre. Ins Leben trat der moderne Sakralbau
mit der 1923 fertiggestellten Eglise Notre-Dame in Le Raincy,
einer Arbeiterstadt in der östlichen Peripherie von Paris. Diese
urbane Kirche von Auguste Perret (1874–1954) bedeutete
eine radikale Zäsur: Das ganze Gebäude besteht aus Stahlbeton,
und zwar von der tragenden Struktur bis hin zu den Wand-
feldern, die als Fertigteile hergestellt und deren Öffnungen mit
farbigen Gläsern geschlossen wurden. Die von Licht durchflu-
tete Kirche, die sich bis heute in einem erstaunlich guten Zustand befindet, wirkte als Fanal und Vorbild. Als herausragender
Folgebau entstand 1926/27 die Antoniuskirche in Basel, ein
Hauptwerk des großen Architekten Karl Moser (1860–1936).
Im Stadtraum durch einen hoch aufragenden Turm markiert,
wird auch diese erste Sichtbetonkirche in der Schweiz durch
neue Materialien und Konstruktionsweisen bestimmt. Wiederum zaubern farbige Glasfenster wechselnde Lichtspiele auf dem
rau verschalten, natürlich belassenen Beton.

Bis zum Ende der zwanziger Jahre konnte sich in mehreren
europäischen Ländern eine Avantgarde des Kirchenbaus heraus-
bilden. Wie der folgende Aufsatz von Albert Gerhards darlegt,
wurde der architektonische Aufbruch in katholischen Kreisen
von einem neuen Kirchenverständnis begleitet. Die Trennung in
ein Presbyterium (Priesterraum, Chor) und Laienraum wurde
aufgehoben, der Altar in die Mitte der Gemeinde gestellt. Neue
Architektur und neue Liturgie kamen dabei nicht immer zur
Deckung: Während die erste deutsche Gemeinschaftsmesse 1921
in der spätromanischen Krypta der Benediktinerabtei Maria
Laach zelebriert wurde, hielt zum Beispiel der moderne Kirchenbaumeister Rudolf Schwarz (1897–1961) zunächst an der
klassischen Wegkirche fest. Die parallele Reformbewegung kam
vor allem in mehreren Kirchen von Martin Weber (1890–1941)
nach dem ›christozentrischen Konzept‹ zum Ausdruck.[2]

Über alle sieben Jahrzehnte hinweg lagen die Schwerpunkte der
neuen Kirchenarchitektur in den mitteleuropäischen Ländern,
besonders in Deutschland, in Österreich und der Schweiz. Doch
auch dort fand der Protestantismus im Wesentlichen erst nach
dem Zweiten Weltkrieg den Anschluss an die Diskussion über

Karl Moser
St. Antonius / St Antonius
Basel, 1927

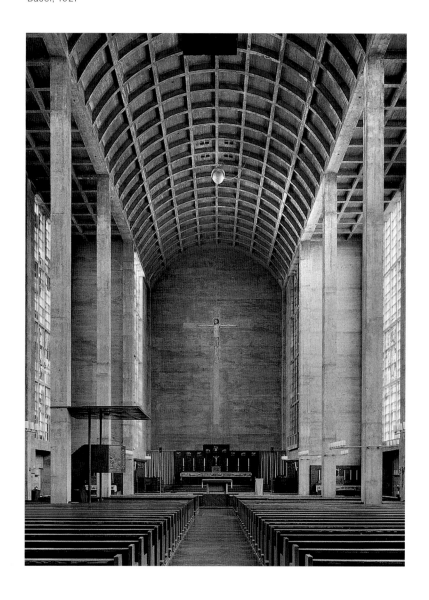

Wolfgang Jean Stock

From Aalto to Zumthor
Fifty Years of European Church Building

An architect should not approach a commission to build a church 'in a routine technical manner', urged the Munich theologian Aloys Goergen in the late 1950s, exactly at the time when European religious building was experiencing a hitherto unknown boom. Since church building was totally different from other architectural projects, not everything would depend on artistic capabilities. Rather, the structure would primarily have to fulfil 'inner requirements', meet precise theological and pastoral needs, 'prerequisites arising from the events inside the church'. Precisely because Goergen, as a former assistant of Romano Guardini, was arguing for fundamental reform of the Roman Catholic Church, indeed even prior to the Second Vatican Council (1962–65) advocating a new liturgy, he declared his emphatic opposition to merely 'atmospheric' or generally 'uplifting' spaces. New churches too must incorporate the spiritual concordance of task and solution.[1]

Central Europe as a Centre of Development

At that time the start of the new church architecture was only one generation old, and even today its history spans no more than seventy years. Modern religious architecture sprang into life with the church of Notre-Dame in Le Raincy, a working-class town on the eastern periphery of Paris. Completed in 1923, this urbane church by Auguste Perret (1874–1954) signified a radical break: the entire building was made of reinforced concrete, from the load-bearing structure to the prefabricated wall sections, whose apertures were filled with coloured glass. Still in a surprisingly good condition today, this light-filled church acted as both signal and exemplar. It was followed in 1926/27 by the superlative church of St Anthony (Antoniuskirche) in Basel, one of the principal works of the great architect Karl Moser (1860–1936). Marked out within the city by its tall tower, this church — the first in Switzerland to employ exposed concrete — is also characterised by new materials and new construction techniques. Here again, stained-glass windows create an enchanting play of light on the raw formwork of concrete which has been left *au naturel*.

An avant-garde of religious construction was able to develop up to the late 1920s in a number of European countries. As the following essay by Albert Gerhards explains, these architectural departures were accompanied in Catholic circles by a new understanding of churches. The separation into presbyterium (chancel and sanctuary, reserved for the officiating priest or clergy) and nave (lay congregation) was abolished and the altar was placed in the middle of the congregation. But new architecture and new liturgy did not always coincide: while the first German communal Mass was celebrated in 1921 in the late Romanesque crypt of the Benedictine abbey of Maria Laach, the modern church architect Rudolf Schwarz (1897–1961), for instance, initially adhered to the classic processional church layout. The parallel reform movement was primarily expressed in several churches built by Martin Weber (1890–1941) in accordance with the 'Christocentric concept'.[2]

Over these seven decades the new church architecture was mainly concentrated in the countries of Central Europe, particularly in Germany, Austria and Switzerland. But even here it was only basically after the Second World War that Protestantism joined in the discussion about the 'church in our time'. One important exception was Finland: modern architecture there was regarded

Karl Moser
St. Antonius / St Antonius
Basel, 1927

›Kirche in unserer Zeit‹. Eine wichtige Ausnahme bildet Finnland: Weil hier die moderne Architektur als ein Sinnbild des jungen, seit 1917 unabhängigen Staates galt, wurde auch die lutherische Staatskirche sehr früh von den neuen Bestrebungen erfasst. Daneben gibt es für die Zeit nach 1950 im europäischen Rahmen mehrere Sonderfälle. Einige seien hier genannt: in den Niederlanden Aldo van Eyck mit seiner ›strukturalistischen‹ Auffassung, in Italien die Versuche von Angelo Mangiarotti mit einem modularen Bausystem, in Schweden die Raumschöpfungen des ›Einzelgängers‹ Sigurd Lewerentz, in Portugal die typologische Neuinterpretation von Álvaro Siza.

Kirchenbau und Architekturgeschichte

Wolfgang Pehnt hat bemerkt, sakrale Bauten zu entwerfen, sei »immer als eine Aufgabe von besonderem Rang empfunden worden«.[3] Weil es im Kirchenbau stets um ganz eigene Dimensionen geht, um Spiritualität und Sinnfälligkeit, hat er auch dazu herausgefordert, dass bei ihm die verschiedenen Richtungen der modernen Architektur seit 1950 in ebenso zugespitzter wie reiner Form zutage treten konnten. Auf diese Weise lässt sich der europäische Kirchenbau als ein prägnanter Ausdruck der Architekturgeschichte lesen – von der jeweiligen Grundströmung bis hin zu experimentellen Ansätzen.

Ohne die verschiedenen Abschnitte über einen Leisten zu schlagen, kann man über die Ländergrenzen hinweg deutliche Parallelen feststellen. In der ersten Nachkriegszeit ist es nicht nur wegen der begrenzten Mittel eine bewusst bescheidene, eine unmonumentale Haltung. Während der fünfziger Jahre werden wieder verstärkt die neuen Materialien wie etwa Stahlbeton in den Kirchenbau eingeführt. Durch die Ausstrahlung von Le Corbusiers 1955 vollendeter Wallfahrtskapelle in Ronchamp, die weithin als ein ›Wendepunkt‹ verstanden wurde, tauchen auch in Belgien und in der Schweiz vermehrt bauplastische Formen auf. Diese konkurrieren im Verlauf der sechziger Jahre mit dem häufig kubisch gestalteten Beton-Brutalismus, vor allem aber mit konstruktivistischen Konzeptionen: organoide, ›weiche‹ Baukörper bilden den Gegensatz zu Montagebauten aus Stahl-Fertigteilen. Während der siebziger Jahre dominiert in vielen Ländern, auch als Folge der 68er Bewegung, die Vorstellung vom kirchlichen Mehrzweckraum – die Gebäude werden anonym bis unscheinbar, nicht zuletzt im städtebaulichen Kontext. In dieser Krisensituation nehmen zugleich die Aufträge aus den beiden großen christlichen Kirchen rapide ab.

Kritik und Krise sakraler Architektur

Für aufmerksame Zeitgenossen hatte die Krise der kirchlichen Baukultur freilich viel früher eingesetzt. Mit guten Gründen erhoben sie ihre kritischen Stimmen bereits nach 1960, als die sakrale Bautätigkeit in ganz Europa quantitativ auf dem Höhepunkt stand. So prangerte der österreichische Jesuit Herbert Muck die »Erfolgsritter« unter den Architekten an, die zusammen mit schwachen Bauherren anstelle von Qualität »faule Kompromisse« verwirklichten.[4] Friedrich Achleitner wies an aktuellen Beispielen einen fatalen Hang zum »Modernismus« nach: Durch die oberflächliche, beliebige Mischung moderner Elemente werde der Kirchenbau zur »marktschreierischen« Mode herabgewürdigt, zu einem neuen Eklektizismus, der nur gefallen wolle.[5]

Le Corbusiers Wallfahrtskapelle in Ronchamp auf einem Buchumschlag von 1956
Le Corbusier's pilgrimage chapel at Ronchamp on a book jacket from 1956

as a symbol of the young state, which had only been independent since 1917, with the result that the Lutheran State Church was influenced by the new aspirations at a very early stage. There were several other exceptions in the post-1950 European context. We should mention a few of them here: in the Netherlands, Aldo van Eyck with his 'structuralist' approach; in Italy, Angelo Mangiarotti's experiments with a modular construction system; in Sweden, the spatial creations of the 'loner' Sigurd Lewerentz; and in Portugal the novel typological interpretations of Álvaro Siza.

Church Building and the History of Architecture

Wolfgang Pehnt has remarked that the design of religious buildings has 'always been considered a task of particular status'.[3] Because church building is always a matter of quite specific dimensions, of spirituality and of 'making manifest', it also invited the various movements in modern architecture after 1950 to be realised in a manner that was as specific as it was pure. European church building can therefore be read as a succinct expression of architectural history — from the underlying trend of a particular period down to experimental attempts.

Without measuring the various phases by the same yardstick, one can identify clear parallels that transcend national borders. In the initial post-war period the approach was deliberately unassuming, unmonumental, and not just because of limited funds. During the 1950s new materials such as reinforced concrete were again increasingly introduced into church building. As a result of the impact of Le Corbusier's pilgrimage chapel in Ronchamp, completed in 1955, which was widely understood as a 'turning point', three-dimensional forms emerged to a greater extent in Belgium and Switzerland too. During the course of the 1960s these competed with the often cubic designs of 'Brutalist' concrete but especially with Constructivist concepts: organoid, 'soft' edifices contrasting with the montage constructions of steel assembly units. During the 1970s, the idea of the church as a multi-functional space was predominant in many countries, also as a consequence of the 1968 movement; churches become anonymous or even inconspicuous, not least in the context of town planning. In this critical situation the commissions from the two major Christian Churches rapidly declined at the same time.

Criticism and Crisis in Religious Architecture

Admittedly, for interested contemporaries the crisis in the culture of religious building had begun much earlier. Critical voices were already being raised after 1960 with good reason, when church building activity all over Europe was at its quantitative peak. Thus the Austrian Jesuit Herbert Muck denounced those architects 'riding the crest of success' who, together with weak clients, were producing 'lazy compromises' instead of works of quality.[4] Using topical examples Friedrich Achleitner demonstrated the fatal tendency towards 'Modernism': as a result of the superficial, arbitrary mix of modern elements church building was degenerating into 'ostentatious' fashion, a new eclecticism that wanted only to please.[5]

Complaints in Great Britain about the lack of pioneering sacred buildings were particularly vehement. In 1965 *Architectural Review* wrote that new towns and housing estates since the war

Frank Hammoutène
Notre Dame de Pentecôte
Paris, La Défense, 2000

Besonders vehement beklagte man in Großbritannien den Mangel an wegweisenden Sakralbauten: »Unsere neuen Städte und Siedlungen wurden seit dem Krieg mit schicken Kirchen übersät, für die man auf amateurhafte Weise unkonventionelle Konstruktionen ausgebeutet hat, mit dem Ergebnis stacheliger Dachformen und dürftiger Ornamente.«[6] Nach seinen ausführlichen Recherchen sparte auch der amerikanische Autor George E. Kidder Smith nicht mit Kritik am neuen Kirchenbau in Europa: »Den heutigen Architekten stehen geradezu atemberaubende Möglichkeiten offen, wobei die neue Freiheit allerdings auch oft missbraucht wurde. Abschreckende Beispiele sind die modernistisch aufgetakelten Kirchen, die man besonders in neuen Vorstadtsiedlungen immer wieder antrifft.«[7]

Renaissance des Kirchenbaus

Weil der Kirchenbau bis in die späten sechziger Jahre hinein eine durch viele Aufträge privilegierte ›Leitaufgabe‹ der Architektur darstellte, kamen bei ihm auch die Fehlentwicklungen und Irrwege besonders deutlich zum Ausdruck. Von den krisenhaften Erscheinungen blieben im Wesentlichen nur die skandinavischen Länder verschont. Gerade Finnland kann auf der Basis seiner breit verankerten Architekturmoderne eine durchgängig hohe Qualität des protestantischen Kirchenbaus vorweisen. Auf katholischer Seite hatten die Liturgische Bewegung und seit dem Zweiten Vatikanum die Liturgiereform viele experimentelle Lösungen angeregt. Besonders bedeutsam waren die radikalen Ansätze des Österreichers Ottokar Uhl, der sich schon früh für »partizipatorische« Sakralräume eingesetzt hatte.[8]

Es gibt etliche Gründe, weshalb der europäische Kirchenbau vor der Jahrtausendwende eine Renaissance erlebt hat – sie reichen von neuen Siedlungsgebieten bis hin zur Beseitigung von Provisorien. In einer Welt, die dem Ökonomismus wie der Unterhaltung verfallen scheint, sind Kirchen und Kapellen oftmals die einzigen ›anderen‹ Orte: Häuser der Stille, der Meditation, der Freiheit und nicht zuletzt der Zuflucht, siehe das Kirchenasyl. Dem wachsenden Bedürfnis nach Schutz vor der lärmigen Außenwelt haben besonders in den letzten Jahren zahlreiche Architekten ebenso angemessene wie beeindruckende Räume geschaffen. Ein vortreffliches Beispiel ist die kleine, aber markante Kirche in der Pariser Bürostadt La Défense.

Zugleich spiegelt sich in diesem wiederum neuen Sakralbau die Vielfalt Europas mit seinen regional so unterschiedlichen Kulturen. Gemeinsam ist den besten Bauten, dass sie, wie es vor einem Jahrhundert der deutsche Baumeister Fritz Schumacher ausgedrückt hat, auf das »Urmaterial« von Architektur vertrauen: auf Raum und Licht. Dabei sind der katholische und der protestantische Kirchenbau einander immer ähnlicher geworden. In der Architektur ist die Ökumene bereits Wirklichkeit. Die Kapelle am schweizerischen Gotthardpass ist sogar der Toleranz unter den Weltreligionen gewidmet.

Die Bilanz für die zweite Hälfte des 20. Jahrhunderts fällt eindeutig aus. Sakrale Baukultur konnte immer dann entstehen, wenn Bauherren mit einem Bewusstsein für Qualität den Mut hatten, eigenwillige Persönlichkeiten zu beauftragen. So schließt sich in diesem Buch nicht nur zeitlich und alphabetisch der Bogen von Alvar Aalto zu Peter Zumthor.

Ottokar Uhl
Kapelle im Stift Melk, Österreich
chapel in the monastery at Melk,
Austria, 1966

1
Aloys Georgen, *Theologische Grundlagen des katholischen Kirchbaues*, in: Konrad Gatz, Willy Weyres, Otto Bartning (Hrsg.), *Kirchen. Handbuch für den Kirchenbau*, München 1959, S. 9 ff.
2
Siehe dazu Günter Rombold, *Katholischer Kirchenbau nach Dettingen. Ein Überblick über 75 Jahre*, in: Michael Pfeifer (Hrsg.), *Sehnsucht des Raumes. St. Peter und Paul in Dettingen und die Anfänge des modernen Kirchenbaus in Deutschland*, Regensburg 1998, S. 156 f.
3
Wolfgang Pehnt, *Glauben ausüben. In der Diaspora – Kirchenbau im 20. Jahrhundert*, in: Romana Schneider, Winfried Nerdinger, Wilfried Wang (Hrsg.), *Architektur im 20. Jahrhundert. Deutschland*, München · London · New York 2000, S. 343.
4
Herbert Muck, *Sakralbau heute*, Aschaffenburg 1961, S. 130.
5
Friedrich Achleitner, *Kirchen, wie sie nicht sein sollen*, in: *Christliche Kunstblätter*, 1962, Heft 4, S. 129–132.
6
The Architectural Review, 1965, Heft 10, S. 246.
7
G. E. Kidder Smith, *Neuer Kirchenbau in Europa*, Stuttgart 1964, S. 9.
8
Siehe dazu Conrad Lienhardt (Hrsg.), *Ottokar Uhl. Werk · Theorie · Perspektiven*, Regensburg 2000.

had been strewn with smart churches for which unconventional constructions had been ransacked in an amateurish way, resulting in spiky roof forms and sparse ornamentation.[6] Following extensive research, the American author George E. Kidder Smith was another who was unsparing with his criticism of Europe's new religious architecture. While acknowledging that the possibilities open to today's architects were absolutely breathtaking, he claimed that the new freedom had also often been misused. His warning examples were the churches, decked out in modernistic fashion that one encountered over and over again, particularly in new suburban housing estates.[7]

Renaissance of Church Building

Until the late 1960s the building of churches was considered one of the architectural world's 'top jobs', benefiting from many commissions, so any aberrations or false moves were also particularly apparent. In essence, only the Scandinavian countries were spared the manifestations of crisis. Finland in particular, on the basis of its broadly grounded modern architecture, can boast a consistently high quality of Protestant church building. On the Catholic side the Liturgical Movement and, since the Second Vatican Council, reform of the liturgy had inspired many experimental solutions. Particularly significant were the radical attempts made by the Austrian Ottokar Uhl, who had early on advocated 'participatory' religious spaces.[8]

There are quite a few reasons why European church building underwent a renaissance before the turn of the millennium, ranging from the development of new residential housing areas to doing away with stop-gap measures. In a world which appears to be given over to economic concerns as well as to entertainment, churches and chapels are often the only 'other' places: houses of stillness, of meditation, of freedom and, not least, of refuge — the church as sanctuary. In the last few years in particular, in response to the growing need for protection from the noisy outside world, numerous architects have created church interiors that are as appropriate as they are impressive. A superb example is the small but striking church in the Parisian 'office city' of La Défense.

At the same time this religious architecture, once again novel, is a reflection of Europe's variety, of its highly diverse regional cultures. A common factor in the best buildings is that, as the German architect Fritz Schumacher expressed it a century ago, they put their trust in the 'original material' of architecture: space and light. Catholic and Protestant church building has become ever more similar. The ecumenical movement is already a reality in architectural terms. The chapel on the St Gotthard Pass in Switzerland is even dedicated to tolerance between the world's religions.

The conclusions for the second half of the twentieth century are clear. A culture of religious architecture was able to emerge when quality-conscious clients had the courage to award commissions to unconventional personalities. Thus in this book it is not just chronologically and alphabetically — from Alvar Aalto to Peter Zumthor — that the circle is complete.

1
Aloys Goergen, 'Theologische Grundlagen des katholischen Kirchbaues', in Konrad Gatz, Willy Weyres and Otto Bartning (eds.), *Kirchen. Handbuch für den Kirchenbau*, Munich, 1959, p. 9ff.
2
See Günter Rombold, 'Katholischer Kirchenbau nach Dettingen. Ein Überblick über 75 Jahre', in Michael Pfeifer (ed.), *Sehnsucht des Raumes. St. Peter und Paul in Dettingen und die Anfänge des modernen Kirchenbaus in Deutschland*, Regensburg, 1998, p. 156f.
3
Wolfgang Pehnt, 'Glauben ausüben. In der Diaspora – Kirchenbau im 20. Jahrhundert', in Romana Schneider, Winfried Nerdinger and Wilfried Wang (eds.), *Architektur im 20. Jahrhundert. Deutschland*, Munich · London · New York, 2000, p. 343.
4
Herbert Muck, *Sakralbau heute*, Aschaffenburg, 1961, p. 130.
5
Friedrich Achleitner, 'Kirchen, wie sie nicht sein sollen', in *Christliche Kunstblätter*, 4 (1962), pp. 129–32.
6
See *Architectural Review*, 10 (1965), p. 246.
7
See G.E. Kidder Smith, *Neuer Kirchenbau in Europa*, Stuttgart, 1964, p. 9.
8
See Conrad Lienhardt (ed.), *Ottokar Uhl. Werk · Theorie · Perspektiven*, Regensburg, 2000.

Guignard & Saner
Kapelle der Weltreligionen
chapel of World Religions
Gotthardpass / St Gotthard Pass, 1998

Lillestrøm
Oslo

Burt

East Kilbride

Den Haag

Neviges
Oudenaarde   Wuppertal
Vaals
Aachen   Wildbergerhütte

Le Havre

Frankfurt

Hasloch

Evry

Karlsruhe

Eichstätt
Ingolstadt

Ronchamp   München   Linz
                                           Wien
Zürich   Steyr
Meggen
Somvix
La Tourette   Hérémence
                   Bollate
                   Milano   San Vito

Marco de Canaveses   Vitória

Riola
Firenze

Lisboa   Madrid

Albert Gerhards

Räume für eine tätige Teilnahme
Katholischer Kirchenbau aus theologisch-liturgischer Sicht

Die zweite Hälfte des 20. Jahrhunderts ist in quantitativer Hinsicht wohl die produktivste Epoche des Kirchenbaus in Europa gewesen – bedingt durch die Zerstörungen des Zweiten Weltkriegs und die vom Wirtschaftswunder geprägte Phase des Wiederaufbaus, die zumindest in Deutschland und einigen anderen mitteleuropäischen Ländern für die Kirchen außergewöhnlich günstige ökonomische Konditionen aufwies. Der Wiederaufbau beziehungsweise Neubau von Kirchen war integraler Bestandteil der Wiedererstehung von Gesellschaft und Kultur.[1] Er spiegelt in mancherlei Hinsicht die jeweilige Zeit wider. Die fünfziger Jahre waren geprägt durch die Rezeption der Moderne. In manchen mutigen Wiederaufbaukonzepten kam der Wille zur Innovation zum Ausdruck, der sich nicht selten über denkmalpflegerische Interessen hinwegsetzte. In den sechziger Jahren neigte sich die Nachkriegsära dem Ende zu. Die Studentenrevolten markierten den Beginn einer Umorientierung des Wertesystems, deren Ende noch nicht abzusehen ist.

Tradition und Innovation

Kirchlich war dies die Zeit der Neugründung vieler Pfarreien, trotz beginnender Erosionserscheinungen. Im expandierenden Kirchenbau standen nicht selten pragmatische Überlegungen im Vordergrund. Die einsetzende Phase der Entsakralisierung tat ihr Übriges. An vielen Orten gab man die zu klein gewordenen Kirchen auf und setzte Mehrzweckräume an deren Stelle, oder man riss die historischen Räume auf und erweiterte sie ohne Rücksicht auf historische und architektonische Gegebenheiten. Diese Tendenz setzte sich durch die siebziger Jahre hindurch fort, wobei bereits erste Zeichen der Rückbesinnung auf verlorene Werte sichtbar wurden. Allerdings kam in dieser Zeit der Kirchenbau mangels Nachfrage fast zum Erliegen. Erstaunlicherweise gelang es in den neunziger Jahren, große Architekten für einige der wenigen Kirchenbauvorhaben zu gewinnen. Hier zeigte sich wie im Bereich der Kunst allgemein, dass die Kirche in der ›säkularen‹ Gesellschaft eine Faszination ausüben kann. So ist auf der Schwelle zum neuen Jahrtausend wider Erwarten die Rede vom »Phönix Kirchenbau«.[2]

Die hier zu behandelnde Periode der Geschichte der katholischen Kirche ist durch die vier Pontifikate der Päpste Pius XII., Johannes XXIII., Paul VI. und Johannes Paul II. geprägt. Die fünfziger Jahre standen unter dem Eindruck der aristokratischen Gestalt Pius' XII. Der Katholizismus galt in der Nachkriegszeit in vielen Ländern Europas als eine unangefochten führende Kraft. Seit Ende der vierziger Jahre machte Pius' XII. mit der Kirchenrefom Ernst, so durch die Erneuerung der Karwoche (1951/55) und die Kirchenmusikinstruktion (1953). Dennoch erschienen die fünfziger Jahre vielen allzu rückwärtsgewandt. Während im Kirchenbau die (gemäßigte) Moderne Einzug hielt, blieben die Strukturen der Kirche unverändert. Da war die Ankündigung eines allgemeinen Konzils durch Papst Johannes XXIII. am Pfingstfest 1959 ein unerhörtes Signal. Mit dem Schlagwort ›aggiornamento‹ verbanden sich Hoffnungen auf eine Öffnung der Kirche gegenüber der Welt, die durch die Beschlüsse des von 1962 bis 1965 abgehaltenen Konzils zumindest teilweise erfüllt schienen. Die am 3. Dezember 1963 verabschiedete Liturgiekonstitution gab den Anstoß für eine Liturgiereform bis dahin unbekannten Ausmaßes, die auch auf die Gestalt des Kirchenraums ungeahnte und von manchen unerwünschte Auswirkungen haben sollte.

Albert Gerhards

Spaces for Active Participation
Theological and Liturgical Perspectives on
Catholic Church Architecture

In sheer volume, the second half of the 20th century was probably the most productive period of church architecture in Europe. It was triggered by the destruction of the Second World War and the phase of reconstruction characterised by the 'economic miracle', which led to extraordinarily favourable economic conditions for the Church at least in Germany and in several other Central European countries. Church restoration or building was an integral aspect of reconstruction[1] and these efforts mirror the spirit of the time in several ways. The 1950s were characterised by a more widespread acceptance of modernism. The desire for innovation was expressed in some courageous reconstruction concepts, frequently winning out over conservation interests. In the 1960s, the post-war era was coming to an end. Student protests marked an emerging re-evaluation of values, a process that continues to this day.

Tradition and Innovation

From a Church perspective, this was the era of founding many new parishes, despite the first signs of erosion. Many expansion projects were primarily driven by pragmatic considerations. The subsequent phase of *de-sacralisation* also took its toll. In many locations, churches, which had become too small, were abandoned in favour of multi-purpose buildings; in other instances, historic structures were opened and expanded with little consideration for historic and architectonic realities. This trend continued throughout the 1970s, although first indications of a return to lost values became noticeable. At the same time, church architecture stagnated almost completely during this period as a result of a lack of demand. It is all the more remarkable that leading architects were persuaded in the 1990s to bring their talents to some of the few church projects. Here, as in the domain of art in general, the fascination of the Church for 'secular' society was clearly in evidence. At the threshold to the new millennium there is talk, surprisingly, of the 'phoenix of church architecture'.[2]

The period of Catholic Church history relevant to this analysis falls into the era spanning from Pope Pius XII, John XXIII and Paul VI to John Paul II. The 1950s were dominated by the aristocratic figure of Pius XII. In the post-war era, Catholicism was universally regarded as an undisputed leading force in many European countries. Pius XII pursued a dedicated campaign of Church reform from the end of the 1940s onward by revitalising Holy Week (1951/55), for example, and introducing ecclesiastical music instruction (1953). Still, many felt that the 1950s were all too focussed on the past. While a moderate modernism was introduced into church architecture, the ecclesiastical structures themselves remained virtually unchanged. In this atmosphere, Pope John XXII's announcement of a universal council at Whitsun 1959 seemed to strike like a thunderbolt. The slogan of *aggiornamento* [lit. updating] was linked to hopes for an opening up of the Church towards the world, hopes that seemed to be answered, at least in part, by the decisions ratified at the council which was held from 1962 to 1965. The liturgical constitution signed on 3 December 1963 unleashed liturgical reform on a hitherto unprecedented scale, which would also have unexpected and, to some members, undesired effects on the physical form of the church space.

The 1960s and 1970s proved to be a time of extraordinary innovation for the Catholic Church, although artistic considerations

Gottfried Böhm
Madonna in den Trümmern
St Columba
Köln / Cologne, 1950

Die sechziger und siebziger Jahre waren für die katholische Kirche außerordentlich innovativ. Allerdings wurden die künstlerischen Belange dem gesellschaftlichen Anliegen vielfach untergeordnet. Kirchenräume hatten zu funktionieren, ein ›Mehrwert‹ wurde ihnen oft nicht zuerkannt. Dementsprechend setzte sich der schon in den fünfziger Jahren begonnene Kahlschlag fort. Neue Kirchenräume wurden oft als Architekturverschnitt von Raumkonzepten der Zeit der Liturgischen Bewegung realisiert, eine über das Funktionale hinausgehende künstlerische und sakrale Qualität wurde kaum zugestanden. Man wird aber dieser Zeit kaum gerecht, wenn man sie nur in ihren Extremen wahrnimmt. Neben vielfach produzierter Meterware gibt es auch hier herausragende Beispiele neuer Kirchengebäude, die Bestand haben. Geistesgeschichtlich kommt der Innovationsschub des Konzils jedoch schon zu Beginn der siebziger Jahre zum Erliegen. Zwar tagen in verschiedenen Ländern Synoden zur Umsetzung der konziliaren Reformen (so die Würzburger Synode 1975), doch drängen universalkirchlich die eher bewahrenden Kräfte in den Vordergrund. Im Kirchenbau zeigte sich der Wandel in dem wiedererwachten Drang nach Ausschmückung, der die Bildaskese der vergangenen Jahrzehnte mitunter in einen »umgekehrten Bildersturm« (Wolfgang Pehnt) verwandelte. Dieser Trend ist nach wie vor nicht abgeschlossen, wenngleich die Bemühungen der neunziger Jahre um künstlerische Qualität zumindest punktuell erste Erfolge zu zeitigen scheinen.[3]

Das Gesamtbild der katholischen Kirche wie auch ihrer architektonischen Repräsentation im Kirchengebäude ist am Ende des 20. Jahrhunderts diffus. Wie das Pontifikat von Johannes Paul II. durch Tradition und Innovation gleichermaßen geprägt ist, so zeigen sich auch im Kirchenbau gegensätzliche Tendenzen, die Ausdruck der ›postmodern‹ anmutenden pluralen Situation der Kirche sein mögen. Um die geistigen Hintergründe des Kirchenbaus in der zurückliegenden Jahrhunderthälfte verstehen zu können, bedarf es eines Rekurses auf seine geistigen Grundlagen.

Katholischer Kirchenbau in der ersten Jahrhunderthälfte

Die katholische Liturgische Bewegung der Zeit nach dem Ersten Weltkrieg war von einem ›christozentrischen Konzept‹ geprägt, wie es durchaus im Zug der Zeit lag.[4] Der rheinische Priester Johannes van Acken (1879–1937) veröffentlichte 1922 ein Büchlein *Christozentrische Kirchenkunst*.[5] Die Anstöße dazu kamen aus dem *Christusprogramm des liturgischen Papstes Pius X.* Zentrale Bestimmung des Raums war für van Acken das Messopfer, symbolisiert im Altar. »Neben und mit dem christozentrischen Gedanken haben wir folglich bei der liturgischen Ausgestaltung des Gebäudes und bei der künstlerischen Verherrlichung der Opferfeier die Tatsache der Opfergemeinschaft besonders zu berücksichtigen.« Die Konsequenz dieses Konzepts einer ›christozentrischen Raumgestaltung‹ für die Architektur war die »Entwicklung eines Einheitsraumes von der Altarstelle aus«. Der christozentrische Gedanke implizierte eine Abkehr vom rein kultisch verstandenen Raumkonzept der Tridentinischen Reform, das den gerichteten Raum mit exzentrischer Aufstellung des Altars als ›Schwelle zum Jenseits‹ favorisierte. Im Unterschied zum trinitarisch begründeten (und vom Konzept der Gegenreform wohl zu unterscheidenden) Modell *Der Weg* von Rudolf Schwarz[6] rückt nun die Altarstelle »aus dem bisherigen Chor in den Laienraum hinein«. Diese Ideen wurden vor allem von Dominikus Böhm und Martin Weber, deren Entwürfe in

Gottfried Böhm
Mariendom / Cathedral
Neviges, 1972

were frequently relegated to second place behind the overall societal goal. Church spaces simply had to function; they were rarely granted a 'surplus value'. Correspondingly, the policy of clearance, which had already begun in the 1950s, continued apace. New church spaces were often realised as an architectonic mixture of spatial concepts reflecting the era of the Liturgical Movement, rarely achieving an artistic and sacred quality that went beyond the purely functional. However, one cannot do full justice to this period by taking note only of the extremes that characterised it. In addition to countless mass-produced exponents, there are nevertheless some outstanding examples of new church buildings from that era whose quality is undiminished. The innovative thrust of the council, however, came to a standstill intellectually as early as the beginning of the 1970s. While synods continued to sit in various regions with the aim of implementing the council reforms (the Würzburg Synod of 1975, for example), the Church as a whole was dominated by conservative forces. In church architecture, this sea change was manifest in a reawakened drive for ornamentation, at times responding to the pictorial asceticism of the preceding decades with a 'reciprocal deluge of images' (Wolfgang Pehnt). This trend has by no means run its course, although the pursuit of artistic quality during the 1990s seems to have yielded at least isolated first successes.[3]

At the close of the 20th century, the overall image of the Catholic Church and of its architectural representation in church buildings is above all vague and confused. Just as the pontificate of John Paul II is marked equally by tradition and innovation, so church architecture is defined by contrary tendencies, which may be an expression of the 'postmodernist' pluralistic situation of the church itself. To fully understand the spiritual background of church architecture in the half century that has just passed, we must refer back to its spiritual foundations.

Catholic Church Architecture in the First Half of the Century

The Catholic Liturgical Movement after the First World War was dominated by a 'Christ-centred concept' that was very much in step with the spirit of the time.[4] In 1922, Johannes van Acken (1879–1937), a priest in the Rhineland, published a booklet entitled *Christ-focussed Ecclesiastical Art*,[5] inspired by the 'Programme of Christ by the liturgical Pope Pius X'. Van Acken held that the central purpose of the space was the office of the sacrament, symbolised by the altar. 'In addition to and in conjunction with the principle of the central focus on Christ, we must therefore pay special heed to the reality of the offertory community for the liturgical layout of the building and the artistic glorification of the sacrament of the offering'. The architectural consequence of this concept of a 'spatial design focused on Christ' was the 'evolution of a uniform space radiating from the locus of the altar'. The principle of the central focus on Christ implied a rejection of the spatial concept formulated in the wake of the Council of Trent, interpreted on a purely cultic level, which favoured directional spaces with eccentrically placed altars as 'thresholds to the beyond'. In contrast to Rudolf Schwarz's model 'The Path' that was founded in the Trinitarian premise (and that is clearly different from the concept of the Counter Reformation)[6] the site of the altar shifted 'from a space reserved for the clergy into the layperson's domain'. Dominikus Böhm and Martin Weber, in particular, embraced these ideas and their designs were incorporated into the second edition of van Acken's

Rudolf Schwarz
St. Anna / St Anna
Düren, 1956

die zweite Auflage des Büchleins van Ackens Eingang fanden, aufgegriffen. Auch Kirchenbauten von Rudolf Schwarz nach dem Modell *Der offene Ring* entsprachen diesen Vorstellungen.

Die von Rudolf Schwarz entwickelten Idealpläne liturgischer Räume beruhen auf hoher architektonischer Kompetenz und auf einem Gespür für das Mysterium der Liturgie in seinen verschiedenen Dimensionen. So kann er in seinem Werk *Vom Bau der Kirche* den entgegengesetzten Konzepten ›Heilige Innigkeit‹ (Der Ring) und ›Heilige Fahrt‹ (Der Weg) gleichermaßen Sinn abgewinnen. Dazwischen steht der ›Heilige Aufbruch‹, die Öffnung des Rings auf die Ewigkeit hin, deren Schwelle der Altar ist. Alles ist zusammengefasst im siebten Plan, dem ›Dom aller Zeiten‹ (Das Ganze).[7] Ein solcher Idealbau lässt sich in der Zeit natürlich nicht verwirklichen, doch wird das Ganze vorab in der gottesdienstlichen Handlung erkennbar: »Sie baut sich ja entlang der Zeit auf und ihre im Verlauf der Zeit hervorgebrachte Gestalt ist in etwa ›das Ganze‹.«[8] Diese Zitate zeigen, dass für Schwarz Ausrichtung und Sammlung kein Gegensatz sein konnten. Sie gehören zur Liturgie wie zum menschlichen Leben insgesamt. Der Kirchenraum sollte den unterschiedlichen Zuständen Entfaltungsspielraum geben.

Hinter diesen Konzepten verbirgt sich ein Problem, das sich auf die Kurzformel bringen lässt: Christozentrik versus Theozentrik. Dies bedeutet: Was bildet die eigentliche Mitte (topographisch und theologisch) des Kirchenraums? Wo ist Christus in diesem ›Heilsdrama‹ anzusiedeln? Ist er Gegenüber der Gemeinde im Sinne des wiederkommenden Herrn, steht er an ihrer Spitze als ihr Haupt oder ist er in ihrer Mitte (Mt 18,20)? Wie verhält sich die Rolle des Priesters als Repräsentant dazu? Handelt er mehr auf Seiten Christi als Haupt seiner Kirche (»in persona Christi«) oder auf Seiten der Kirche als »Braut Christi« (»in persona ecclesiae«)? Diese Fragen markieren ein erhebliches Konfliktpotential im katholischen Kirchenraum der hier zu behandelnden Epoche, das auch in jüngster Zeit Auswirkungen zeitigt, etwa bei der Diskussion um die Herz-Jesu-Kirche in München-Neuhausen aus dem Jahr 2000.[9]

Leitideen zum katholischen Kirchenraum nach dem Zweiten Weltkrieg

In der Phase des Wiederaufbaus in Deutschland gab die Liturgische Kommission der Fuldaer Bischofskonferenz »Richtlinien für die Gestaltung des Gotteshauses aus dem Geist der römischen Liturgie« in Auftrag, die 1949 unter der Federführung des Bonner Kirchenhistorikers Theodor Klauser zusammengestellt wurden.[10] Die Richtlinien beginnen mit folgender Zweckbestimmung: »Das christliche Gotteshaus ist das geweihte und – schon unabhängig von der Eucharistie – von Gottes besonderer Gegenwart erfüllte Gebäude, in dem sich das Volk versammelt. Und zwar versammelt es sich hier (die Reihenfolge bedeutet hier zugleich Rangordnung): Erstens und vor allem, um die Erneuerung des Erlösungsopfers Christi zu begehen; zweitens, um die Früchte des Erlösungsopfers Christi in den heiligen Sakramenten entgegenzunehmen; drittens, um das Wort Gottes zu hören; viertens, um dem im eucharistischen Brote gegenwärtigen Christus seine Huldigungen darzubringen; fünftens, um sich außerliturgischen Andachten hinzugeben.«[11]

Aus der Unterschiedlichkeit der Zweckbestimmungen ergibt sich eine Aufgabenstellung an die Erbauer. Als Erfordernisse

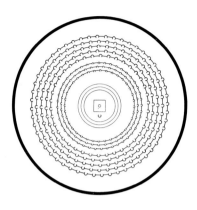

Rudolf Schwarz
oben / above:
›Heilige Innigkeit‹ / 'Holy Intimacy'
unten / below:
›Heilige Fahrt‹ / 'Holy Journey'
1947

booklet. Churches designed by Rudolf Schwarz according to the 'Open Ring' model also corresponded to this philosophy.

Rudolf Schwarz's idealised plans for liturgical spaces are rooted in great architectonic knowledge and a sensibility for the mystery of the liturgy in all its different dimensions. In his seminal work *Vom Bau der Kirche* [*The Incarnate Church*], Schwarz was able to make sense of both concepts, however contrary, namely that of the 'Holy Intimacy' (the ring) and the 'Holy Journey' (the path). Between these lies the 'Holy Departure', the opening of the ring on to eternity, whose threshold is represented by the altar. All these concepts are summarised in the seventh plan, the 'Cathedral for All Time' (the entirety).[7] While this kind of idealised building cannot be executed within the framework of time, the entirety is manifest in the act of performing the service: 'After all, the service adheres to a temporal structure and its "form" which emerges over the course of time is roughly that of "the entirety"'.[8] These quotes demonstrate how Schwarz could never regard orientation and gathering as opposites. They belong to the liturgy as they do to human life. The church space should therefore allow a variety of conditions to flourish.

These concepts overlay a basic problem, which can be expressed in abbreviated form as: Christ-centred versus theology-centred. In other words: what is the true centre (topographically and theologically) of the physical church space? What is Christ's place in this 'history of salvation'? Is He facing the community in the sense of the resurrected Lord, does He lead the community or is His rightful place in the middle of the community (Matthew: 18, 20)? What is the role of the priest as His representative? Does the priest act for Christ as the head of His church (*in persona Christi*) or for the church as the 'Bride of Christ' (*in persona ecclesiae*)? These questions outline a tremendous potential for conflict with regard to Catholic church buildings during the period relevant to this investigation, whose impact has been felt even in recent times, evidenced by the debate surrounding the church of the Sacred Heart in Neuhausen, Munich (2000).[9]

Central Ideas on Catholic Sacred Spaces after the Second World War

During the phase of Germany's reconstruction, the liturgical commission of the bishops' conference at Fulda commissioned the drafting of 'guidelines for the design of the house of God in the spirit of the Roman liturgy', which were compiled in 1949 under the stewardship of the church historian Theodor Klauser from Bonn.[10] The guidelines begin with the following definition: 'The Christian house of God is the consecrated building that is filled by God's unique presence — even independently of the Eucharist — where the people gather. They gather (sequence also denotes importance in the list that follows): first and foremost, in order to renew Christ's sacrifice; secondly, in order to receive the fruits of Christ's sacrifice in the holy sacraments; thirdly, to hear God's word; fourthly, to pay homage to Christ embodied in the bread of the Eucharist; fifthly, to engage in extra-liturgical contemplation'.[11]

The differences in definition translate into tasks that the builder must fulfil. The following demands are placed on 'God's people of our time' from a human perspective: 'A desire for community, a need for truth and authenticity, a wish to move from the peripheral to the central and essential, a longing for clarity, brightness and transparency, a yearning for tranquillity and

Rudolf Schwarz
oben / above:
›Heiliger Aufbruch‹ / 'Holy Departure'
unten / below:
›Der Dom aller Zeiten‹
'The Cathedral for All Time'
1947

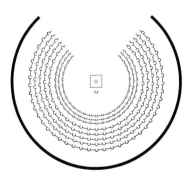

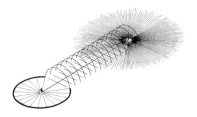

»für das Gottesvolk unserer Tage« werden von seiten der Menschen aufgeführt: »der Drang nach Gemeinschaft, das Verlangen nach Wahrheit und Echtheit, der Wunsch, vom Peripherischen zum Zentralen und Wesentlichen zu kommen, der Drang nach Klarheit, Helle und Übersichtlichkeit, die Sehnsucht nach Stille und Frieden, nach Wärme und Geborgenheit.«[12] Daraus werden konkrete Folgerungen gezogen. In Bezug auf die ästhetische Gestalt des Äußeren heißt es: »Unser Bestreben müßte wohl sein, das ganz Andere, das Überweltliche, das Göttliche dessen, was im Inneren des Gotteshauses geschieht, auf eine ebenso würdige wie beredte Weise in seinem Äußeren anzukündigen und das Gotteshaus dabei doch auf eine harmonische Weise in seine Umgebung einzuordnen.«[13]

Die primäre Ausrichtung auf die eucharistische Opferfeier gibt dieser den Vorrang vor dem eucharistischen Anbetungskult, wobei einer zentralen Aufstellung des Altars sowie dem Zentralbau, wie von Teilen der Liturgischen Bewegung gefordert, eine Absage erteilt wird. Dagegen setzt man ein Liturgieverständnis, das die Liturgie als Aktion Christi und seines Repräsentanten, des priesterlichen Liturgen, aber auch als Aktion der Gemeinde begreift. »Das Zusammenspiel dieser Aktionen fordert einen irgendwie zum Altar hin ausgerichteten Raum, der Spieler und Gegenspieler, Priester und Gemeinde, einander klar gegenüberstellt und einen Prozessionsweg herüber und hinüber eröffnet.«[14] Gegenüber älteren Raumkonzepten wird der frei stehende, umschreitbare Altar gefordert, der in seiner Dimensionierung und Positionierung als das »Herz der Gesamtanlage« erfahrbar sein soll. Daher soll auch alles »überflüssige Beiwerk« beiseite gelassen werden. Die Zelebration *versus populum* wird als möglich erachtet. Sie steht nicht im Gegensatz zur beizubehaltenden Ost-West-Richtung, da der Altar den eigentlichen Orientierungspunkt von Priester und Gemeinde darstellt.

Dieser Text markiert den status quo katholischen Kirchenbaus in der Nachkriegszeit. Die Raumdisposition ist einerseits von Gedanken der Liturgischen Bewegung inspiriert, etwa in der ›Klärung‹ des Raums, der positiven Bewertung der Zelebration zum Volk hin oder der Forderung nach optimaler Kommunikation zwischen Presbyterium und Gläubigenraum. Doch werden diese deutlich voneinander abgesetzt, so dass die klassische Zweiteilung entgegen manchen Konzepten der Liturgischen Bewegung festgeschrieben wird. Die Trennung ist zum Beispiel durch die Altarschranken beziehungsweise Kommunionbank noch als selbstverständlich vorausgesetzt. Allerdings gab es schon in dieser Zeit bemerkenswerte Abweichungen von der Regel, etwa bei Bauten von Emil Steffann. Das Zueinander von Altarraum und Gemeinderaum blieb eine strittige Frage.

Unter Bezug auf die französischen Dominikaner P. Pie Regamey und P. Marie-Alain Couturier plädierte Ekkart Sauser für die begriffliche Unterscheidung, aber für die sachliche Verwiesenheit der scheinbar gegensätzlichen Ideen vom Haus Gottes und vom Haus der Gläubigen. Kurz: die Ehre Gottes ist der geheiligte Mensch, und das Glück des Menschen ist die Verherrlichung Gottes. Dies führt zu einer besonderen Akzentuierung des Altars (der nach Sauser zugleich Sinnbild Christi und des Abendmahlstisches ist). Regamey: »Der mystische Leib Christi, oder genauer gesagt, der Teil des mystischen Leibes Christi, den eine bestimmte Versammlung von Gläubigen darstellt, findet seinen Daseinsgrund nur in der Teilnahme am wahren Leib, der Eucharistie.«[15] Der Einfluss der französischen Dominikaner

peace, warmth and shelter'.[12] These demands translate into concrete consequences. With regard to the aesthetic form of the external, the guidelines state: 'We should strive to announce the Otherness, the otherworldliness, the godliness of what occurs in the House of God in a manner that is both dignified and eloquent, and moreover integrate the House of God harmoniously into its environment'.[13]

The primary orientation towards the eucharistic celebration of the sacrament gives it precedence over the eucharistic cult of adoration, rejecting the idea of either a centrally placed altar or a centrally planned building, which had been one of the demands that arose out of the Liturgical Movement. The counter-interpretation is one where the liturgy is understood as an act of Christ and his representative, the priest as liturgist, but also an act performed by the community. 'The interplay of these actions calls for a space that is in some manner oriented toward the altar and brings protagonists and antagonists, that is priests and congregation, face to face with each other and opens a processional path in both directions.'[14] In contrast to older spatial concepts, the new ideal calls for a free-standing altar with 'ambulatory', which would be experienced as the 'heart of the structure' both in size and position, further enhanced by abolishing all 'superfluous accessories'. The authors of the guidelines can see no reason why a celebration *versus populum* should not be possible. Nor do they view it as a contrast to the east-west orientation, which they continue to support, since the altar is the true focal point for priest and congregation.

This guideline documents the *status quo* of post-war architecture in the Catholic Church. The spatial disposition is inspired on the one hand by the ideas formulated by the Liturgical Movement, the 'purification' of the space, for example, or the positive reading of the celebration *versus populum*, and on the other hand by the challenge to optimise communication between the chancel area and the congregation area. A clear distinction is nevertheless made between the two domains, thereby entrenching the classic division in direct conflict with some of the concepts expressed in the Liturgical Movement. Thus the division is still assumed as natural, for example, in the form of elements such as the altar, or more precisely the communion rails. There were some notable exceptions to the rule, however, even during that time, for example in buildings designed by Emil Steffann. Still, the relationship of chancel to congregation remained a contentious issue.

Supporting his argument with references to the French Dominican friars P. Pie Regamey and P. Marie-Alain Couturier, Ekkart Sauser advocated a distinction in terms, but a material reference between the seemingly contradictory ideas of the House of God and the House of Worship. In short: God's glory is the sanctified human being, and human happiness lies in glorifying God. Hence the accentuation of the altar (which is simultaneously a symbol of Christ and of the table of the Last Supper according to Sauser). Regamey writes: 'The existential foundation of the mystical Body of Christ, or more precisely, that part of the mystical Body of Christ represented by a specific gathering of believers, lies exclusively in partaking of the true Body, the Eucharist'.[15] The influence which the French Dominican friars exerted on church architecture in the second half of the 20th century through their journal *L'Art Sacré* cannot be overestimated.[16]

Emil Steffann
St. Laurentius / St Laurentius
München / Munich, 1955

mit ihrer Zeitschrift *L'Art Sacré* auf den Kirchenbau der zweiten Hälfte des 20. Jahrhunderts kann nicht hoch genug veranschlagt werden.[16] Die von ihnen binnen weniger Jahre inspirierten Kirchenbauten bilden bis heute einen Maßstab: die Pfarrkirche Unsere Liebe Frau aller Gnaden in Plateau d'Assy (1950), die Rosenkranzkapelle der Dominikanerinnen in Vence (1951), die Herz-Jesu-Kirche in Audincourt (1951), die Wallfahrtskirche Unsere Liebe Frau auf der Höhe in Ronchamp (1955), der Konvent Sainte-Marie-de-la-Tourette in l'Abresle (1960).

Das Zweite Vatikanische Konzil und die Folgen

Das Zweite Vatikanische Konzil nimmt in seinem Kirchen- und Liturgieverständnis den christologisch-eucharistischen Gedanken des Mystischen Leibes auf, ergänzt diesen aber durch das pneumatologische Bild vom »Tempel des Hl. Geistes« und vor allem durch das theologische des »pilgernden Gottesvolkes«. Diese trinitarische Sichtweise hat für die theologische Konzeption des Kirchenraums nicht geringe Auswirkungen: ein ausschließlich auf den Altar bezogenes christozentrisches Konzept erscheint nicht mehr angemessen. Dies wird auch durch die Aussage von den verschiedenen Gegenwartsweisen Christi in der Liturgiekonstitution »Sacrosanctum Concilium« (SC 7) bestätigt, wo nicht mehr nur von der Gegenwart in den eucharistischen Gaben und im geweihten Priester, sondern auch von der Gegenwart im Wort, in der versammelten priesterlichen Gemeinde, ihrem Beten und Singen, die Rede ist. Das Konzil hat zwar keine konkreten Aussagen zur Raumgestalt gemacht, doch sind insbesondere die Aussagen der Liturgiekonstitution über die bewusste, fromme und tätige Teilnahme der Gläubigen (SC 48) von grundlegender Bedeutung.

Die Folgen der Liturgiereform für den Kirchenraum waren erheblich, wenngleich vieles durch die Liturgische Bewegung vorbereitet und in den Bauten der fünfziger und frühen sechziger Jahre vorweggenommen wurde. Die wichtigsten Neuerungen:
– Konzentration auf einen einzigen, frei stehenden Altar unter Verzicht auf Seiten- oder Nebenaltäre (möglich geworden durch die Einführung der Konzelebration).
– Trennung von Altar und Aufbewahrungsort der Eucharistie (Tabernakel), der nun in einer eigenen Kapelle aufgestellt werden kann.
– Einführung eines festen Ortes der Wortverkündigung (Ambo) im Altarbereich, wodurch die Kanzel im Kirchenschiff obsolet wird.
– Einführung eines festen Priestersitzes für die Gottesdienstleitung.
– Änderung des Kommunionritus (Kommunionprozession), wodurch die Kommunionbänke funktionslos werden, deren ursprüngliche Funktion als Abschrankung des Chorbereichs ebenfalls nicht mehr notwendig erscheint.
– Funktionsänderung des Taufsteins aufgrund der Bestimmung, das Wasser in jeder Feier außerhalb der Osterzeit zu weihen; Verlagerung des Taufortes vom Eingangsbereich ins Angesicht der Gemeinde.
– Änderung der Bußpraxis, Einführung von Beichtzimmern und Reduzierung der Beichtstühle.

Der Gemeinschaftsgedanke, ausgelöst durch das Konzil, hat das schon vorher ad experimentum erprobte Konzept der Zelebration *versus populum* zur allgemeinen Norm werden lassen, obwohl die Dokumente dies niemals vorgeschrieben haben.

The church buildings, which they inspired in the space of a few years, set a standard even today: the parish church Our Blessed Lady in Plateau d'Assy (1950), the Dominican Rosary Chapel at Vence (1951), the church of the Sacred Heart in Audincourt (1951), the pilgrimage church of Notre Dame du Haut in Ronchamp (1955) and the Sainte-Marie-de-la-Tourette convent in l'Abresle (1960).

The Second Vatican Council and its Consequences

Ecclesiastically and liturgically, the Second Vatican Council abandoned the Christ-centred, Eucharistic idea of the Mystical Body, replacing it instead with the pneumatological concept of the 'Temple of the Holy Spirit' and above all the theological image of 'God's people on a pilgrimage'. This Trinitarian perspective had considerable influence on the theological concept of the sacred space: a Christ-centred concept entirely focussed on the altar no longer seemed appropriate. This is further reinforced by the broadened definition of Christ's presence contained in the liturgical constitution, the 'Sacrosanctum Concilium' (SC 7): Christ, the constitution specifies, is not only present in the Eucharist and the officiating priest, but also in the gospel, the community of priests, their prayers and chants. While the Council made no specific statements with regard to spatial design, the passages in the liturgical constitution that address the conscious, devout and active participation of the believers (SC 48) are of a fundamental order.

The liturgical reform had far-reaching consequences for Catholic church interiors, although much groundwork had been done by the Liturgical Movement and the buildings of the 1950s and early 1960s. The principal innovations were:
– the focus on a single, free-standing altar without side or secondary altars (made possible through the introduction of con-celebration);
– the separation of altar and tabernacle, which could now be placed in a separate chapel;
– the introduction of a fixed place for the ambo near the altar, making the pulpit in the aisle obsolete;
– the introduction of a fixed celebrant's chair;
– changes to the rite of communion (communion procession), which rendered the communion rail superfluous, whose original function as a barrier between nave and chancel now also seemed unnecessary;
– functional change with regard to the baptismal font owing to the stipulation that the water should be blessed during each service (with the exception of the Easter period); shifting the position of the baptismal font from the entrance into the congregation's field of vision at the front;
– changes in the practice of confession; introduction of confessional rooms and phasing out of confessionals.

The communal ideal, promoted by the Council, meant that the celebration *versus populum*, a previously experimental concept, became the norm, even though the documents never stipulated that this should be so. The transition occurred with surprising rapidity and often with little consideration for existing situations. Critics soon raised their voices, but were given little credence by those responsible for the liturgy. One of the critics during the early 1980s was sociologist Alfred Lorenzer with his book *The Council of Accountants*, a relentless review of liturgical reform. His criticism of the redesigned sanctuaries was particu-

Le Corbusier
Kapelle / chapel
Ronchamp, 1955

Die Umsetzung geschah in erstaunlicher Schnelligkeit und oft
ohne nennenswerte Rücksicht auf die bestehende Situation.
Schon bald traten Kritiker auf den Plan, die aber seitens der für
die Liturgie Verantwortlichen nicht besonders beachtet wurden.
Zu den kritischen Stimmen zählte Anfang der achtziger Jahre
der Soziologe Alfred Lorenzer mit seinem Buch *Das Konzil der
Buchhalter*. Darin rechnet er mit der Liturgiereform gründlich
ab. Besonders hart geht er mit der Umgestaltung der Kirchenräume ins Gericht. Die unbekümmerte Verlagerung des Altars
zerstört, so Lorenzer, die Raumstruktur, bringt den Raum als
Sinngestalt »zum Einsturz«.[17]

Erst in jüngster Zeit verdichten sich die Stimmen derer, die
eine kritische Revision des Bestehenden anmahnen.[18] Kardinal
Ratzinger bringt seine Position auf den Punkt: »Der Altar ist
gleichsam der Ort des aufgerissenen Himmels; er schließt den
Kirchenraum nicht ab, sondern auf – in die ewige Liturgie
hinein.«[19] Die Einwände gegen die gängige Praxis verdienen
zweifelsohne Beachtung. Das Problem liegt jeweils in der Ver-
absolutierung eines Aspekts. Kommt es in einer verkürzten
Sicht des Gemeinschaftscharakters der Liturgie oft zu einem
rein ›horizontalen‹, auf die diesseitige Feiergemeinschaft be-
zogenen Verständnis christlichen Gottesdienstes, so tendiert
die andere Seite zu einer Absolutsetzung des Gedankens der
eschatologischen Ausrichtung »versus orientem« oder des rein
latreutisch verstandenen Anbetungscharakters. Beide Dimensionen, die der zentrierten Versammlung und die der exzen-
trischen Ausrichtung, gehören im christlichen Gottesdienst
(wie auch in dem der Synagoge) zusammen und müssen in einem instabilen Gleichgewicht gehalten werden.[20] Dabei können
die Schwerpunkte unterschiedlich liegen, wie die Vielfalt der
Raumkonzepte der zweiten Hälfte des 20. Jahrhunderts belegt.

Die erwähnte Pluralität von Kirchenbildern und die verschiedenen Weisen der Gegenwart Christi bei der Liturgie suggerieren
eine Pluralität von Raumkonzepten, welche die 1989 zuerst
publizierten und im Jahr 2000 in revidierter Form wieder aufge-
legten *Leitlinien für den Bau und die Ausgestaltung von gottesdienstlichen Räumen*[21] ausdrücklich bejahen. Im Unterschied zu
den Richtlinien von 1949 geht der jüngere Text von der grund-
sätzlichen Einheit des Kirchenraumes aus. Die Gemeinsamkeit
des Taufpriestertums wird durch die hierarchische Binnenstruk-
turierung nicht aufgehoben. Daher ist die Differenzierung in
Orte besonderer Teilnehmer (zum Beispiel der Ort des Vorsitzes)
und besondere Funktionsorte (zum Beispiel der Altar) nach-
geordnet. Dabei geht es nicht um eine Nivellierung der Unterschiede. Die 1996 publizierte Arbeitshilfe *Liturgie und Bild*
sieht diese geradezu als Chance für eine spannungsvolle Raumgestalt an.[23]

Diese jüngere Entwicklung zeigt eine Modifizierung dessen,
was sich vielfach als »katholischer Kirchenraum« in den vergangenen Jahrzehnten durchgesetzt hat: die Abkehr von einem rein
aktionistischen Verständnis des Prinzips der ›tätigen Teilnahme‹,
das in plakativen Umsetzungen zu containerartigen Gebilden
mit einer Vorstandstribüne geführt hatte. Statt dessen wird Wert
auf Differenzierung gelegt, auch was die Vielfalt der Feierfor-
men anbetrifft. Dabei sind architektonische Qualität und liturgische Dignität ebenbürtig. Dies hatte Überlegungen und
Gestaltungen in Richtung von ›Communio-Räumen‹ zur Folge,
die das Spezifische der Gott-menschlichen Gemeinschaft im
Gottesdienst erfahrbar machen sollten. Der bekannteste Neubau

Dieter G. Baumewerd
St. Christophorus
St Christophorus
Sylt, 2000

larly harsh. The carefree attitude toward repositioning the altar, Lorenzer held, destroys the spatial structure, precipitating a 'collapse' of the symbolic content of the space.[17]

Voices of discontent, clamouring for a critical review of existing conditions have only recently become more numerous.[18] Cardinal Ratzinger put it succinctly: 'The altar is, as it were, the place where heaven opens up; it is not the termination of the sanctuary but its opening — toward the eternal liturgy'.[19] No doubt critiques of the common practice deserve consideration. The problem lies in the absolutist interpretation of individual aspects. While a myopic view of the communal character of the liturgy often leads to a purely 'horizontal' reading of the Christian mass, too focussed on the worldly community of celebrants, the other side tends to place the idea of the eschatological focus *versus orientem* or the latreutic reading of the supreme worship on an unreachable pedestal. Both dimensions — the centralised gathering and the eccentric orientation — are present in the Christian mass (and indeed in the synagogue) and it is important to maintain a delicate balance between them.[20] The focus may shift, as is evident in the variety of spatial concepts developed in the second half of the 20th century.

The aforementioned plurality of what a church should look like and the various manners of Christ's presence in the liturgy suggest a plurality of spatial concepts, clearly endorsed in the *Guidelines for the Building and Design of Spaces for Reading the Mass*,[21] first published in 1989 and reissued in a revised edition in 2000.[22] In contrast to the guidelines from 1949, the more recent text assumes the fundamental unity of the church space. The community of the Christian priesthood is not abolished by the hierarchical internal structure. Hence, the differentiation is subordinated according to sites for special participants (for example, the presiding chair) and sites for special functions (for example, the altar). It is not a question of levelling differences. The pamphlet *Liturgy and Image* published in 1996 identifies the differentiation as an opportunity for creating a stimulating spatial design.[23]

This more recent development reveals a modification of the established 'Catholic church space' of the past decades: rejecting the reading of the principle of 'active participation' on the basis of activism alone, which had led to simplified interpretations resulting in container-like structures with platforms for the 'executive'. Differentiation is valued instead, equally with regard to the variety in celebratory rituals. Architectonic quality and liturgical dignity are given equal status. This led to explorations and designs for so-called 'communio spaces' which aimed to make tangible in the service the specificity of the unity between God and people. The best-known new building in this category is Dieter G. Baumewerd's St Christopherus in Westerland, Sylt, erected at the end of the 1990s.[24] Faced with these spatial concepts, we must once again explore what constitutes the 'centre' of the church space.

The Theological Symbolic Form: the Encounter between God and Man as the Centre of the Gathering

The liturgy offers an experience of community as one of the fundamental characteristics of the Church. In 1918 Romano Guardini, one of the leaders of the Liturgical Movement, published a slim volume entitled *On the Spirit of the Liturgy*.

Dieter G. Baumewerd
St. Christophorus
St Christophorus
Sylt, 2000

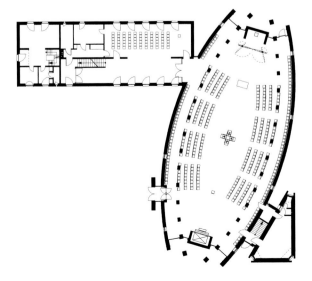

dieser Kategorie ist die von Dieter G. Baumewerd Ende der neunziger Jahre errichtete St.-Christopherus-Kirche in Westerland/Sylt.[24] Anhand dieser Raumkonzepte stellt sich noch einmal neu die Frage nach der ›Mitte‹ des Kirchenraumes.

Zur theologischen Sinngestalt: Gott-menschliche Begegnung als Mitte der Versammlung

Die Liturgie bringt als einer der Wesensvollzüge der Kirche Gemeinschaft in die Erfahrung. Romano Guardini, eine der großen Persönlichkeiten der Liturgischen Bewegung, veröffentlichte 1918 ein Bändchen mit dem Titel: *Vom Geist der Liturgie.* Das zweite Kapitel lautet: *Liturgische Gemeinschaft.* Guardini bemerkt darin, dass die Liturgie nicht ›ich‹ sagt, sondern ›wir‹. Als Grund gibt er dafür an, dass die Liturgie nicht vom Einzelnen, sondern von der ganzen Kirche getragen werde, dass das Subjekt also nicht »die einfache Zusammenzählung aller gleichgläubigen Einzelnen« sei, sondern die Kirche. Für Guardini blieb Gemeinschaft in der Liturgie jedoch stets etwas Vermitteltes. Das Individuelle hat darin keinen Stellenwert. Die Vereinigung der Glieder der Gemeinschaft geschieht nicht unmittelbar von Mensch zu Mensch, sondern durch Ausrichtung auf dasselbe Ziel.[25]

Diese Überlegungen stehen im Kontrast zu heutigen Vorstellungen von Gemeinschaft. Zwischen der Zeit nach dem Ersten Weltkrieg und der Gegenwart geschah das, was wir »anthropologische Wende« der Theologie nennen. Es geht in Theologie und Kirche nicht primär um die Verkündigung objektiver Wahrheiten, sondern um »die Vermittlung des Anrufs Gottes an die Subjektivität des Menschen« (Karl Rahner). Damit wird das Subjekt zum Ort der Begegnung von Gott und Mensch, und Intersubjektivität ist nicht nur auf der ›vertikalen‹ Ebene zwischen Gott und Mensch, sondern auch auf der ›horizontalen‹ Ebene zwischen den einzelnen Menschen eine liturgische Gegebenheit. Nicht nur die persönliche Gottesbeziehung der einzelnen Gläubigen, auch nicht die gemeinsame Ausrichtung allein, sondern die Erfahrung gläubigen Miteinanders wird zum Prüfstein für geglückten Gottesdienst. Das Zweite Vatikanische Konzil hat sich in zentralen Aussagen (zum Beispiel Kirchenkonstitution »Lumen Gentium« Art. 26) eindeutig zum Prinzip der erfahrbaren Gemeinschaft bekannt und damit einer rein universalistischen Sicht den Rücken gekehrt. Diese Impulse wurden auf verschiedene Weise umgesetzt. Wichtige theoretische Einsichten und praktische Erfahrungen wurden durch Herbert Muck vermittelt und durch Ottokar Uhl realisiert.[26] Am Ende des 20. Jahrhunderts wird deutlich, dass Kirchenbau weniger eine monumentale als eine prozessuale Größe ist: »Kirchenbau ist [...] als eine fortschreitende, miteinander parallel verlaufende Gestaltwerdung von Raum und Gemeinde zu begreifen, als ein dynamischer, auf verschiedenen Ebenen (organisatorisch wie inhaltlich) verlaufender Gestaltwerdungsprozeß.«[27] Der letzte Bau einer katholischen Kathedrale im 20. Jahrhundert, die von Mario Botta errichteten Kathedrale von Evry, löste international eine Diskussion über die Bedeutung des Kirchenbaus in den Gesellschaften Europas aus. Im Hintergrund standen die Erfahrungen der ›Wende‹, die einerseits eine rege Kirchenbautätigkeit in den Ländern des ehemaligen Ostblocks auslöste, andererseits aber die Notwendigkeit der Umnutzung oder Aufgabe von Kirchengebäuden akut erscheinen ließ. Kann, soll die Kirche durch Gebäude noch Zeichen setzen wie in früheren Zeiten? Ein vorläufiges Fazit: »Die Kirche kann Zeichen setzen, wenn sie

Ottokar Uhl
Judas Thaddäus
Karlsruhe, 1989

The heading of chapter two is: 'Liturgical Community'. In it, Guardini notes that the liturgy does not speak in the first person singular ('I') but in the first person plural ('we'). He proposes that this is based on the fact that the liturgy is not supported by the individual but by the Church, that the subject is more than 'the mere sum of all individuals sharing the same faith' but the Church as a whole. However, Guardini always understood community in the liturgy as being mediated. The individual aspect has no place in it. The individual members of the community are not unified on a direct level from one person to another, but by virtue of being dedicated to the same goal.[25]

These observations are in stark contrast to contemporary ideas of community. The years that passed between the end of the First World War and the present have witnessed an evolution that theologians refer to as an 'anthropological turning point'. Theology and Church are no longer primarily focussed on pronouncing objective truths, but on 'bringing the call to God to the subjectivity of the human being' (Karl Rahner). Thus the subject becomes the locus of the encounter between God and Man, and intersubjectivity is a liturgical fact not only on the 'vertical' plane between God and Man, but also on the 'horizontal' plane among individuals. The litmus test of a successful mass is no longer the personal relationship of the individual believers with God or even the common goal itself, but the experience of devout togetherness. The Second Vatican Council has taken a clear stance in favour of the experiential community in several key statements (for example the *Lumen Gentium*, article 26 in the Constitution), thus turning its back on a purely universalistic perspective. These impulses have been implemented in a variety of ways. Important theoretical insights and practical experiences were formulated by Herbert Muck and implemented by Ottokar Uhl.[26] At the end of the 20th century, it has become evident that church architecture is less a monumental force than one that is concerned with process: 'Church architecture [...] should be understood as a continuous "forming" where space and community evolve together, a dynamic process of formation that occurs at different levels (both in terms of organisation and in terms of content)'.[27] The last building project of a Catholic cathedral in the 20th century, Mario Botta's cathedral in Evry, inspired an internal debate on the meaning of church architecture in European society. The discussions were held in the wake of the 'turning point', which had initiated much activity in church building in the former East German states but also emphasised the need for conversion or at least redefining the task of church buildings. Can the Church, or should it, still create symbols by means of buildings as it did in the past? A preliminary conclusion might be: 'The Church can create symbols if it wishes to do so. It must itself become a symbol of proximity to God, of the encounter between God and the world, between God and Man and between people. As part of a constant striving for this quality, church buildings can also allude to God's presence among humans and to the world that is yet to come'.[28]

The Belgian Benedictine Frédéric Debuyst, on the other hand, proposes that the focus at the end of the 20th century be on the sheltering space created for a small community, a return to the origins of the Church.[29] Debuyst regards Emil Steffann and P. Couturier as the leading exponents. Steffann, whose design for St Martin in Dornbirn was an early predecessor of the 'communio space' at the end of the 1960s, interpreted space not as

Mario Botta
Kathedrale / Cathedral
Evry, 1995

es will. Sie muß selbst zum Zeichen der Nähe Gottes, der Begegnung von Gott und Welt, von Gott und Mensch und von Mensch und Mensch werden. Im ständigen Bemühen um diese Qualität können auch Kirchengebäude etwas vom Wohnen Gottes unter uns Menschen und von der kommenden Welt erahnen lassen.«[28]

Für den belgischen Benediktiner Frédéric Debuyst steht am Ende des 20. Jahrhunderts dagegen der bergende, auf eine kleine Gemeinde bezogene Raum im Vordergrund, gleichsam eine Rückkehr zu den Anfängen.[29] Dabei sind für ihn die Namen Emil Steffann und P. Couturier maßgeblich. Für Steffann, der mit seinem Entwurf für die Kirche St. Martin in Dornbirn bereits Ende der sechziger Jahre einen der Vorläufer des ›Communio-Raums‹ geschaffen hatte, war Raum nicht Richtung, sondern Mitte.[30] Debuyst führt als Beispiele neben St. Laurentius in München die Kirche von Westerland/Sylt, eine Studentenkapelle in Pordenone/Venetien, die neue Kirche der deutschsprachigen Gemeinde St. Paulus in Brüssel (2001)[31] sowie zwei Klosterkirchen an. Die Räume haben bei aller Verschiedenheit die sammelnde Dimension gemeinsam, die Kirchen von Sylt und Brüssel die Gruppierung der Gemeinde um die ›Brennpunkte‹ Altar und Ambo. Dieses Raumkonzept versucht, die Gegensätze Zentralität und Longitudinalität miteinander zu verbinden. Wesentlich ist der freie Raum in der Mitte zwischen den ›Polen‹ Altar und Ambo (im Entwurf für Dornbirn: Altar und Taufort). Der ›Osten‹ als Zielpunkt Gott-menschlicher Begegnung wird in die Mitte der Versammlung mit den Kristallisationspunkten Wort und Sakrament gelegt, wobei der Freiraum die Unverfügbarkeit der göttlichen Gegenwart symbolisiert. Durch die Axialität der elliptischen Grundgestalt bleibt zudem der Verweischarakter über die Feierversammlung hinaus erhalten. In der Kirche Notre Dame de l'Arche de l'Alliance in Paris wird der Verweischarakter durch einen angedeuteten Lettner betont, der ein Spannungsmoment innerhalb der gemeinschaftsbetonten Grundgestalt bildet.[32]

Bei aller Unterschiedlichkeit ist diesen neuen Raumkonzepten der theologische Grundgedanke gemeinsam: »Wesen des christlichen Gottesdienstes ist die Verherrlichung Gottes durch Jesus Christus im Heiligen Geist – ein Nachvollziehen der Bewegung, die Gott selber ist. [...] Die feiernde Gemeinde ist niemals Selbstzweck, der um sich selber kreist, sondern ist verwiesen auf den ganz Anderen, auf Gott. Daher ist auch nicht einfach Christus die Mitte des Gottesdienstes, erst recht nicht die eucharistischen Gaben, die ihn vergegenwärtigen, sondern die wechselseitige Begegnung von Gott und Menschen durch Christus im Heiligen Geist. Mitte des Gottesdienstes ist also die heilige Handlung, der gnadenhafte Wesensaustausch zwischen Gott und Mensch.«[33] Von da aus stellt sich auch die Frage nach der angemessenen künstlerischen Ausgestaltung auf neue Weise. Ist die frontale Anordnung eines monumentalen Altarbildes wie das von Georg Meistermann in der Kirche Maria Regina Martyrum in Berlin nach wie vor beispielhaft, oder sollte eine solch beherrschende Bildkomposition nicht besser an anderer Stelle platziert sein, etwa hinter einer im Halbkreis versammelten Gemeinde?

Katholischer Kirchenbau ist im Laufe des 20. Jahrhunderts anspruchsvoller geworden, da er sich weder auf einen kirchlichen Stil (im Sinne des Historismus) noch auf institutionelle Absicherung zurückziehen kann. Die Suche vieler – auch religiös

ungebundener – Menschen nach künstlerisch verantworteten sakralen Räumen, die der »universalen Erlösungserwartung« (Papst Johannes Paul II.) Stimme geben,[34] nimmt die Christen jedoch in die Pflicht, solche Räume bereitzuhalten und bereitzustellen, die von der Gegenwart des Anderen in der heutigen Welt zeugen. Der katholische Kirchenbau der vergangenen fünf Jahrzehnte in Europa gibt hierzu wertvolle Anregungen.

Catherine de Bie
St. Paulus / St Paulus
Brüssel / Brussels, 2001

direction but as the centre.[30] In addition to St Laurentius in Munich, Debuyst cites the church in Westerland, Sylt, a student chapel in Pordenone, Venice, the new church for the German-speaking congregation of St Paulus in Brussels (2001)[31] and two monastery churches as examples. Despite their differences, the spaces share a common collective dimension — the churches in Sylt and Brussels by grouping the congregation around the 'focal points' of altar and ambo. This spatial concept seeks a unifying element between the contrasts of central and longitudinal focus. One essential characteristic is the open space in the centre between the 'poles' of the altar and the ambo (in the design for Dornbirn: altar and baptismal font). The 'East' as the destination for encounters between God and Man is shifted to the centre of the congregation, crystallised in gospel and sacrament, whereby the open space symbolises the unattainability of the divine presence. The axes of the elliptical figure nevertheless preserve the referential character beyond the gathered congregation. In Notre Dame de l'Arche de l'Alliance in Paris, the referential character is emphasised by an allusion to a wood screen, which adds an element of tension to the community-focussed plan.[32]

All other differences aside, these new spatial concepts share one fundamental theological principle: 'The essence of the Christian mass is to glorify God through Jesus Christ in the Holy Spirit — a re-enactment of the movement that is God Himself. [...] The community gathered in celebration is never a purpose in its own right, circling around itself and introspective; instead it is addressed to the wholly Other, to God. Therefore Christ alone is not the centre of the mass, nor the Eucharistic offerings that embody Him, but the reciprocal encounter between God and Man through Christ in the Holy Spirit. At the centre of the mass lies the divine act, the merciful exchange of being between God and Man'.[33] This interpretation casts a new light on the question of the appropriate artistic approach to the interior. Is the frontal arrangement of a monumental altar image, such as Georg Meistermann's work in the church Maria Regina Martyrum in Berlin, still the exemplary solution? Or should such a dominant pictorial composition be moved to a different position, perhaps behind the congregation gathered in a half circle?

Over the course of the 20th century, Catholic church architecture has become more discriminating, since it can no longer seek refuge in an ecclesiastical style (in the sense of Historicism) or in institutional assurances. Many people — even those without religious allegiance — are searching for genuinely artistic sacred spaces, which express the 'universal expectation of salvation' (Pope John Paul II).[34] At the same time, this universal search charges Christians with the duty of preserving and offering spaces that bear witness to the presence of the Other in today's world. European Catholic church architecture of the past five decades provides valuable stimuli on how to meet this challenge.

Hans Schädel
Maria Regina Martyrum
Berlin, 1963

Frank Hammoutène
Notre Dame de Pentecôte
Paris, 2000

1
Die immense Bautätigkeit ist in zahlreichen diözesanen und überdiözesanen Publikationen dokumentiert. Vgl. z.B. Hugo Schnell, *Der Kirchenbau des 20. Jahrhunderts in Deutschland. Dokumentation, Darstellung, Deutung*, München 1973; Barbara Kahle, *Deutsche Kirchenbaukunst des 20. Jahrhunderts*, Darmstadt 1990; Wolfgang Bergthaler u.a. (Hg.), *Funktion und Zeichen. Kirchenbau in der Steiermark seit dem II. Vatikanum*, Graz 1992; Fabrizio Brentini, *Bauen für die Kirche. Katholischer Kirchenbau des 20. Jahrhunderts in der Schweiz* (= Brückenschlag zwischen Kunst und Kirche), Luzern ⁴1994; Karl Josef Bollenbeck, *Neue Kirchen im Erzbistum Köln. 1955–1995*. 2 Bde., Brühl 1995; Paloma Gil, *El templo del siglo XX*, Barcelona 1999 (Arquitectura/teoría – 5).
2
Vgl. das gleichnamige Themenheft der Zeitschrift *Kunst und Kirche* 3/2001; darin besonders: Wolfgang Pehnt, *In der Diaspora. Kirchenbau im 20. Jahrhundert*, S. 136–147.
3
Vgl. das Ausstellungsprojekt 1994/95 der Deutschen Gesellschaft für christliche Kunst: *Initiativ. Kunst und Kirche mit herausragenden Beispielen aus den Jahren 1969–1994*.
4
Ich beziehe mich hier im Wesentlichen auf : Walter Zahner, *Rudolf Schwarz – Baumeister einer neuen Gemeinde. Ein Beitrag zum Gespräch zwischen Liturgiewissenschaft und Architektur in der Liturgischen Bewegung* (= MThA 15), Altenberge 1992; ders., *Raumkonzepte der Liturgischen Bewegung*, in: Albert Gerhards/ Theodor Sternberg/Walter Zahner, *Communio-Räume. Auf der Suche nach der angemessenen Raumgestalt katholischer Liturgie*, Regensburg 2002 (im Druck).
5
J. van Acken, *Christozentrische Kirchenkunst. Ein Entwurf zum liturgischen Gesamtkunstwerk*, Gladbeck 1922, ²1923.
6
Vgl. Rudolf Schwarz, *Vom Bau der Kirche*, Heidelberg 1938, ²1947.
7
Ebd. (1947), S. 130 f.
8
Ebd., S. 132.
9
Vgl. Klemens Richter, *Verschiedene Wege nach Rom? Prozessionskirche versus Communio-Raum*, in: *Kunst und Kirche* 64 (2001), S. 148–150.
10
Zuerst veröffentlicht 1955; in der Originalfassung wieder veröffentlicht als Anhang in: Theodor Klauser, *Kleine Abendländische Liturgiegeschichte. Bericht und Besinnung*, Bonn 1965, S. 161–172.
11
Ebd., S. 163.
12
Ebd., S. 164.
13
Ebd., S. 165.
14
Klauser (s. Anm. 10), S. 166.
15
P. Pie Regamey, *L'art sacré au XX siècle?*; dt. Übersetzung: *Kirche und Kunst im XX. Jahrhundert*, Graz 1954, S. 32; zitiert nach Ekkart Sauser, *Symbolik des katholischen Kirchengebäudes*, in: Josef Andreas Jungmann, *Symbolik der katholischen Kirche*, Stuttgart 1960, S. 53–95, hier S. 70.
16
Vgl. H. Bischof, *Der Geist weht, wo er kann. Marie-Alain Couturier ›im Gespräch‹ mit Matisse, Picasso, Braque ...*, Salzburg 1999.
17
Vgl. Alfred Lorenzer, *Das Konzil der Buchhalter. Die Zerstörung der Sinnlichkeit. Eine Religionskritik*, Frankfurt 1981, S. 201 f.
18
Vgl. Albert Gerhards, *Versus orientem – versus populum. Zum gegenwärtigen Diskussionsstand einer alten Streitfrage*, in: *Theologische Revue* 98 (2002), S. 15–22.
19
Joseph Kardinal Ratzinger, *Der Geist der Liturgie*. Eine Einführung, Freiburg–Basel–Wien 2000, S. 62 f.
20
Vgl. dazu die in Anm. 4 angezeigte Publikation *Communio-Räume*.
21
Sekretariat der Deutschen Bischofskonferenz (Hg.), *Leitlinien für den Bau und die Ausgestaltung von gottesdienstlichen Räumen* (= Die deutschen Bischöfe. Liturgiekommision 9), Bonn 1989, ⁵2000. Vgl. dazu: Albert Gerhards, *Liturgiereform am Kirchenraum vorbei? Zur Rezeption der ›Leitlinien für den Bau und die Ausgestaltung von gottesdienstlichen Räumen‹* (1988), in: *Kunst und Kirche* 57 (1994), S. 11–13.
22
Leitlinien (s. vorige Anm.) Abschnitt 1.3.
23
Sekretariat der Deutschen Bischofskonferenz (Hg.), *Liturgie und Bild. Eine Orientierungshilfe. Handreichung der Liturgiekommission der Deutschen Bischofskonferenz* (= Arbeitshilfen 132), Bonn 1996, ²1999, Abschnitt 3.1.
24
Vgl. Dieter Baumewerd, *Katholische Pfarrkirche St. Christophorus in Westerland/Sylt*, in: *Kunst und Kirche* 64 (2001), S. 151–153.
25
Vgl. Romano Guardini, *Vom Geist der Liturgie*, Freiburg ¹⁷1952, S. 26 f.
26
Vgl. Herbert Muck, *Der Raum. Baugefüge, Bild und Lebenswelt*, Wien 1986; Lehrstuhl für Bauplanung und Entwerfen Professor Ottokar Uhl (Hg.), *Kirche Neureut Workshop 1992*, Karlsruhe 1992; vgl. auch Dirk Ansorge u.a. (Hg.), *Raumerfahrungen. Raum und Transzendenz. Beiträge zum Gespräch zwischen Theologie, Philosophie und Architektur*, Münster–Hamburg–London 1999.
27
Anja Künzel, *Kirche bauen – Gemeinde bilden. Zur Beziehung von Architektur und Liturgie im Leben katholischer Pfarrgemeinden. Fünfzehn Skizzen aus dem Bistum Aachen*, Darmstadt 1996, S. 248.
28
Albert Gerhards, *Die Kirche – ›Feste Burg‹ oder ›Zelt Gottes unter den Menschen‹? Der Auszug aus dem Gotteshaus und die ›Denkmale anderer Götter‹ bei uns: Können und wollen die Kirchen in einer pluralistisch-materialistischen Gesellschaft noch Zeichen setzen?*, in: Konrad-Adenauer-Stiftung/ Wolfgang Schuster (Hg.), *Kirche im Mittelpunkt*. Fachtagung Schwäbisch Gmünd 4. bis 6. September 1991 im Tagungszentrum Stadtgarten, Schwäbisch Gmünd 1991, S. 39–44, hier S. 44.
29
Vgl. Frédéric Debuyst, *Réflexions théologiques et liturgiques sur la situation actuelle de l'architecture chrétienne*, in: Ephrem Carr (Hg.), *Architettura e arti per la liturgia*. Atti del V congresso internazionale di liturgia, Roma, Pontificio Istituto Liturgico, 12–15 ottobre 1999, Rom 2001, S. 117–130; ders., *Le génie chrétien du lieu*, Paris 1997.
30
Vgl. Johannes Heimbach, *Der Kirchenbaumeister Emil Steffann. Eine biografische Erinnerung mit Blick auf den Dom zu Münster*, in: Theodor Sternberg (Hg.), *Kirchenbau zwischen Aufbruch und Abbruch*, Münster 2000, S. 27–50.
31
Vgl. Gottfried Stracke, *Textile Kunst und Paramentik im 20. Jahrhundert. Einführung*, in: *Münster* 54 (2001), S. 290–300, hier S. 297–299.
32
Vgl. Bischof (s. Anm. 16), S. 152 f. Zu diesem Raumkonzept insgesamt: Gerhards/ Sternberg/ Zahner (s. Anm. 4).
33
Albert Gerhards, (Hg.), *In der Mitte der Versammlung. Liturgische Feierräume* (= Liturgie & Gemeinde. Impulse & Perspektiven 5), Trier 1999, S. 22 f.
34
Vgl. ders., *'Stimme der universalen Erlösungserwartung' – der theologische Ort der Kunst in Hinblick auf das Verhältnis von Liturgie und Bild*, in: Carr (s. Anm. 29), S. 77–103.

1

The building boom is documented in numerous documents issued on the diocesan and higher levels. Cf., for example H. Schnell, *Der Kirchenbau des 20. Jahrhunderts in Deutschland. Dokumentation, Darstellung, Deutung*, Munich 1973; B. Kahle, *Deutsche Kirchenbaukunst des 20. Jahrhunderts*, Darmstadt 1990; W. Bergthaler et al. (eds.), *Funktion und Zeichen. Kirchenbau in der Steiermark seit dem II. Vatikanum*, Graz 1992; F. Brentini, *Bauen für die Kirche. Katholischer Kirchenbau des 20. Jahrhunderts in der Schweiz* = Brückenschlag zwischen Kunst und Kirche 4, Lucerne 1994; K. J. Bollenbeck, *Neue Kirchen im Erzbistum Köln. 1955–1995*, 2 vols., Brühl 1995; P. Gil, *El templo del siglo XX*, Barcelona 1999 (*Arquitectura/teoría* – 5).

2

See the pamphlet of the same title included in the 3/2001 issue of the journal *Kunst und Kirche*, especially the contribution by W. Pehnt, 'In der Diaspora. Kirchenbau im 20. Jahrhundert', pp. 136–47.

3

Cf., the 1994/95 exhibition project organised by the German Society for Christian Art Initiative 'Kunst und Kirche' [Art and Church] with outstanding examples from 1969–94.

4

I am referring chiefly to W. Zahner, *Rudolf Schwarz – Baumeister einer neuen Gemeinde. Ein Beitrag zum Gespräch zwischen Liturgiewissenschaft und Architektur in der Liturgischen Bewegung* = MThA 15 (Altenberge 1992); ibid., 'Raumkonzepte der Liturgischen Bewegung', in A. Gerhards, Th. Sternberg, W. Zahner, *Communio-Räume. Auf der Suche nach der angemessenen Raumgestalt katholischer Liturgie*, Regensburg 2002.

5

J. van Acken, *Christozentrische Kirchenkunst. Ein Entwurf zum liturgischen Gesamtkunstwerk*, Gladbeck 1922, 1923.

6

Cf., R. Schwarz, *Vom Bau der Kirche*, Heidelberg 1938, 1947.

7

Ibid., (1947), pp. 130 f.

8

Ibid., p. 132.

9

Cf., K. Richter, 'Verschiedene Wege nach Rom? Prozessionskirche versus Communio-Raum', in *Kunst und Kirche* 64 (2001), pp. 148–50.

10

First published in 1955; original version reprinted as an appendix in Th. Klauser, *Kleine Abendländische Liturgiegeschichte. Bericht und Besinnung*, Bonn 1965, pp. 161–72.

11

Ibid., p. 163.

12

Ibid., p. 164.

13

Ibid., p. 165.

14

Klauser (see note 10), p. 166.

15

P. Regamey, *L'art sacré au XX siècle?*, Graz 1954, p. 32; quoted in E. Sauser, 'Symbolik des katholischen Kirchengebäudes', in J. A. Jungmann, *Symbolik der katholischen Kirche*, Stuttgart 1960, pp. 53–95; here p. 70.

16

Cf., H. Bischof, *Der Geist weht, wo er kann. M.-A. Couturier 'im Gespräch' mit Matisse, Picasso, Braque...*, Salzburg 1999.

17

Cf., A. Lorenzer, *Das Konzil der Buchhalter. Die Zerstörung der Sinnlichkeit. Eine Religionskritik*, Frankfurt 1981, pp. 201f.

18

Cf., A. Gerhards, 'Versus orientem – versus populum. Zum gegenwärtigen Diskussionsstand einer alten Streitfrage' in *Theologische Revue* 98 (2002), pp. 15–22.

19

J. Kardinal Ratzinger, *Der Geist der Liturgie. Eine Einführung*, Freiburg, Basel, Vienna 2000, p. 62f.

20

Cf., the publication "Communio-Räume" referenced in note 4.

21

Sekretariat der Deutschen Bischofskonferenz (ed.), *Leitlinien für den Bau und die Ausgestaltung von gottesdienstlichen Räumen* = Die deutschen Bischöfe. Liturgiekommision 9, Bonn, 1989, 2000. Cf. A. Gerhards, 'Liturgiereform am Kirchenraum vorbei? Zur Rezeption der Leitlinien für den Bau und die Ausgestaltung von gottesdienstlichen Räumen' (1988), in *Kunst und Kirche* 57 (1994), pp. 11–13.

22

Guidelines (see previous note.), paragraph 1.3.

23

Sekretariat der Deutschen Bischofskonferenz (ed.), *Liturgie und Bild. Eine Orientierungshilfe. Handreichung der Liturgiekommission der Deutschen Bischofskonferenz* = Arbeitshilfen 132, Bonn 1996, 1999, paragraph 3.1.

24

Cf., D. G. Baumewerd, 'Kath. Pfarrkirche St. Christophorus in Westerland/Sylt' in *Kunst und Kirche* 64 (2001), pp. 151–53.

25

Cf., R. Guardini, *Vom Geist der Liturgie*, Freiburg 1952, p. 26f.

26

Cf., H. Muck, *Der Raum. Baugefüge, Bild und Lebenswelt*, Vienna, 1986; Lehrstuhl für Bauplanung und Entwerfen Professor Ottokar Uhl (ed.), *Kirche Neureut Workshop 1992*, Karlsruhe 1992; see also: D. Ansorge et al. (eds.) *Raumerfahrungen. Raum und Transzendenz. Beiträge zum Gespräch zwischen Theologie, Philosophie und Architektur*, Münster, Hamburg, London 1999.

27

A. Künzel, *Kirche bauen – Gemeinde bilden. Zur Beziehung von Architektur und Liturgie im Leben katholischer Pfarrgemeinden. Fünfzehn Skizzen aus dem Bistum Aachen*, Darmstadt 1996, p. 248.

28

A. Gerhards, 'Die Kirche – "Feste Burg" oder "Zelt Gottes unter den Menschen"? Der Auszug aus dem Gotteshaus und die "Denkmale anderer Götter" bei uns: Können und wollen die Kirchen in einer pluralistisch-materialistischen Gesellschaft noch Zeichen setzen?' in Konrad-Adenauer-Stiftung/Wolfgang Schuster (eds.), *Kirche im Mittelpunkt. Fachtagung Schwäbisch Gmünd 4. bis 6. September 1991 im Tagungszentrum Stadtgarten*, Schwäbisch Gmünd 1991, pp. 39–44, here p. 44.

29

Cf., F. Debuyst, 'Réflexions théologiques et liturgiques sur la situation actuelle de l'àrchitecture chrétienne', in E. Carr (ed.), *Architettura e arti per la liturgia. Atti del V congresso internazionale di liturgia, Roma, Pontificio Istituto Liturgico, 12–15 ottobre 1999*, Rome 2001, pp. 117–30; F. Debuyst, *Le génie chrétien du lieu*, Paris 1997.

30

Cf., J. Heimbach, 'Der Kirchenbaumeister Emil Steffann . Eine biografische Erinnerung mit Blick auf den Dom zu Münster' in Th. Sternberg (ed.), *Kirchenbau zwischen Aufbruch und Abbruch*, Münster 2000, pp. 27–50.

31

Cf., G. Stracke, 'Textile Kunst und Paramentik im 20. Jahrhundert. Einführung', in *Münster* 54 (2001), pp. 290–300, here pp. 297–99.

32

Cf., Bischof (see note 16), p. 152f. On this spatial concept in general Gerhards, Sternberg, Zahner (see note 4).

33

A. Gerhards, (ed.), *In der Mitte der Versammlung. Liturgische Feierräume* = Liturgie & Gemeinde. Impulse & Perspektiven 5, Trier 1999, p. 22f.

34

Cf., 'Stimme der universalen Erlösungserwartung – der theologische Ort der Kunst in Hinblick auf das Verhältnis von Liturgie und Bild', in Carr (see note 29), pp. 77–103.

Fritz Metzger

St. Felix und Regula
Zürich, Schweiz
1950

Saints Felix and Regula
Zurich, Switzerland
1950

Mit dieser Kirche, die in einem dicht bebauten Wohnviertel von Zürich liegt, setzte eine Neuorientierung im schweizerischen Kirchenbau ein. Erstmals wurde hier die Wegeordnung des längs gerichteten Grundrisses zugunsten einer engeren Verbindung von Gemeinde- und Altarraum aufgegeben – das große Queroval entsprach den Bestrebungen der Liturgischen Bewegung. Der Entwurf von Fritz Metzger (1898 bis 1973) ging bereits 1945 aus einem Wettbewerb hervor. Der geschwungene, niedrige Baukörper setzt einen Kontrast zu den Kuben der Miethäuser in der Nachbarschaft. Der frei stehende Turm ist weithin sichtbar, wirkt aber durch seine Höhe überzogen. Charakteristisch für den Kirchenraum ist die bewusste Verwendung einfacher Materialien: Asphalt für den Boden, Beton für die Decke, Zementsteine für die Wände. 1954 setzte der Künstler Ferdinand Gehr farbige Fenster ein. Neben dem Eingang befindet sich die Marienkapelle. Die Deckenkalotte über dem Oval ist eine außerordentliche Ingenieurleistung. Mit einer Stichhöhe von nur 1,60 Metern galt sie seinerzeit als das flachste Gewölbe, das bis dahin ausgeführt wurde. Adresse: Zürich-Aussersihl, Hardstraße.

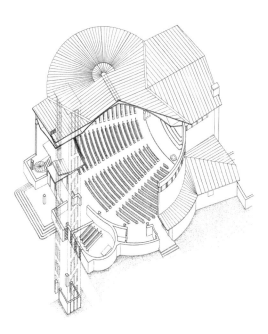

Axonometrie
axonometric projection

A new orientation in Swiss church building began with this church, located in a heavily built-up residential district. Here for the first time a longitudinal ground plan was waived in favour of a closer link between the congregation and the chancel: the large transverse oval corresponded with the endeavours of the Liturgical movement. The design by Fritz Metzger (1898–1973) had already been drafted in 1945 for a competition. The low, curved building forms a contrast to the cubes of the apartment blocks in the neighbourhood. The free-standing bell tower is visible over a long distance but gives the impression of being exaggerated because of its height. Characteristic of the church interior is the deliberate use of simple materials: asphalt for the floor, concrete for the ceiling, and cement blocks for the walls. In 1954 the artist Ferdinand Gehr added stained-glass windows. Beside the entrance stands the Lady chapel. The ceiling calotte over the oval represents an extraordinary engineering achievement. With a camber of only 1.6 metres, it was at the time considered to be the shallowest vault ever constructed. Address: Hardstrasse, Aussersihl, Zurich.

Luigi Figini · Gino Pollini

Madonna dei Poveri
Mailand, Italien
1952

Madonna of the Poor
Milan, Italy
1952

Luigi Figini (1903–1984) und Gino Pollini (1903–1991), deren gemeinsames Hauptwerk die Olivetti-Werke in Ivrea sind, haben mit dieser Kirche in einem westlichen Vorort von Mailand ein besonderes Beispiel des Sakralbaus geschaffen. Der längs gerichtete Baukörper, der auf seiner Westseite in einer Spitze endet, zeigt in seiner äußeren Erscheinung eine Nähe zum Industriebau. Die absichtlich schlichte Gestalt wird vor allem durch das Stahlbetonskelett geprägt, das auf der Eingangsseite durch Wandfelder aus Ziegelsteinen ausgefacht wurde. Beim Kirchenraum für 1000 Personen haben die Architekten den Typus der frühchristlichen Basilika aufgenommen, wobei die wechselnde Lichtführung aus indirekten Quellen das Raumerlebnis bestimmt. Die dunklen Seitenschiffe sollen der Meditation dienen, während das Hauptschiff sein Dämmerlicht durch niedrige Öffnungen in den Obergaden aus Betonblocksteinen erhält. Strahlend hell ist hingegen das Sanktuarium unter dem Turm: Durch eine Kassettendecke ergießt sich das Licht auf die erhöhte Altarzone, die durch zwei durchbrochene Betonbalken zusätzlich betont ist. Adresse: Mailand-Baggio, Via Osteno.

Luigi Figini (1903–84) and Gino Pollini (1903–91), whose principal joint work is the Olivetti factory in Ivrea, created a particular example of religious architecture with this church, located in a western suburb of Milan. In its outward appearance the longitudinal building, which terminates in a point at its western end, shows an affinity with industrial architecture. The intentionally simple form is characterised primarily by the reinforced steel skeleton, which on the entrance side was filled with brick wall sections. For the church interior, which can hold a thousand people, the architects adopted the type of the early Christian basilica, whereby the changing light from indirect sources determines one's experience of the space. The dark side aisles are intended for meditation, while the nave receives half-light via low openings in the clerestory made of concrete blocks. The sanctuary below the tower, on the other hand, is brilliantly lit: light pours in through the coffered ceiling on to the raised altar zone, which is given additional emphasis by two perforated concrete beams. The crypt with a gently vaulted ceiling has an archaic feel. Address: Via Osteno, Milano-Baggio.

0   10 m

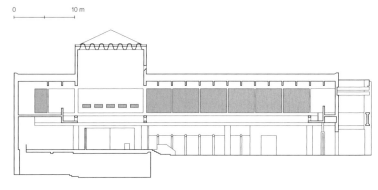

Längsschnitt
longitudinal section

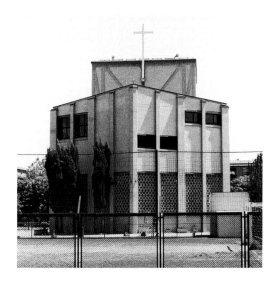

Im strahlend hellen Sanktuarium steht der Altar frei im Raum, so dass der Priester den Gottesdienst zur Gemeinde gerichtet abhalten kann. Blickfang ist das mit leuchtenden Juwelen besetzte Kreuz.

The altar stands alone in the brilliantly lit sanctuary so that the priest can hold services facing the congregation. The cross, set with gleaming jewels, attracts the eye.

Rudolf Schwarz

St. Michael
Frankfurt am Main, Deutschland
1954

St Michael
Frankfurt am Main, Germany
1954

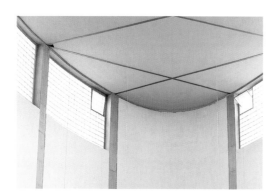

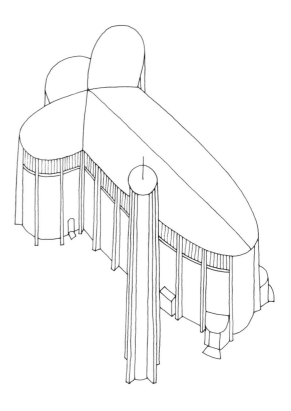

Der burgartige Baukörper hat einen
Grundriss, in dem sich zwei ungefähr
elliptische Flächen durchdringen. Der
später errichtete Glockenturm wurde
von Karl Wimmenauer entworfen.

The castle-like building has a ground
plan in which two roughly elliptical
areas overlap. The bell tower, erected
at a later date, was designed by Karl
Wimmenauer.

Seit der asketischen, 1930 vollendeten Fronleichnamskirche in Aachen
[Seite 156] entwickelte sich Rudolf
Schwarz (1897–1961) zu einem der
bedeutenden modernen Kirchenarchitekten des 20. Jahrhunderts.
Den Auftrag für St. Michael erhielt er
durch einen Wettbewerb. Dieses Bauwerk in einem Frankfurter Wohnviertel »ist in seiner ganzen Gestalt so
stark durch seine Bauweise bestimmt,
dass man diese kennen muss, um
den Bau zu verstehen« (Schwarz).
Wegen des schlechten Baugrunds besteht die Konstruktion aus einem
Stahlbetonskelett mit sich nach oben
hin verjüngenden Pfeilern. Die Wände
sind mit Sichtziegelmauerwerk ausgefacht, das innen verputzt und weiß
gestrichen wurde. Die Kirche für rund
600 Personen hat einen fast elliptischen Grundriss, der im Chorbereich
durch zwei ebenfalls elliptische
Apsiden erweitert wurde. Tageslicht
erhält der Kirchenraum durch ein
umlaufendes Fensterband aus Glasbausteinen, das in den Hauptapsiden
unterbrochen ist. Das flache Dach
hat einen eleganten Überstand.

Rudolf Schwarz (1897–1961) developed into one of the major modern
church architects of the 20th century
following his ascetic Fronleichnamskirche (Corpus Christi) in Aachen
[p.156], completed in 1930. He received the commission for the church
of St Michael as the result of a competition. This edifice in a residential
district of Frankfurt 'is in its entire form
so strongly determined by its building method that one has to become
acquainted with this in order to understand the building' (Schwarz).
Because of a poor-quality site, the
construction consists of a reinforced-
concrete skeleton with pillars that
taper as they rise. The walls are filled
with visible brickwork, plastered inside and painted white. The church for
around 600 people has an almost elliptical ground plan, which in the area
of the choir was widened by means
of two apses, likewise elliptical. The
church interior receives daylight
through a surrounding band of glass-
brick windows which is interrupted
in the two main apses. The flat roof
has an elegant projection.

Der 51 Meter lange und 16 Meter hohe Kirchenraum soll die Gläubigen vor der Außenwelt abschirmen: Die Metapher »Burg« verwendete Schwarz im Sinne einer »Urgestalt«. Innen wirkt die Kirche durch die weiß gestrichenen Wände zwischen den lasierten Betonstützen sowie durch das von oben einfallende Licht hell und freundlich. Die ebene Decke ist hellblau gestrichen, im Kontrast dazu haben die Flansche der kreuzweise verlegten Stahlbinder einen goldfarbenen Anstrich. Was die Liturgie betrifft, ist der Raum »sorgsam bedacht« (Schwarz). Anstelle einer Sängerempore gibt es in der Ostapside ein Sängerpodest. Die erhöhte Altarinsel steht frei im Raum, so dass der Gottesdienst sowohl im Kirchenschiff als auch zur Werktagskapelle in der Westapside hin stattfinden kann. Das versetzbare Kreuz wurde von Ewald Mataré geschaffen. Unter dem Hochaltar liegt die Krypta mit farbigen Fenstern von Georg Meistermann. Adresse: Frankfurt-Nordend, Gellertstraße.

The church, 51 metres long and 16 metres high, is intended to shield the faithful from the outside world: Schwarz used the metaphor 'castle' in the sense of 'archetype'. The church's interior makes a light and friendly impression because of the white walls between varnished concrete supports and the light falling in from above. The level ceiling is painted light blue. In contrast, the flanges of the steel girders, laid crossways, are painted gold. From the liturgical perspective the space is 'carefully thought out' (Schwarz). Instead of a gallery there is a platform for singers in the eastern apse. The raised altar island is freestanding so that services can be held both in the nave and facing towards the workday chapel in the western apse. The movable cross was created by Ewald Mataré. Under the high altar lies the crypt with stained-glass windows by Georg Meistermann. Address: Gellertstrasse, Nordend, Frankfurt.

Ursprünglich war die Kirche der neu gegründeten Frankfurter Gemeinde von allen Seiten aus zu sehen. Heute wird ihre markante Gestalt durch Bäume und Büsche weitgehend verdeckt.

This church for the newly established Frankfurt community was originally visible from all sides. Today its striking shape is largely hidden by trees and shrubs.

0   10 m

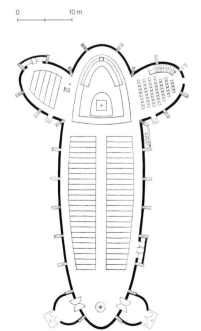

Grundriss
floor plan

Emil Steffann

St. Laurentius
München, Deutschland
1955

St Laurentius
Munich, Germany
1955

Die Kirche St. Laurentius, von Emil Steffann (1899–1968) zusammen mit Siegfried Östreicher entworfen, hat im modernen deutschen Sakralbau eine Schlüsselstellung inne. Ein Jahrzehnt vor dem Zweiten Vatikanum nimmt sie durch ihre räumliche Konzeption die römische Liturgiereform vorweg. Erstmals wird in Deutschland der Gedanke, die Gemeinde um eine ›Mitte‹ zu versammeln, baulich umgesetzt. Die nur leicht erhöhte Altarinsel ist in den zur Konche quer gelagerten Hauptraum vorgezogen, so dass die Gläubigen in drei Blöcken am Gottesdienst teilnehmen können. Der schmucklose, jedoch ausdrucksstarke Innenraum findet seine Entsprechung im schlichten Außenbau. Als bewusst scheunenartiges Gehäuse liegt die Kirche in der Mulde einer großen Grünanlage und bildet das Zentrum eines baulichen Ensembles mit Pfarrhof, Jugendräumen und Kindergarten. Ebenfalls franziskanischen Geist verkörpert das Mauerwerk aus hart gebrannten Ziegeln, dessen feine Farbabstufungen die Fassaden lebendig machen.

The church of St Laurentius, designed by Emil Steffann (1899–1968) with Siegfried Östreicher, holds a key position in modern German religious architecture. It anticipated the Roman Catholic liturgical reforms in its spatial concept a decade before the Second Vatican Council. Here the idea of gathering the congregation together around a 'centre' is translated into architecture for the first time in Germany. The only slightly elevated altar island is drawn forward into the main body of the church, positioned diagonally to the concha, so that the congregation can participate in the service in three blocks. The plain, yet expressive interior finds a counterpart in the simple exterior. The deliberately barn-like church building lies in a hollow in a large green space and forms the centre of an architectural ensemble together with the presbytery, premises for young people's activities and a kindergarten. The masonry, consisting of fired bricks with delicate gradations of colour that en-liven the appearance of the façades, likewise incorporates the Franciscan spirit.

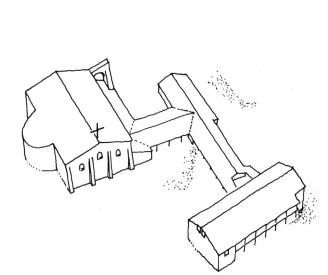

Anstelle eines Kirchenturms dient ein
gemauerter Bogen als Glockenträger.
Nur das große Kreuz über der Westfassade weist auf die sakrale Bestimmung des Bauwerks hin.

Instead of a church tower, a masonry
arch acts as a support for the bells.
Only the large cross over the western
façade points to the building's religious purpose.

Der Eingang zur Kirche befindet sich am Ende eines Verbindungsgangs. Die offene Flügeltür leitet den Blick über den dämmrigen Vorraum hinweg in den quer liegenden Hauptraum.

The entrance to the church lies at the end of a connecting corridor. The open double door leads the eye beyond the dimly lit anteroom into the diagonally positioned main body of the church.

Sorgfältig wurde auch die Wegeführung geplant, der allmähliche Übergang von außen nach innen. Vom Kirchenplatz aus gelangt man über einen Verbindungsgang und den dämmrigen Vorraum zunächst in einen Seitengang mit fünf großen Bögen. Erst hier öffnet sich der quer angeordnete Hauptraum, der von hoch liegenden Fenstern belichtet wird. Mit Ausnahme der Taufkapelle, die Steffann 1961 als eigenen Bauteil auf der Südseite angefügt hat, ist die Kirche in ihrem ursprünglichen Zustand erhalten. Neben dem weiß geschlämmten Mauerwerk wirken als Materialien die blaugrau gestrichenen Fichtenholzbretter der Decke, der graue Naturstein als Fußboden sowie das dunkel gebeizte Eichenholz der Türen, Bänke und Beichtstühle. Unverändert bis heute ist auch der den Altarbereich hervorhebende Lichterkranz aus einfachen Glühbirnen in abgehängten Kupferfassungen. Der ganze Raum strahlt Ruhe und Geborgenheit aus. Weil die Architekten entgegen den seinerzeit gültigen liturgischen Bestimmungen geplant hatten, blieb der Kirche jeder Umbau erspart. Adresse: München-Gern, Nürnberger Straße.

The directional flow was also carefully planned as a gradual transition from outside to inside. From the square outside one first enters a side aisle with five large arches via a connecting corridor and the dimly lit anteroom. Only here does the diagonally postioned main body of the church, lit by windows set high up, open out. With the exception of the baptistry, which Steffann added on the south side in 1961 as a separate part of the building, the church is still in its original condition. Besides the whitewashed masonry, the spruce planks of the ceiling, painted a bluish grey, the grey natural stone of the flooring and the dark smoked oak of the doors, pews and confessionals make effective materials. Also still unchanged is the crown of light, made from simple light bulbs in suspended copper holders, which emphasises the altar zone. The entire space radiates a sense of peace and security. Since the architects' plan ran contrary to the liturgical stipulations of that time, the church was spared any need for modification. Address: Nürnberger Strasse, Gern, Munich.

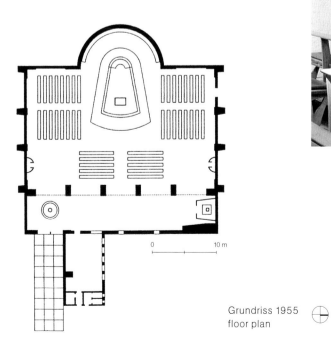

Grundriss 1955
floor plan

Angelo Mangiarotti

Mater Misericordiae
Bollate, Italien
1957

Mater Misericordiae
Bollate, Italy
1957

Die Aufnahme aus der Bauzeit zeigt, dass das Tragwerk einen mächtigen Baldachin aus Stahlbeton bildet. Die überwiegend transluzenten Wände wurden später unabhängig von der tragenden Konstruktion geschlossen.

The photograph taken during construction shows that the supporting framework forms a massive canopy of reinforced concrete. The predominantly translucent walls were later filled independently of the supporting structure.

Als Zentrum eines neuen Wohnquartiers in einem Industrievorort nordwestlich von Mailand geplant, stellt die Pfarrkirche auch eine ingenieurtechnische Meisterleistung dar. Angelo Mangiarotti, der sie zusammen mit seinem damaligen Partner Bruno Morassutti entwarf, hat sich als Architekt besonders mit modularen Bausystemen aus Beton beschäftigt. Die Tragstruktur der Kirche besteht aus vier hohen, leicht konisch zulaufenden Rundstützen, auf denen zwei kastenförmige Hauptträger lagern. Quer zu ihnen verlaufen sechs Nebenträger, welche die Richtung der Wegkirche betonen. Auf den X-förmigen Nebenträgern, die jeweils aus 30 vorgespannten Fertigteilen bestehen, liegen die flachen, ebenfalls vorgefertigten Dachplatten. Das Grundstück der ursprünglich solitären, heute dicht umbauten Kirche wird durch eine nach oben geschweifte Feldsteinmauer eingefasst, in welche die Kreuzwegstationen eingefügt sind. In diesem ›Klostergarten‹ nimmt der Kubus wegen des Grundwasserstandes eine erhöhte Position ein. Zwischen dem Eingang zur Werktagskapelle im Erdgeschoss und der Freitreppe zur Kirche steht ein markantes Kreuz.

Planned as the centre of a new residential district in an industrial suburb to the north-west of Milan, this parish church is also a masterly feat of technical engineering. Angelo Mangiarotti, who designed it together with his then partner Bruno Morassutti, was as an architect particularly concerned with modular concrete systems. The church's load-bearing structure consists of four tall, slightly tapering circular supports on which lie two box-type main girders. Six secondary beams which accentuate the direction of the processional church run diagonally to them. On the X-shaped secondary beams, which each consist of 30 pre-stressed assembly pieces, lie the flat roofing plates, also prefabricated. The plot of the church, which originally stood alone but is now closely surrounded by other buildings, is enclosed by a wall of uncoursed rubble, curved at the top, in which the Stations of the Cross are inserted. In this 'cloister garden' the cube of the church occupies an elevated position because of the groundwater level. Between the entrance to the workday chapel on the ground floor and the flight of steps leading up to the church stands an imposing cross.

Grundriss
floor plan

0   10 m

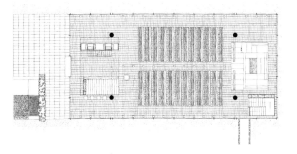

Den eleganten Kirchenraum prägen zum einen die unverhüllt gezeigten Elemente der Konstruktion: die acht Meter hohen Rundstützen und die Kastenträger aus Ortbeton sowie die Nebenträger und Deckenplatten als Betonfertigteile. Mangiarotti hat dabei die Potentiale des frei formbaren Werkstoffs Beton gestalterisch genutzt. Die Anschlusspunkte der Stützen zu den Kastenträgern sind figürlich ausgebildet, bei den Nebenträgern drückt sich der X-förmige Querschnitt aus, die Untersicht der Dachplatten zeigt eine diagonale Struktur. Von gleicher Bedeutung für die Klarheit des Kirchenraums sind die unabhängig vom Tragwerk geschlossenen Wände. Bis zur Höhe der Hauptträger handelt es sich um Stahl-Glas-Fassaden mit lichtdurchlässigen Sandwich-Paneelen, die auch zur Dämmung dienen. Zwischen den beiden Einfachgläsern liegt eine transluzente Schicht aus Schaumstoff, die für eine diffuse Helligkeit sorgt. Auf diese Weise dringt die Außenwelt nur durch das wechselnde Licht in den Raum ein. Umgekehrt wird der Kirchenkubus bei Dunkelheit zu einem prägnanten Leuchtkörper. Adresse: Bollate-Baranzate, Via della Conciliazione.

The elegant church interior is characterised on the one hand by the exposed constructional elements: 8-metre-high circular supports and the box girders of concrete cast *in situ*, as well as secondary beams and roofing plates in the form of prefabricated concrete units. Mangiarotti made creative use here of the potential of the freely malleable concrete material. The points of connection of the supports to the box girders are built up figuratively, in the case of the secondary beams the X-shaped cross-section is effective, and the bottom view of the roofing plates displays a diagonal structure. Of equal importance for the clarity of the interior are the walls, filled independently of the supporting framework. Up to the height of the main supports they consist of steel and glass façades with translucent sandwich panels which also serve as insulation. Between the two simple panes of glass lies a translucent layer of foam which ensures a diffuse light. The outer world thus penetrates into the church interior only in terms of the changing light. On the other hand, in the darkness the cube of the church becomes a clear-cut, luminous body. Address: Via della Conciliazione, Bollate-Baranzate.

Im Laufe der Jahre ist der Schaumstoff in den Sandwich-Paneelen gerissen oder fleckig geworden. Seit 2001 setzt sich ein internationales Komitee für die Sanierung dieses bedeutenden Kirchenbauwerks ein.

Over the years the foam material in the sandwich panels has become torn or blotchy. An international committee has been supporting a project to renovate this important church since the beginning of 2001.

Hans Schädel

St. Josef
Hasloch am Main, Deutschland
1958

St Josef
Hasloch am Main, Germany
1958

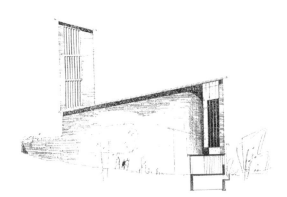

Über 80 Kirchen hat der Würzburger Dombaumeister Hans Schädel (1910 bis 1997) entworfen. Sein bedeutendster Sakralbau ist St. Josef im Dorf Hasloch bei Wertheim am Main. Die kleine, zweigeschossige Filialkirche sitzt außerhalb des Ortes in einem Wiesenhang, dessen Richtung von dem markanten Pultdach gegenläufig aufgenommen wird. Aufgrund seiner massiven Fassaden aus örtlichem Rotsandstein wirkt das Bauwerk von außen unscheinbar. Seine Bedeutung erschließt sich im Inneren: Die drei voneinander unabhängigen, völlig geschlossenen Wandschalen, die jeweils an einem Ende in einer Kurve einschwingen, umgreifen einen offenen Raum mit dynamischem Qualitäten. Die Wandschalen definieren zugleich die liturgischen Orte von Taufstein, Ambo und Altar. Im Kontrast zum Halbdunkel des Eingangsbereichs liegt die Altarzone in strahlendem Licht, das von Süden her durch ein verdecktes Glasband zwischen zwei Wandschalen einfällt. In die Nordwand ist ein Glasmosaik von Markus Prachensky eingefügt. Der Innenraum diente als Vorbild für die Kirche von Miguel Fisac in Vitória [Seite 74].

Würzburg Cathedral's architect Hans Schädel (1910–97) designed more than 80 churches. His most important religious building is the church of St Josef in the village of Hasloch, near Wertheim am Main. The small, two-storeyed daughter church is located outside the village on a sloping meadow, the opposite direction to that adopted by the prominent pent roof. Seen from outside, the building appears to be conventional because of its massive façades in local red sandstone. Its significance is revealed in the interior: the three completely filled wall shells, independent of one another and each curving inwards at one end, enclose an open, dynamic space. At the same time the wall shells define the liturgical sites of baptismal font, ambo (lectern) and altar. In contrast to the half-darkness of the entrance area, the altar zone lies bathed in radiant light that enters from the south via a concealed band of glazing, set between two of the wall shells. A glass mosaic by Markus Prachensky occupies the north wall. The church interior served as a model for Miguel Fisac's Church of the Coronation of Our Lady in Vitória [p. 74].

Das auf den Wandschalen lagernde Pultdach steigt zur Altarzone hin an. Der wiederkehrende Christus, eine Holzplastik von Julius Bausenwein, scheint in dem von Süden einfallenden Licht zu schweben.

The pent roof resting on the wall shells rises continuously up to the altar zone. The Returning Christ, a wood sculpture by Julius Bausenwein, seems to float in the light pouring in from the south.

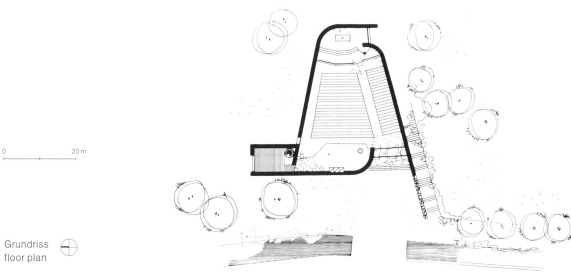

0   20 m

Grundriss ⊕
floor plan

51

Winfried Nerdinger

Architektur ist Bewegung
Le Corbusiers Sakralbauten

Der junge Charles Edouard Jeanneret wurde zwar protestantisch erzogen, aber er entwickelte keine religiösen Neigungen und bezeichnete sich später als Nonkonformisten. Um seine eigene unerbittliche Wahrheitssuche zu erklären, verwies Jeanneret, der sich seit 1923 Le Corbusier nannte, allerdings gerne auf seine Vorfahren, die angeblich von den Katharern, mittelalterlichen Ketzern und Reinheitsfanatikern abstammten. In den zwanziger und dreißiger Jahren war für ihn der Sakralbau kein Thema, erst nach dem Zweiten Weltkrieg setzte er sich mit dieser Bauaufgabe insgesamt vier Mal auseinander. Während die Planung für ein Wallfahrtszentrum in La Sainte-Baume noch nicht zur Ausführung kam, konnte er die Wallfahrtskirche Notre-Dame-du-Haut in Ronchamp und das Dominikanerkloster La Tourette bei Arbresle verwirklichen. Die Kirche in Firminy blieb als halbfertiger Rohbau liegen und ist trotz Bemühungen einer Bürgerinitiative bis heute nicht weitergeführt worden.

La Sainte-Baume: Entwurf ohne Ausführung

Den ersten Impuls zu einer sakralen Planung erhielt Le Corbusier 1946 durch ein Zusammentreffen mit Edouard Trouin, der ein 200 Hektar großes Grundstück bei La Sainte-Baume im Val d'Aups besaß. Das Gelände ist gegen Süden von einer Felswand eingefasst, mit einer Grotte auf halber Höhe, in der nach der Legende Maria Magdalena lebte. Da Trouin plante, hier einen »Ort des Zusammenschlusses und der Meditation« zu schaffen, war Le Corbusier, den seit einem Besuch des Kartäuserklosters in Ema bei Florenz 1907 die Verbindung von Klosterzelle, Gemeinschaft und Natur faszinierte, sofort so begeistert, dass er ein gewaltiges Programm entwickelte: Von einer kleinen Wohnstadt mit vorgelagerter Hotelzone sollte ein Prozessionsweg durch einen neu angelegten Park zu einem Eingang unterhalb des Magdalenenheiligtums führen. Von hier hätte man eine ›unterirdische Basilika‹ betreten, eine durch Stollen verknüpfte Grottenanlage, die aus dem Inneren des Berges heraus gearbeitet werden sollte. Die drei Hauptgrotten dieser von außen nicht sichtbaren ›Basilika des Friedens und der Vergebung‹ sollten durch Rampen und Galerien erschlossen und über schmale, ans Tageslicht geführte Stollen belichtet und belüftet werden. Als Vorbild für diese »Trouinade«, wie Le Corbusier die ganze Anlage in einem Wortspiel mit dem Namen seines Auftraggebers nannte (trou = Loch, trouer = durchlöchern), verwies er auf eine Reiseskizze des Serapeiums in der Villa Hadriana, auf der er schon 1910 die raffinierte indirekte Belichtung einer höhlenartigen Anlage durch ein *trou de mystère* aufgezeichnet hatte.

Das Projekt von La Sainte-Baume blieb zwar nach dem Einspruch einiger hoher Kirchenführer liegen, aber Le Corbusier griff seine Ideen, wie häufig bei seiner Arbeit, bei anderen Planungen wieder auf. Die Wohnstadt mit Hotels variierte er im mediterranen Siedlungstyp *Roq et Rob* und das *trou de mystère* sowie die Mediationshöhle verwirklichte er in der Kirche von Ronchamp. Das Studium von Landschaft, Lage und Ort, das schon die Planung in La Sainte-Baume bestimmt hatte, wurde in Ronchamp besonders bedeutungsvoll. In seinen Erläuterungen und Texten zum Bau der kleinen Wallfahrtskirche hob Le Corbusier diesen Ausgangspunkt seiner Arbeit hervor: »Juli 1950, auf dem Hügel, ich bemühe mich drei Stunden, den Ort und die Horizonte zu erfassen. Allmählich habe ich mich damit angefüllt. [...] Ronchamp? Kontakt mit einem Ort, Situierung in einen Ort, Sprache des Ortes, Worte an den Ort gerichtet. Nach allen vier Himmelsrichtungen.«

Projekt / project
La Sainte-Baume, 1948
Handskizze / sketch

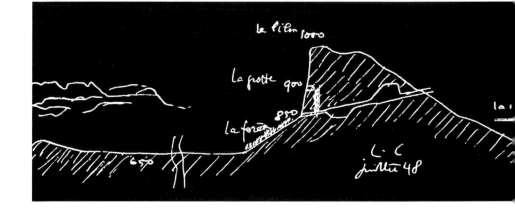

Architecture is Movement
Le Corbusier's Sacred Buildings

Although the young Charles-Édouard Jeanneret was raised in a Protestant home, he was never religiously inclined and later described himself as a non-conformist. To explain his relentless search for truth, Jeanneret — who called himself Le Corbusier after 1923 — often pointed to his forefathers, presumed descendants of the Cathars, members of a severely rigorous ascetic sect in medieval Europe. Sacred architecture was not a theme that interested him in the 1920s and 1930s; only after the Second World War did he devote himself to this particular building task, realising a total of four projects on the theme. While the plan for a pilgrimage centre in La Sainte Baume never reached completion, Corbusier did realise the pilgrimage church Notre-Dame-du-Haut in Ronchamp and the Dominican Friary of La Tourette near Arbresle. The church in Firminy has remained a half-finished skeleton structure that still awaits completion despite the efforts of a citizens' initiative.

La Sainte Baume: Design without Execution

Le Corbusier was first inspired to develop a plan for a sacred building by an encounter in 1946 with Edouard Trouin, who owned a 200-hectare property near La Sainte Baume in the Val d'Aups. The plot terminates in a rock face at its southern end and includes a grotto at mid-elevation, once inhabited, as local legend has it, by Mary Magdalene. Trouin planned to create a 'site for communal union and meditation' and Le Corbusier, who, since visiting the Carthusian monastery in Ema near Florence in 1907, had been fascinated by the connection between monastic cell, community and nature, was so taken with the idea that he devised an ambitious programme. From a small residential town with a hotel district at its entrance, a processional path would lead through a landscaped park to an entrance just below the Magdalene shrine. Visitors would step into a 'subterranean basilica' — a sequence of grottoes linked by a gallery, which was to be excavated from the interior of the mountain. Access to the three principal grottoes of this 'basilica of peace and forgiveness' (invisible from the outside) would be provided via ramps and galleries, while natural light and ventilation would be provided through narrow galleries excavated up to the surface. Le Corbusier referred to a sketch of the *Serapeium* in the Villa Hadrian. Already in 1910, he had outlined a clever strategy for indirect lighting in the cave-like space by means of a so-called *trou de mystère*, which now stood model for the trouinade he designed for his client's complex. ("Trouinade" was a word creation by Le Corbusier, from the French *trou* = hole, and *trouer* = to dig, to perforate).

Although the La Sainte Baume project was shelved after objections from several High-Church leaders, Le Corbusier returned to his ideas, as he so often did, for other planning projects. He varied the residential town with hotels in his *Roq et Rob* Mediterranean housing scheme and applied the *trou de mystère* and the idea of the meditation cave to the chapel at Ronchamp. The study of landscape, location and site, which had already defined the plan for La Sainte Baume, took on particular importance at Ronchamp. In his commentaries and essays on the construction of the small pilgrimage chapel, Le Corbusier emphasised this departure point of his work: 'July 1950, on the hill, I've been trying for three hours to grasp the site and the horizons. Gradually, I have fully absorbed them. [...] Ronchamp? Contact with a location, situating in a location, language of the site, words addressed to the site. In all four cardinal directions'.

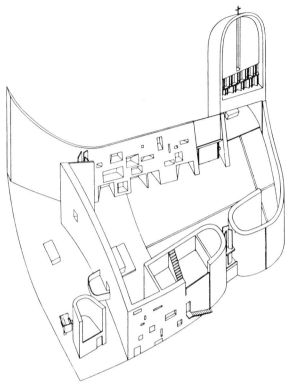

Kapelle / chapel
Ronchamp, 1955
Axonometrie
axonometric projection

Für dieses Sprechen mit dem Ort fand Le Corbusier sogar neue Begriffe: ›visuelle Akustik‹ und ›akustische Form‹. Die Landschaft spricht aus allen Richtungen auf den Ort, und der Architekt antwortet darauf mit den von ihm geschaffenen Formen. In diesem Sinne kann Ronchamp als Reaktion auf den genius loci beschrieben werden, als Schwung und Gegenschwung zu den umliegenden Vogesenhügeln, als Akzentuierung dieses beherrschenden Hügels an der burgundischen Pforte beim Aufblick von der Saône-Ebene oder als Aufnahme und Fortsetzung der Höhenlinien auf dem Hügelplateau. Diese Interpretationen erschließen aber nur eine Seite der Architektur, ihr Gegenstück ist eine Funktionsanalyse. Erst beides zusammen führt zu einem Verständnis des kleinen Kirchenbaus, der seit seiner Einweihung 1955 für viele zur architektonischen Offenbarung und für manche sogar Anlass zum Architekturstudium wurde.

Versöhnung zwischen Kirche und moderner Kunst

Bei der Planung und der Auseinandersetzung mit dem Sakralbau standen Le Corbusier zwei Dominikanerpatres, Lucien Ledeur und Alain Couturier, zur Seite, die sich beide seit den dreißiger Jahren um eine Reform der katholischen Kirche bemühten. In der von Couturier seit 1937 herausgegebenen Zeitschrift *L'Art Sacré* wurde die Ansicht vertreten, dass sich die traditionellen Bilder und Typen der Kirche erschöpft hätten und dass nur die wirklich essentiellen Ideen in eine neue, lebenskräftige Form gebracht werden müssten. Couturier hatte es sich deshalb zur Lebensaufgabe gemacht, eine Versöhnung zwischen Kirche und moderner Kunst herbeizuführen. Immer wieder erklärte er, das Ideal für eine Renaissance der christlichen Kirche wäre es, Genies zu haben, die gleichzeitig Heilige sind; da eine derartige Verbindung in der Gegenwart aber nicht vorhanden sei, sei es besser, sich an Genies ohne Glauben zu wenden als an Gläubige ohne Talent. Die Kirche sollte den Anschluss an die Kunst finden, nicht umgekehrt, und deshalb verhalf er beispielsweise Léger, Lipchitz, Rouault oder Matisse (Kapelle in Vence) zu kirchlichen Aufträgen.

Die wichtigste Verbindung entwickelte sich jedoch zu Le Corbusier. Couturier machte ihn mit christlichem Denken, Symbolen und Problemen vertraut, nannte ihm Literatur und Vorbilder und war der religiöse Pate nicht nur von Ronchamp, sondern auch für das Kloster La Tourette, dessen Bau er an Le Corbusier vermittelte und dafür ebenfalls entscheidende Hinweise gab. Mit Ronchamp und La Tourette, den beiden vielleicht bedeutendsten Sakralbauten des 20. Jahrhunderts, erfüllte Le Corbusier den Lebenswunsch Couturiers, die zeitlosen Elemente des Sakralen mit den modernsten künstlerischen Ideen der Zeit wieder in Einklang zu bringen und damit ihre Lebensfähigkeit zu beweisen.

Der Hügel an der burgundischen Pforte war seit dem 6. Jahrhundert Ort einer Marien-Wallfahrtsort. Seit 1270 ist eine Kirche nachweisbar, die aber aufgrund der exponierten Lage immer wieder zerstört und anschließend wieder aufgebaut wurde. So entstand nach dem Ersten Weltkrieg ein neogotischer Neubau (1924), den deutsche Truppen 1944 zerbombten. Der Hügel war also ein heiliger Ort, an dem sich nach christlicher Auffassung das Transzendente gezeigt hatte, und er war ein höchst geschichtsträchtiger Ort, auf dem sich Geschichte in vielen Schichten übereinander abgelagert hatte. Die Wallfahrts- und Gnadenidee blieb dabei immer gleich, nur die äußeren

Kapelle / chapel
Ronchamp, 1955
Rückseite / rear view

Le Corbusier even coined new expressions for this dialogue with the site: *visual acoustics* and *acoustic form*. The landscape speaks to the site from all directions and the architect responds with the forms he creates. Ronchamp can thus be read as a reaction to the *genius loci*, an oscillating and counter-oscillating response to the surrounding Vosges hills, an accentuation of this particular hill at the Burgundian gateway, which dominates the view from the plains of the Saône River, or a gesture of embracing and continuing the contour of the hilltop. But these interpretations address only one aspect of the architecture. The other approach is to undertake a functional analysis. Only a combination of both leads to a full understanding of the small chapel, which has become an architectural revelation to many since its inauguration in 1955 and has even inspired some to study architecture.

Reconciliation between Church and Modern Art

In the planning and study of sacred buildings, Le Corbusier found support in two Dominican friars, Lucien Ledeur and Alain Couturier, who had been committed to reforming the Catholic Church since the 1930s. From 1937 onwards, Couturier published a journal, *L'Art Sacré*, which postulated that the traditional images and models were superannuated and that the essential ideas of the Church must be translated into a new and vital form. Couturier devoted himself to mediating between the Church and modern art. He insisted that the Christian Church would achieve a renaissance by recruiting members who, ideally, combined artistic genius with a saintly spirit. Since such 'ideal candidates' could not be found at the time, it would be better, he continued, to engage individuals of genius who were non-believers rather than believers who had no genius. The Church must establish a connection to art, not vice versa, and to this end Couturier negotiated ecclesiastic contracts for Léger, Lipchitz, Rouault and Matisse (the chapel at Vence).

But the most important connection he forged was the one with Le Corbusier. Couturier familiarised the architect with Christian thought, symbols and ideals, and advised him on the relevant literature and precedents. He was religious 'godfather' not only for the Ronchamp project but also for the monastery at La Tourette, a commission he had negotiated for Le Corbusier and for which he also provided important impulses. With Ronchamp and La Tourette, perhaps the two most important sacred buildings of the 20th century, Le Corbusier fulfilled Couturier's lifelong desire to bring the timeless elements of the sacred once again into harmony with contemporary artistic ideas to reinforce the viability of the former.

The hill at the Burgundian gateway had been a pilgrimage site dedicated to the Virgin Mary since the 6th century. Records show that a church has occupied the site since 1270, although it was repeatedly destroyed as a result of its exposed and vulnerable location, and each time reconstructed. Thus, after the First World War, a new building was erected in a neo-Gothic style (1924) and later bombed by German forces in 1944. The hill was therefore clearly a sacred site, a place where the Christian belief in the transcendent had become manifest and, moreover, a locale marked by layers of its rich history. Notions of pilgrimage and grace remained unchanged; only the external forms changed in the course of the centuries. The goal of giving a site of such longstanding constancy a new 20th-century form cor-

Kloster / monastery
La Tourette
Eveux-sur-Abresle, 1960

Formen änderten sich im Laufe der Jahrhunderte. Einer Konstante durch die Zeit eine neue, dem 20. Jahrhundert adäquate Form zu geben, dies entsprach sowohl den Bemühungen Couturiers als auch Le Corbusiers, der nach neuen ›Standards‹ suchte, nach Formen, mit denen die Kräfte und Ideen seiner Gegenwart adäquat ausgedrückt werden könnten.

Die Konstante durch alle geschichtlichen Ablagerungen hindurch ist in Ronchamp die Wallfahrt auf den Hügel zum Marien-Gnadenbild, vor dem Messen und Bittgebete stattfinden. Das Gnadenbild ist aber nur ›wirksam‹ am konkreten Ort, an dem der Gnadenakt – Erscheinung oder Hilfeleistung – stattgefunden hat. Da es nicht um die durch den Menschen geschaffenen Formen geht, wird an solchen sakralen Orten häufig die alte Substanz bei Neubauten beibehalten und überformt. So steckt beispielsweise in der barocken Wallfahrtskirche in Ettal, dem Auge unsichtbar, noch der gotische Vorgängerbau. Der äußere Anlass für derartige Transformationen mag oft die Wiederverwendung des Baumaterials sein, die sakrale Bedeutung erschließt sich aber nicht auf dieser Ebene. Auch Le Corbusier stellte sich in diese Tradition und errichtete seinen Neubau wieder mit den Steinen der zerstörten Vorgängerkirche. Davon ist an der verputzten Betonkonstruktion von Notre-Dame-du-Haut nicht das Geringste zu sehen, aber die ›Idee‹ blieb erhalten. Gerade diese Umformung alter Substanz in einen Bau aus neuem Geist dürfte Le Corbusier fasziniert haben und Umformung, Transsubstantiation von Brot und Wein in Fleisch und Blut Christi, ist ja wieder eine zentrale Idee des christlichen Glaubens.

Kapelle in Ronchamp: Architektur und Liturgie

Schon auf den ersten Skizzen fixierte Le Corbusier in wenigen Strichen die Grundform des Baus, indem er den Bewegungsverlauf einer Wallfahrt auf diese Anhöhe im Zusammenklang mit der Liturgie präzise in Architektur umsetzte. Die exakte Übereinstimmung von Grundriss und Formen der Kirche mit der Liturgie betonten sowohl Couturier als auch Le Corbusier in verschiedenen Beiträgen für *L'Art Sacré*. Alle Pilger müssen von Süden einen schmalen Prozessionsweg heraufsteigen und werden beim Austritt auf die Hügelkuppe durch eine in Bewegungsrichtung abgeknickte Wand zum Eingang gewiesen, der sich am höchsten Punkt des Hügels befindet. Dort lenkt der Schwung des Südturms die Pilger in den Innenraum.

Die Pilgerschaft kann in zwei verschiedenen Formen durchgeführt werden. An den Marienfeiertagen kommen Tausende auf den Hügel, für sie wird eine Messe im Freien gelesen. Die Ostwand schwingt nach innen, gibt Raum für den Außenaltar und antwortet damit dem Halbkreis der Versammlung, die Le Corbusier in einem großem Bogen skizzierte und die er ursprünglich auf eine vom Hügel abgehobene Betonschale stellen wollte. Das Gnadenbild kann zu diesen Anlässen gedreht werden, so dass die Marienfigur nach außen blickt.

Einzelpilger suchen dagegen das stille Gebet, die Zwiesprache mit Maria, um eine Gnade zu erbitten. Für sie schuf Le Corbusier den circa 25 mal 15 Meter großen grottenartigen Innenraum, das ›Meditationsschiff‹, das sich durch dicke gerundete Mauern von der Außenwelt abgrenzt und in ein mystisches Dunkel getaucht ist. Im Eingangsbereich ist das schwere, dunkle

Kapelle / chapel
Ronchamp, 1955
Ostwand mit Außenaltar
east wall with exterior altar

responded to Couturier's and Le Corbusier's ambition to create new 'standards' — forms that could adequately express the forces and ideas of their time.

The common factor in all the historic depositories at Ronchamp is the pilgrimage up the hill to the sacred image of the Virgin Mary, in front of which mass is read and prayers of supplication are spoken. But the sacred image is only 'effective' at the concrete site where the act of grace — apparition or miracle — occurred. Since these are not manifestations fashioned by human hands, most new developments of such sacred sites tend to preserve and incorporate the existing substance. Thus the baroque pilgrimage church in Ettal still contains its Gothic predecessor, albeit invisible to the human eye. The outward motivation for such transformations is often the practicality of reusing the existing building material; but their spiritual significance cannot be understood on this plane. Le Corbusier, too, accepted the challenge of this tradition and constructed his new building with reclaimed stone from its destroyed predecessor. None of this is evident in the plaster-finished concrete structure of Notre-Dame-du-Haut, but the 'idea' has been preserved. Le Corbusier was surely fascinated by this translation of an old substance into new form in a spirit of transformation: an allusion to the transubstantiation of bread and wine into the flesh and blood of Christ and, hence, a reflection of the central tenet of Christian faith.

The Chapel at Ronchamp: Architecture and Liturgy

Even Le Corbusier's earliest sketches for the chapel capture the basic shape of the building with a few strokes by translating the sequential movements of a pilgrimage to this hilltop into architecture that is in harmony with the liturgy. Both Couturier and Le Corbusier emphasised the exact agreement between the plan and shape of the chapel with the Christian liturgy in various contributions to *L'Art Sacré*. All pilgrims ascend a narrow processional path from the south, following it to the entrance at the apex of the hill. From this point, the curved wall of the south tower guides the pilgrims into the interior.

The pilgrimage can be undertaken in two different ways. On the days consecrated to the Virgin Mary, thousands arrive at the hill and a mass is read for them under the open skies. The east wall swerves inward, making way for an outdoor altar and mirroring the half circle of the congregation, which Le Corbusier had sketched with a large curve and which he originally planned to position on a concrete shell elevated from the hill. The sacred image can be rotated on such occasions, turning the image of the Virgin Mary so that it faces outward.

Solitary pilgrims, on the other hand, seek silent prayer, a private dialogue with the Virgin to ask for grace. For this group, Le Corbusier created the approximately 25-by-15 metre grotto-like interior — the 'meditation aisle' sheltered from the outside world by thick, rounded walls and shrouded in mystical darkness. At the entrance area, the heavy, dark fair-faced concrete roof is drawn far down in a pronounced curve, only to rise suddenly and steeply in the direction of the altar. The floor, on the other hand, follows the gradient in the direction of the altar, opening the space into a wedge-like shape and offering each pilgrim an individual view of the altar: 'Dedans tête-à-tête avec soi-même

Le Corbusier
in seinem Atelier / in his studio
24, rue Nungesser et Coli
Paris

Sichtbeton-Dach in einer starken Kurve tief herab gezogen und steigt in Altarrichtung steil und straff an. Der Fußboden dagegen fällt, dem natürlichen Bodenverlauf folgend, zum Altar hin ab, so dass sich der Raum keilförmig öffnet. Damit wird jedem Pilger ein individueller Blick zum Altar ermöglicht: »Dedans tête-à-tête avec soi-même – dehors 10 000 pèlerins devant l'autel.« Die völlig unterschiedliche Gestaltung und Wirkung des Äußeren und Inneren entspricht somit auch den beiden Formen der Wallfahrt.

Der Altar steht traditionell genau in der Mittelachse, die Bänke für die Pilger schwenken jedoch aus der Achse und folgen der Südwand, so dass sich der in der Bank Betende buchstäblich dem Altar zuwenden muss. Blickt er geradeaus, so sieht er auf halber Höhe in der Ostwand das in einen Lichtkasten gestellte Gnadenbild. Damit ist Maria architektonisch genau ihr liturgischer Platz zugewiesen, denn Maria ist die Fürbitterin. Sie ist nicht die Mitte, sondern die Vermittlerin zwischen Mensch und Gott. An sie werden die Gebete gerichtet, sie leitet sie weiter, dieser Bewegung folgt die Architektur.

Das Gebet der Pilger an Maria ist das Ave-Maria, das auch in die farbigen Glasfenster der Südwand eingeschrieben ist. Während die Pilger also beten, fällt das in Licht aufgelöste Ave-Maria durch die tiefen Luken der Südwand auf sie und hüllt sie in ihr eigenes stummes Gebet ein. Die ganze Südwand ist ein architektonisches Ave-Maria. Die Architektur wird zum Gebet, das empor getragen wird zum Gnadenbild der Marienfigur, die im Morgenlicht wie eine strahlende Sonne erscheint. Dieses eindringliche Bild machte Le Corbusier zum Signet von Ronchamp: »Marie brillante comme le soleil.« Kleine Löcher in der Wand umgeben diese Sonne wie Sterne eine Gloriole und diese ›Sterne‹ sind wiederum so platziert, dass sie vom Marienbild zum Altar hinüber leiten.

Kunst der Lichtführung

Diese Gebetsgrotte ist nochmals unterteilt, denn die drei Türme grenzen aus dem Raum verschieden große Nebenkapellen aus, so dass ohne gegenseitige Störung fünf Gottesdienste für Gruppen verschiedener Größe gleichzeitig abgehalten werden können. Die drei Türme sind mit ihren Öffnungen genau nach Norden, Osten und Westen orientiert, zu jeder Tageszeit fällt also in die Kapellen ein jeweils anderes Licht ein. Die Lichtführung stammt von dem *trou de mystère* der Villa Hadriana, aber Le Corbusier steigerte die Wirkung noch, indem er das von oben herab rieselnde Licht – er selbst sprach von einem »Lichtbrunnen« – auf einem besonders grobkörnigen, aufgespritzten Beton sich in allen Brechungen materialisieren ließ. Durch die kräftige Färbung der Lichtschächte entsteht darüber hinaus fast der Eindruck einer archaischen Opferhöhle. Die Liturgie wird also durch die Architektur auf ihre Ursprünge zurückverwiesen und gleichzeitig in neuer Formensprache gefasst.

Das Licht spielt die entscheidende Rolle bei der Wirkung der Formen. »Der Schlüssel ist das Licht«, schrieb Le Corbusier, denn Licht schafft erst die Formen. Er hob deshalb auch die Dachschale auf Stützen von den Wänden ab, so dass von einem umlaufenden, 10 Zentimeter hohen Lichtschlitz die Unterseite des Daches modelliert wird. Dadurch wird eine fast irreale Wirkung erzeugt, denn das schwere dunkle Sichtbeton-Dach drückt

Kapelle / chapel
Ronchamp, 1955
Wand mit Glasfenstern
wall with stained-glass
windows

— dehors 10.000 pèlerins devant l'autel' ['Inside, face to face with oneself — outside, 10,000 pilgrims before the altar']. Thus, the contrast in design and impact between exterior and interior reflects the two types of pilgrimage.

The altar is positioned precisely on the middle axis in the traditional manner, while the pews for the pilgrims swerve away from the axis and follow the line of the south wall, an arrangement that compels the person kneeling in prayer to literally turn from the pew toward the altar. Looking straight ahead, the pilgrim sees the sacred image set into a light box halfway up the east wall. Architecturally the Virgin is allocated to a precise liturgical position. For Mary is the intercessor, she is not the centre but the mediator between God and man. The prayers are addressed to her and she passes them on; and the architecture replicates this sequence.

The prayer of the pilgrims is the Hail Mary, which is also inscribed in the stained-glass windows on the south wall. While the pilgrims pray, light penetrates through the Hail Mary inscription in the deep skylights on the south wall, falling down on them and enveloping them in their silent prayer. The entire south wall is an architectural Hail Mary. The architecture becomes a prayer that is carried upward to the votive picture of the Virgin, illuminated by the morning light like a glowing sun. Le Corbusier chose this memorable image as the motto of Ronchamp: 'Marie brillante comme le soleil'. Small holes in the wall surround this sun like stars around a halo and these 'stars' in turn are arranged to guide the eye from the image of Mary to the altar.

The Art of Illumination

This prayer grotto is once again divided, for the three towers separate side chapels of varying sizes from the principal space, creating areas where mass can be read simultaneously for five different groups of varying size without interference. The three towers and their openings are oriented precisely towards north, east and west, allowing a different type of light to penetrate into the chapels at any time of day. The lighting strategy is based on the *trou de mystère* in the Villa Hadrian. But Le Corbusier enhanced the effect by allowing the top light — the architect called it a 'light well' — to bounce off the coarse-grained, shotcrete concrete floor. Moreover, the strong colouring of the shafts of light creates an effect that is not unlike a 'sacrificial cave'. In other words, the architecture returns to the very origins of the liturgy, while at the same time couching it in a new formal language.

The light plays the decisive role in the effect of the forms. 'Light is the key element', Le Corbusier wrote, for light creates form in the first place. To this end, he also separated the roof shell from the walls with columns, creating a 10-centimetre-high band of light that sculpts the circumference of the roof on the underside. The result is almost surreal, for the heavy, dark fair-faced concrete roof presses downward, enveloping the space and yet somehow floating: a suspension of causality that creates an ambivalence ideally suited to the meditative space.

Le Corbusier explained that a crab shell he had found on Long Island and which lay next to his drawing table stood model for

Kapelle / chapel
Ronchamp, 1955
Blick zum Altar
view of the altar

nieder, umschließt und scheint doch gleichzeitig zu schweben: eine Ambivalenz, die dem Meditationsraum, dem Entheben von kausalen Gesetzmäßigkeiten kongenial entspricht.

Als Vorbild für das Dach nannte Le Corbusier eine Krabben-schale, die er auf Long Island gefunden hatte und die neben sei-nem Zeichentisch lag. Erste Schnittskizzen durch das Dach ver-weisen allerdings auch auf einen Flugzeugflügel oder eine Art Raumtragwerk. Außerdem zeigt eine Studie von 1948 für einen Damm bereits jene doppelte Einrollung am Ende der Beton-wand, die er dann bei dem vielfach kopierten Wasserspeier an der Westseite von Ronchamp verwendete. Es ist also anzunehmen, dass Le Corbusier, wie häufig bei seinen Arbeiten der Nach-kriegszeit, sowohl die Architektur wieder auf einfache ursprüng-liche Bedeutungen zurückführen wollte und daher Begriffe wie Brunnen, Grotte, Schale, Schiff Petri oder Zelt Mariens verwen-dete, als auch den Ausdruck des Maschinenzeitalters suchte.

Das zweischalige Dach besteht aus sieben unterschiedlich ge-krümmten, 2,26 Meter hohen Stahlbetonbindern, zwischen de-nen oben und unten Balken liegen, die mit einer 6 Zentimeter dicken Betonschale vergossen sind. Diese ›Stahlbetonmuschel‹ liegt an der Südseite auf den Pfosten eines Stahlbeton-Rahmen-fachwerks auf, das sich von 3,70 Meter Bodenfläche auf 50 Zentimeter verjüngt. Die Hohlräume sind mit Maschendraht überspannt und mit einer grob aufgespritzten, 4 Zentimeter starken Betonschicht überdeckt, in welche die vielgestaltigen tiefen Lichtluken mit unterschiedlicher Laibungsneigung einge-schnitten sind, so dass das Licht im Wechsel des Tages und der Jahreszeiten in zahllosen Varianten buchstäblich in den Innen-raum geführt wird.

Hinweise auf seine Entwurfsideen gab Le Corbusier in der gro-ßen, nach seinem Entwurf emaillierten mittelachsigen Ein-gangstür: Zwei sich berührende Fünfecke bilden die Basis einer Komposition, die ganz auf der Geometrie des goldenen Schnitts, nach dem er den *Modulor* entwickelt hatte, aufgebaut ist. So-weit möglich diente der *Modulor* auch als Maßsystem für den Bau, von der Binderhöhe bis zur Traufkante am Wasserspeier. Im ersten Satz seiner Publikation über Ronchamp betonte er deshalb: »Notre-Dame-du-Haut est un fruit des nombres.« Die menschliche Ratio durchwaltet also die Architektur und kein barocker Expressionismus, wie Le Corbusier empört gegen seine Kritiker schrieb, die diesen Bau zumeist nicht mit seinen bis-herigen Werken in Einklang bringen konnten.

Die Gestaltung der Tür zeigt aber nicht nur die von Le Cor-busier geliebte cartesianische Klarheit von Zahl und Geometrie, sondern sie umfasst auch den zweiten Pol seines Weltbilds: Archaische Zeichen und die Symbole des Lebens im kosmi-schen Kreislauf, wie Stern, Wolke, Vegetation oder die ›kreative Hand‹ des Schöpfers, sind mit der geometrischen Ordnung verknüpft. Die Bildwelt des Eingangs verweist darauf, dass die kleine Wallfahrtskirche nicht nur präzise Umsetzung von Funk-tion und Liturgie in eine neue Architektursprache ist, sondern auch Spiegel von Le Corbusiers Denken und Fühlen. Ronchamp ist von Le Corbusier gestaltet wie ein Szenario menschlichen Lebens und Strebens, das sich zwischen individueller Gottsuche in der Abgeschlossenheit der Grotte und kollektivem Erleben des Transzendenten in der freien Natur, zwischen sich schließen-den und sich öffnenden Räumen, zwischen Urformen und dem Geist des Maschinenzeitalters entfaltet.

the roof. Initial sketches of the roof section, however, also allude to an aircraft wing or a kind of spatial framework. And a 1948 sketch for a dam already features the dual scroll at the termination of the concrete wall, which he later used in the oft-copied concrete rainspout on the west side of Ronchamp. Le Corbusier's language — well, grotto, shell, arc and tent — seems to reflect his intention of taking architecture back to its simple original roots, as he did in much of his post-war work, while at the same time seeking an architectural expression for the Machine Age.

The double-shell roof consists of seven 2.26-metre-high reinforced steel girders bent into differing curvatures, between which beams are placed top and bottom, which are fused with a 6-centimetre-thick cast concrete shell. On the south side, this 'reinforced concrete shell' rests on the posts of a reinforced concrete framework, which diminishes from 3.7 metres to 50 centimetres. The cavities are overlaid with wire-mesh and covered in a 4-centimetre-thick layer of rough shotcrete concrete into which the deep, randomly shaped openings are cut at different angles, virtually guiding the light into the interior at different times of the day and seasons in sheer endless variations.

The large entrance portal is in line with the centre aisle and features an enamelled design created by the architect. The latter provides some insight into Le Corbusier's design ideas: two tangential pentagons form the basis of a composition founded entirely on the geometry of the Golden Section, from which he had developed the Modulor. The Modulor also served as the principal measuring system for the construction, from the girder height to the eaves' edge at the rainspout. In the first sentence of his publication on Ronchamp, Le Corbusier stressed: 'Notre-Dame-du-Haut est un fruit des nombres' ['Notre-Dame-du-Haut is the fruit of numbers']. In other words, the architecture is governed by the human scale and not by a baroque expressionism, to paraphrase Le Corbusier's indignant reply to his critics, most of whom had trouble placing this building in the context of his previous work.

But the design on the portal is more than a mere testament to Le Corbusier's love of Cartesian clarity in numbers and geometry. It also embodies his passion for archaic signs and the symbols of life — star, cloud, plant forms or the 'creative hand' of God — set into a cosmic circle and woven into the geometric order. The pictorial world at the entrance reveals that the small pilgrimage chapel is not only a precise translation of function and liturgy into a new architectural language, but also a mirror of Le Corbusier's thoughts and feelings. The architect designed Ronchamp as a scenario of human life and endeavour, staged between extremes: the individual search for God in the seclusion of the grotto and the collective experience of the transcendent in open nature, closed and open space, primordial forms and forms in the spirit of the Machine Age.

Dialectic of the Monastery

In an essay on Ronchamp, Le Corbusier anticipated potential misconceptions and explained that his use of organic forms in the church should by no means be interpreted as his having abandoned the *boîte à miracles* of his invention, the geometric figure with an animated inner life. Instead, the curvatures he chose simply corresponded to this particular building task.

Kapelle / chapel
Ronchamp, 1955
Haupteingang
main entrance

Dialektik des Klosters

In einer Schrift über Ronchamp griff Le Corbusier selbst möglichen Missverständnissen voraus und erklärte, dass er mit den organischen Formen der Kirche keineswegs die von ihm entwickelte Form der *boîte à miracles*, der geometrischen Figur mit bewegtem Innenleben, aufgegeben habe, sondern dass die gewählten gekurvten Formen der Bauaufgabe entsprochen hätten und dass er für eine andere Aufgabe, wenn sie entsprechend gelagert sei, natürlich wieder die *boîte* verwenden werde. Diese Form ergab sich dann auch geradezu zwingend für seinen nächsten Sakralbau, das Dominikanerkloster La Tourette in Arbresle bei Eveux, das ihm sein Freund Couturier 1953, wenige Monate vor dessen Tod, vermittelte. Als Couturier den Bau des Klosters vorschlug, berichtete ihm Le Corbusier von seinem eigenen architektonischen Urerlebnis, dem Besuch der Kartause in Ema, wo er aus der Gestaltung von individuellem und kollektivem Leben gelernt habe, was eine Architektur zum Glück der Menschen sei. Le Corbusier integrierte deshalb auch die U-förmige Anlage des Kartäuserklosters mit aneinander gereihten Zellen und Erschließungskorridor in die Konzeption von La Tourette. Nachdem ihn ein Leben lang das Erlebnis der Kartause von Ema und die Dialektik von individuellem und kollektivem Leben begleitet hatten, konnte er nun selbst ein Kloster errichten, also letztlich auch sich selbst verwirklichen.

Couturier führte ihn in die Regeln des Klosterlebens ein, skizzierte das Schema einer Klosteranlage und erläuterte ihm die über Jahrhunderte in Architektur fixierten Funktionsabläufe. Auf seine Anregung besichtigte Le Corbusier das Zisterzienserkloster Le Thoronet in der Provence, das nach Couturier »den wahren Geist hat, den ein Kloster haben muss«. Die Klosteranlagen der Zisterzienser, eine Abspaltung von den Cluniazensern im 11. Jahrhundert, sind dadurch gekennzeichnet, dass sie entsprechend den strengen Ordensregeln äußerst karg und schmucklos erscheinen, denn der Gründer Bernard von Clairvaux wollte sie vom Prunk und Glanz des mächtigen Benediktinerklosters in Cluny abgrenzen. Die Kirchen der Zisterzienser wurden deshalb treffend als »Betscheunen« bezeichnet. Eine offen gezeigte Armut bestimmt auch Le Corbusiers Stahlbeton-Kloster La Tourette. Der monastischen Strenge, aber auch dem knappen Etat der Dominikaner, entspricht eine Architektur, die nur von Licht und Schatten ›lebt‹. Allerdings kam es doch zu einer fast fünfzigprozentigen Kostenübersteigung, obwohl zahlreiche Einsparungen vorgenommen und sogar alle Leitungen offen verlegt wurden.

Neben der Kargheit lernte Le Corbusier von Le Thoronet die Umsetzung des Klosterlebens in Architektur. Besonderes Kennzeichen der circa 1400, über ganz Europa verstreuten Zisterzienserklöster ist ein nahezu gleichbleibender, strenger architektonischer Aufbau. Die Klöster liegen in einem Tal, die geostete Kirche befindet sich im Norden, nach Süden schließt sich der Kreuzgang an, dem die einzelnen Räume in funktionaler Entsprechung des Klosterlebens immer in der selben Folge zugeordnet sind. Einzelne Elemente aus diesem Schema wie die abgesetzte Kirche im Norden, das Brunnenhaus im Kreuzgang oder der Kapitelsaal mit zwei Säulen sind in entsprechender Abwandlung auch an La Tourette sofort ablesbar.

Le Thoronet ist nun insofern eine der ganz wenigen Ausnahmen vom Zisterzienserschema, oder in Le Corbusiers Sprache vom

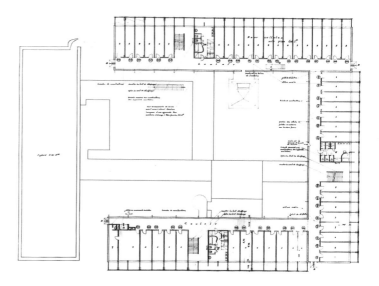

Kloster / monastery
La Tourette
Eveux-sur-Arbresle, 1960
Grundriss mit Zellen
floor plan showing cells

Naturally, Le Corbusier maintained, he would return to the *boîte* for a different task, as long as it was suitable. This form turned out to be the only rational solution for his next sacred building, the Dominican Friary La Tourette in Arbresle near Eveux, a commission negotiated for him by his friend Couturier in 1953, a few months prior to his death. When Couturier suggested the idea of building the monastery, Le Corbusier shared his own architectural ur-experience, the visit to the Carthusian monastery in Ema, where he learned to understand the meaning of architecture for the happiness of mankind through the manner in which individual and collective life was organised. Le Corbusier therefore included the U-shaped plan of the Carthusian monastery with rows of cells and circulation corridor in his concept for La Tourette. Having cherished for so many years the experience at the Carthusian monastery of Ema and the dialectic of individual and collective life, he finally had the opportunity to build a monastery himself — ultimately, an act of self-realisation.

Couturier introduced him to the rules of monastic life, sketched the scheme for a monastery complex and explained the functional sequences that had become fixed in architecture over the centuries. He encouraged Le Corbusier to visit the Cistercian monastery Le Thoronet in Provence, which 'has the true spirit, which a monastery must have' as Couturier put it. The Cistercians were a group that had split from the Cluniac Order in the 11th century. Their monasteries are characterised by a rigorous sparseness and absence of ornamentation in accordance with the strict rules of the order, for the founder Bernard de Clairvaux wanted to distinguish them clearly from the opulence and glory of the powerful Benedictine monastery at Cluny. Cistercian churches were therefore fittingly referred to as 'prayer sheds'. An open emphasis on poverty also characterises Le Corbusier's reinforced concrete monastery La Tourette. The monastic austerity and the limited financial resources of the Dominican friars are perfectly matched by the architecture that 'lives' only through light and shadow. In the end, the final costs still exceeded the original budget projections by fifty per cent, despite numerous economising efforts and the fact that all pipelines and conduits were installed above ground.

In addition to austerity, Le Thoronet also taught Le Corbusier how to translate monastic life into architecture. The approximately 1,400 Cistercian monasteries scattered throughout Europe are characterised by an almost uniform, uncompromising layout. The monasteries lie in a valley, and the east-facing church is located in the northern section of the complex, followed by the cloister to the south, to which the individual rooms are invariably allocated in the same sequence based on the functions of monastic life. Variations on individual elements from this scheme, such as the detached church on the north side, the well-house in the cloister or the capital hall with two columns, are immediately apparent in La Tourette.

It is important to note that Le Thoronet represents one of the few exceptions in the Cistercian scheme — and in Le Corbusier's vocabulary — because the topography of the site suggested a different orientation for this complex, which features a trapezoid cloister and is adapted to the site with a series of stairs. This variation within a rigid scheme corresponded perfectly to the task, for the Dominicans had no fixed monastic architecture. Moreover, La Tourette was to serve as a seminary, where novices

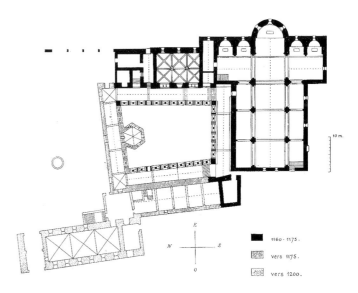

Kloster / monastery
Le Thoronet
Grundriss / floor plan

Standard, als dort die Anlage auf Grund der Topographie nicht wie üblich orientiert ist, einen trapezoiden Kreuzgang besitzt und mit Treppen dem Gelände angepasst ist. Diese Variation innerhalb eines rigiden Schemas entsprach genau der Aufgabe, denn die Dominikaner hatten zum einen keine fixierte Ordens-architektur, zum anderen sollte in La Tourette eine Ordens-hochschule entstehen – die Novizen lernten dort sieben Jahre Philosophie und Theologie, dafür waren besondere Funktionen unterzubringen – und letztlich lag der Bauplatz an einem rela-tiv steilen Hang. Le Corbusier konnte also in Le Thoronet das Schema und gleichzeitig dessen Variation und Adaption an die Topographie studieren.

La Tourette: Geometrie in der Landschaft

Die Einpassung in die spezifische Situation betrieb Le Corbusier wie immer mit äußerster Sorgfalt und stundenlangem Skizzie-ren vor Ort. Dem Gelände folgen nur die abgesetzte Kirche und die beiden Arme des Kreuzgangs, die mit Rampen so geführt werden, dass der Hang – wie in Le Thoronet – erlebbar ist. Das Kloster selbst hob Le Corbusier »wie einen Teller« auf Stützen an und ließ die Natur nahezu unberührt. Er schuf damit eine klare, von der Landschaft abgesetzte geometrische Umrissform, an der er die innere Organisation sichtbar machen konnte. Einerseits bestimmt das jahrhundertealte Schema die Kloster-anlage – die geostete Kirche mit Krypta und Sakristei liegt im Norden, sämtliche übrigen Räume umschließen einen nach Süden angefügten Hof – andererseits ermöglicht die Lage am Hang eine vertikale Gliederung, mit der Le Corbusier die spezi-fische Aufgabenstellung löste, ohne das Schema zu verlassen.

Ein besonderes Kennzeichen von La Tourette ist die präzise Differenzierung der Räume nach Funktionen beziehungsweise Lebensbereichen: individuelles – gemeinsames – geistliches Leben. Dieser Teilung entsprechen privater – kollektiver – sakraler Raum. Der private Bereich der Mönche ist nach oben gehoben, abgegrenzt und streng im Raster der Zellen geglie-dert. Private Räume erhalten präzise geführtes Licht, das den Tagesablauf erlebbar macht. Der kollektive Bereich ist weit-räumig, mit freiem Grundriss und vielfältiger Belichtung durch rhythmisch gegliederte Lichtwände, den *ondulatoires* und *pans de verre*. Kollektive Räume greifen ineinander, ziehen sich vom Eingang nach unten und stellen die Verbindung zum Boden her. Der sakrale Bereich ist mit der Erde verbunden, in sich ab-geschlossen und mit dramatischer Inszenierung der Belichtung gestaltet. Ein viertes Element, die Bewegung, verbindet alle Bereiche. »Architektur ist Bewegung«, dieser Grundsatz Le Cor-busiers gilt auch für La Tourette, wo alle Teile mit einem viel-fältigen System von Treppen, Rampen und Gängen zu einer *promenade architecturale* verknüpft sind.

Trotz der klaren Gliederung und der kargen Erscheinung bietet La Tourette einen unerschöpflichen Reichtum an architekto-nischen Erfindungen. Über eine Brücke betritt man das Kloster durch ein Eingangstor, das mit 226 mal 126 Zentimetern ge-nau nach dem *Modulor* dimensioniert ist, der somit bereits am Eingang das Maß vorgibt, das die ganze Anlage durchzieht und ordnet. Am Eingangsbereich befinden sich vier abgesonder-te, organisch geschwungene Sprechzellen. Es sind die einzigen ›körperlichen‹ Formen im Kloster, denn hier treffen sich die Mönche mit ihren Angehörigen und kommen in Kontakt mit dem weltlichen Leben. Der streng geometrische Klosterbereich,

Kloster / monastery
La Tourette
Eveux-sur-Arbresle, 1960
Innenhof / inner courtyard

would study philosophy and theology for seven years, and the relevant functions had to be accommodated in the design. Finally, the construction site was located on a fairly steep slope. The combination of these factors allowed Le Corbusier to study the scheme at Le Thoronet while also taking note of the variations it offered and its adaptation to the topography.

La Tourette: Geometry in the Landscape

As always, Le Corbusier took great care to adapt to the specific situation and spent hours sketching on site. Only the detached church and the two wings of the cloister follow the topography. The latter are arranged with ramps in such a manner as to render the slope experiential, as is the case at Le Thoronet. Le Corbusier elevated the cloister itself on pilotis, presenting it as if 'on a platter' and leaving the natural environment virtually untouched. The result is a clean, primordial geometric form, distinctly separate from the landscape, which enables the architect to expose the internal organisation. On the one hand, the monastery complex is defined by the centuries-old scheme — the east-facing church with crypt and sacristy at the northern end of the grounds, and all other spaces arranged around a courtyard attached to the south. On the other hand, the hillside location allowed for a vertical disposition, which Le Corbusier used to solve the specific task without abandoning the scheme.

One distinct characteristic of La Tourette is the precise differentiation of spaces according to functions or living areas respectively, into areas for individual, communal and spiritual life. This division is complemented by private, communal and sacred spaces. The friars' private area is elevated, demarcated and strictly divided in accordance with the grid of the cells. Private rooms are lit with great precision to render the passage of the day experiential. The collective area is spacious, with an open ground plan and varied lighting through rhythmically articulated light walls, the *ondulatoires* and *pans de verre*. The communal rooms flow into one another, progress downward from the entrance and establish a connection to the ground. The sacred area is linked to the earth, self-contained and notable for the dramatically staged lighting scheme. A fourth element — movement — connects all areas. 'Architecture is movement' — Le Corbusier's fundamental principle — also applies to La Tourette, where all parts are linked into a *promenade architecturale* by means of a diverse system of stairs, ramps and corridors.

Despite its clear division and frugal appearance, La Tourette offers an inexhaustible abundance of architectonic invention. Access to the monastery is via a bridge and through an entrance portal, whose measurements of 226 x 126 centimetres correspond precisely to the Modulor; the scale that defines the entire complex is thus already established at the entrance. Four detached, organically curved meeting cells are located at the entrance area. These are the only 'corporeal' forms in the monastery, for this is where the monks meet with relatives and come into contact with worldly life. The strictly geometric monastic area, the world of the sacred and the spiritual, remains untouched by this contact. From the entrance, the movement of the communal space proceeds through tall study rooms to the library, which acts as a fluid link between two wings of the monastery. This change in direction is structurally illustrated in the halved round-shafted pillars. Seminar rooms of varying sizes

Kloster / monastery
La Tourette
Eveux-sur-Arbresle, 1960
Gang vor den Zellen
corridor outside the cells

Winfried Nerdinger

die Welt des Sakralen und Geistigen, bleibt davon unberührt. Vom Eingang verläuft die Bewegung des kollektiven Raums durch hohe Studierräume zur Bibliothek, die fließend zwei Flügel des Klosters verbindet. Diese Schwenkung ist konstruktiv an den halbierten Rundpfeilern ablesbar. Auf der Westseite schließen sich Seminarräume verschiedener Größe an. Innerhalb dieses kollektiven Bereichs steigt man hinab zum Sammelpunkt der Mönche, dem Atrium, das als Verteiler zu Kapitelsaal, Refektorium, Kreuzgang und Kirche dient.

Der private Bereich wird ebenfalls von der Eingangsebene erschlossen, von der man zu den zwei Geschossen mit einhundert Arbeitszellen hinaufsteigt, die alle im Modulormaß 183 mal 226 mal 592 Zentimeter (10,8 Quadratmeter) dimensioniert sind. Der Raum kann somit in Höhe und Breite mit ausgestreckten Armen berührt und körperlich erfahren werden. Mit der Loggia ergibt sich eine Raumtiefe von 766 Zentimetern, die in einzelne Bereiche – Hygiene, Schlafen, Arbeiten, Ausblick – differenziert ist. Diese Differenzierung unterstreicht der Wechsel im Verputz, der auch das Licht unterschiedlich moduliert: rau im Schlaf-, glatt im Arbeitsbereich.

Krypta mit ›Lichtkanonen‹

Abgetrennt vom privaten und kollektiven Bereich liegt die Kirche im Norden. Der Block aus *béton brut* wird etwa in der Mitte betreten und bietet grandiose Licht-Schattenwirkungen. Der Raum der Mönche im Westen ist durch Lichtschlitze in Sehhöhe und einen schmalen Streifen unter der Decke erhellt. Der Altar steht erhöht und wird durch ein vertikales Lichtband sowie über einen nach Norden geschobenen Seitenaltar dramatisch inszeniert. Im Zusammenwirken des kargen Sichtbetons mit den modulierenden Lichtstreifen entsteht ein überwältigender Raum, der Meditation und Reflexion gleichermaßen ermöglicht und umschließt. Von der Sakristei führt ein unterirdischer Gang zu den Einzelaltären der Krypta, die sich »wie ein Ohr« in den Hang hinausschiebt und durch farbige Lichtkanonen belichtet wird. Trotz der kargen Sichtbetonwände ist die Akustik gut. Ursprünglich wollte Le Corbusier sogar die Gesänge der Mönche mit einem großen Schalltrichter ins ganze Tal übertragen. Das abgeschirmte, geschlossene Kloster sollte »immateriell« in die Welt hinaus wirken.

»Das weise Spiel der Volumen in Licht und Schatten«, Le Corbusiers Definition von Architektur, spielt die entscheidende Rolle auch in La Tourette. So erfand er insgesamt 26 verschiedene Formen, nicht nur um Licht in das Kloster zu bringen, sondern um mit Licht zu gestalten, zu leiten, zu differenzieren und zu wirken. Das Spiel des Lichts, auch im Wechsel zwischen Tag- und Nachtwirkung, ist an kaum einem anderen Bau von Le Corbusier so großartig nachzuvollziehen wie an La Tourette. Ganz bewusst stellte Le Corbusier La Tourette in die große Tradition der christlichen Lichtmetaphysik, die Abt Suger als *per visibilia ad invisibilia* umschrieben hatte und die in den Lichtwänden der Kathedralen, mit denen das göttliche Licht eingefangen werden sollte, kulminierte. Bezeichnenderweise sprach Le Corbusier im Zusammenhang mit den von ihm entwickelten Lichtkanonen über den Altären der Krypta vom »bombardement de la lumière divine«.

Die *pans de verre ondulatoires*, die Jannis Xenakis, ein griechischer Mitarbeiter in Le Corbusiers Büro, entwickelte, kön-

Kloster / monastery
La Tourette
Eveux-sur-Arbresle, 1960
Ostwand mit Krypta
east wall and crypt

are attached on the west side. Within this collective area, one descends towards the monks' gathering place, the atrium, which serves as a circulation zone leading to the main hall, refectory, cloister and church.

The private area is also accessed from the entrance level leading up to the two floors with one hundred work cells, all with the same Modulor measurements of 183 x 226 x 592 centimetres (10.8 square metres). Each cell is therefore on a scale that allows the occupant to experience it physically, to be able to touch walls and ceilings with outstretched arms. With the addition of the loggia, the total room depth is 776 centimetres, divided into individual areas for personal hygiene, sleeping, working and contact with the outside. This differentiation is underscored by the change in the wall rendering, which also modulates the light: a rough surface in the sleeping area, a smooth surface in the working area.

Crypt with 'Light Cannons'

The church to the north lies separate from the private and communal areas. The entrance into the *béton brut* block lies approximately in the middle; the interior offers stunning *chiaroscuro* effects. The area set aside for the monks on the west side is lit through light bands at eye level and a narrow strip below the ceiling. The altar is elevated and dramatically staged through a vertical band of light and a side altar, shifted to face north. The sparse fair-faced concrete and the modulating strips of light combine to create a powerful space; at the same time, it is a sheltering space that promotes meditation and reflection. A subterranean corridor leads from the sacristy to the individual altars of the crypt, which penetrates into the hill 'like an ear' and is lit through coloured light cannons. The acoustics are excellent, despite the bare fair-faced concrete wall. Le Corbusier's original intent was to broadcast the chant of the monks across the entire valley through a large sound funnel, the idea being that the hermetic, enclosed monastery would radiate 'immaterially' into the world.

'The masterly, correct and magnificent play of masses brought together in light', Le Corbusier's definition of architecture, is also the dominant feature at La Tourette. Thus he invented a total of 26 different forms, not only to bring light into the monastery, but to design, direct and differentiate light and to enhance its varied qualities. More than in any other building Le Corbusier created, the play of light and its alternating diurnal and nocturnal effects are most splendidly realised in La Tourette.

The architect placed La Tourette deliberately in the venerable tradition of the Christian metaphysics of light, which the Abbot Suger had paraphrased as *per visibilia ad invisibilia*, and which culminated in the illuminated cathedral walls designed to capture the divine light. Characteristically, Le Corbusier referred to his light cannons above the altars in the crypt as a *'bombardement de la lumière divine'*.

The *pans de verre ondulatoires*, developed by Jannis Xenakis, a Greek staff member in Le Corbusier's office, can justly be described as a modern translation of the medieval illuminated walls. Xenakis' 'wave walls' are composed like musical pieces with rhythm, *glissandi*, *crescendo* and *decrescendo*. Le Corbusier also referred to them as *pans de verre musicaux* for this reason.

Kloster / monastery
La Tourette
Eveux-sur-Arbresle, 1960
Krypta mit Lichtkanonen
crypt with 'light cannons'

nen geradezu als moderne Umsetzung der mittelalterlichen Lichtwände bezeichnet werden. Seine ›Wellenwände‹ sind wie Musikstücke mit Rhythmus, glissendi, crescendo und decrescendo komponiert. Le Corbusier nannte sie deshalb auch »pans de verre musicaux«. Die Abstände der Betonstreben nahm Xenakis aus der roten und blauen Modulorreihe, wodurch ein harmonischer Teilungsrhythmus nahezu selbständig entsteht. Er komponierte also eine ›Lichtsymphonie‹ mit Strecken analog zur Tonharmonie (die allerdings nicht auf dem goldenen Schnitt basiert).

Die vollendete Proportionierung des Ganzen wie der Teile, das kontrolliert inszenierte Spiel der Volumina in Licht und Schatten zur Vermittlung präziser architektonischer Wirkungen und die unendliche Fülle an Eindrücken und Erfindungen kennzeichnen nicht nur Ronchamp und La Tourette, sondern insgesamt Le Corbusiers Architektur, die er immer im engen Zusammenhang mit seiner bildnerischen Tätigkeit sah. Er selbst erklärte, dass das Wesen seiner Architektur erst aus seiner Arbeit an der Malerei verständlich sei. Bekanntlich verbrachte er jeden Vormittag, also die Hälfte seiner Schaffenszeit, in seinem Atelier mit Malen, Bildhauern und Schreiben. Auch zu Zeiten mit vielen großen Bauaufträgen kam er erst nachmittags ins Architekturbüro. Die von funktionalen, konstruktiven und finanziellen Zwängen freie, künstlerische Tätigkeit sowie die unablässige Schulung der ästhetischen Wahrnehmung ermöglichten ihm offensichtlich, Architektur als gestalterische Einheit, als vollendetes Kunstwerk zu konzipieren.

Dem am 1. Juni 1961 eingeweihten Kloster mangelte es schon in den sechziger Jahren an Novizen und Studenten. In den siebziger Jahren wurde die Ausbildung nach Lyon verlegt, seitdem leben in La Tourette nur noch eine Handvoll Mönche, und das Kloster dient als Bildungsstätte ›Centre Thomas Morus et Albert Le Grand‹. Aus dem geschlossenen Konvent wurde ein offenes Haus, eine Pilgerstätte für Architekten aus aller Welt.

Firminy: unvollendetes Projekt

Den letzten Auftrag für einen Sakralbau erhielt Le Corbusier über den mit ihm befreundeten Bürgermeister von Firminy, Claudius-Petit, der seine Stadt mit Le Corbusiers Genie verbinden wollte und ihm die Planung einer Unité, eines Stadions, eines Jugendheims und einer Kirche zuwies. Ganz bewusst suchte er wieder eine neue gestalterische Lösung, um neben Ronchamp und La Tourette einen »dritten neuartigen Kirchentyp« zu schaffen. Über quadratischem Grundriss sollte sich eine mächtige hyperbolische Schalenkonstruktion in der Form eines Kegelstumpfs erheben. Beim Parlament in Chandigarh konnte er diese Form, die für ihn Kuppel und Kühlturm, Sakrales und Profanes, Tradition und Fortschritt vereinigte, verwirklichen. In Firminy war bei Le Corbusiers Tod nur der Unterbau hergestellt und als sich dann ein politischer Wechsel vollzog, blieb der Rohbau leider liegen. Mit Notre-Dame-du-Haut und La Tourette hatte er jedoch schon zwei unsterbliche Meisterwerke der Sakralarchitektur geschaffen.

Projekt / project
Firminy, 1955
heutiger Zustand
present state

Xenakis based the distance between the concrete mullions on the red and blue Modulor series, which leads quite naturally to a harmonious rhythm of divisions. In other words, he composed a 'symphony of light' in sections that are analogous to tonal harmony (although the latter is not based on the Golden Section).

The perfect proportion of the whole as well as of its parts, expressed with great precision in the carefully staged play of light and shadow to bring out the architectonic volumes, and the infinite variety of effects and inventions are not only characteristic of Ronchamp and La Tourette. They define Le Corbusier's architecture in its entirety, which he always understood as being closely linked to his work as a visual artist. He explained that the nature of his architecture could only be understood on the basis of his art. It is well known that he spent every morning, that is the first half of his creative day, in his studio occupied with painting, sculpting and writing. Even during periods when he was dealing with major building contracts, he would only arrive at the architecture office in the afternoon. Artistic activity free from functional, constructional and financial constraints and continuous training in aesthetic perception obviously enabled him to conceive of architecture as an aesthetic whole, a complete work of art.

The monastery, which was consecrated on 1 June 1961, already had a shortage of novices and students in the 1960s. In the following decade, seminary training was moved to Lyon and since then only a handful of monks reside at La Tourette and the monastery serves as a training site, the *Centre Thomas Morus et Albert Le Grand*. The closed convent became an open house, a pilgrimage site for architects from all corners of the world.

Firminy: Incomplete Project

Le Corbusier's final commission for a sacred building came to him through his friend Claudius-Petit, the mayor of Firminy, who wanted to link his town to the architect's genius and assigned him the task of planning a Unité d'Habitation, a stadium, a youth hostel and a church. Le Corbusier deliberately embarked on a search for an entirely new design solution to create a 'third, new type of church' in addition to Ronchamp and La Tourette. A massive hyperbolic shell structure would rise above a square ground plan in the shape of a cone stump. In the Parliament of Chandigarh project, he was able to realise this form, a convergence, in his eyes, of cupola and cooling tower, of the sacred and the profane, of tradition and progress. At the time of Le Corbusier's death, only the substructure was complete at Firminy. With the political change that followed in the town, the skeleton construction was unfortunately left unfinished. Yet in Notre-Dame-du-Haut and La Tourette, Le Corbusier had achieved two lasting masterpieces of sacred architecture.

Le Corbusier
in seinem Büro / in his office
35, rue de Sèvres
Paris

Auguste Perret

St. Joseph
Le Havre, Frankreich
1959

St Joseph
Le Havre, France
1959

Der 109 Meter hohe Turm der Betonkirche dominiert die nach 1945 wieder aufgebaute Stadt Le Havre. Bei
Dunkelheit strahlen der von innen illuminierte Schaft und seine Laterne
wie ein Leuchtfeuer über dem Hafen.

The 109-metre-high tower of the concrete church dominates the town of
Le Havre, rebuilt after 1945. At night
the tower shaft, illuminated from
within, and its lantern, shine out over
the harbour like a beacon.

Auguste Perret (1874–1954), ein Pio-
nier der Stahlbetonbauweise, plädierte auch bei sakralen Bauten für die
Verwendung von Sichtbeton. Nach
dem Zweiten Weltkrieg übernahm er
mit dem Wiederaufbau der Stadt
Le Havre seinen größten Auftrag. Im
Rahmen der nach klassischen Prinzipien, aber mit Betonfertigteilen neu
errichteten Stadt entstand auch der
postum fertiggestellte Kirchenbau,
wobei der mit seinem Kreuz 109 Meter
hohe Turm einen monumentalen
Kontrast zu den horizontalen Häuser-
zeilen bildet. Alle tragenden Bauteile
sind in Ortbeton ausgeführt. Der für
960 Personen ausgelegte Kirchenraum mit einem zentralen Altar befindet sich im quadratischen Unterbau.
Mächtige, vierteilige Pfeiler in seinen vier Ecken tragen den Turm, wobei
V-förmige Diagonalstützen zwischen
dem Unterbau und dem achteckigen Turmschaft vermitteln. Auch die
Seitenwände des Turms sind mit
Betonelementen ausgefacht, in deren Öffnungen viele tausend Glasscheiben in 50 verschiedenen Farben
sitzen. Die von Marguerite Huré entworfene Komposition erzeugt tagsüber faszinierende Lichtspiele auf dem
schalungsrauen Beton.

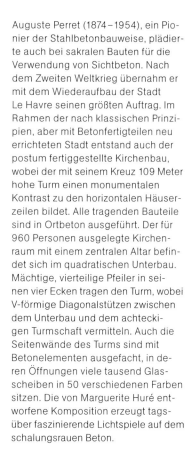

Auguste Perret (1874–1954), a pion-
eer of building with reinforced concrete, advocated the use of exposed
concrete even for religious buildings.
After the Second World War he under-
took his greatest commission: the
reconstruction of Le Havre. The church,
completed posthumously, was also
created within the context of this
rebuilding of the town on the basis
of classical principles but using prefabricated concrete components.
The tower, 109 metres high including its cross, forms a monumental
contrast to the horizontal rows of
houses. All the load-bearing parts of
the building are executed in concrete
which was cast in situ. The church
interior designed to hold 960, with a
central altar, is located in the square
substructure. Massive four-part pillars
in its four corners carry the tower,
whereby V-shaped diagonal supports
connect the substructure with the
octagonal tower shaft. The side walls
of the tower are also faced with concrete elements in which there are
apertures holding many thousands
of panes of glass in 50 different colours. During the daytime, this composition, designed by Marguerite Huré,
creates a fascinating play of light on
the raw, exposed concrete.

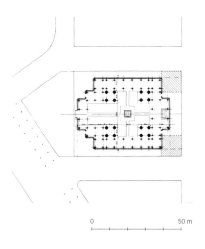

0   50 m

Lageplan mit Grundriss
site with floor plan

Joachim und Margot Schürmann

Christkönig
Wuppertal, Deutschland
1959

Christ the King
Wuppertal, Germany
1959

Der kubische Kirchenbau gehört zu einem Ensemble mit Pfarrhaus, Kindergarten und Jugendheim, das in ein vorstädtisches, nach Westen abfallendes Gelände eingebettet ist. Von der in Kurven ansteigenden Straße aus lässt sich das einfache, aber markante Gebäude deutlich wahrnehmen. Der Baukörper gliedert sich in hoch geführte, fast völlig geschlossene Wände aus Bruchsteinmauerwerk und ein umlaufendes Fensterband unter dem flachen Dach. Beim Eintreten erkennt man sofort, dass die Architekten die Hanglage des Gebäudes geschickt genutzt haben. Obwohl ein ›Einraum‹ mit durchlaufender Decke, hat das Gebäude zwei Ebenen. Unmittelbar bei den Eingängen liegt die Tauf- und Beichtkapelle, fast ein Geschoss höher und durch zwei seitliche Treppenaufgänge erschlossen die Wegkirche, die ebenfalls durch Bruchsteinwände aus örtlicher Grauwacke bestimmt wird. Seinen besonderen Charakter erhält der bescheidene Kirchenraum außerdem durch das von hoch oben einfallende Licht sowie durch das räumliche Holzfachwerk, dessen filigrane Konstruktion das Dach trägt. Adresse: Wuppertal-Elberfeld, Nevigeser Straße.

This cubical church forms part of an ensemble, together with vicarage, kindergarten and young people's home, which is embedded in a suburban plot sloping down towards the west. The simple but striking building can clearly be seen from the road, which winds uphill. The church's exterior is structured by high, almost completely closed walls of undressed masonry and a surrounding band of windows set below the flat roof. On entering the church one immediately recognises that the architects have made skilful use of the building's location on a slope. Although a 'single-room' building with a continuous ceiling, the church is on two levels. Right by the entrances lies the baptismal and confessional chapel. Almost a storey higher and opened up by two side staircases is the church; it too is defined by rough masonry walls made from the local graywacke. The special character of the unassuming interior is further enhanced by the light falling in from high above and by the three-dimensional timber framing, the filigree construction of which bears the roof. Address: Nevigeser Strasse, Elberfeld, Wuppertal.

Die bis auf ein farbiges Fenster schmucklose Tauf- und Beichtkapelle dient zugleich als Vorhalle für die eigentliche Kirche. Das sorgfältig ausgeführte Bruchsteinmauerwerk der Wände wirkt als bergende Hülle.

Undecorated except for one stained-glass window, the baptismal and confessional chapel also serves as an ante-room to the church proper. The carefully executed stonework of the walls provides a protective shell.

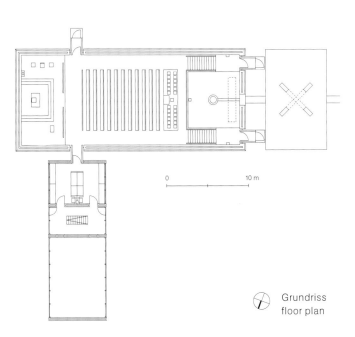

Grundriss
floor plan

0 _____ 10 m

Miguel Fisac

Iglesia de la Coronación de
Nuestra Señora
Vitória, Spanien
1960

Church of the Coronation
of Our Lady
Vitória, Spain
1960

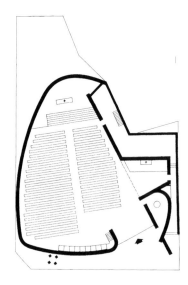

 Grundriss
floor plan

Der Innenraum der kleinen Dorfkirche in Hasloch [Seite 50] stand hier Pate, nicht Le Corbusiers Kapelle in Ronchamp, wie zuweilen behauptet wird. Miguel Fisac, der im Spanischen Bürgerkrieg auf nationalistischer Seite gekämpft hatte, entwarf mit der neoromanischen, 1943 fertiggestellten Heiliggeist-Kirche in Madrid seinen ersten Sakralbau. Nach mehreren Auslandsreisen löste er sich Anfang der fünfziger Jahre vom Historismus. Die Krönungskirche in Vitória, der Hauptstadt des Baskenlandes, ist sein reifstes Bauwerk. Eine geschwungene, völlig geschlossene Wand aus örtlichem Naturstein umfasst auf drei Seiten den Kirchenraum mit 700 Sitzplätzen. Die tragende Wand ist innen weiß verputzt. Im Kontrast dazu steht die gerade Westwand aus Naturstein mit einem Muster aus regelmäßig versetzten Fensterschlitzen. Durch ein hohes, vom Raum aus unsichtbares Glasband zwischen den beiden Wänden fällt das Licht in dramatischer Weise auf den blockhaften Altar, über dem an dünnen Drähten ein Kruzifix von Pablo Serrano aufgehängt ist. Der Raum unter der hellen, dynamisch ansteigenden Holzdecke ist ernst und würdevoll. Adresse: Calle de Eulogio Serdan.

The interior of the small village church at Hasloch [p. 50] was the inspiration for this church, not — as is sometimes claimed — Le Corbusier's chapel of Notre Dame du Haut at Ronchamp. The first religious building designed by Miguel Fisac, who had fought in the Spanish Civil War on the nationalist side, was the Neo-Romanesque Chapel of the Holy Spirit in Madrid, completed in 1943. After several trips abroad, in the early 1950s Fisac turned away from historicism. The Church of the Coronation of Our Lady in Vitória, capital of the Basque region, is his most mature work. A curved, completely closed wall of local natural stone encloses the church interior, which seats 700 people, on three sides. Inside, the load-bearing wall is plastered white, in contrast to the straight west wall of natural stone with a pattern of regularly staggered window slits. Light falls dramatically via a high band of glazing between the two walls that is invisible from below on to the block-like altar, over which a crucifix by Pablo Serrano is suspended on thin wires. The interior space below the light, dynamically rising wooden ceiling is solemn and dignified. Address: Calle de Eulogio Serdan, Vitória.

Nach drei Seiten schließt sich die berühmt gewordene Kirche von ihrer Umgebung ab. Neben der hermetischen, das ansteigende Dach tragenden Natursteinwand steht ein Glockenturm aus Stahlbeton.

This now famous church is closed off from its surroundings on three sides. Beside the hermetically sealed wall of natural stone, which carries the rising roof, stands a bell tower of reinforced concrete.

Sep Ruf

St. Johannes von Capistran
München, Deutschland
1960

St John of Capistrano
Munich, Germany
1960

Bei dieser Kirche in einem Münchner Wohnviertel mit niedriger Bebauung hat Sep Ruf (1908–1982) den Typus des Pantheons aufgenommen, wobei die Außenansicht die Struktur des Gebäudes verbirgt. Der Zentralbau besteht aus zwei massiven, gemauerten Schalen mit unterschiedlichem Durchmesser (32 und 28 Meter), die sich im Eingangsbereich berühren. In dem sichelförmigen, bis zu vier Meter breiten Zwischenraum befinden sich unter anderem die Sakristei und die Taufkapelle. Der Eingang liegt auf der Rückseite der Kirche in einer raumhohen Glaswand, welche in die äußere Schale aus roten Klinkersteinen eingeschnitten wurde. Auch der Kirchenraum mit dem weit vorgezogenen Altar wird vor allem durch das Sichtmauerwerk geprägt. Ein niedriges Lichtband trennt den Zylinder vom Dach, so dass die Decke zu schweben scheint. In der Mitte der Decke aus Holzstäben vor dunklem Hintergrund öffnet sich ein ›Lichtauge‹ von fünf Metern Durchmesser, das zusammen mit der verglasten Eingangswand die Hauptquelle der Lichtführung darstellt. Adresse: München-Bogenhausen, Gotthelfstraße.

Sep Ruf (1908–82) adopted the Pantheon type, in which the exterior conceals the structure of the building, for this church, which is situated in a low-density residential district. The central construction consists of two solid masonry shells of differing diameters (32 and 28 metres) which touch in the entrance zone. Up to 4 metres wide, the sickle-shaped gap between them accommodates, among other elements, the sacristy and the baptismal chapel. The entrance lies at the rear of the church in a full-height glass wall inserted into the outer shell of red clinker bricks. The church interior too, with the altar drawn forward, is characterised primarily by exposed masonry. A low band of windows separates the cylinder from the roof so that the ceiling seems to float. An 'eye of light', 5 metres in diameter, opens up against the dark background in the middle of the slightly canted ceiling of wooden slats. This, together with the glass entrance wall, represents the main source of light. Address: Gotthelfstrasse, Bogenhausen, Munich.

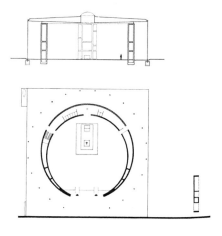

⊕ Grundriss und Schnitt
floor plan and section

0   20 m

Um die einprägsame Rundform der Kirche nicht zu stören, wurde auf einen Turm verzichtet. Umgeben wird der Zylinder von einem ›Schleier‹ aus 22 stählernen Pendelstützen, die das weit überstehende Dach tragen.

In order not to detract from the memorable circular form of the church, it has no tower. The cylinder is surrounded by a 'veil' of 22 steel pendulum stanchions which support the wide overhang of the roof.

Arbeitsgruppe 4
mit Johann Georg Gsteu

Seelsorgezentrum Ennsleiten
Steyr, Österreich
1961/1971

Ennsleiten Pastoral Centre
Steyr, Austria
1961/1971

Diese Anlage bildet im österreichischen Kirchenbau eine Zäsur. Mit der Arbeitsgruppe 4 (Friedrich Kurrent, Johannes Spalt) und Johann Georg Gsteu tritt hier erstmals jene konstruktivistische Richtung auf, die durch die Salzburger Sommerseminare von Konrad Wachsmann geprägt wurde. Zudem ist die Anlage ein Sinnbild für die reformerische Tendenz zur ›Entsakralisierung‹ von Kultbauten. Oberhalb der Steyr-Werke gelegen, umschließen die beiden Häuser des Pfarrzentrums zusammen mit dem höheren Kirchenbau einen Hof. Die Anlage ist aus einem tragenden Element entwickelt, einer Doppelstütze in X-Form. Sechs Stützen ergeben in Verbindung mit einem Betonrahmen ein räumliches Element, das beliebig gereiht oder gestapelt werden kann. Das zweite Prinzip ist die Trennung von ›Gerüst‹ und ›Haut‹: Das Skelett ist dauerhaft, die Raumhülle indes veränderbar. Schließlich nimmt das Bauwerk die Vorstellung vom ›multifunktionalen Raum‹ vorweg. Weil das Pfarrzentrum beim Diözesanbaumeister auf Ablehnung gestoßen war, wurde die Kirche erst zehn Jahre später errichtet.

This complex marks a break in Austrian church building. With Arbeitsgruppe 4 (Friedrich Kurrent, Johannes Spalt) and Johann Georg Gsteu, this was the first appearance of the Constructivist trend that was influenced by Konrad Wachsmann's summer seminars in Salzburg. Moreover, the complex also symbolises the Church's reforming tendency to 'secularise' religious buildings. Overlooking the Steyr-Werke factory, the two houses that make up the parish centre together with the taller church building enclose a courtyard orientated towards the road. The complex has been developed from a load-bearing element — a counterbracket in the shape of an 'X'. Six of these in combination with a concrete frame produce a three-dimensional element that can be lined up or stacked as required. The second principle is the strict separation of 'skeleton' and 'skin': the skeleton is permanent, but the interior skin can be changed. Finally, the edifice anticipates the concept of multi-functional space. Since the parish centre was rejected by the diocesan architect, the church was erected ten years later.

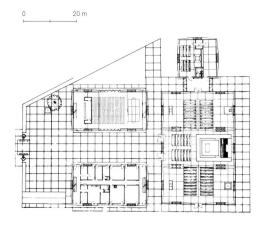

0 ⊢—⊣ 20 m

Grundriss
floor plan

Der anfangs viergeschossig geplante Kirchenraum wirkt sehr nüchtern, lässt sich aber gut nutzen. An den Anschlusspunkten des Skeletts sind die Längsträger plastisch ausgebildet, um den Kräfteverlauf zu zeigen.

The church interior, initially planned to be four-storeyed, makes a very sober impression but is practical in use. The longitudinal supports are built up three-dimensionally at the points of attachment to the skeleton in order to demonstrate the flow of forces.

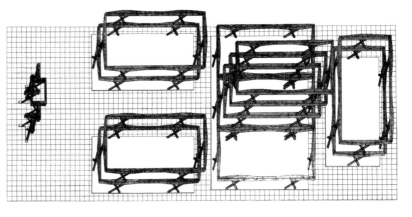

Rudolf Schwarz

St. Theresia
Linz, Österreich
1962

St Theresia
Linz, Austria
1962

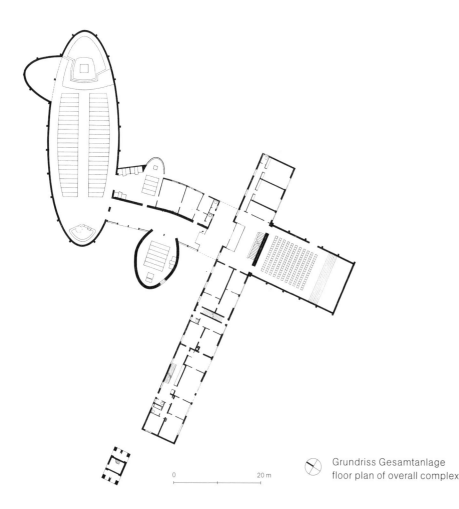

Grundriss Gesamtanlage
floor plan of overall complex

0   20 m

Der Kirchenbau mit seinem hohen Campanile aus offenem Betonmaßwerk liegt südlich der Eisenbahnlinie München–Wien auf einem Hügel und ist daher weithin sichtbar. Er zählt zu den bedeutenden Spätwerken des deutschen Kirchenbaumeisters Rudolf Schwarz (1897–1961) und wurde von Maria Schwarz vollendet. Zusammen mit dem lang gestreckten Pfarrhaus bildet er einen nach Westen orientierten Hof. Die Kirche hat einen ovalen Grundriss, der auf seiner Nordseite um eine Seitenkonche für Orgel und Sänger erweitert wurde. Altar und Taufstein stehen sich in den beiden Rundungen gegenüber: »Den Raum umkreist eine elliptische Bewegung, die vom Altar ausgeht, die Kirchengemeinde einbezieht und dort, in ihrem Rücken, sich wendet.« (Schwarz) Der Eingang zur Kirche liegt neben ihrem Schiff in einer Glaswand, aus der die in Bruchstein gemauerte Marien- und Werktagskapelle mit farbigen Fenstern von Georg Meistermann hervorspringt. Das Tragwerk der Kirche ist ein schlank dimensioniertes Stahlbetonskelett, das mit Ziegelwänden und einem Fensterkranz ausgefacht wurde, der auf den beiden Längsseiten dynamisch nach unten gezogen ist.

The church with its tall campanile of open concrete tracery is set on a hill to the south of the Munich–Vienna railway line and is therefore visible from a long way off. It is considered to be one of the important late works by the German church architect Rudolf Schwarz (1897–1961) and was completed by Maria Schwarz. In conjunction with the long presbytery it forms a courtyard orientated towards the west. The church has an oval ground plan, widened on its northern side by a concha for organ and singers. Altar and font stand opposite each other in the two curvatures: 'An elliptical movement which starts at the altar, includes the congregation and then turns round there, behind them, revolves around the space' (Schwarz). The entrance to the church lies alongside the nave in a glass wall from which projects the combined Lady chapel and workday chapel, built of rubble masonry and with stained-glass windows by Georg Meistermann. The church's supporting framework is a reinforced-concrete skeleton of slender dimensions, filled in with brick walls and a crown of windows that descends dynamically on the two long side walls.

Die eindrucksvolle, aber nüchterne Gestalt der Kirche ist auch eine Referenz an die Industriestadt Linz. Außen springen die schlanken Stützen des Skeletts vor, während die waagrechten Riegel bündig in der Wand liegen. Oben ein farbiges Glasfenster von Georg Meistermann.

The impressive, but restrained form of the church is also a reference to the industrial city of Linz. On the exterior the slim supports of the skeleton protrude, whereas the horizontal bars lie flush in the wall. At the top there is a stained-glass window by Georg Meistermann.

Nach Norden hin erweitert sich das
Kirchenoval durch eine Seitenkonche
für Orgel und Sänger, die sich zum
Altar öffnet. Ein schlanker, im Raum
stehender ›Stab‹ setzt den Stützenraster von fünf Metern fort.

The oval of the church widens to the
north to form a side concha for organ
and singers that opens out to the
altar. A slender, free-standing 'rod'
continues the 5-metre support grid.

Bei einer maximalen Breite von 16
Metern ist der Kirchenraum 48 Meter
lang. Die geschlossenen Felder im
Betonskelett zeigen innen ein rotes
Sichtmauerwerk, in das dunklere Steine eingestreut sind, um die hohen
Wände lebendiger zu machen. Zwischen den Wänden und der Decke
sorgt ein umlaufender, doppelter
Fensterkranz aus schmalen Hoch-
rechtecken für eine großzügige Belichtung. Zum Altarbereich hin sinken
die mit Glasbausteinen ausgefüllten
Fenster stufenweise ab, um danach
wieder aufzusteigen: »So teilt sich der
Bau von unten nach oben in Zonen,
vergleichbar den Notenlinien eines
Musikstücks.« (Schwarz) Die im ganzen Raum unverhüllte Decke ist
ein Plattenbalken mit schmalen Rippen und nach beiden Köpfen des
Bauwerks hin leicht erhöht. Die Stahl-
betonrippen liegen vor der blauen
Decke. Obwohl seine Gestalt aus der
Konstruktion entwickelt ist, vermittelt
der weite Raum ein Gefühl von Erhabenheit. Dieser Eindruck stellt sich
vor allem abends ein, wenn die ›Fest-
beleuchtung‹ eingeschaltet ist.
Adresse: Linz-Keferfeld, Losensteiner
Straße.

The church is 48 metres long with a
maximum width of 16 metres. Inside,
the closed areas of the concrete
skeleton reveal the exposed red masonry in which darker stones are
scattered to enliven the high walls. Between walls and ceiling, a surrounding double crown of windows consisting of narrow, vertical rectangles ensures that there is generous light.
These windows, filled with glass bricks,
gradually descend towards the altar
zone, then climb again: 'The building
is thus divided into zones from bottom to top, comparable to the lines of
a stave in a piece of music' (Schwarz).
The ceiling, exposed throughout, is
a T-beam with narrow ribs and is
raised slightly at both heads of the
structure. The reinforced-concrete
ribs lie in front of the blue ceiling. Although its form is derived from the
construction, the wide space produces a feeling of the sublime. This
impression is particularly strong in the
evening when the festive illumina-
tions are switched on. Address:
Losensteiner Strasse, Keferfeld, Linz.

Längsschnitt
longitudinal section

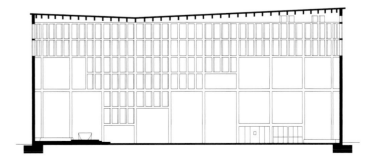

Friedrich Achleitner

Künstlerische Vielfalt und typologische Strenge
Kirchenbau in Österreich zwischen 1950 und 2000

Die Impulse für den Kirchenbau in der Zweiten Republik
kamen nicht aus dem ›Schoß der Kirche‹, sondern von ein paar
kaum wahr- und schon gar nicht ernst genommenen ›Rand-
figuren‹. Etwa von Monsignore Otto Mauer, dem Studentenseel-
sorger und späteren Domprediger zu St. Stephan mit seinem
aktiven Diskussionsforum, der von ihm gegründeten Galerie
St. Stephan, die aus Gründen amtlicher Distanzierung in Galerie nächst St. Stephan umgetauft werden musste. Otto Mauer
hatte aus dem Umfeld der Neuländer – einer aus dem christlich-
deutschen Studentenbund hervorgegangenen, 1921 gegründeten reformerischen katholischen Jugendbewegung – einige
Mitstreiter, darunter Monsignore Karl Strobl, den Initiator der
Studentenkapellen, Joseph Ernst Mayer, den Pfarrer der Rosen-
kranzkirche in Wien-Hetzendorf, und Otto Schulmeister, Redakteur der Zeitschrift *Wort und Wahrheit* und Chefredakteur der
Tageszeitung *Die Presse*.

Eine österreichische ›Parallelaktion‹

Kräftig unterstützt wurde der Versuch, zwischen Kirche und
zeitgenössischer Kunst einen Dialog aufzubauen, von Günther
Rombold in der Zeitschrift *Christliche Kunstblätter* (später
Kunst und Kirche) und dem von Clemens Holzmeister von der
Universität Innsbruck nach Wien geholten Jesuitenpater Herbert Muck, der an der Akademie der bildenden Künste das
Institut für Kirchenbau (später Riten und Verhalten) begründe-
te. Nach Ständestaat und Drittem Reich war die Amtskirche
zunächst kaum imstande, auf die eigenen, vor allem liturgischen
Reformkräfte zu reagieren, geschweige denn auf die in der Kunst
einsetzenden vielfältigen Erneuerungsbestrebungen. So kam es
zur klassisch-österreichischen ›Parallelaktion‹, die sehr spät
wahr- und ernst genommen, in den beiden letzten Jahrzehnten
aber auch wieder halb verdrängt wurde.

Für den österreichischen Kirchenbau der Nachkriegszeit war die
Meisterschule von Clemens Holzmeister an der Wiener Akademie bestimmend. Holzmeister, wenngleich in seiner Spätzeit
keine wegweisenden Bauten mehr realisierend, war der per-
sonalisierte Mythos eines modernen Kirchenbaus. Seine Bio-
graphie war mit dem legendären Aufbruch der zwanziger und
dreißiger Jahre in Deutschland verbunden (Professur an der
Akademie in Düsseldorf), seine besten Bauten standen im Saarland, im Rheinland und Berlin. Für seine Schüler Johann Georg
Gsteu, Wilhelm Holzbauer, Friedrich Kurrent, Josef Lackner
und Johannes Spalt, um nur die bekanntesten zu nennen, war
die frühe Auseinandersetzung mit der deutschen Entwicklung
(Rudolf Schwarz, Dominikus Böhm) neben der Wiederent-
deckung der österreichischen Moderne eine Art ›Logik der For-
schung‹.

Holzmeister, der in seinen lichtbestimmten Räumen eine barocke Sinnlichkeit mit franziskanischem Geist verband, hatte in
seiner ›kulturalistischen‹ und motivreichen Architektur bei den
Schülern einen schweren, aber auch wackeligen Grundstein
gelegt. Sein ›Dreiklang der Künste‹, sein ständestaatlicher Uni-
versalismus, seine ebenso emotionale wie autoritäre Ganzheits-
doktrin enthielt neben einer bewundernswerten ›sinnlichen
Präzision‹ eine demonstrative Abneigung gegen alles Rationale,
Analytische und aufklärerisch Aufmuckende, was er schlicht als
Spinnerei von Nichtskönnern abtat. Die Heiligsprechung der
Zeichenkohle und des 6B-Bleistifts provozierte die ersten Zwei-
fel bei seinen für die Architektur entflammten ›Aposteln‹. Sie

Clemens Holzmeister
oben / above:
St. Peter / St Peter
Mönchengladbach 1933
unten / below:
St. Adalbert / St Adalbert
Berlin 1933

Friedrich Achleitner

Creative Variety and Typological Rigour
Church Architecture in Austria between 1950 and 2000

The impulse for church architecture in the Second Republic did not come from the 'heart of the Mother Church' but from a few 'marginal figures', who received little attention and were certainly not taken seriously, for example, Monsignor Otto Mauer, the student priest and later cathedral preacher at St Stephan's and his lively discussion forum, the St Stephan Gallery, which he was forced to rename 'Gallery near St Stephan' in order to distance himself from the church establishment. Otto Mauer found some comrades-in-arms among the so-called Neuländer — a Catholic reform youth movement founded in 1921, which had split from the Christian-German Student Association — among them Monsignor Karl Strobl, the initiator of the student chapels, Joseph Ernst Mayer, parish priest at the Rosenkranz-kirche in Vienna-Hetzendorf, and Otto Schulmeister, editor of the magazine *Wort und Wahrheit* and later editor-in-chief of the daily *Die Presse*.

A 'Parallel Action' in Austria

Attempts to establish a dialogue between the Church and contemporary art were passionately supported by Günther Rombold in his magazine *Christliche Kunstblätter* (later *Kunst und Kirche*) and by the Jesuit priest Herbert Muck, who was called to Vienna from the University of Innsbruck and who founded the Institute for Church Architecture at the Academy of Fine Arts (later *Riten und Verhalten* [lit. 'Rites and Behaviour']). After decades of existence within a corporative state and the Third Reich, the official Church was barely able to react to the reform movements in its own ranks, which focussed on liturgical reform, never mind the abundance of new directions proposed by the art world. The result was a classic Austrian 'parallel action', recognised and appreciated only very late, only to be denied once again over the last two decades.

Post-war Austrian church architecture was dominated by the leading school of Clemens Holzmeister at the Viennese Academy. Although he no longer created important buildings in his mature years, Holzmeister was the personification of modern church architecture. His name was linked to the legendary awakening in Germany in the 1920s and 1930s (as a professor at the Academy in Düsseldorf), and his best buildings were in the Saarland, in Rhineland and in Berlin. His students — Johann Georg Gsteu, Wilhelm Holzbauer, Friedrich Kurrent, Josef Lackner and Johannes Spalt, to name only the best known — understood the early study of developments in Germany (Rudolf Schwarz, Dominikus Böhm) as a kind of 'logical research' process that went hand-in-hand with the rediscovery of Austrian modernism.

Holzmeister, whose light-flooded spaces combined Baroque sensuality with the Franciscan spirit, had laid a heavy, albeit unstable, foundation stone for students in his architecture which is rich in motifs and cultural references. His 'triad of the arts', his corporative universality, and his holistic doctrine — as emotional as it was authoritarian — promoted not only an admirable 'sensual precision' but also a demonstrative rejection of all that was rational, analytical and enlightening, which he dismissed as incompetent tomfoolery. The sanctification of the charcoal crayon and the 6-B pencil instilled the first signs of doubt among his 'apostles' who were passionately devoted to architecture. They began to yearn for a more finely drawn spirituality, which they found in Rudolf Schwarz, for example,

Porträt / portrait
Monsignore Otto Mauer
Wien / Vienna

entwickelten die Sehnsucht nach einer feiner strukturierten Spiritualität, die sie etwa bei Rudolf Schwarz fanden, der gerade im Stift Wilhering am Entwurf seiner Theresienkirche von Linz arbeitete [Seite 80]. Noch stärker aber wirkte das Auftreten des ›rationalen Utopisten‹ und ›Propheten‹ Konrad Wachsmann in Salzburg. Dieser entwickelte in seinem futuristischen Positivismus eine fantastische Perspektive von baulichem Fortschritt, dessen Wirkung zumindest für die später Kirchen bauenden Holzmeisterschüler – und darüber hinaus, etwa für Ottokar Uhl – grundlegend wurde.

Die architektonische Diskussion wurde dank der engagierten Kirchenmänner permanent von einer liturgischen begleitet und, je nach religiösem Engagement der Architekten, natürlich auch zum zentralen Thema gemacht, obwohl sie – das ist eine riskante Behauptung – für die architektonischen Raumerfindungen nur bedingt maßgebend war. Wie wären sonst so konträre ästhetische Raumkonzepte denkbar, wie sie von Rudolf Schwarz, der Arbeitsgruppe 4 und Johann Georg Gsteu, von Josef Lackner und Ottokar Uhl, von Ferdinand Schuster oder von Günther Domenig und Eilfried Huth entwickelt wurden? Tatsache ist, dass es heute möglich wäre, an Hand der architektonischen Vielfalt im Kirchenbau in den fünfziger und sechziger Jahren eine österreichische Architekturgeschichte dieses Zeitraums zu schreiben.

1955–1970: Ein überschaubares Spannungsfeld

Mit dem Blick von heute stellt sich diese heroische Phase des österreichischen Kirchenbaus fast als geschlossenes Spannungsfeld dar. Wenn man vom frühen Auftakt absieht, der Kirche in Salzburg-Parsch, dem Umbau eines Bauernhofes unter der Protektion Holzmeisters, bei dem ein Jahrzehnt vor dem Zweiten Vatikanischen Konzil ein gewaltiger Schritt in der liturgischen Konzeption gemacht wurde, dann gibt es trotz der ›sprachlichen‹, formalen und gestalterischen Vielfalt ein enges typologisches Beziehungsnetz. Herbert Muck hat einmal vom »Quadratroman« des österreichischen Kirchenbaus gesprochen, weil, angefangen von der Kirche im Innsbrucker Stadtteil Neu-Arzl (einschließlich aller späteren Lackner-Kirchen), über die Kapelle im Kolleg St. Joseph in Salzburg-Aigen der Arbeitsgruppe 4 sowie Gsteus Wiener Seelsorgezentrum Baumgarten bis hin zu den Montagekirchen von Ottokar Uhl und der Kirche in der Grazer Eisteich-Siedlung von Ferdinand Schuster, Räume über dem Quadrat ein zentrales Thema blieben. Gerade diese typologische Fixierung auf einen neutralen, flexiblen Grundriss macht aber auch die architektonischen Unterschiede sichtbar, die sich vor allem im Umgang mit dem Licht, in der Wahl der Materialien und Konstruktionen und auch in den Ordnungen der Altarbereiche ausdrücken.

Obwohl die Arbeitsgruppe 4 (Wilhelm Holzbauer, Friedrich Kurrent und Johannes Spalt) mit dem Projekt für die Wiener Florianikirche die Auseinandersetzung mit der quadratischen Raumfigur ausgelöst hatte, hat sie sich als Gruppe kaum mehr damit beschäftigt. Bei dem basilikal gerichteten Querraum von Steyr-Ennsleiten, zwischen 1958 und 1972 mit Gsteu ausgeführt [Seite 78], wird räumlich ein Dialog mit Schwarzschen Raumgedanken geführt, für das konstruktive Konzept und die bauliche Verwirklichung stand aber sichtbar Wachsmann Pate. Später allerdings tauchen bei Holzbauer (St. Vitalis, Salzburg, 1967–72), bei einigen Entwürfen von Kurrent, darunter

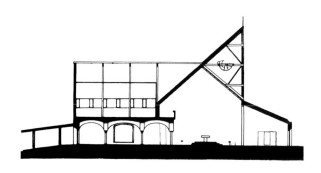

Arbeitsgruppe 4
Pfarrkirche / parish church
Salzburg-Parsch, 1956

who was then working on his design for the Theresienkirche in Linz at the Wilhering Seminary [p. 80]. But the presence of the 'rational Utopian' and 'prophet' Konrad Wachsmann in Salzburg had an even greater impact. In his futuristic positivism, Wachsmann developed a fantastical view of architectonic progress, whose influence was to be fundamental especially for those among Holzmeister's students, who went on to build churches — and beyond that also for Ottokahr Uhl.

Thanks to the efforts of dedicated church officials, the debate on architecture was constantly intermingled with discussions of the liturgy. Depending on the religious attitude of the architects, the latter often became the central theme, although — and this may be a daring proposition — it was only marginally important for architectural and spatial innovations. How else would the dramatically opposed aesthetic spatial concepts of Rudolf Schwarz, the Arbeitsgruppe 4 and Johann Georg Gsteu, of Josef Lackner and Ottokar Uhl, Ferdinand Schuster or even Günther Domenig and Eilfried Huth have been possible? One could write an entire history of Austrian architecture during this period based solely on the variety in church architecture of the 1950s and 1960s.

1955–70: A Manageable Area of Tension

From today's perspective, this heroic phase in Austrian church architecture could almost be seen as a discrete area of tension. Early overtures aside — the church in Salzburg-Parsch, Holzmeister's conversion of a farm house that represented a giant leap forward in the liturgical movement a full decade prior to the Second Vatican Council — one can clearly discern a tight web of typological similarities, despite the variety in 'language', form and design. Herbert Muck once spoke of the *Quadratroman*[1] of Austrian church architecture because spaces projected from the square remained a central theme, starting with the church in Innsbruck's Neu-Arzl district (and all subsequent Lackner churches), to the chapel at the St Joseph Seminary in Salzburg-Aigen (Arbeitsgruppe 4), Gsteu's Viennese Baumgarten parish centre, Ottokar Uhl's modular churches and Ferdinand Schuster's church for the Eisteich housing scheme in Graz. It is precisely this typological basis in a neutral, flexible ground plan that sheds light on the architectonic differences, which are chiefly expressed in the treatment of light, the choice of material and construction as well as the layout of the altar areas.

Although the members of the Austrian group known as Arbeitsgruppe 4 (Wilhelm Holzbauer, Friedrich Kurrent and Johannes Spalt) had instigated the exploration of the square spatial figure with their project for the Viennese Florianikirche, they spent little time working on the problem as a group. The basilical transept of Steyr Ennsleiten, executed in collaboration with Gsteu between 1958 and 1972 [p. 78], enters into a spatial dialogue with the Schwarzian concept of space; the structural concept and the constructional execution, however, were visibly indebted to Wachsmann. Later, highly impressive and independent spatial creations re-emerge, notably in the work of Holzbauer (St Vitalis, Salzburg, 1967–72), in several of Kurrent's designs (among others the church erected between 1992 and 1996 in Aschheim near Munich) but also in Spalt's Salvatorkirche on the Wienerberg (1970–79). Johann Georg Gsteu had translated an exploration of the square — the three-dimensional cube — into a self-contained, highly complex and yet wholly exclusive

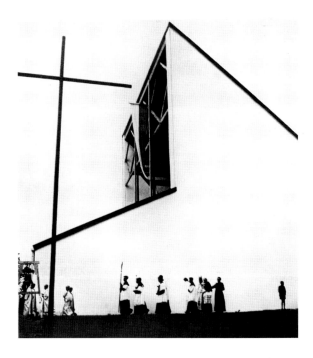

Arbeitsgruppe 4
Pfarrkirche / parish church
Salzburg-Parsch, 1956

---

[1] Literally 'story of the square'; also the title of a 1973 work by the present author.

die in Aschheim bei München von 1992 bis 1996 erbaute Kirche, aber auch bei Spalts Salvatorkirche am Wienerberg (1970–79) sehr eindrucksvolle und selbständige Raumschöpfungen wieder auf. Johann Georg Gsteu hatte bei dem zwischen 1960 und 1965 entstandenen Seelsorgezentrum Baumgarten in Wien [Seite 98] die Auseinandersetzung mit dem Quadrat – dem räumlichen Würfel – auf der Grundlage einer konstruktiven, modularen Ordnung zu einem in sich geschlossenen, sehr komplexen, aber auch alles aus- und abschließenden Raumthema gemacht. Gleichwohl ist mit diesem scheinbar rationalistischen Entwurf ein starker stimmungsvoller und stimmiger Raum gelungen, der kaum mehr überboten werden konnte.

Ähnlich ist es bei Josef Lackner: Für ihn ist der Raum über dem Quadrat das eigentliche Thema seiner Kirchen – schwebende Decken und von oben belichtete Wände, in unterschiedlichen Materialien und betont konstruktiv artikuliert. Die ›sprachliche‹ Spannweite reicht von einer expressiven Zeichenhaftigkeit (in Völs) über die extreme Kontrastierung von Materialien, etwa schwere Betonquader und filigrane Blechkonstruktionen (Wien-Lainz, 1965–68), bis zu komplexen Faltwerken vieler Entwurf gebliebener Projekte. Während Lackners feste und visuell stabilisierte Gehäuse nur im Inneren offen bleiben, geht Ottokar Uhl bei seinen Montagekirchen einen Schritt weiter: Die ›strategischen‹ Bauten auf Widerruf, welche die Entstehung von Gemeinden begleiten und ermöglichen sollten, sind schon in ihrer Herstellung und Konstruktion Bauten auf Zeit. Sie teilen, unter Verzicht auf sakrale Symbole, ihr provisorisches Dasein mit, was nicht besagt, dass es Uhl nicht gelungen wäre, kontemplative, spirituell gestimmte Räume zu schaffen wie in Wien-Kundratstraße (1966/67), die noch heute – trotz Umbau – eine starke Aura besitzen und eine bewusste Beziehung von Kirche und Welt signalisieren.

Zeichen einer Aufbruchstimmung

Merkwürdig: Diese radikale Tendenz zur ›Entsemantisierung‹ von Architektur, der Verzicht auf Redseligkeit und formale Erinnerung – siehe die Wiener Studentenkapellen – hat heute eine stärkere Botschaft, sagt mehr über das Denken dieser Zeit aus als die betont sakralen Konzepte, wie sie etwa noch von Clemens Holzmeister vertreten wurden. In diesen Kontext gehören auch die Arbeiten von Ferdinand Schuster, vor allem seine Mehrzweckhalle der Grazer Kirche in der Eisteich-Siedlung, Symbol einer bedingungslosen Öffnung der Kirche, die allerdings bald wieder zurückgenommen wurde.

Diese Gruppe von Kirchen, die aus dem Diskussionsfeld der späten fünfziger Jahre hervorgegangen sind, verbindet heute viel mehr als man in ihrer Entstehungszeit wahrhaben konnte oder wollte. Der Kunst wurde a priori religiöse Kompetenz zuerkannt (die großen Beispiele, wie etwa die Wallfahrtskirche von Ronchamp [Seite 56], entstanden in Frankreich), wenngleich deren Schöpfer sich oft als Außenstehende oder gar Atheisten erklärten. Auch Otto Mauer und Joseph Ernst Mayer fragten keinen Künstler nach einem religiösen Bekenntnis. Alle diese Kirchen signalisieren die Aufbruchstimmung in eine neu zu entdeckende und neu zu formulierende Welt. So gesehen war Rudolf Schwarz ein großer, in der kirchlichen Tradition stehender Außenseiter: Seine Räume trugen alte Gedanken in die Gegenwart, er baute Erinnerungen an Kathedralen und versuchte, nicht in einem ›kulturalistischen‹ Sinne wie Clemens

Josef Lackner
Kirche / church
Innsbruck, Neu-Arzl, 1960

Ferdinand Schuster
Seelsorgezentrum / parish centre
Graz, 1971

and conclusive spatial theme in his Baumgarten parish centre in Vienna, which was built between 1960 and 1965 [p. 98]. Nevertheless, this seemingly rationalistic design succeeded in creating an atmospheric and harmonious space, unmatched in perfection.

In the case of Josef Lackner, too, the space projected from a square is the principal theme in his churches — floating ceilings and top-lit walls, in a variety of materials and with a pronounced structural articulation. The breadth of 'language' ranges from expressive symbolism (in Völs) to extreme material contrasts, for example heavy concrete blocks and filigree sheet metal structures (Vienna-Lainz, 1965–68), to the complex fold structures in many unbuilt designs. While Lackner's solid and visibly stabilised shells remain exposed only in the interior, Ottokar Uhl takes it one step further in his modular churches: the 'strategic' buildings, devised to encourage the development of community, are unabashedly temporary in terms of construction alone. They announce their provisional existence, doing without sacred symbols. Nevertheless, Uhl succeeded in creating contemplative spaces imbued with a spiritual feeling, as in Vienna-Kundratstrasse (1966/67), which still possess a powerful aura today — despite renovation — and signal a deliberate relationship between 'Church and world'.

Signs of a Spirit of Departure

Paradoxically, this radical trend towards 'de-semanticising' architecture, relinquishing loquacity and formal remembrance (see the student chapels in Vienna, for example) communicates a more powerful message today and speaks more to the philosophy of that time than the emphatically 'sacred' concepts that were, for example, still promoted by Clemens Holzmeister. The work of Ferdinand Schuster also belongs in this context, above all his 'multipurpose hall' in the Grazer Church of the Eisteich housing scheme — symbol of an unconditional opening of the Church, which was, however, revoked soon afterwards.

This group of churches, which emerged from the debates in the late 1950s, has much more in common today than one was able — or willing — to concede at the time they were created. Art was *a priori* viewed as competent in matters religious (the leading exponents, such as the pilgrimage church at Ronchamp [p. 57] were created in France), although the artists themselves frequently declared themselves to be outsiders or even atheists. Nor did Otto Mauer and Joseph Ernst Mayer demand a religious declaration from any artist. All these churches indicate a spirit of departure into a world to be discovered and formulated anew. From this perspective, Rudolf Schwarz was a great outsider firmly planted in the tradition of the Church: his spaces transported ancient ideas into the present, he built memories of the cathedral type and tried (although not in the sense of Clemens Holzmeister's cultural references) to breathe new life into the typological legacy. Schwarz was very much admired by the younger generation, but I doubt that he was truly understood. His language sprang from a different culture and a different time; his 'Rhenish mysticism' had little hope of holding its own in the buoyant atmosphere of the 1960s against the technological myth of a Konrad Wachsmann. As outlandish as it may sound, the route to Rudolf Schwarz's thinking was only possible via the detour of 'Post-modernism', in other words, through yet another misunderstanding.

Ottokar Uhl
Studentenkapelle / students' chapel
Wien / Vienna, 1958

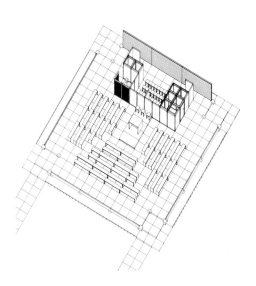

Ottokar Uhl
Kirche / church Kundratstraße
Wien / Vienna, 1967

Holzmeister, das typologische Erbe neu zu beleben. Schwarz wurde von den Jungen zwar verehrt, aber ich vermute, nicht wirklich verstanden. Seine Sprache kam aus einer anderen Kultur und aus einer anderen Zeit, seine ›rheinische Mystik‹ hatte im Aufwind der sechziger Jahre keine Chance, gegenüber dem technologischen Mythos eines Konrad Wachsmann zu bestehen. So verquer es auch klingen mag – der Zugang zum Denken von Rudolf Schwarz war erst wieder über den Umweg der Postmoderne, also über ein weiteres Missverständnis möglich.

1970–2000: Zufälle und Sternstunden

Mit dem Auftreten von Walter M. Förderer und mit der Kampfansage der steirischen Expressionisten Günther Domenig und Eilfried Huth an den Wiener Klassizismus begann in ganz Österreich eine neue Art der Konfrontation. Der Versuch einer Weiterführung der klassischen Moderne, symbolisiert in den Varianten der Mies-van-der-Rohe-Rezeption, wurde von vielen Seiten energisch in Frage gestellt. Erstes Zeichen war die Kirche in Oberwart (Burgenland) von Domenig und Huth, die den vitalen Schweizer Sichtbeton-Brutalismus aufnahm und auch ein betont urbanistisches Moment in die Diskussion einbrachte. Der ›Ausritt‹ des zum Monumentalen neigenden Bildhauers Fritz Wotruba bei der Kirche am Georgenberg in Wien (mit Fritz G. Mayr, 1965–76), mit dem gewaltigen, an archaische Kultstätten erinnernden Skulpturenreigen als Raumkonzept, schuf eine tabula rasa, die scheinbar alles öffnete, in Wirklichkeit aber einen Wendepunkt setzte. Von dieser Phase an, die mit dem starken Rückgang des Kirchenbaus zusammenfiel und zugleich – im Zuge der Ölkrise – dem Bauen generell neue Bedingungen stellte, waren für die Architektur und damit auch für den Kirchenbau neue Zeiten angebrochen.

Die folgenden Kirchen, die man als Schlüsselbauten für die letzten Jahrzehnte ansprechen kann, sind solitäre Leistungen und unter ganz verschiedenen, oft wenig vergleichbaren Bedingungen entstanden, eingebettet in künstlerische Biographien und kaum in einem Zusammenhang zu sehen. Sie reflektieren die architektonische Vielfalt, die sich in den sehr unterschiedlichen Bundesländern entwickelt hat, sie sind Statements zu architektonischen Positionen. Die liturgischen Konzepte sind bestimmt von einem ›nachkonziliaren Standard‹ und weniger von innerkirchlichen, kämpferischen Strategien.

Es bedürfte schon einer sehr ausgreifenden und tief gehenden Analyse, wenn man etwa die Salvatorkirche am Wienerberg von Johannes Spalt (1976–79) in der Architektur der siebziger Jahre positionieren wollte. Der wohltemperierte Raum, aus Holz gebaut und eine zentral- bis osteuropäische Baukultur reflektierend, ist im neueren Kirchenbau kein zweites Mal – nicht einmal als Variation – zu finden. Zwischen der Bergkapelle in Ramingstein von Friedrich Kurrent (1990/91), in geschälten Stämmen von Forstarbeitern über einem Dreiecksgrundriss pagodenartig aufgetürmt, und der Aigener Dorfkirche, im Talboden der Enns von Volker Giencke gebaut (1990–92), besteht so gut wie keine Beziehung, wenn man nicht den Kontrast zwischen stringenter Geometrie und freier Form, zwischen elementarer Bauweise und zeitgenössischer High-Tech-Konzeption als oppositionelle Positionen akzeptieren will. Trotzdem können beide nur in der Gegenwart entworfen und gebaut worden sein. Und beide haben in ihrem Umfeld eine in sich ruhende, starke und eindrucksvolle Wirkung. Kurrents Kapelle ist viel-

Fritz Wotruba
Kirche zur Heiligsten Dreifaltigkeit
Holy Trinity church
Wien / Vienna, 1976

Johannes Spalt
Salvatorkirche
Wien / Vienna, 1979

With the arrival on the scene of Walter M. Förderer and the declaration of the Styrian 'Expressionists' Günther Domenig and Eilfried Huth against 'Viennese Classicism', a new type of confrontation began to dominate the scene in Austria in the guise of a vigorous questioning of how to pursue *classic modernism*, symbolized by the various receptions of Mies van der Rohe. The first sign was the church in Oberwart (Burgenland province) by Domenig and Huth, which adopted the Swiss fair-faced concrete brutalism and also introduced an emphatically urbanist factor into the debate. Fritz Wotruba's 'excursion' — the church on the Georgenberg in Vienna (where the sculptor, known for his penchant for the monumental, collaborated with Fritz G. Mayr in 1965–76) — with its massive *rondo* of sculptures as a spatial concept, reminiscent of archaic cult sites, made a clean sweep that seemed to throw the doors wide open but in reality marked a turning-point. After this moment, which coincided with a pronounced decrease in church building and simultaneously with new demands for development in general in the wake of the 'oil crisis', a new era dawned for architecture on the whole and thus also for church architecture.

The subsequent churches, which can be discussed as key buildings in the last decades, were isolated achievements, created under a wide variety of conditions, often with little in common, embedded in artistic biographies and almost without shared context. They reflect the architectonic variety that developed in the distinctly different Federal states; they are statements of architectonic position. The liturgical concepts are defined by a 'post Vatican-Council standard' and less by internal, combative strategies within the Church.

One would need to embark on a broad and in-depth analysis to position the Salvatorkirche on the Wienerberg by Johannes Spalt (1976–79), for example, in the architecture of the 1970s. This well-tempered space, constructed from timber and reflecting a Central- to East-European culture of building, has no equal in more recent church buildings, not even as a variation. There is virtually no relationship between the mountain chapel in Ramingstein by Friedrich Kurrent (1990/91), a pagoda-like construct of shaven tree trunks raised by forest workers on a triangular ground plan, and the village church in Aigen, built by Volker Giencke at the bottom of the Enns River valley (1990–92), unless one is willing to accept the contrast between stringent geometry and free form, between elemental building method and contemporary high-tech concept as diametrically opposed positions. Still, both exponents could only have been designed and built in the present time. And both exude a self-contained, strong and memorable effect on their surroundings. Kurrent's chapel is perhaps a farewell to a waning culture within a still-resistant landscape, and Giencke's light space is among the most atmospheric and contemplative I have ever encountered.

The church designed by Franz Freytag and Felix Orsini-Rosenberg at Welzenegg in Carinthia (1993) is proof that conversions — of a hall into a church, for example — can also establish a completely new spatial idea through a dialogue with the existing fabric. From a historical perspective, this building can also be regarded as a distillation of fifty years of debate on Austrian church architecture.

Friedrich Kurrent
Bergkapelle / mountain chapel
Ramingstein, 1991

Volker Giencke
Kirche / church
Aigen im Ennstal, 1992

leicht der Abgesang auf eine verschwindende Kultur in einer
noch resistenten Landschaft, Gienckes Lichtraum gehört zu den
stimmungsvollsten und kontemplativsten, die ich kenne.

Dass es auch bei Umbauten – etwa von einem Saal zu einer
Kirche – möglich ist, aus einem Dialog mit dem Bestand einen
absolut neuen Raumgedanken zu entwickeln, zeigt die von
Franz Freytag und Felix Orsini-Rosenberg entworfene Kirche
von Welzenegg in Kärnten (1993). In historischer Perspektive
dürfte man diesen Bau auch als ein Konzentrat aus einer fünfzig-
jährigen Diskussion im österreichischen Kirchenbau ansehen.

Nachklänge von Reformation und Gegenreformation

Schließlich, und nicht zuletzt, könnte man an den beiden
Kirchen von Heinz Tesar, der evangelischen von Klosterneuburg
(1993–95) und der katholischen in Wien-Donaustadt (2000),
den ganzen Konflikt österreichischer Aufklärung und Gegenreformation abhandeln, die innere Dynamik einer sich nie auf-
lösenden Polarität, die bis in die Kunst der Gegenwart lebendig geblieben ist und sich offenbar schon in einem Lebenswerk,
subtilerweise aber mit umgekehrten Vorzeichen, auszudrücken
vermag. So atmet die Kirche von Klosterneuburg [Seite 294],
eingebettet in eine barocke Szenerie, mit dem ovalen Grundriss
und dem expressiv-sinnlichen Umgang mit Licht, fast einen
gegenreformatorischen ›propagandistischen‹ Geist, während
der versenkte Würfel in der Donaustadt, durch eine leichte Dre-
hung sich vom Höhenspektakel der Bebauung distanzierend,
fast einen protestantischen Widerstand inszeniert. Natürlich ist
der schlichte, holzverkleidete Raum mit dem Symbol der Ver-
letzung (des Wundmals) mehr als eine protestantische Prediger-
kirche, doch atmet er zumindest einen ökumenischen Geist.

Man könnte abschließend für den österreichischen Kirchenbau
nach 1950 die These wagen, dass er seine künstlerische Kraft
und Vielfalt, seine typologische Strenge, seine Ausfälle ins
Expressive, ja Sinnlich-Phantastische, seine Offenheit, die Sen-
sibilität für den Ort und die Landschaft, die kulturelle Spannweite, die geringe Berührungsangst mit der Geschichte, das
deklarierte Beziehen von künstlerischen Positionen mit einer
gewissen Risikobereitschaft, dass er alles dies noch immer
aus dem traumatischen Konflikt von Reformation und Gegenreformation, von Aufklärung und universalistischen Traditionen
bezieht. So gesehen, bedurfte die Schule von Clemens Holzmeister des Stachels der Wachsmann-Doktrin. Und dennoch
haben, was man hier verraten darf, beide großen Lehrer in
der Moser-Weinstube in Salzburg zusammen in Eintracht ihre
Viertel Veltliner getrunken.

Franz Freytag · Felix Orsini-Rosenberg
Herz-Jesu-Kirche
church of the Sacred Heart
Welzenegg, 1993

Grundrisse alt / neu
ground plans old / new

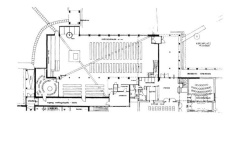

Echoes of Reformation and Counter-reformation

Last but not least, the two churches by Heinz Tesar, the Protestant church at Klosterneuburg (1993–95) and the Catholic church in Vienna-Donaustadt (2000), could serve as a model for the entire conflict between Austrian enlightenment and counter-reformation. This internal dynamic of a still unresolved polarity, whose force remains undiminished even in contemporary art, can it seems be expressed even in the work of one architect, but in an indirect way when the usual characteristics are reversed. Thus the church at Klosterneuburg [p. 294] with its oval ground plan and an expressively sensual treatment of light is almost counter-reformatory and 'propagandistic' in spirit, enveloped as it is in a baroque setting; while the sunken cube in the capital on the Danube, whose gentle rotation establishes a distance to the 'vertigo' of the built environment that surrounds it, seems to stage a Protestant resistance. Of course the plain, timber-clad space with the symbol of the wound (the stigmata) is more than a Protestant preaching church, but at least it is ecumenical in spirit.

To conclude this summary of Austrian church architecture after 1950 one might even propose the thesis that its artistic vitality and variety, typological rigour, expressive, even imaginatively sensual excursions, its openness, sensibility to the site and the landscape, cultural breadth, its mild fear of coming into contact with history, and its declarations of artistic positions with a certain willingness to take risks — that all this still derives from the traumatic conflict between reformation and counter-reformation, enlightenment and universalistic traditions. Seen in that light, the school of Clemens Holzmeister needed the impetus of the Wachsmann doctrine. And yet — as we have revealed here — these two teachers were able to sit together companionably in the Moser wine bar in Salzburg, and share a jug of Veltliner wine.

Heinz Tesar
Kirche / church Donaustadt
Wien / Vienna, 2000

Heinz Tesar
Kirche / church Donaustadt
Wien / Vienna, 2000

Giovanni Michelucci

San Giovanni Battista
Florenz, Italien
1964

St John the Baptist
Florence, Italy
1964

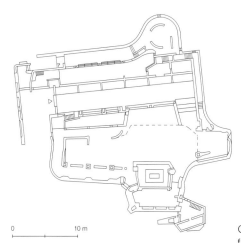

Grundriss
floor plan

0   10 m

Drei Materialien – heller Naturstein, Stahlbeton und Kupfer – prägen die expressiv aufgeladene Kirche am Autobahnkreuz Florenz-Nord. Das bei einer Raststätte in einem gepflegten Park eingebettete Bauwerk soll nicht nur eine Stätte der Besinnung für die Autofahrer sein, sondern auch der beim Bau der ›Autostrada del Sole‹ verunglückten Arbeiter gedenken. Ein modisch gestaltetes Vorprojekt des Ingenieurs Lamberto Stoppa wurde beendet, als die Arbeiten an den Fundamenten begonnen hatten. Giovanni Michelucci (1891–1990), übernahm zunächst widerstrebend die Aufgabe, das Projekt zu vollenden. Seine Bildvorstellung war eine Zeltform als Symbol für das irdische Leben: »Diese Kirche ist eine kleine Stadt, in der die Menschen, wenn die architektonische Sprache ihre Wirkung entfaltet hat, sich wiederfinden sollen.« Vom höhlenartigen Eingang gehen zwei Wege ab: Einer führt über eine Treppe in die Kirche, der andere in die große ›Halle der Regionen‹, wo kitschige Bronzereliefs der Schutzheiligen ausgestellt sind. Der zerklüftete Kirchenraum mit einer konvexen Betondecke fasst als ›Aula‹ den großen Altar, eine Seitenkapelle und den Altar der Hochzeiten auf einer Galerie zusammen.

Three materials — light natural stone, reinforced concrete and copper — characterise this expressive, highly charged church at the Florence North motorway intersection. Situated beside a motorway service, the building is intended to be not just a place of contemplation for motorists but also a memorial to the workmen who lost their lives during the construction of the Autostrada del Sole. A stylish preliminary project by the engineer Lamberto Stoppa was halted after work on the foundations had already begun. Giovanni Michelucci (1891–1990) took over the task of completing the project with some initial reluctance. He visualised a tent shape as a symbol of earthly life: 'This church is a small town in which people should be able to rediscover themselves if the architectural language has been fully effective'. There are two possible routes from the cave-like entrance: one leads via steps into the church, the other into the large 'Hall of the Regions', where kitsch bronze reliefs of patron saints are on display. In the manner of an aula, the rugged church interior with its convex concrete ceiling brings together the large altar, a side chapel and the altar for weddings, located up in a gallery.

Die gespreizten Stützen des Stahlbetonskeletts tragen das mehrfach gefaltete Kupferdach. Die organoiden Pfeiler sollen den Kräftefluss im Tragwerk ausdrücken.

The splayed supports of the reinforced-concrete skeleton bear the high copper roof with its multiple folds. The organic forms of the pillars are intended to express the flow of power in the supporting framework.

Rudolf Schwarz

St. Bonifaz
Aachen, Deutschland
1964

St Boniface
Aachen, Germany
1964

Im Vergleich zu St. Michael in Frankfurt am Main [Seite 38] und St. Theresia in Linz [Seite 80] entwickelte Rudolf Schwarz hier – zusammen mit seiner Frau Maria – eine völlig andere sakrale Baugestalt. Die als Betonkonstruktion mit einer Ausfachung aus Backsteinen postum errichtete Kirche bezeichnete Schwarz als »Stufenberg«. Der dreifach aufgestufte Innenraum drückt sich exakt im Außenbau aus, an dem die Materialien natürlich belassen sind. Im Gotteshaus mit einer maximalen Höhe von 16 Metern versammelt sich die Gemeinde in »drei Armen« um die wenig erhöhte, aber weit vorgezogene Altarinsel. Diese T-Form ist im Deckenbereich aufgenommen: Zwei längs und ein quer laufender Träger bilden den Rost für einen ebenfalls T-förmigen Obergaden, auf dem über der Altarzone wiederum ein rechteckiger Gaden aufgesetzt ist. Die Decken der ›Nebenschiffe‹ sind im unteren Bereich des Rostes eingehängt. Drei nach oben höher werdende Fensterbänder umziehen die verschiedenen Raumgevierte und sorgen für ein intensives Tageslicht: »Der ganze Raum bildet gewissermaßen das Innere eines Berges aus Licht.« (Schwarz) Adresse: Aachen-Forst, Mataréstraße.

Rudolf Schwarz — together with his wife Maria — developed a totally different type of religious building here compared with the churches of St Michael in Frankfurt am Main [p. 38] and St Theresia in Linz [p. 80]. Built posthumously as a concrete structure with brick cladding, this church was described by Schwarz as a 'Stufenberg' (literally, 'stepped hill'). The interior, laid out as three rising steps or levels, is mirrored exactly on the exterior, where the materials are left in their natural state. In the church, with a maximum height of 16 metres, the congregation gathers in three 'arms' around the altar island, which is only slightly elevated but is positioned far forward. This T-shape is repeated in the ceiling area: two longitudinal supports and one transverse support form the grill for a clerestory, likewise T-shaped, on which in turn a rectangular upper storey is set over the altar zone. The ceilings of the 'side aisles' are suspended in the lower area of the grill. Three bands of windows, becoming higher towards the top, surround the various areas of the interior and guarantee strong daylight: 'The entire space forms, so to speak, the interior of a hill of light' (Schwarz). Address: Mataréstrasse, Forst, Aachen.

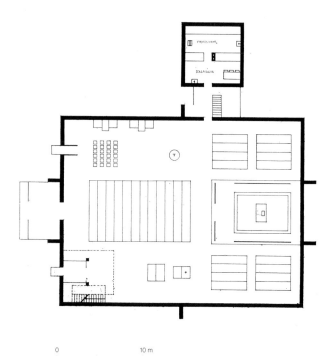

Grundriss
floor plan

0   10 m

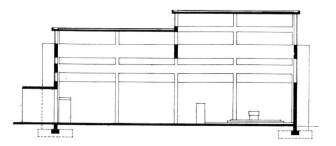

Längsschnitt
longitudinal section

Der von oben großzügig belichtete
Altarbereich bildet das Zentrum der
dreifach aufgestuften Kirche. Der
ganze Raum ist stützenfrei, so dass
der Blick von Wand zu Wand reicht.

The altar area, lit generously from
above, forms the centre of the church
which is built on three levels. The entire space is free of supports, so that
the eye can move from wall to wall.

Johann Georg Gsteu

Seelsorgezentrum Baumgarten
Wien, Österreich
1965

Baumgarten Pastoral Centre
Vienna, Austria
1965

Der Geist des Zweiten Vatikanischen Konzils drückt sich in dieser zentral-räumlichen Kirche aus. In einer westlichen Vorstadt von Wien liegt sie in einem leicht abfallenden Hang an einer dreieckigen Straßenmündung. Die prominente Lage wird durch den hohen Betonsockel betont. Grundlage des Entwurfs war das Quadrat, dessen Geometrie die modulare Ordnung von der Großform bis zum kleinsten Detail bestimmt. Alle Maße sind aus der Betonkonstruktion mit einem Stützenraster von 180 Zentimetern abgeleitet. Nach einem langen Entwurfsprozess ergab sich ein einheitlicher Hallenraum, der von den Stützen und Rippen des Tragwerks geradezu dramatisch geprägt ist. Tageslicht erhält die Kirche durch Öffnungen, die sich in einer Kreuzform von der Deckenmitte bis hinab in die Wände ziehen. Die ursprünglich transluzenten, aus Kunststoff bestehenden Lichtzonen wurden wegen Materialmängeln durch Glas ersetzt. Ebenso streng wie die kubische Kirche selbst ist der Außenraum gestaltet: Vier quadratische ›Satelliten‹ nehmen die Funktionen von Pfarrhof, Sakristei, Pfarrsaal und dem aufgestelzten Glockenträger auf. Adresse: Wien-Penzing, Hütteldorfer Straße.

The spirit of the Second Vatican Council is expressed through this centrally organised church. It is located on a slight downward slope at a three-way road junction in a western suburb of Vienna. The prominent position is emphasised by the high concrete base. The design is based on the square, whose geometry determines the modular arrangement from the overall form down to the tiniest detail. All the dimensions derive from the concrete structure with a 180-centimetre support grid. The long design process resulted in a uniform hall-type space which is characterised in truly dramatic fashion by the supports and ribs of the load-bearing framework. Daylight enters via openings which radiate out in a cruciform shape from the centre of the ceiling and into the walls. The originally translucent plastic light zones were replaced by glass as a result of faults in the material. The exterior is shaped just as strictly as the cubical church itself: four square 'satellites' assume the functions of presbytery, sacristy and parish hall, plus the belfry on an elevated pile foundation. Address: Hütteldorfer Strasse, Penzing, Vienna.

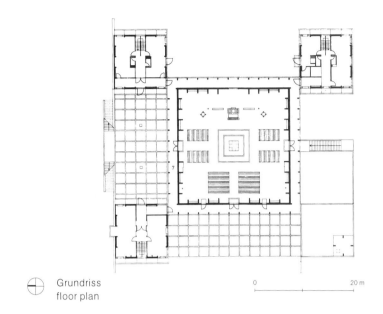

Grundriss
floor plan

0   20 m

Eine Altarinsel nimmt die Mitte des
quadratischen Hallenraums ein,
der durch die Stützen und Rippen der
Sichtbetonkonstruktion charakterisiert ist. Die kreuzförmig angeordneten, nunmehr mit Glas geschlossenen Lichtzonen reichen vom Scheitel-
punkt der Decke bis hinab in die
Wände.

The middle of the square hall, characterised by the supports and ribs of
the exposed concrete structure, is
occupied by the altar island. The light
zones, arranged in a cruciform
manner and nowadays made of glass,
stretch from the crown of the ceiling
down into the walls.

Gillespie, Kidd and Coia

St. Bride
East Kilbride, Großbritannien
1965

St Bride's
East Kilbride, Great Britain
1965

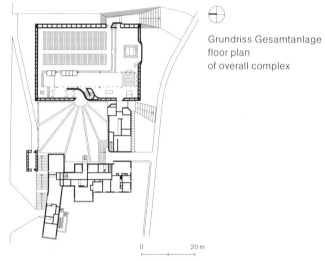

Grundriss Gesamtanlage
floor plan
of overall complex

0   20 m

Die anspruchsvolle britische Kirchenarchitektur der sechziger Jahre
zeichnet sich durch einen Hang zur
Nüchternheit aus, durch einfache
geometrische Formen sowie durch
die Verwendung von Sichtmauerwerk. In Schottland gehörten Gillespie,
Kidd und Coia zu den ganz wenigen
Architekten, die auch im Sakralbau
über konventionelle Lösungen hinaus
dachten. Ein Beispiel ist diese große
Kirche mit Gemeindezentrum in East
Kilbride, einer ›New Town‹ südlich
von Glasgow. Das auf einem Hügel
gelegene Ensemble gliedert sich
in den mächtigen Kirchenbau mit 800
Sitzplätzen, das flache Pfarrzentrum
und die 32 Meter hohe Scheibe des
Campanile. Der Hauptzugang führt
über eine breite Treppe zwischen Turm
und Pfarrhaus auf eine sanft ansteigende ›Piazza‹, an deren Ostseite der
Eingang zur Kirche in den kubischen
Außenbau eingekerbt ist. Durch eine
geschwungene Wand bildet sich
der Eingang im Innenraum ab, einer
Halle mit Galerie. Eindrucksvoll ist
die Lichtführung: Sie erfolgt durch
eine lamellenartig ausgebildete Holzdecke unter dem Glasdach sowie
durch Einschnitte in den doppelschaligen, tragenden Wänden.

The ambitious British church architecture of the 1960s is distinguished
by a tendency to sobriety, by simple
geometric shapes and by the use of
exposed masonry. In Scotland, Gillespie, Kidd and Coia were among the
very few architects who, even in the
context of religious buildings, thought
beyond conventional solutions. One
example is this large church with
a community centre in East Kilbride,
a new town south of Glasgow. The
complex, located on a hill, consists
of the massive church with seating
for 800, the flat presbytery and the narrow, 32-metre-high campanile. The
main access is via broad steps between tower and presbytery to a
gently rising piazza, on the eastern
side of which the entrance to the
church is cut into the cubical exterior.
The entrance is created in the interior by means of a curved wall —
a galleried hall characterised by the
exposed masonry of its walls. The
movement of light in the church is impressive: it comes in through the slat-
ted wooden ceiling below the glass
roof, as well as through incisions in the
double-skinned, load-bearing walls.

Im Kirchenraum wird das Mauerwerk durch Licht und Schatten belebt. Tageslicht fällt zum einen durch die Decke ein, zum anderen durch Einschnitte in den doppelschaligen Wänden.

Inside the church the masonry is enlivened by the play of light and shadow. Daylight enters, on the one hand, through the ceiling and, on the other, through incisions in the double-skinned walls.

Liam McCormick

St. Aengus
Burt in Donegal, Irland
1965

St Aengus
Burt, Donegal, Ireland
1965

Das in Braun- und Grautönen chan-
gierende Bruchsteinmauerwerk
der tragenden Außenwand ist leicht
gewölbt. Ein umlaufendes Fensterband trennt die Wand vom zeltartigen
Dach. Der Kirchenraum wird durch
eine runde Deckenöffnung über dem
Altar belichtet, außerdem durch die
transluzente Glasmalerei von Helen
Moloney.

The variegated brown and grey rubble
masonry of the load-bearing outer
wall is slightly curved. A surrounding
band of windows separates the wall
from the tent-like roof. The church
interior is lit by a round aperture in the
ceiling over the altar as well as by
the translucent stained-glass window
by Helen Moloney.

Mit großer Verspätung konnte sich in Irland ein moderner Kirchenbau durchsetzen. Der eigentliche Wandel begann in den sechziger Jahren unter dem Einfluss des Zweiten Vatikanums. Die Abkehr von rechteckigen Grundrissen war auch hier mit der Absicht verbunden, die Gemeinschaft der Gläubigen architektonisch hervorzuheben. Der bedeutendste irische Kirchenbaumeister seiner Generation ist Liam McCormick, ein besonders überzeugendes Werk von ihm diese Dorfkirche an der irischen Nordküste. In einer Hügellandschaft über dem Meeresarm Lough Swilly gelegen, nimmt der Bau durch seine Rundform wie auch durch das Bruchsteinmauerwerk der Außenwände die Gestalt einer benachbarten alten Fortifikation auf. Der Grundriss zeigt zwei Kreise mit unterschiedlichem Durchmesser, die sich beim Eingang fast berühren. Im sichelförmigen Zwischenraum sind das Baptisterium und Büros untergebracht. Die Gemeinde versammelt sich auf drei Seiten um den Altar, der durch eine unter der Dachlaterne liegende Öffnung in der Decke effektvoll belichtet wird. Das exzentrisch ansteigende Kupferdach mit einem konisch geformten Turm wird innen von runden Stahlstützen getragen.

Modern church-building was eventually accepted in Ireland, but very late. The real change began in the 1960s under the influence of the Second Vatican Council. Here too, the move away from rectangular ground plans was linked to the aim of emphasising the community of the faithful in architectural terms. Liam McCormick is the most important Irish church architect of his generation, and this village church on the north coast of Ireland is a particularly convincing example of his work. Set in a hilly landscape overlooking Lough Swilly, the building takes on the form of a nearby old fortification through its circular shape and the rough masonry of the outer walls. The ground plan shows two circles of differing diameters that almost touch at the entrance. The sickle-shaped space in between houses the baptistry and offices. The congregation gathers on three sides around the altar, which is effectively lit by an aperture in the ceiling positioned below the roof lantern. The copper roof, rising off-centre with a conical tower, is borne internally by a ring of round steel supports.

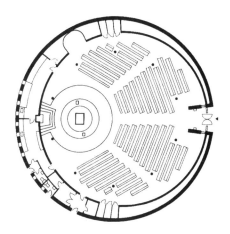

Grundriss
floor plan

Lund & Slaatto

St. Hallvard
Oslo, Norwegen
1966

St Hallvard
Oslo, Norway
1966

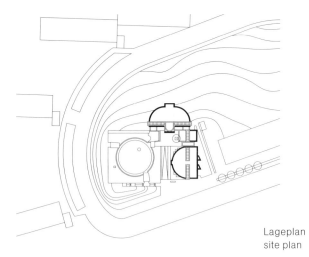

Lageplan ⊗
site plan

Enerhaugen ist ein traditionelles Arbeiterquartier östlich des Osloer Stadtzentrums. Im Mittelpunkt des Viertels, das heute von vielen Ausländern bewohnt wird, liegt das Kloster St. Hallvard mit Kirche und Pfarrzentrum auf einem felsigen Hügel. In den Kubus aus rotem Backsteinmauerwerk, der sich nur nach Süden durch die Fensterreihen des Klosters großzügig öffnet, ist die Kreisform der völlig umbauten Kirche einbeschrieben. Durch schlitzartige Einschnitte im Außenbau sind die drei Bereiche der Anlage voneinander getrennt. Im nördlichen Einschnitt liegt der zurückgesetzte Eingang zur Kirche, die zu den eindrucksvollsten Räumen von ganz Norwegen zählt: Im Dämmerlicht dieser ›Höhle‹ zwischen dem Zylinder aus rauem, breit verfugtem Sichtmauerwerk und der hängenden Betondecke stellt sich sofort eine Atmosphäre der Geborgenheit ein. Eine der wenigen Lichtquellen ist die Glassteinwand über dem Eingang. Der dunkle Boden steigt zu der nach Osten gerichteten Altarinsel leicht an. Der Tiefpunkt der unteren Deckenschale liegt nicht in der Mitte des Raums, sondern auf einem Backsteinpfeiler am Eingang.

Enerhaughen is a traditional working-class district to the east of Oslo city centre. In the middle of the district, where many foreigners live today, is the monastery of St Hallvard, its church and presbytery located on a rocky hill. The circular shape of the church, which is completely surrounded by buildings, is inscribed within the cube of red brickwork, which forms the monastery, and opens out generously towards the south only through its rows of windows. The three zones of the complex are separated from each other by slit-like recesses on the exterior. Set back in the northern recess lies the entrance to the church, which is considered to be one of the most impressive in the whole of Norway. In the half-light of this 'cave', between the cylinder of raw, broadly disposed, exposed masonry and the suspended concrete ceiling, an atmosphere of safety prevails. One of the few sources of light is the glass-brick wall over the entrance. The dark floor rises slightly to the altar island, which faces east. The lowest point of the bottom roof shell lies not in the middle of the space but on a brick pillar at the entrance.

Die schlichten Materialien – Mauerwerk, Sichtbeton und Holz – sind
sorgfältig aufeinander abgestimmt.
Die Kirche beeindruckt auch durch
die Qualität der sachlichen Details.

The simple materials — masonry,
exposed concrete and wood — have
been carefully harmonised. The
church also impresses the visitor
through the quality of its functional
detail.

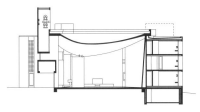

Grundriss und Schnitt
floor plan and section

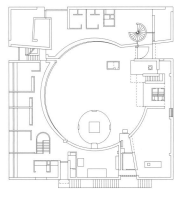

0   20 m

Juliaan Lampens

Wallfahrtskapelle
Oudenaarde, Belgien
1966

Pilgrimage Chapel
Oudenaarde, Belgium
1966

Le Corbusiers Sakralbauten haben
auch in Belgien vielfach nachgewirkt.
Juliaan Lampens ahmte den Meister
aber nicht nach, sondern orientierte sich lediglich an seiner unkonven-
tionellen Haltung. Die mit Rutger
Langaskens entworfene Wallfahrtskapelle ist ein grandioser Betonkörper wie aus einem Guss. Südlich
der flämischen Kleinstadt Oudenaarde liegt sie fast versteckt in einem
bewaldeten Hang. Der Weg zu ihr
steigt zunächst an, um dann in eine
betonierte Zufahrt überzugehen,
die hinunter bis zu dem Vorplatz am
Eingang führt. Als Fußgänger kann
man von einer erhöhten Rasenterras-
se aus direkt in die Kapelle schauen.
Die von einem weit auskragenden
Betonschirm gefasste Südfassade
wirkt sehr einladend. Geteilt wird die
Glaswand von einer Betonwanne
mit integriertem Glockenträger. Das
Bauwerk mit sehr großen Spann-
weiten und einer Lichtkuppel über
dem Altar erstreckt sich über 56
Meter Länge in einer extremen Keil-
form. Sie fällt bis zu einer Seitenkapelle hin ab, die vom Hauptbau
durch ein Wasserbecken getrennt ist.
Adresse: Oudenaarde-Edelare.

In Belgium too Le Corbusier's religious buildings continued to exert an
influence in many ways. Juliaan
Lampens did not however copy the
master but took the latter's unconventional attitude as a basis. Designed in association with Rutger
Langaskens, the pilgrimage chapel
is a magnificent concrete body forming a unified whole. It lies almost
hidden on a wooded slope south of
the small Flemish town of Oudenaarde. The road leading to it initially ascends, then a concrete drive
leads down to the forecourt at the entrance to the chapel. Approaching
on foot, one can look straight into the
chapel from a raised grassy terrace.
The southern façade, framed by a
deep concrete overhang, has a very
inviting look. The glass wall is divided up by a concrete tub with integral
belfry. The building with very large
spans and a dome-light over the altar
extends for a length of 56 metres in
an extreme wedge shape. It slopes
down towards a side chapel, separated from the main building by a pond.
Address: Edelare, Oudenaarde.

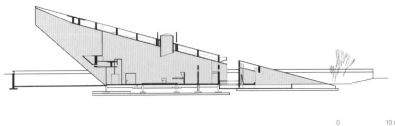

Längsschnitt
longitudinal section

0   10 m

Ein Wasserbecken trennt den Hauptbau von der Seitenkapelle. Die Innenaufnahme zeigt die ursprünglich karge Möblierung des großen Raums durch Sitzelemente aus Beton.

A pond separates the main building from the side chapel. The interior view shows the originally austere furnishing of the large space with concrete seating elements.

Franz Füeg

St. Pius
Meggen, Schweiz
1966

St Pius
Meggen, Switzerland
1966

Längsschnitt
longitudinal section

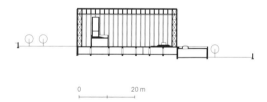

0   20 m

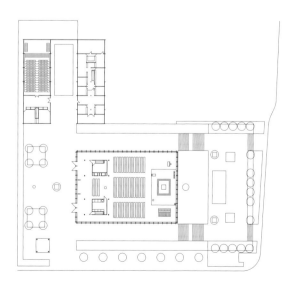

Grundriss
floor plan

Um 1960 gehörte Franz Füeg zur so genannten Solothurner Schule, die vor allem in der Nachfolge von Mies van der Rohe das analytische Bauen gegen die neu aufkommende plastische Architektur vertrat. Als Redakteur der Zeitschrift *Bauen + Wohnen* hatte er sich auch zum Kirchenbau geäußert: »Für den Architekten steht nur fest, dass er die Kirche als Bauwerk so gestaltet, dass sie den gottesdienstlichen und seelsorgerischen Ansprüchen genügt, dass er die Architektur korrekt aus diesen und aus der Konstruktion gewinnt und dass der [...] Raum mit den Bewegungen und Handlungen, die darin geschehen, identisch ist.« Auf die Probe wurde diese Feststellung 1961 beim Wettbewerb für St. Pius in Meggen bei Luzern gestellt. Die Vorprüfung wies nämlich den von Füeg eingereichten Entwurf ab, weil die Werktagskapelle außerhalb des Kirchenraums angeordnet war. Trotzdem empfahl die Jury den Entwurf zur Ausführung: »Der Kirchenraum wirkt auf Grund des konstruktiv durchsichtigen Gefüges klar und rein. Der Raum mit seiner konsequenten Abstraktion und die Proportionen schaffen jene Ruhe und Besinnung, die für [...] die Mitfeier des Mysteriums gefordert sind.«

Around 1960 Franz Füeg belonged to the so-called Solothurn School which, primarily in emulation of Mies van der Rohe, supported analytical building as opposed to the newly emerging sculptural architecture. Füeg had also expressed his opinion of religious architecture as editor of the magazine *Bauen + Wohnen*: 'For the architect, all that is certain is that he shapes the church as a building in such a way that it meets liturgical and pastoral requirements, that he arrives at the architecture correctly from these requirements and from the construction, and that the [...] space is identical with the movements and actions that take place within it'. This statement was put to the test in 1961 with the competition for the church of St Pius near Lucerne. The design of Füeg was rejected on preliminary examination because the workday chapel was placed outside the church interior. Despite this, the jury recommended that the plan should be implemented: 'The church interior gives a clear and pure impression as a result of the structurally transparent arrangement. The space with its logically consistent abstraction and proportions create that [sense of] peace and contemplation that are required for the celebration of the mystery'.

Die Kirche steht auf einem Sockel in Hanglage über dem Vierwaldstätter See. Das Stahlskelett des Kubus ist mit nicht tragenden, transluzenten Marmorplatten geschlossen.

The church stands on a plinth on a hillside overlooking Lake Lucerne. The steel skeleton of the cube is filled with non-load-bearing, translucent slabs of marble.

Den Kirchenraum bestimmt die paradoxe Erscheinung der Marmorplatten: Obwohl eigentlich massiv, wurde das Material durch den dünnen Schnitt zu einem changierenden Lichtfilter.

The paradoxical appearance of the marble slabs determines the interior: although actually solid, owing to the thinness of the slabs the material becomes a filter for the changing light.

Durch den Einsatz von zwei Techniken aus ganz verschiedenen Zeiten, des modernen Stahlbaus sowie der überlieferten Verwendung von dünn geschnittenen Natursteinplatten, verbindet sich in der Kirche eine rationale Konstruktion mit transzendentaler Stimmung. Das tragende Skelett ist ein Montagebau aus Fertigteilen, der durch die schmalen, gereihten Doppel-T-Profile gegliedert ist. Das flache Dach liegt auf einem Fachwerkträgersystem. Als Ausfachung der hohen Wände dienen 2,8 Zentimeter dünne, durchscheinende Marmorplatten, die eine bernsteinfarbene Membran für das Tageslicht erzeugen. Weil in jeder Ausfachung die Platten desselben Marmorblocks aufeinander gesetzt sind, wiederholt sich in der Vertikalen das Bild der spezifischen Äderung. Diese Hülle, die einzigartige Raumerlebnisse vermittelt, macht das Gebäude zu einem wechselnden Lichtkörper: Tagsüber leuchten die Wände nach innen, bei Dunkelheit wie eine riesige ›Laterne‹ nach außen. Der vom Architekten bis hin zur Einrichtung gestaltete Raum ist nach Osten auf den großen, mehrfach abgestuften Altarbereich ausgerichtet.

Rational construction is combined with transcendental atmosphere in this church through the use of two techniques from very different eras — modern steel construction and traditional usage of thinly sliced slabs of natural stone. The load-bearing skeleton is a montage of assembly units that is organised via narrow double-T profiles in rows. The flat roof lies on a framework girder system. Translucent marble slabs 2.8 centimetres thick, which produce an amber-coloured membrane allowing for the passage of daylight, serve as infill for the high walls. Since in every section of infill slabs cut from the same marble block are placed above one another, the particular veining of the marble is repeated down the vertical axes. This skin, which makes the interior a unique experience, turns the building into a changing body of light: during the day the walls glow inwardly, while at night they shine out like a gigantic lantern. The interior space, shaped by the architect right down to the furnishings, is focused eastwards towards the large altar zone built on several stepped levels.

Urbild aller Architektur
Kirchenbau in Belgien und den Niederlanden nach 1950

Erst nach dem Zweiten Vatikanischen Konzil (1962–1964) wurde in den siebziger Jahren in Brüssel die Basilique de Koekelberg fertig gestellt. Größe und Kosten des 1921 von dem Architekten Albert Van Huffel entworfenen, gleichermaßen monumentalen wie symbolischen Bauwerks erwiesen sich für das belgische Episkopat als rechter Alptraum.[1] Zwischenzeitlich hatte sich die soziale Position der Kirche gründlich verändert und die Liturgie eine neue Dimension angenommen.

Bislang gibt es weder eine gründliche Untersuchung der verschiedenen, die Kirchenarchitektur in Belgien bestimmenden Bewegungen noch eine Studie, welche diese Kirchenarchitektur in einen größeren europäischen Zusammenhang einordnet. Entsprechend beschränkt sich dieser Text auf eine Reihe wichtiger Bauten und Richtungen. Er erwähnt darüber hinaus die bedeutendsten Architekten, die dazu beitrugen, dem Kirchenbau neue Inspirationsquellen zu erschließen. Zeitschriften und andere Publikationen spielen eine wichtige Rolle, wenn es darum geht, sich ein Bild von der modernen Kirchenarchitektur, der neuen Fassung der Liturgie und der Entwicklung der religiösen Kunst zu machen. Die einflussreichste Zeitschrift in Belgien war *Art d'Eglise*, eine französischsprachige Publikation, die von den Benediktinermönchen der Abtei Sint Andries bei Brügge herausgegeben wurde. Diese vierteljährlich erscheinende Zeitschrift erschien zwischen 1926 und 1980.[2] Sie beschränkte sich nicht nur auf Belgien, sondern enthielt – dank ihrer zahlreichen internationalen Kontakte – Artikel zu anderen europäischen Ländern und sogar zu Amerika.

Darüber hinaus spielte der ehemalige Jesuit Geert Bekaert eine wichtige Rolle. In der Zeitschrift *Streven* veröffentlichte er zahlreiche seiner Aufsätze, und dank seiner häufigen Artikel in der Zeitung *De Standaard* zur Debatte über moderne Kirchenarchitektur und ihr Verhältnis zu einer neuen Gottesdienstordnung erreichte er eine breitere Öffentlichkeit. Seine zahlreichen internationalen Kontakte führten zur Publikation von *Gewijde Kunst* (Religiöse Kunst), einer Sondernummer mit einem Überblick über Neuerungen in der europäischen Kirchenarchitektur.[3] Bekaert befasste sich ständig mit der Frage der direkten Verbindung zwischen Leben und Kirche, zwischen Gottesdienst und Bauwerk.

Seiner Ansicht nach sollte der Zweck des modernen Kirchengebäudes verknüpft sein mit dem Wunsch nach einer gänzlich auf irdische Realität ausgerichteten religiösen Erfahrung. »Tatsächlich sollte diese Erfahrung während und durch den Gottesdienst geschehen. Dies führt zu einer doppelten Bewegung: Die Architektur fordert vom Gottesdienst eine menschliche Realität, indes der Gottesdienst auch den tiefen Sinn der Architektur offenbart und sie zum Urbild aller Architektur erhebt. Mit anderen Worten, dass das ganze Leben ein Gottesdienst und jedes Haus eine Kirche ist, und dass im Widerspruch dazu der Gottesdienst im Kirchengebäude einzig einen bestimmter Moment im religiösen Leben selbst darstellt und auch nicht mehr sein darf.«[4] Bekaert betonte häufig, die Kirche oder *ecclesia* sei gleichbedeutend mit der Zusammenkunft von Gläubigen und nicht mit einem Bauwerk. Das Aufspüren neuer Inspirationsquellen bedeute die Rückkehr zu den Anfängen, der Versammlung von Christen in »dem einen oder anderen Haus«, und es enthalte den Appell zum völligen Bruch mit einem uralten Typus. Dies erklärt den Titel von *In een of ander huis*, Bekaerts 1967 erschienenem Buch über europäische Architektur.[5]

Primal Image of all Architecture
Churches in Belgium and The Netherlands after 1950

It was only after the 1970s, following the Second Vatican Council (1962–64), that the Basilica of Koekelberg in Brussels was completed. Designed in 1921 by the architect Albert Van Huffel, the size and cost of this monumental and symbolic edifice proved to be a veritable nightmare for the Belgian episcopate.[1] In the meantime the social position of the Church changed drastically and the liturgy acquired a new dimension.

There are as yet no plans for a thorough study of the different movements which have prescribed church architecture in Belgium, or for a study that places church architecture within a broader European context. Consequently, this text is restricted to a number of important buildings and movements. It also includes a brief overview of the most important architects who contributed towards providing new sources of inspiration for church architecture. Periodicals and other publications play an important role in building up a picture of modern church architecture, the new version of the liturgy, and the development of religious art. The most important periodical in Belgium was the French-language *Art d'Eglise*, published by the Benedictine monks of the abbey of Sint Andries near Bruges. This quarterly magazine was published between 1926 and 1980.[2] It focused not only on Belgium, but through its many international contacts it included articles on other European countries, and even America.

In addition to this, the former Jesuit Geert Bekaert played an important role in the circulation of and debates on the position of religious architecture. He had numerous publications in the magazine *Streven*, and through his many articles in *De Standaard* newspaper he managed to bring the debate on modern church architecture in relation to a new version of the service to a wide general public. His many international contacts led to the publication of *Gewijde Kunst* [Sacred Art], a special issue with an outline of innovation in European church architecture.[3] Bekaert has constantly addressed the question of the direct link between life and the church, between the service and the building.

In his view, the purpose of the modern church building should be related to a desire for a religious experience that is entirely orientated towards an earthly reality: 'This experience should in fact occur in and by way of the service. This gives rise to a double movement: the architecture demands a human reality from the service, but the service also reveals the deep purpose of the architecture and elevates it to the prototype of all architecture. In other words, that all life is one service and every house a church, and in contradiction to this, that the service in the church building is only, and cannot be allowed to be more than, an explicit moment in religious life itself.'[4] Bekaert often emphasised that the church, the ecclesia, was a coming-together of believers, and not a building. Finding new sources of inspiration means going back to the beginning, the coming together of Christians in 'some house or other' and a plea for making a clean break with an age-old type. This explains the title of Bekaert's book on European architecture published in 1967, *In een of ander huis* [In One House or Another].[5]

Foreign journals too undoubtedly had a circulation and their own influence, such as the French magazine, *L'Art Sacré*, in which two important religious buildings by Le Corbusier, Ronchamp and La Tourette, were extensively documented.[6]

Zeitschrift / magazine
Art d'Eglise
Nr. / No. 134

Zweifellos hatten auch ausländische Zeitschriften eine Leser-
schaft und übten ihren eigenen Einfluss aus, wie etwa die
französische Zeitschrift *L'Art Sacré*, in der Ronchamp und La
Tourette, zwei wegweisende sakrale Bauten Le Corbusiers,
ausführlich vorgestellt wurden.[6]

Neue Kirchen in Flandern

Bei Belgien handelt es sich um eine Schöpfung des 19. Jahrhunderts, entstanden aus der Vereinigung zweier kultureller Einhei-
ten. Es kann deshalb nicht überraschen, dass in Flandern und
Wallonien, den holländisch- bzw. französischsprachigen Regionen dieses Landes, bei der Entwicklung des Kirchenbaus jeweils
andere Einflüsse vorherrschen. Während der ersten Hälfte des
20. Jahrhunderts orientierten sich viele Architekten in Flandern
an den Niederlanden.[7] Als besonders anregend erwiesen sich
das Schaffen von H. P. Berlage und W. M. Dudok. Auf dem Gebiet der Kirchenarchitektur verdienen zwei Architekten besondere Erwähnung: Granpré Molière, Dozent an der Universität
von Delft, und A. J. Kropholler. Kropholler, der auch in Belgien
tätig war, baute im Jahr 1932 ein Kloster in Affligem bei Aalst.

Nach dem Zweiten Weltkrieg war vorwiegend der Einfluss der
›Bosschen Schule‹ spürbar. Deren wichtigster Exponent war
der Holländer Jos Ritzen (1896–1961).[8] Als sein erstes Bauwerk
wurde 1924 die Heilig-Hartkerk, ein überkuppelter Kirchenbau, in Maastricht fertig gestellt, bei dem er mit dem Architekten
Boosten zusammengearbeitet hatte. Ritzen war der bedeutendste Vertreter der Bosschen Schule in Belgien, und er verfügte
über viele Kontakte zu holländischen Kollegen. Er erhielt die
wichtigsten Aufträge für Kirchenbauten, wie die Abtei von Achel
und das Jesuitenkolleg für Philosophische Theologie in Heverlee bei Löwen. Für die Kirche in Tongeren (1954) wählte Ritzen
die Form einer frühchristlichen Basilika. Sein größter, 1955
fertig gestellter Kirchenbau steht in Knokke. Der über einem
basilikalen Grundriss entstandene Bau wird durch einen frei
stehenden Glockenturm ergänzt. Die beträchtliche Größe der
Kirche in Knokke verdankt sich dem nennenwerten Zuwachs
von Touristen, die an die belgische Küste reisen.

Obgleich es sich bei der 1955 von Paul Felix (1913–1981) erbauten Kapelle des Studentenwohnheims Pius X. in Löwen um
ein sehr kleines Projekt handelt, kann man sie doch als Ausgangspunkt der Erneuerung in Flandern betrachten.[9] Ferner
wuchs diesem bescheidenen Bau durch die erfolgreiche Zusammenarbeit des Bildhauers Bonduel und des Glaskünstlers
Martens symbolische Bedeutung zu. Im Laufe der zweiten Hälfte der fünfziger Jahre setzte sich in Belgien und besonders in
Flandern eine weitreichende Dynamik durch – die Weltausstellung in Brüssel im Jahr 1958 regte eine Vielzahl von Initiativen
an. Tatsächlich erklärt dies die Organisation der ersten Ausstellung zu religiöser Kunst und Architektur in Löwen, die unter
dem Titel *Ars Sacra 58* stattfand. Ein unbestritten zentrales
Werk aus dieser Periode stellt das Klarissinnenkloster Zonnelied
in Ostende dar, ein 1957 von Paul Felix geschaffenes Meisterwerk. Der Konvent dieser geschlossenen Anlage gruppiert sich
um sieben Innenhöfe verschiedener Größe. Der Gebrauch
von gelbem Backstein sowohl im Innen- wie im Außenbereich
führt zu einer ausgeprägten Geschlossenheit. Hier ist die Architektur auf ihre einfachsten Elemente reduziert: Backstein, Beton
und naturbelassenes Kiefernholz. Die Kapelle ist streng axial
angelegt, und die Proportionen des Innenraums sind auf das

Belgium is a creation of the 19th century, a combination of
two cultural communities. It is therefore unsurprising that in
Flanders and Wallonia, the Dutch-language and the French-
language regions of this country, there is a different emphasis in
the development of church architecture. During the first half
of the 20th century, many architects in Flanders were oriented
towards the Netherlands.[7] Especially inspiring was the work of
H. P. Berlage and W. M. Dudok. In the field of church architecture, special mention must be made of two architects, Granpré
Molière, a lecturer at Delft University, and A. J. Kropholler.
Kropholler also built in Belgium: a monastery in Affligem near
Aalst in 1932.

After the Second World War the influence of the 'Bossche School'
had the most impact. The most important figure was the Dutch-
man Jos Ritzen (1896–1961).[8] His first completed building
was the H. Hartkerk [Church of the Sacred Heart], a domed
church in Maastricht (1924), which was realised in collaboration with architect A. J. N. Boosten. Ritzen was the most
important exponent of the Bossche School in Belgium, and he
had many contacts among his Dutch colleagues. He was given
the most important briefs for churches, such as the Abbey
at Achel and the Jesuit College of Philosophical Theology at
Heverlee near Leuven. For the church in Tongeren (1954)
Ritzen chose the form of the early Christian basilica. His largest
church is in Knokke and was completed in 1955. The plan is
that of the basilica and the high belltower relates to the tradition
of the freestanding campanile tower. The substantial size of
the church in Knokke was due to an important increase in the
number of tourists visiting the Belgian coast.

Although the chapel of the Pius-X students' hostel in Leuven
from 1955 by Paul Felix (1913–81) was a very small project, it
may be regarded as the starting point of innovation in Flanders.[9]
It was also through the successful co-operation of the sculptor
Bonduel and the glass artist Martens that this modest work
acquired a symbolic significance. During the second half of the
1950s an important dynamism came into being in Belgium
and especially in Flanders: the World's Fair in Brussels in 1958
stimulated a variety of initiatives. Indeed, this explains the
organisation of the first exhibition on religious art and architecture in Leuven under the title *Ars Sacra 58*. An unarguably
crucial work from this period is the *Zonnelied* nunnery of the
Sisters of St. Clare in Ostend (1959), which is a masterpiece
by Paul Felix. The nunnery of this enclosed order is built around
seven patios of different sizes. A high degree of unity results
from the use of yellow brick both inside and out. Here the architecture is reduced to its simplest elements: brick, concrete and
natural pinewood. The chapel is strongly axial and the basic
proportions of the interior space are focused on the large window
behind the altar. Here too Felix worked together with the two
aforementioned artists. This authentic work became a point of
reference in religious architecture and was extensively documented in *Art d'Eglise*.[10]

An important initiative was *Pro Arte Christiana*[11] in 1959, the
first architectural competition for a church building in Flanders.
The international jury, consisting of Hermann Baur, Rudolf
Schwarz, Xavier Arsène-Henry and Michel Margot, awarded
first prize to the young architect Marc Dessauvage (1931–84).

Paul Felix
Kloster / nunnery
Ostende / Ostend, 1957

große Fenster hinter dem Altar ausgerichtet. Auch hier arbeitete Felix mit den beiden oben erwähnten Künstlern zusammen. Dieser maßgebliche Bau wurde zu einer Bezugsgröße in der kirchlichen Architektur und in *Art d'Eglise* ausführlich dokumentiert.[10]

Als wesentliche Initiative erwies sich *Pro Arte Christiana*, der erste, im Jahr 1959 veranstaltete Architekturwettbewerb für einen Kirchenbau in Flandern.[11] Die international besetzte Jury, bestehend aus Hermann Baur, Rudolf Schwarz, Xavier Arsène-Henry und Michel Margot, erkannte den ersten Preis dem jungen Architekten Marc Dessauvage (1931–1984) zu. Der Entwurf umfasste ein großflächiges, horizontales Dach sowie eine von frei stehenden Pfeilern getragene Metallbinderkonstruktion. Unter dieser »großen Plattenkonstruktion« fügten sich die Wände in fließender Bewegung ein – dadurch ergab sich ein äußerst subtiler Übergang zwischen Außen- und Innenraum. Bei diesem Entwurf verband Dessauvage den Einfluss Mies van der Rohes mit dem Gedanken von Le Corbusiers *plan libre*. Auch wenn dieser Entwurf nie realisiert wurde, so kennzeichnet er gleichwohl den Beginn einer großen Zahl von Kirchenbauaufträgen Dessauvages. Im Jahr 1960 erhielt er den Auftrag, in der Abtei von St. Andries in Loppem eine kleine Gästekapelle zu errichten. Dem folgten Aufträge für Kirchenbauten in ganz Flandern. Während der sechziger Jahre erwies sich Dessauvage als führender Architekt bei der Suche nach einer neuen Richtung für die Kirchenarchitektur in Flandern.[12] Dessauvage war auf der Suche nach einem Ort, der den Wunsch, anderen zu begegnen, stimulieren sollte. Bekaert machte häufig auf diese Bauten aufmerksam und darüber hinaus wurden diese Kirchen in *Art d'Eglise* umfassend vorgestellt.[13] Dessauvage ging von der herkömmlichen axialen Grundrissgestaltung ab – die räumliche Anlage betont nicht mehr die zentrale Stellung des Altars, sondern eher den Aspekt des gemeinsamen Aufenthaltes in einem kontinuierlichen Raum. In den meisten Kirchen umstehen die in drei Zonen angeordneten Bänke den Altar. Im Hinblick auf die Architektursprache steht dieser Bau in der Tradition des international so benannten »New Brutalism«.

Dessauvages Entscheidung, den Innenraum seiner Kirchen neu zu orientieren, steht in diametralem Gegensatz zu der Richtung, die weiterhin glaubte, ein Kirchengebäude solle eine bestimmte Expressivität, ja Monumentalität ausstrahlen. Bei der Pilgerkapelle in Edelare (1961) von Juliaan Lampens (geb. 1926) handelt es sich zweifelsohne um den augenfälligsten Vertreter dieser Strömung.[14] Der Bau [Seite 102] erscheint als imposante, monolithische Betonmasse, die aus dem Boden aufsteigt und sich zum Himmel erhebt. Während Le Corbusier seinen Entwurf für die Kirche in Firminy schuf, entwarf Léon Stynen (1899–1990) eine hiervon deutlich beeinflusste Kirche.[15] Die Kirche in Harelbeke (1966) hat die Form einer unregelmäßigen, oktagonalen Betonpyramide mit gekappter Spitze. Dieser Bereich ist als Oberlicht gestaltet, welches das Tageslicht spektakulär in den Innenraum einfallen lässt. Stynen war ein Freund Le Corbusiers, und auch sein übriges Werk zeigt seine Bewunderung für ihn.

Der berühmte holländische Mönch Dom Hans van der Laan (1904–1991) führte in der Gemeinde Waasmunster zwei Projekte aus. Im Dorfzentrum baute er ein bestehendes Kloster um, und in einer bewaldeten Gegend errichtete er die neue Abtei Roosenberg (1977). Der Komplex zeichnet sich durch Zurück-

Marc Dessauvage
Wettbewerb / competition
Pro Arte Christiana, 1958
1. Preis / first prize

Léon Stynen
St. Rita / St Rita
Harelbeke, 1962

The design comprised a large horizontal roof, a metal truss construction supported by freestanding columns. Under this 'large table' construction, the walls were introduced in a flowing movement thus creating an extremely gentle transition between exterior and interior. In this design he combined the influence of Mies van der Rohe with the concept of Le Corbusier's *plan libre*. This design was never realised however, but was the start of a large number of church briefs for Dessauvage. In 1960 he was commissioned to construct a small guest chapel in the abbey of St Andries in Loppem. This was followed by commissions for churches all over Flanders. During the 1960s Dessauvage would prove himself to be the most important architect to give a new direction to church architecture in Flanders.[12] Dessauvage sought a place that stimulated the desire to meet others. Bekaert frequently focused attention on these buildings and the churches were also extensively documented in *Art d'Eglise*.[13] The traditional axial construction of the ground plan was abandoned; the composition of the space no longer emphasised the central position of the altar but rather the aspect of being together in one continuous space. In most churches the pews are grouped around the altar in three zones. When it comes to the idiom of architectural form, this work links up more readily with the internationally used term New Brutalism.

The choice of Dessauvage for the reorientation of the church interior is diametrically opposed to the tendency that continued to believe that a church building should have a certain emphatic expressiveness, even monumentality. The pilgrims' chapel in Edelare (1961) by Juliaan Lampens (b. 1926) is undoubtedly the most explicit example of this trend [p. 102].[14] The building is a monolithic and imposing mass of concrete that rises out of the ground and raises itself towards the heavens. While Le Corbusier was creating his design for the church at Firminy, Léon Stynen (1899–1990) designed a church with strong associations.[15] The church at Harelbeke (1966) is an irregular, octagonal concrete pyramid truncated at the top. The sliced section forms a skylight that allows daylight dramatically into the interior. Stynen was a friend of Le Corbusier and his other work also shows his admiration for him.

The renowned Dutch monk Dom Hans van der Laan (1904–91) worked at two places in the borough of Waasmunster. In the village centre he transformed an existing monastery and in a wooded area he built the new 'Roosenberg' abbey (1977). The complex is a unity of restraint and representativeness. The church with its octagonal upper section is very different from the abbey church at Vaals, which is undoubtedly his masterpiece (p. 172). According to Bekaert this work possesses 'no mysticism, no ecstasy. But it does have a subtle precision and asceticism'.[16]

New Churches in Wallonia

It was to the great credit of the diocese of Namur that after the Second World War it employed a number of young architects and artists for the reconstruction of several small churches.[1] It called in a number of talented people from Brussels. The first was the moderate Modernist Josse Franssen for the church at Jemeppe (1945), a building with a circular ground plan. It is indisputable that the main figure who greatly stimulated church architecture in Wallonia was Roger Bastin (1913–86).[2] The design for his first church at Saint-Gilles in Brussels dates from

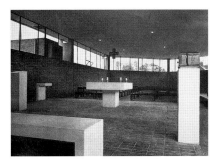

Marc Dessauvage
St. Josef / St Joseph
Willebroek, 1964

Marc Dessauvage
St. Rochus / St Roch
Aarschot, 1965

Marc Dessauvage
St. Paulus / St Paul
Westmalle, 1967

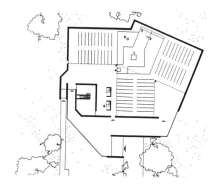

haltung und Symbolkraft aus. Die Kirche mit ihrem oktagonalen Oberbau unterscheidet sich stark von der Klosterkirche
im niederländischen Vaals, seinem Meisterwerk [Seite 168].
Bekaert zufolge ist seinem Werk »keine Mystik, kein Über-
schwang eigen. Aber es verfügt über eine subtile Präzision und
Askese«.[16]

Neue Kirchen in Wallonien

Es gereicht der Diözese Namur zu großer Ehre, dass sie nach
dem Zweiten Weltkrieg junge Architekten und Künstler für den
Wiederaufbau mehrerer kleiner Kirchen einstellte.[1] Eine Reihe
begabter Leute wurde aus Brüssel berufen. Der erste war der
gemäßigte Modernist Josse Franssen für die Kirche in Jemeppe
(1945), ein Bau mit kreisförmigem Grundriss. Zweifelsfrei war
Roger Bastin (1913–1986) derjenige, der die Kirchenarchitektur
in Wallonien am nachhaltigsten beflügelte.[2] Der Entwurf für
seine Kirche in Saint-Gilles, Brüssel, datiert aus dem Jahr 1938,
wurde aber erst 1951 fertig gestellt. Der Einfluss von Dominikus
Böhm ist sehr deutlich, und bezüglich der Form kann man sogar Anklänge an das Werk des italienischen Architekten Libera
entdecken.

Von 1945 bis 1951 arbeitete Bastin mit Jacques Dupuis (1914
bis 1984) zusammen, einer der faszinierendsten Figuren in der
belgischen Nachkriegsarchitektur.[3] Beide unternahmen mehrere
Studienreisen in skandinavische Länder, was zur Folge hatte,
dass sich der Einfluss von Aalto und Asplund in ihrem Schaffen
deutlich verfolgen lässt, wie etwa im Fall der vier kleinen Kapellen in Bertrix. Ihr Ausgangspunkt ist die Suche nach einer
Verbindung zwischen regionalen Bautraditionen und Materialien und einer auf der Grundlage der Moderne entwickelten
Formensprache. Die Kirche in Jéhonville ist dafür ein gutes Beispiel. Der erste Entwurf stammt von 1947, wurde jedoch in
leicht abgewandelter Form erst zehn Jahre später realisiert. Der
Gebrauch von Stein stellte die regionale Verbindung her,
während die Gestaltungselemente, beispielsweise das durchge-
hende, horizontale Fenster zwischen Dach und Wänden sowie der Abschluss des Turms, einer stärker international geprägten Formensprache entstammen. Bastin schuf mehrere kleine
Kirchen mit beachtlichen räumlichen Qualitäten, wie die in
Heer-Agimont (1962). Er war sehr darum bemüht, das neue
Bauwerk in die bestehende dörfliche Struktur einzufügen, sowohl
im Hinblick auf die verwendeten Materialien wie auch in
der Form des Daches. Das beste Beispiel hierfür ist die Kirche in
Sart-en-Fagne (1965). Bastin baute eine Vielzahl kirchlicher
Gebäude, darunter die Priesterseminare in Namur und Floreffe.
Ferner erhielt er den Auftrag, das Gelände der Pilgerstätte in
Beauraing umzugestalten und durch eine große Pilgerkirche zu
erweitern (1958–68). Er entwarf zwei übereinander situierte
Kirchenräume und nutzte so das abschüssige Gelände optimal
aus. Der unten liegende kleine Gebetsraum ist recht dunkel,
während der darüber liegende, ausgedehnte Versammlungs-
bereich eher einem überdachten Marktplatz gleicht. Vor allem
durch das Wiederholen der V-förmigen Dachträger aus Beton
schuf Bastin einen außergewöhnlichen Raum. Mit seiner Verwendung schmaler, vertikaler Fensteröffnungen unterschiedlicher Breite nimmt er deutlich Bezug auf das von ihm geschätz-
te Werk Le Corbusiers. Die Tatsache, dass er selbst im Bistum
große Achtung genoss, geht aus seiner Berufung zum leitenden
Architekten des vatikanischen Pavillons auf der Weltausstellung
1958 in Brüssel hervor.

Roger Bastin · Jacques Dupuis
Kapelle / chapel
Bertrix, 1950

Roger Bastin
Kirche / church
Sart-en-Fagne, 1965

1938 but it was only completed in 1951. The influence of Dominikus Böhm is very obvious, and in terms of form one can even see associations with the work of the Italian architect Adalberto Libera.

From 1945 to 1951 Bastin collaborated with Jacques Dupuis (1914–84), one of the most fascinating figures in post-1945 Belgian architecture.[3] Both went on several study trips to Scandinavian countries, with the result that the influence of Aalto and Asplund can be clearly traced in their work, as in the four small chapels at Bertrix. Their starting point is the search for a link between a regional building tradition and materials and a formal idiom developed on the basis of modernity. The church at Jéhonville is a good example of this. The first design dates from 1947 but was only built, in a slightly modified form, ten years later. The use of stone laid the link with the region, while the compositional elements, such as the continuous horizontal window between the roof and walls and the end of the tower, come from a more internationally oriented idiom. Bastin built several small churches with considerable spatial qualities, such as the one at Heer-Agimont (1962). He took great care to fit the new building into the existing fabric of the village, both in the materials he used and the shape of the roof. The finest example of this is the church at Sart-en-Fagne (1965). Bastin built a great many religious edifices, including the seminaries at Namur and Floreffe. He was also commissioned to reorganise the site of the place of pilgrimage at Beauraing (1958–68) and to expand it, with a large church for the pilgrims. He designed two church spaces, one above the other, making optimal use of the existing slope. The small prayer space underneath is quite dark, while the large assembly area at the top seems more like a covered marketplace. Bastin creates an extraordinary space primarily by repeating the V-shaped concrete roof structure. His choice of narrow vertical windows of varying widths is a clear reference to his great appreciation of the work of Le Corbusier. The fact that he himself was held in high regard in the episcopate is also apparent from his appointment as chief architect for the Vatican pavilion at the 1958 World's Fair in Brussels.

The finest example of Le Corbusier's influence is the College of Christ the King (le collège du Christ-Roi) at Ottignies, designed by the architects P. Caulier and P. Lepère on commission to the Redemptorist Brothers (1967).[4] This large complex consists of a college and a monastery for 24 monks with a chapel attached. The complex is located on a slope and, as in Le Corbusier's La Tourette, the inner patio is linked to the surroundings. References to Le Corbusier are also very striking in the composition of the facade, the materials and the details.

Little research has been done up to now on the influence of the church architecture of the German Rhineland and the German-speaking part of Switzerland on religious architecture in Belgium. At about the same time as the church in Jéhonville, the architect V. Sarlet was building one in Marloie (1948–55). Its compact basic volume and the freestanding lofty campanile were clearly inspired by Swiss examples. The church in Tubize, built in 1958, was even designed by the Swiss architect Ellenberger, in collaboration with A. Marin.[5] In this church with its circular ground plan, several details refer to Frank Lloyd Wright's formal language.

Apart from Bastin, it was mainly Jean Cosse (b. 1931) who received many briefs for churches and monasteries.[6] In his formal

Roger Bastin
Wallfahrtsort / place of pilgrimage
Beauraing, 1968

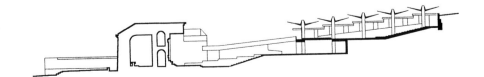

Das beste Beispiel für Le Corbusiers Einfluss stellt das Collège du Christ-Roi in Ottignies dar, das die Architekten P. Caulier und P. Lepère im Auftrag der Congrégation de Rédemptoristes entwarfen (1967).[4] Dieser große Komplex besteht aus einem Kollegium sowie einem Konvent für 24 Mönche mit angeschlossener Kapelle. Die Gebäude liegen auf einem Abhang, und wie bei La Tourette von Le Corbusier bestehen Verbindungen zwischen dem Innenhof und der Umgebung. Darüber hinaus lassen sich bei der Fassadengestaltung, den Materialien und Details deutliche Bezüge zu Le Corbusier erkennen.

Der Einfluss der Kirchenarchitektur des Rheinlandes sowie der deutschen Schweiz auf Belgien ist ein bislang wenig erforschtes Gebiet. Etwa zu der Zeit, als die Kirche in Jéhonville gebaut wurde, entstand nach Entwürfen des Architekten V. Sarlet ein solcher Bau in Marloie (1948–55). Die Nähe von dessen kompaktem Baukörper und dem hoch aufragenden, frei stehenden Glockenturm zu Schweizer Beispielen ist augenfällig. Bei der 1958 errichteten Kirche in Tubize handelt es sich tatsächlich um einen in Zusammenarbeit mit A. Marin entstandenen Entwurf des Schweizer Architekten Ellenberger.[5] Bei diesem Bau mit kreisförmigem Grundriss nehmen mehrere Details Bezug auf die Formensprache von Frank Lloyd Wright.

Neben Bastin erhielt überwiegend der 1931 geborene Jean Cosse zahlreiche Aufträge für Kirchen und Klöster.[6] Hinsichtlich seiner Formensprache entschied sich Cosse für eine subtil eingepasste, bodenständige Architektur. Es gibt keine Anzeichen einer wie auch immer gearteten expliziten Aussage wie im Werk Dessauvages. Sein wichtigster Bau ist die Kirche in Louvain-la-Neuve, der einzigen im 20. Jahrhundert in Belgien neu entstandenen Stadt, die in der Folge der Spaltung der katholischen Universität Löwen gegründet wurde. Diese 1984 geweihte Kirche erweckt trotz ihres prägnanten Glockenturms den Eindruck eines ausgesprochen streng gestalteten Bauwerks.

In einem Aufsatz über die Neuausrichtung der Kirchenarchitektur führt Dom Frédéric Debuyst ein Gebäude von Emil Steffann bei Thionville als Beispiel einer »Grande-église« an. Ausgangspunkt ist nicht neues Bauen, sondern die Umnutzung des vorhandenen Erbes. Das schönste Beispiel hierfür ist das Dominikanerkloster in Froidmond (1975) von Lucien Kroll (geb. 1927). In einem alten Brabanter Gehöft baute man die große Scheune zu einem Gebetshaus um, das gleichzeitig als Gemeindekirche dient. Zwischen 1952 und 1957 arbeitete er mit dem ebenfalls 1927 geborenen Charles Vandenhove zusammen. Auch die 1952 in Huy errichtete kleine Kapelle verdient Erwähnung. Ferner entwarf Lucien Kroll für die Benediktinerabtei in Chevetogne (1961) ein ökumenisches Zentrum über organischem Grundriss sowie eine Kapelle in Linkebeek (1963).[7] Wie Bastin plante auch Kroll in den sechziger Jahren Kirchen in Ruanda. Für Sainte-Catherine-de-Sienne, einen Wallfahrtsort in Astenet in der Nähe von Aachen, entwarf Emile José Fettweis (geb. 1927) eine kleine Kapelle, die den Einfluss Le Corbusiers deutlich erkennen lässt. Für die zweite Bauphase, bei der er mit dem Ingenieur René Greisch zusammenarbeitete, ordnete er die Funktionen eines Versammlungsplatzes unter einem durchgehenden Dach um einen fächerförmigen Platz an, ein Verweis auf den weltberühmten Platz in Siena.

Wie in Flandern kam auch in Wallonien der Kirchenbau in der Mitte der achtziger Jahre völlig zum Erliegen. Sämtliche Finanz-

idiom Cosse opted for a vernacular architecture of gentle integration. There was no sign of any outspoken statement as in the work of Dessauvage. His most important building is the church at Louvain-la-Neuve, the only new town created in Belgium in the 20th century, founded as a result of the division of the Catholic University of Leuven. This church, with its pronounced belltower, was consecrated in 1984 but remains an extremely formal composition.

In an article on the reorientation of church architecture, Dom Frédéric Debuyst refers to a building by Emil Steffann near Thionville, as an example of a *grande-église*. The point of departure is not new building but the reuse of the existing heritage. The finest example of this is the Dominican monastery at Froidmont (1975) by Lucien Kroll (b. 1927). In an old Brabant farmstead the large barn was transformed into a prayer building which also acts as a parish church. Between 1952 and 1957 he collaborated with Charles Vandenhove (b. 1927). The small chapel at Huy from 1952 is worth mentioning. Lucien Kroll also designed an ecumenical centre with an organic ground plan for the Benedictine abbey at Chevetogne (1961) and a chapel at Linkebeek (1963).[7] Like Bastin, in the 1960s Kroll designed church buildings in Rwanda. For Sainte Catherine de Sienne, a place of pilgrimage in Astenet (near Aachen), Emile José Fettweis (b. 1927) designed a small chapel which clearly shows the influence of Le Corbusier. For the second phase, in collaboration with the engineer René Greisch, he grouped the functions of a meeting place under a single roof and round a fan-shaped square, a reference to the world-famous square in Siena. As in Flanders, church building came to a complete standstill in the mid-1980s. All financial resources were put into revaluating the historical heritage, and there was barely a sign of any significant new building projects.

New Churches in the Netherlands

Unlike Belgium, the Netherlands has both a Catholic and a Protestant church community that commission architectural designs. Round about 1950 church architecture was greatly influenced by the views of M. J. Granpré Molière. His preference for the early Christian basilica type of church and solid brick architecture was expressed in his church in Breda, from 1951–53. A.J. Kropholler's church designs were similar.[1] Kropholler tried to combine a Romanesque austerity with a Dutch building tradition and the influence of H. P. Berlage. The work of Koldeweij and Molenaar is also to be situated in the more traditional tendency. These architects also wrote for the *Katholiek Bouwblad* [Catholic Architecture Magazine], the magazine which regularly documented new church building from 1949 to 1959.[2]

As already mentioned, one major figure was the Benedictine monk Dom Hans van der Laan.[3] He gradually distanced himself from the views of Granpré Molière and the 'Delft School' and worked towards a more timeless architecture. The number of his designs that were built is extremely small, and the monastery at Vaals, completed in 1967, is his masterpiece [p. 172]. Van der Laan explored the philosophical background and elementary principles of architectural design. This was demonstrated by his many writings, including *Le nombre plastique* (1960) and most especially the book *De architectonische ruimte* (1977). In the 1940s and 1950s, Dom van der Laan made his insights into

Hans van der Laan
Abtei St. Benediktusberg
St Benediktusberg abbey
Vaals, 1986

mittel wurden in die Aufwertung des historischen Erbes gesteckt, und es gab kaum Anzeichen nennenswerter, neuer Bauprojekte.

Neue Kirchen in den Niederlanden

Anders als in Belgien gaben in den Niederlanden sowohl die katholische als auch die protestantische Kirche Architekturentwürfe in Auftrag. Um 1950 war der Kirchenbau stark vom Einfluss der Ansichten M.J. Granpré Molières geprägt. Seine Vorliebe für den Kirchentyp der frühchristlichen Basilika und für massive Backsteinarchitektur schlug sich in seiner 1951 bis 1953 errichteten Kirche in Breda nieder. Die Kirchenentwürfe A. J. Krophollers fielen ähnlich aus.[1] Kropholler versuchte, romanische Strenge mit niederländischer Bautradition und dem Einfluss H.P. Berlages zu verknüpfen. Auch die Arbeiten Koldewijs und Molenaars sind einer eher traditionellen Ausrichtung zuzuordnen. Diese Architekten schrieben darüber hinaus für das *Katholiek Bouwblad*, jene Zeitschrift, die von 1949–1959 regelmäßig neue Kirchenbauten behandelte.[2]

Einer der führenden Köpfe war der bereits erwähnte Benediktinermönch Dom Hans van der Laan.[3] Er distanzierte sich allmählich von den Ansichten Granpré Molières und der ›Delfter Schule‹ und bemühte sich um eine Architektur mit zeitloserem Ausdruck. Die Zahl seiner realisierten Entwürfe ist ziemlich klein, darunter ist die 1987 vollendete Klosteranlage in Vaals zweifellos sein Hauptwerk [Seite 168]. Van der Laan lotete den philosophischen Hintergrund und die Grundprinzipen des architektonischen Entwerfens aus. Dies belegen seine vielen Schriften, etwa *Le nombre plastique* (1960) und besonders *De architectonische ruimte* (1977). In den vierziger und fünfziger Jahren verdeutlichte Dom van der Laan seine Erkenntnisse zu Architektur und Kirchenbau in mehreren, in ‹s-Hertogenbosch veranstalteten Kursen, und seine Ideen lagen der so genannten Bosschen Schule zugrunde.

In der katholischen Provinz Limburg erfreute sich der Kirchenbau stets großer Aufmerksamkeit und einer Fülle von Gelegenheiten. Zum faszinierenden Werk von F. P. J. Peutz (1916 bis 1966) zählen mehrere Kirchen.[4] Im Jahr 1940 entwarf er eine Kuppelkirche für 1000 Menschen, die neben seinem Rathausbau in Heerlen zu stehen kommen sollte; allerdings wurde die Kirche erst 1951 an anderer Stelle errichtet. Der quadratische Grundriss mit oktagonalem Obergeschoss wird von einer Kuppel mit Laterne gekrönt. Peutz, der zahlreiche Betonbauten für Zechenanlagen entworfen hatte, wählte für den gesamten Kirchenbau das gleiche Material. 1954 errichtete er in Roermond eine zweite Kuppelkirche. Im Zusammenhang mit Limburg gilt es, die Kirchen von Alfons Boosten (1873 bis 1951)[5] zu erwähnen sowie die 1958 entstandene Kirche in Vaals von J.H.A. Huysmans, eine bemerkenswerte Synthese von Tradition und Moderne, die in der *Architectural Review* als »Rokkoko aus Beton« beschrieben wurde.

Die späten fünfziger Jahre erwiesen sich als eine für den Kirchenbau bedeutsame Zeitspanne. Zu den erwähnenswerten Neubauten zählen Karel Sijmons Kirche in Aerdenhout (1958), H. Nefkens Kirche in Haarlem (1958) sowie M. Duintjers Bau in Amsterdam (1956). Häufig ist der Einfluss des schweizerischen Kirchenbaus sowie der Arbeiten von Rudolf Schwarz sichtbar. Während dieser Zeit entstand überdies eine Erneuerungsbewegung, die eine direkte Verbindung zu anderen öffent-

F. P. J. Peutz
Kuppelkirche / domed church
Heerlen, 1951

architecture and church building more explicit in several courses organised at 's-Hertogenbosch, and his ideas lay behind the so-called 'Bossche School'.

In the Catholic province of Limburg, church building always received much attention and plenty of opportunities. The captivating work of F. P. J. Peutz (1916–66) includes several churches.[4] In 1940 he designed a domed church for 1,000 people next to his town hall in Heerlen. The church was only built in 1951, and then on another site. The basic shape of the ground plan is a square with an octagonal upper section, topped by a dome with a lantern. Peutz, who had designed many concrete structures for mine buildings, chose the same material for the whole church. In 1954 he built a second domed church in Roermond. While in Limburg, we must mention the churches by A. J. N. Boosten (1873–1951)[5] and the church at Vaals (1958) by J. H. A. Huysmans, a remarkable synthesis of tradition and modernism which *Architectural Review* described as 'rococo in concrete'.

The late 1950s was a busy time for church building. Projects worth mentioning include Karel Sijmons' church in Aerdenhout (1958), H. Nefkens' church at Haarlem (1958) and M. Duintjer's in Amsterdam (1956). One can often clearly see the influence of Swiss church building and of the work of Rudolf Schwarz. During this period a movement for renewal also came into being which sought a direct relationship with other public briefs. One example of this is the Reformed Church at Nagele (1962) by Van den Broek and Bakema. The appearance of the church is determined by the freestanding belltower. This campanile defines the forecourt of the church and forms a gradual transition from the public domain to the enclosed nature of the church interior. Its modernity is also emphasised by replacing the traditional brick by grey concrete blocks, a choice of material that played an extremely defining role in Dutch architecture in the 1960s and 1970s. Two other interesting buildings from this period are the church in Haarlem (1961) by the architect G. H. M. Holt, with a steel skeleton that is left visible, and the glazed auditorium at the cemetery in Haarlemmermeer (1958–67) by Gerrit Rietveld, built by Van Dillen & Van Tricht. Rietveld also designed the church at Uithoorn (1960–65). He accepted the brief on condition that the building would also be used for other purposes. It contains a theatre, a refreshment room and a nursery.

A pivotal moment was the limited competition for a Protestant church in Driebergen. In 1964 seven prominent architects were invited to submit a design: P. Blom, G. Boon, H. Hertzberger, J. Jelles, J. van Stigt, J. Verhoeven and A. van Eyck. The jury unanimously chose Aldo Van Eyck's (1918–1999) design for 'The Wheels of Heaven'. Francis Strauven emphasises the fact that Van Eyck was able to translate his hesitation about how a new church space can develop, as a form of ambivalence, into an innovative spatial concept.[6] The design is not for a neutral, centreless space. Van Eyck chose a clearly articulated cohesion of four distinct centres: four circular places with two different diameters. The basic idea, which was also formulated in the brief, was a pathway through the interior, a church in the form of a 'house of passage'. A new place to come together, a space with an 'openness' without an explicit centre or axiality. Bekaert even went so far as to attribute a paradigmatic shift to this design, to call it an architectural manifesto for new church spaces.[7]

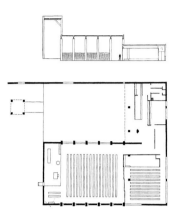

Van den Broek & Bakema
Kirche / church
Nagele, 1962

lichen Bauaufträgen anstrebte. Ein Beispiel hierfür ist die reformierte Kirche in Nagele (1962) von Van den Broek und
Bakema. Das Erscheinungsbild der Kirche wird von ihrem frei
stehenden Glockenturm bestimmt. Dieser Turm bezeichnet
den Vorhof der Kirche und fungiert als Vermittler des allmähli-
chen Übergangs vom öffentlichen Bereich zum abgeschlossenen
Charakter des Kircheninneren. Die Modernität der Anlage
wird durch die Tatsache unterstrichen, dass an die Stelle des
traditionellen Backsteins graue Betonblöcke treten, ein Material,
das in den sechziger und siebziger Jahren in der holländischen
Architektur eine äußerst bestimmende Rolle spielte. Zwei weitere interessante Bauten aus dieser Zeit sind die Kirche in
Haarlem (1961) von G.H.M. Holt mit ihrem sichtbaren Stahlskelett sowie das von Gerrit Rietveld konzipierte und von Van
Dillen & Van Tricht erbaute, verglaste Auditorium auf dem
Friedhof in Haarlemmermeer (1958–67). Von Rietveld stammt
außerdem der Entwurf für die zwischen 1960 und 1965 errich-
tete Kirche in Uithoorn. Er übernahm den Auftrag unter der
Bedingung, dass der Bau auch für andere Zwecke genutzt würde.
Er enthält ein Theater, eine Cafeteria sowie einen Kindergarten.

Als entscheidend sollte sich der eingeladene Wettbewerb für eine
protestantische Kirche in Driebergen erweisen. Hierzu bat man
1964 sieben bekannte Architekten um die Vorlage eines Entwurfs: P. Bloom, G. Boon, H. Hertzberger, J. Jelles, J. van Stigt,
J. Verhoeven und A. Van Eyck. Die Jury entschied sich einstim-
mig für Aldo Van Eycks »The Wheels of Heaven« genannten
Entwurf. Francis Strauven zufolge war Van Eyck (1918–1999)
in der Lage, sein Zaudern bei der Planung eines neuen Kirchenraumes als eine Ausprägung von Zwiespältigkeit in ein inno-
vatives Raumkonzept zu übertragen.[6] Bei dem Entwurf geht es
nicht um einen neutralen Raum ohne Mittelpunkt. Statt dessen
entschied sich Van Eyck für eine klar gegliederte Abfolge von
vier gesonderten Räumen in Form kreisförmiger Felder, von denen jeweils zwei den gleichen Durchmesser aufweisen. Die auch
in der Ausschreibung enthaltene Grundidee war die eines
Weges durch den Innenraum, eine Kirche in Form eines »Hau-
ses des Übergangs«. Ein neuer Versammlungsort, ein offener
Raum ohne ausdrückliches Zentrum oder festgelegte Axialität.
Bekaert ging sogar so weit, diesem Entwurf eine paradigmati-
sche Verschiebung zuzuschreiben und ihn als architektonisches
Manifest für neue Kirchenräume zu bezeichnen.[7]

Van Eycks erste Skizzen für die katholische Pastoor Van Ars Kirche
in Den Haag [Seite 124] weisen eine deutliche Ähnlichkeit mit
dem Projekt in Driebergen auf. Die Entwürfe entstanden zwischen 1963 und 1966, wurden jedoch erst 1969 realisiert. Der
Außenbau gleicht einem geschlossenen, rechteckigen Kasten,
doch in dem von einer Fülle von Räumen geprägten Interieur
gelang Van Eyck hohe Eindrücklichkeit. Er schuf, was man als
»labyrinthische Klarheit« bezeichnen könnte. Zwischen den
beiden tiefer liegenden Bereichen fügte er eine »Innenstraße«
ein, ein 11 Meter hohes Hauptschiff, mit dem diese Kirche die
Bedeutung einer via sacra annnimmt. Es ist interessant, dass
Dom van der Laan dieses Projekt den Kirchenoberen gegenüber
verteidigte.[8] Darüber hinaus entwarf Aldo Van Eyck eine Kirche
für die molukkische Gemeinde in Deventer (1984–92).

In den siebziger Jahren entstand noch die von L. Bisscheroux
konzipierte unterirdische Kirche in Heerlen (1977). Danach
nahmen die Aufträge für neue Kirchen rasch ab und versiegten
zu Beginn der neunziger Jahre nahezu gänzlich.

Gerrit Rietveld
Kirche / church
Uithoorn, 1965

The first sketches for the Roman Catholic Pastoor Van Ars church in The Hague [p. 128] show a close resemblance to the project in Driebergen. It was designed between 1963 and 1966 but was only built in 1969. The exterior is a closed rectangular box; on the inside, Van Eyck was able to achieve great intensity, an interior with an abundance of spaces. He creates what one might call a 'labyrinthine clarity'. Between the two lower sections he set an 'indoor street', an 11-metre-high nave which in this church takes on the significance of a *via sacra*. It is interesting to note that Dom Hans van der Laan defended this project to the church authorities.[8] Aldo Van Eyck also designed a church for the Moluccan community in Deventer (1984–92).

In the 1970s, there was the underground church in Heerlen (1977), designed by L. Bisscheroux. After this the briefs for new churches decreased rapidly and by the 1990s this had almost entirely dried up.

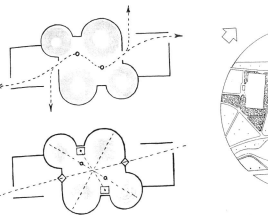 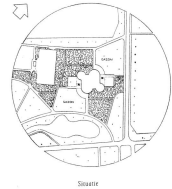

Situatie

Aldo van Eyck
Projekt / project
'The Wheels of Heaven'
1964

Aldo van Eyck
Pastoor van Ars Kirche / church
Den Haag / The Hague, 1969

Flandern

1
Marc Dubois, *Albert Van Huffel 1877–1935*, Gent 1983;
Pierre Rion, *De Basiliek van Koekelberg/Architectuur en Hedendaagse Geschiedenis*, Louvain-la-Neuve 1986.
2
Die französischsprachige Zeitschrift *Art d'Eglise* wurde von der Abbaye de Saint-André-lez-Bruges herausgegeben. Die erste Ausgabe erschien 1926 mit dem Titel *L'Artisan Liturgique*, die letzte im Jahr 1980; insgesamt kamen 193 Hefte heraus. Es fällt auf, dass diese Zeitschrift Werk und Denken des Benediktinermönchs Dom Hans van der Laan keinerlei Aufmerksamkeit widmete.
3
1961 veröffentlichte die Zeitschrift *Nieuwe Stemmen* eine von Geert Bekaert zusammengestellte Sonderausgabe (Nr. 6–7) über religiöse Kunst; Geert Bekaert, *Moderne kerkelijke kunst in Vlaanderen*, in: *De Kerk in Vlaanderen*, Tielt 1962.
4
Geert Bekaert, *De nieuwe kapel van het St.-Lievenscollege te Gent*, in: *Verzamelde Opstellen/Stapstenen 1950–1965*, Gent 1985.
5
Geert Bekaert, *In een of ander huis: kerkbouw op een keerpunt*, Tielt–Den Haag 1967.
6
Die französische Zeitschrift *L'Art Sacré* wurde auch in Belgien gelesen. Sie publizierte Kirchenentwürfe des Institut Supérieur d'Architecture Saint-Luc in Tournai (Nr. 3 & 4/1954). In *L'Art Sacré* erschienen ausführliche Artikel über Le Corbusiers Bauten in Ronchamp (Nr. 1 & 2/1955) und La Tourette (Nr. 7 & 8/1960).
7
Marc Dubois, *Architectuurrelatie Vlaanderen/Nederland*, in: *Ons Erfdeel*, Nr. 2, 1983.
8
Frans De Blauwe, *Jos Ritzen*, Antwerpen 1957.
9
Geert Bekaert, R. De Meyer, *Paul Felix 1913–1981 Architectur*, Tielt–Bussum 1981.
10
Frans Debuyst, *Le Monastère des Clarisses d'Ostende*, in: *Art d'Eglise*, Nr. 107, 1959.
11
Pro Arte Christiana, in: *Art d'Eglise*, Nr. 111, 1960.
12
Geert Bekaert, Luc Verpoest, *Marc Dessauvage 1931–1984*, Wommelgerm 1987.
13
Das Werk Marc Dessauvages war Bestandteil der folgenden Ausgaben: 111 (1960), 134 (1966), 139 (1967), 146 (1969).
14
Gerard Vandenhaute, Paul Vermeulen, *Juliaan Lampens 1950–1991*, Antwerpen 1991.
15
Albert Bontridder, *Gevecht met de rede: Léon Stynen/Leven en werk*, Antwerpen 1979.
16
Geert Bekaert, *Landschap van Kerken/10 eeuwen bouwen in Vlaanderen*, Antwerpen–Löwen 1987.

Wallonien

1
André Lanotte, *Présentation d'un effort diocésain: Namur 1945–1950*, in: *Art d'Eglise*, Nr. 2 & 3, S. 25–72. Im Jahr 1960 erschien eine zweite Sonderausgabe (Nr. 112) mit einem Überblick über die Bauten von 1950 bis 1960.
2
Pierre Puttermans, Henry Pouillon, Thibaut Parage, et. al., *Roger Bastin/Architecte 1913–1986*, Hayen 2001.
3
Maurizio Cohen, Jan Thomaes, *Jacques Depuis: l'architecte*, Brüssel 2000.
4
Paul Caulier, Philippe Lepère, *Le Collège du Christ-Roi à Ottignies*, in: *Art d'Eglise*, Nr. 141, 1967.
5
Art d'Eglise, Nr. 107, 1959.
6
Geert Bekaert, F. Strauven, *Bouwen in België 1945–1970*, Brüssel 1971.
7
Quelques réalisations religieuses de Lucien Kroll, in: *Art d'Eglise*, Nr. 152, 1970.

Niederlande

1
Alexander Jacobus Kropholler, *Bouwkunst in de 20ste eeuw*, Amsterdam 1953.
2
Diese Zeitschrift trat die Nachfolge des von 1928 bis 1940 erschienenen *Rooms Katholiek Bouwblad* an.
3
Richard Padovan, *Dom Hans van der Laan: Modern Primitive*, Amsterdam 1994. Alberto Ferlenga, P. Verde, *Dom Hans van der Laan: le opere, gli scritti*, Mailand 2000.
4
Wiel Arets, Wim Van den Bergh, William Graatsma, *FPJ Peutz Architect 1916–1966*, Eindhoven 1981.
5
Werk Alphonse Boostens in: *Katholiek Bouwblad*, Nr. 10, 1951.
6
Francis Strauven, *Aldo Van Eyck: The Space of Relativity*, Amsterdam 1998.
7
Geert Bekaert, *In een of ander huis: kerkbouw op een keerpunt*, Tielt–Den Haag 1967.
8
Francis Strauven, *Aldo Van Eyck: The Space of Relativity*, Amsterdam 1998.

Flanders

1
M. Dubois, *Albert Van huffel 1877–1935*, Ghent, 1983. P. Rion, *De Basiliek van Koekelberg/Architectuur en Hedendaagse Geschiedenis*, Louvain-la-Neuve, 1986.
2
The French-language magazine *Art d'Eglise* was published by L'Abbaye de Saint-André-lez-Bruges. The first issue appeared in 1926 under the title 'L'Artisan Liturgique'. The last issue appeared in 1980. There was a total of 193 issues. It is notable that this magazine did not pay any attention to the work and thinking of the benedictine monk Dom Hans van der Laan.
3
In 1961, the magazine *Nieuwe Stemmen* published a special issue (nos. 6–7) on 'Sacred Art', compiled by Geert Bekaert. G. Bekaert, 'Moderne kerkelijke kunst in Vlaanderen' in *De Kerk in Vlaanderen*, Tielt, 1962.
4
G. Bekaert, 'De nieuwe kapel van het St.-Lievenscollege te Gent' in *Verzamelde Opstellen/Stapstenen 1950–1965*, Ghent, 1985.
5
G. Bekaert, *In een of ander huis: kerkbouw op een keerpunt*, Tielt-The Hague, 1967.
6
The French magazine *L'Art Sacré* also circulated in Belgium. It published church designs from St. Luke's architectural college in Tournai (nos. 3 and 4/1954). *L'Art Sacré* published exhaustive articles on Le Corbusier's two buildings, at Ronchamp (nos. 1 and 2/1955) and La Tourette (nos. 7 and 8/1960).
7
M. Dubois, 'Architectuurrelatie Vlaanderen / Nederland' in *Ons Erfdeel* no. 2, 1983.
8
F. De Blauwe, *Jos Ritzen*, Antwerp, 1957.
9
G. Bekaert, R. De Meyer, *Paul Felix 1913-1981 Architectuur*, Tielt-Bussum, 1981.
10
F. Debuyst, Le Monastère des Clarisses d'Ostende in *Art d'Eglise* no. 107, 1959.
11
'Pro Arte Cristiana' in *Art d'Eglise* no. 111, 1960.
12
G. Bekaert, L. Verpoest, *Marc Dessauvage 1931–1984*, Wommelgem, 1987.
13
The work of Marc Dessauvage appeared in the following issues: 111 (1960), 134 (1966), 139 (1967), 146 (1969)
14
G. Vandenhaute, P. Vermeulen, *Juliaan Lampens 1950–1991*, Antwerp, 1991.
15
A. Bontridder, *Gevecht met de rede: Léon Stynen/Leven en werk*, Antwerp, 1979.
16
G. Bekaert, *Landschap van Kerken/10 eeuwen bouwen in Vlaanderen*, Antwerp-Leuven, 1987.

Wallonia

1
A.Lanotte, 'Présentation d'un effort diocésain: Namur 1945–1950' in *Art d'Eglise* nos. 2 and 3, 1950, pp. 25–72. In 1960 a second special issue appeared (no. 112), with a survey of buildings from 1950 to 1960.
2
P. Puttemans, H. Pouillon, T. Parage, et al., *Roger Bastin/Architecte 1913–1986*, Hayen, 2001.
3
M. Cohen, J. Thomaes, *Jacques Dupuis: l'architecte*, Brussels, 2000.
4
P. Caulier, P. Lepère, 'Le Collège du Christ-Roi à Ottignies' in *Art d'Eglise* no. 141, 1967.
5
Art d'Eglise, no. 107, 1959
6
G. Bekaert, F. Strauven, *Bouwen in België 1945-1970*, Brussels, 1971.
7
'Quelques realisations réligieuses de Lucien Kroll' in *Art d'Eglise*, no. 152, 1970.

The Netherlands

1
A. J. Kropholler, *Bouwkunst in de 20ste eeuw*, Amsterdam, 1953.
2
This magazine was the successor to the *Rooms Katholiek Bouwblad*, published from 1928 to 1940.
3
R. Padovan, *Dom Hans van der Laan: Modern Primitive*, Amsterdam, 1994.
A. Ferlenga, P. Verde, *Dom Hans van der Laan: le opere, gli scritti*, Milan, 2000.
4
W. Arets, W. Van den Bergh, W. Graatsma, *FPJ Peutz Architect 1916–1966*, Eindhoven, 1981.
5
Work by Alphonse Boosten, in *Katholiek Bouwblad*, no.10, 1951.
6
F. Strauven, *Aldo Van Eyck: The Space of Relativity*, Amsterdam, 1998.
7
G. Bekaert, *In een of ander huis: kerkbouw op een keerpunt*, Tielt-The Hague, 1967.
8
F. Strauven, *Aldo Van Eyck: The Space of Relativity*, Amsterdam, 1998.

Aldo van Eyck

Pastoor van Ars Kirche
Den Haag, Niederlande
1969

Pastoor van Ars Church
The Hague, Holland
1969

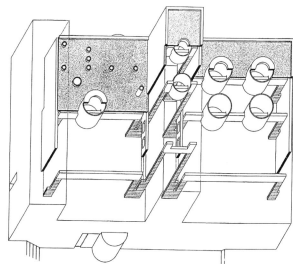

Axonometrie
axonometric projection

Aldo van Eyck (1918–1999) ist in die Geschichte als ein Begründer des ›Strukturalismus‹ eingegangen, jener niederländischen Bauschule, die um 1960 die schematisch gewordene Architekturmoderne bekämpfte. Während die analytische Moderne das Verhältnis zwischen Funktion und Raum statisch bestimmte, sahen die Strukturalisten ihre Aufgabe darin, den Nutzern ihrer Gebäude einen flexiblen Rahmen zu liefern, der individuelle Aktivitäten fördern sollte. Dass dabei ›Archetypen‹ aufgegriffen wurden, zeigt diese Kirche in einem südwestlich gelegenen Wohnviertel von Den Haag. Das fensterlose, nur durch Dachkuppeln belichtete Gebäude ist im Sinne der frühchristlichen Tradition wie eine Krypta auf den Innenraum ausgerichtet.

Aldo van Eyck (1918–99) has gone down in history as a founder of Structuralism, the Dutch school of architecture opposed to Modernism, which in the architectural world around 1960 had grown rather formulaic. Whereas the analytical modernists determined the relationship between function and space in static terms, the structuralists saw it as their task to provide their buildings' end-users with a flexible framework that was intended to promote individual activities. The fact that 'archetypes' were followed in this process is demonstrated by this church which was built in a residential area south-west of The Hague. The windowless building, lit only by cupolas in the roof, is laid out inside like a crypt from the early Christian tradition.

129

Das 11 Meter hohe Hauptschiff bildet eine ›via sacra‹. Unter den Betonträgern öffnet es sich durch fünf Portale zu den flachen Bereichen von Kirchenraum und Gemeindesaal.

The 11-metre-high nave forms a 'via sacra'. Below the concrete supports it opens out through five portals into the flat areas of the interior and the community hall.

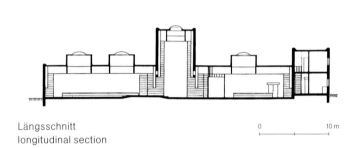

Längsschnitt
longitudinal section

0   10 m

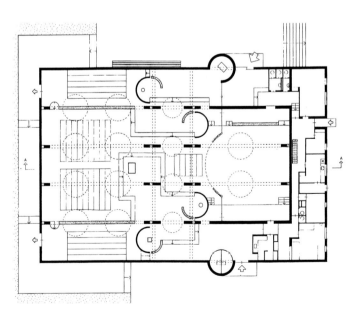

Grundriss
floor plan

Die asketische Ausstrahlung der Kirche beruht nicht zuletzt auf den einfachen Materialien. Mit Ausnahme der betonierten Elemente wurden außen wie innen helle Zementsteine verwendet. Das natürlich belassene Sichtmauerwerk gliedert durch sein Fugenbild alle Wände, auch die halbkreisförmigen Schalen der kleinen Kapellen. Der Grundriss der Kirche ist polyzentral, so dass der Besucher zur Bewegung durch das Gebäude angeregt wird. Der 400 Plätze umfassende Kirchenraum kann während der Sommersaison (in der Nähe befindet sich ein Feriengebiet) auf 600 Plätze erweitert werden. Im Gegensatz zum kirchlichen Zeitgeist der späten sechziger Jahre wollte Aldo van Eyck keinen neutralen Mehrzweckraum schaffen, sondern differenzierte Räume mit spiritueller Atmosphäre. Dazu trägt neben dem als ›via sacra‹ gestalteten Hauptschiff die ausschließliche Lichtführung von oben bei. Durch die runden, regelmäßig angeordneten Dachkuppeln fällt mildes, gleichmäßiges Licht nach innen, auch auf den Altar. Adresse: Den Haag-Loosduinen, Aaltje Noordewierstraat.

The church's ascetic aura is due not least to its simple materials. With the exception of the concrete elements, light-coloured cement blocks were used both inside and out. The exposed masonry, left au naturel, gives structure to all the walls — including the semicircular shells of the small chapels — through its jointing. The church is polycentric in ground plan, so that the visitor is encouraged to move around it. The seating capacity of 400 can be increased to 600 during the summer season (there is a resort area nearby). By contrast with the ecclesiastical mood of the late 1960s, Aldo van Eyck did not wish to create a neutral, multipurpose space but rather differentiated spaces with a spiritual atmosphere. The arrangement of the nave as a 'via sacra' contributes to this, as does the light entering exclusively from above. Soft, even light falls into the church, including on to the altar, through round, regularly spaced cupolas in the roof. Address: Aaltje Noordewierstraat, Loosduinen, The Hague.

Nuno Portas · Teotónio Pereira

Igreja do Sagrado Coração de Jesus
Lissabon, Portugal
1970

Church of the Sacred Heart
Lisbon, Portugal
1970

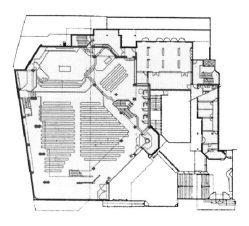

 Grundriss
floor plan

0   20 m

In der Nähe der berühmten Praça de Pombal gelegen, verkörpert das Bauwerk den Neubeginn der sakralen Architektur in Portugal. Angesichts der konservativen, vordemokratischen Zustände bedeutete es eine Zäsur, den kirchlichen mit dem öffentlichen Raum zu verbinden. Auf dem umbauten Grundstück zwischen zwei Seitenstraßen waren neben der großen Kirche auch ein Gemeindezentrum sowie andere Einrichtungen unterzubringen. Die ganze Anlage ist derart eng in ihre Umgebung eingefügt, dass sie nur von einem erhöhten Standpunkt aus zu erfassen ist. Wegen der nach Osten hin extremen Hanglage haben die Architekten die Gebäude auf mehreren Ebenen angeordnet. Eine Fußgängerpassage mit zahlreichen Treppen stellt die Verbindung zwischen den beiden Straßen her. Der Eingang zur Kirche liegt am oberen Hof. Ihr Außenbau wird bestimmt durch vorgefertigte Betontafeln, die ersten, die in Portugal hergestellt wurden. Im hohen, seitlich belichteten Innenraum ist das Tragwerk aus gegossenem Beton sichtbar. Die Innenschale der Wände besteht aus hellen Zementsteinen mit einer Reliefstruktur. Adresse: Rua Castelo Branco.

Situated close to the famous Praça de Pombal, this edifice is the embodiment of a new beginning for religious architecture in Portugal. In view of the conservative, pre-democratic conditions prevailing at the time, the combination of ecclesiastical with public space signified a complete break. A community centre and other facilities, in addition to the large church, were also to be housed on the enclosed plot of land set between two side streets. The entire complex is so tightly squeezed into its setting that it can only be understood from an elevated viewpoint. Because of the site's extreme slope down to the east the architects arranged the buildings on several levels. A pedestrian passage with innumerable steps acts as a link between the two streets. The church is entered from the upper courtyard. Its outer appearance is characterised by prefabricated concrete panels — the first to be produced in Portugal. In the high interior, lit from the side, the supporting cast-concrete structure is visible. The inner shell of the walls consists of light-coloured cement blocks with a relief structure. Address: Rua Castelo Branco.

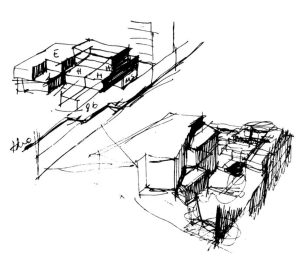

Durch eine große Öffnung im Dach fällt das Licht effektvoll auf die gemauerte Wand hinter dem Altar. Nur von einem erhöhten Standpunkt aus ist die völlig umbaute Kirche in der Stadtsilhouette zu erkennen.

Light falls dramatically on to the masonry wall behind the altar through a large aperture in the roof. Completely hemmed in by other buildings, the church can only be picked out in the city's skyline from a raised vantage point.

Erhard Fischer

St. Christophorus
Ingolstadt, Deutschland
1970

St Christophorus
Ingolstadt, Germany
1970

Dieses Gebäude war der Auftakt einer vorausschauenden Planung. Noch bevor während der siebziger Jahre in einem nordwestlichen Vorort von Ingolstadt neue Wohngebiete entstanden, wurde die Kirche als künftiges Zentrum des Stadtteils errichtet. Dabei verfolgte der Architekt das Ziel, die sakrale Aufgabe so eng wie möglich mit dem Alltag der kirchlichen Gemeinde zu verbinden. Deshalb enthält der zusammen mit Klaus Weissenfeldt entworfene Bau nicht nur den Kirchenraum mit Sakristei, sondern auch die Amtszimmer der Gemeinde, die Wohnung des Pfarrers sowie im Untergeschoss einen Jugendraum: »Die übliche Isolierung des eigentlichen kirchlichen Bereichs wird bewusst durchbrochen und jegliche ›feierliche‹ Abgeschiedenheit verhindert.« Anfangs frei stehend, ist der Kirchenbau aus monolithischem Sichtbeton inzwischen von mehrgeschossigen Wohngebäuden umgeben. Außerdem wurde er bis zum Ende der siebziger Jahre schrittweise zu einem Gemeindezentrum erweitert: Ebenfalls von Fischer entworfen, umschließen ein Kindergarten, ein Pfarrsaal und mehrere Altenwohnungen zusammen mit der kompakten Kirche einen intimen Hof.

This building was the first step in a forward-looking plan. Even before new residential areas were developed in a north-western suburb of Ingolstadt during the 1960s, the church was constructed as the future centre of the district. In so doing, the architect pursued the objective of linking religious duty as closely as possible with the everyday life of the congregation. The building, designed in conjunction with Klaus Weissenfeldt, therefore contains not just the church and sacristy but also parish offices, the presbytery and premises for youth activities in the basement: 'The customary isolation of the actual spiritual zone is deliberately broken down, and any kind of "solemn" seclusion is prevented'. Although it initially stood alone, the church in monolithic exposed concrete is now surrounded by multi-storey residential blocks. In addition, until the end of the 1970s it underwent step-by-step expansion to form a community centre. Also designed by Fischer, a kindergarten, parish hall and several old people's apartments, together with the compact church, enclose an intimate courtyard.

Im Grundriss ist der großzügig wirkende Kirchenraum ein Quadrat, das durch eine Diagonale vom Haupteingang über das mittlere Gestühl bis hin zum Altar überlagert wird.

In its ground plan the interior, which has a spacious feel, is a square overlaid by a diagonal that runs from the main entrance via the middle pews to the altar.

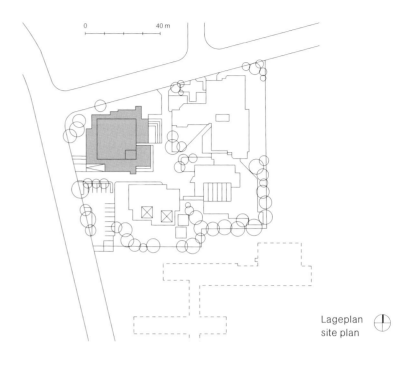

Lageplan
site plan

Gottesdienste in dem Kirchenraum
mit 400 Sitzplätzen wurden öfters
vom Fernsehen übertragen. Am Rand
des erhöhten Altarbereichs befindet
sich die Tabernakelstele.

Services in the church, which has
seating for 400, used to be broadcast
frequently on television. The tabernacle stele is positioned at the edge
of the raised altar zone.

Im Sinne des nachkonziliaren Kirchenbaus wurde das Sanktuarium diagonal in die Nordwestecke gelegt, so dass sich die Gemeinde in drei Blöcken um den Altar versammelt. Nach Osten hin erweitert sich der Kirchenraum durch eine Sängerempore, westlich von ihm liegt mit eigenem Eingang die Werktagskapelle. Der Hauptkirchenraum hat ein erhöhtes, als Trägerrost in Holz konstruiertes Dach, das durch eine verglaste Zone von den massiven Wänden abgesetzt ist. Diese Zone versorgt den winkelförmigen, vom Raum aus nicht sichtbaren ›Lichtschacht‹ hinter dem Altar: Auf diese Weise fällt das Licht zwischen Außen- und Innenwand indirekt ein. Der sorgfältig detaillierte Baukörper öffnet sich außerdem an den Ecken durch verglaste Schlitze, die dezentes Tageslicht eindringen lassen. Aus kubischen Formen komponiert, wird der Außenbau auch durch die vorgezogenen Wasserspeier akzentuiert. Eine Betonsanierung hat den ursprünglichen Charakter des rau verschalten Materials leider verändert. Adresse: Ingolstadt-Friedrichshofen, Jurastraße.

In accordance with church-building principles following the Second Vatican Council, the sanctuary was positioned diagonally in the northwestern corner so that the congregation could gather around the altar in three blocks. The interior is widened on the east by a singers' gallery, while on the west lies the workday chapel with its own entrance. The main body of the interior has a raised wooden roof, constructed in the form of a grid, which is offset from the solid walls by a glazed zone. This zone supplies the angled 'light well' — not visible from inside the church — behind the altar; light thus enters indirectly between the outer and the inner wall. The carefully detailed building is also opened up in several corners by glazed slits, which let in muted daylight. Composed of cubical forms, the exterior is further accentuated through projecting water spouts. Renovation of the concrete has unfortunately altered the original character of the roughly moulded material. Address: Jurastrasse, Friedrichshofen, Ingolstadt.

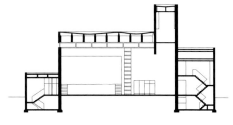

Schnitt
section

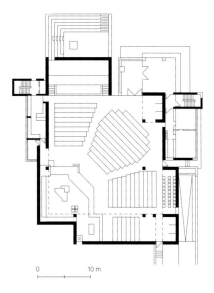

Grundriss
floor plan

0   10 m

Walter M. Förderer

St. Nicolas
Hérémence, Schweiz
1971

St Nicolas
Hérémence, Switzerland
1971

Eingebettet in einen Steilhang, überragt die Betonkirche das ganze Dorf.
Die Fenstereinschnitte in dem burgartigen Baukörper wirken wie Schieß-
scharten.

Embedded in a steep slope, the concrete church towers over the whole
village. The irregular window openings cut in the fortress-like building
have the effect of embrasures.

1964 veröffentlichte Walter M. Förderer seine Schrift *Kirchenbau von heute für morgen? Fragen heutiger Architektur und Kunst*. Darin forderte er die Kirche dazu auf, sie solle sich »nicht aufdrängen und mit ihren Bauten unbedingt beherrschend in Erscheinung treten wollen«. Aufgrund des Wertepluralismus in der modernen Welt könne ein Kirchenbau nicht mehr »die Mitte« einnehmen. Diese Aussage lässt sich mit Förderers Kirchen nicht in Übereinstimmung bringen. Der Widerspruch löst sich dadurch auf, dass er in seiner Schrift von allgemeinen Kriterien spricht, seine eigenen Sakralbauten aber als Kunstwerke versteht. Als Architekt ein Autodidakt, hat sich Förderer in mehreren Kirchen als Bildhauer verwirklicht. Sein Meisterwerk ist die Kirche im Dorf Hérémence, das südlich von Sion in den Alpen liegt. In diesem Fall hat der Sichtbeton einen starken örtlichen Bezug, da in den sechziger Jahren oberhalb der Ortschaft ein großer Staudamm fertiggestellt worden war. Wie ein begehbarer Felsen ragt die Kirche inmitten der Holzhäuser auf – ein Durchgang mit Gassen und Plätzen verbindet die obere mit der unteren Dorfstraße.

Walter M. Förderer published *Kirchenbau von heute für morgen? Fragen heutiger Architektur und Kunst* [Today's church-building for tomorrow? Questions about contemporary architecture and art] in 1964. In this document he asked the Church not to 'impose itself and seek to appear absolutely dominant through its buildings'; because of the pluralism of values in the modern world, a church could no longer occupy 'the centre'. These statements do not however accord with Förderer's own churches. The inconsistency is resolved when one realises that in his text he is talking about general criteria, while he regards his own religious buildings as works of art. Self-taught as an architect, Förderer achieved his ambition as a sculptor in a number of sculptural churches. His masterpiece is the church in the village of Hérémence, which lies south of Sion in the Valais Alps. The exposed concrete that he used has strong local associations in this case, as the gigantic Grande Dixence Dam was constructed above the village in the 1960s. The church towers like a cliff over the wooden houses: a public thoroughfare with alleys and squares links the upper and lower village streets.

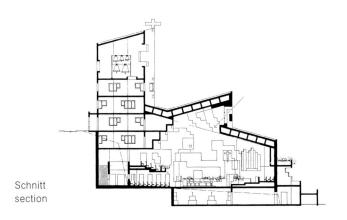

Schnitt
section

Der mit Vorsprüngen, Einbuchtungen und Galerien expressiv durchgestaltete Außenbau drückt sich körperhaft in dem bis zu 22 Meter hohen Innenraum aus, den Förderer als »Kathedrale« bezeichnet. Wie seine anderen Bauten entwickelte er St. Nicolas anhand eines Modells, dessen Proportionen und Maße anschließend in Pläne übertragen wurden. Die technische Ausführung des Entwurfs war aber derart kompliziert, dass das Modell auf der Baustelle als Arbeitshilfe dienen musste. Weil die gegossenen Wände und Mauern 40 bis 50 Zentimeter dick sind, hat sich der Sichtbeton trotz des rauen Klimas bewährt. Der hohe Schalungsdruck führte zu reliefartigen, lebendigen Oberflächen. Auch im Kirchenraum mit 500 Sitzplätzen, die den Altar auf drei Seiten einfassen, gehen alle Bauteile homogen ineinander über: Vom dunklen Umgang aus wächst das durch einen Balkon, eine auskragende Empore und mehrere Tribünen gegliederte Innenvolumen mit Stufen und Deckenfalten dramatisch in die Höhe. Das Licht fällt von oben ein, vor allem auf den liturgischen Bezirk.

The expressive styling of the exterior, with projections, bays and open galleries, is reflected in the interior, up to 22 metres high, which Förderer terms a 'cathedral'. As with his other constructions, he developed St Nicolas with the assistance of a model, the proportions and dimensions of which were subsequently converted into plans. However, the technical realisation of the design proved so complicated that the model had to be used as a working aid on the building site. Since the cast walls are 40 to 50 centimetres thick, the concrete has survived despite the raw climate. The high pressure of the moulding process produced lively, relief-like surfaces. In the interior, with seating for 500 that encloses the altar on three sides, all the building's components merge homogeneously into one another: from the dark ambulatory the inner volume — structured by means of a balcony, an overhanging gallery and several platforms — swoops upwards dramatically by way of tiers and roof folds. Light enters from above, falling chiefly on to the liturgical zone.

Der Wechsel von Licht und Schatten macht den öffentlichen Weg durch das Bauwerk zu einem Erlebnis. Zwischen den Dorfstraßen liegt ein Höhenunterschied von 15 Metern.

Changes of light and shade turn a walk along the public thoroughfare through the edifice into an experience. There is a 15-metre difference in altitude between the two village streets.

0   20 m

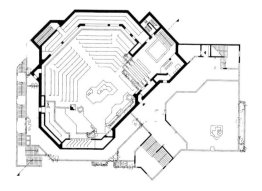

Grundriss
floor plan

Gottfried Böhm

Mariendom mit Pilgerweg
Neviges, Deutschland
1972

Cathedral of the Virgin Mary
with Pilgrims' Way
Neviges, Germany
1972

Zusammen mit dem etwa gleichzeitig entstandenen Rathaus in Bensberg bildet der Mariendom bei Velbert im Bergischen Land den Höhepunkt im Schaffen von Gottfried Böhm, der 1986 mit dem renommierten Pritzker Prize ausgezeichnet wurde. Der erste Bauabschnitt war die 1968 fertiggestellte Wallfahrtskirche Maria, Königin des Friedens, anschließend wurden die Bauten und Anlagen des Pilgerwegs errichtet. Im Gegensatz zum eher bescheidenen Kirchenbaustil der sechziger Jahre entwarf Böhm, Sohn des berühmten Kirchenarchitekten Dominikus Böhm, den Dom als eine monumentale, auf die weitere Umgebung hin bezogene Plastik: »Die eigenwillige Architektur der Betonkirche spiegelt die hügelige Landschaft des Bergischen Landes wider.«

Together with the town hall in Bensberg which was constructed at roughly the same time, the Mariendom near Velbert in the Bergisches Land (a hilly region in the Ruhr Valley) forms the pinnacle of the creative œuvre of Gottfried Böhm, recipient of the prestigious Pritzker Prize in 1986. The first phase of the project involved the pilgrimage church of 'Mary, Queen of Peace', completed in 1968, following which the buildings and installations of the pilgrims' way were constructed. In contrast to the rather modest religious architectural style of the 1960s, Böhm, son of the famous church architect Dominikus Böhm, designed the cathedral as a structure of monumental plasticity, integrated into its wider environment: 'The unconventional architecture of the concrete church reflects the undulating landscape of the Bergisches Land'.

Lageplan
site plan

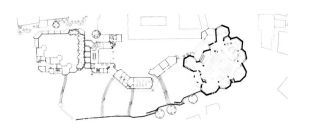

0   10 m

Die Strecke vom Bahnhofsvorplatz zum Mariendom hat Böhm als breiten ›Pilgerweg‹ mit mehreren, wellenförmigen Treppenanlagen gestaltet.

Böhm laid out the terrain leading from the forecourt of the railway station to the cathedral as a broad 'pilgrims' way' with several wave-like flights of steps.

Gottfried Böhm gewann den Wettbewerb 1964 in der zweiten Stufe. Die Kohlezeichnung zeigt die scharfkantige Dachlandschaft, deren höchste Spitze 35 Meter erreicht. Das Dach, ein freitragendes Betonfaltwerk, soll ein großes Zelt darstellen.

Gottfried Böhm won the 1964 competition at the second stage. The charcoal drawing shows the sharp-edged roof 'landscape', 35 metres high at its peak. The roof, a cantilevered structure of folded concrete, is meant to represent a large tent.

Auch im Kirchenraum drücken sich Elemente einer ›kleinen Stadt‹ aus: Die Pflasterung und die Straßenlaternen des Pilgerwegs setzen sich bis in den Zentralraum hinein fort, seitliche Emporen sowie raumhohe Wandnischen für Altäre und Betkapellen fordern die Pilger zur Bewegung im Gebäude auf, das 800 Sitzplätze hat und insgesamt 6000 Besucher aufnehmen kann. Die in ein mystisches Dunkel gehüllte Oberkirche ist als ›sakraler Marktplatz‹ gestaltet. Wie schon beim Pfarrzentrum St. Gertrud in Köln (1961) hat Böhm einen monolithischen Betonkörper geschaffen: »Mich begeisterte die Möglichkeit, Decken und Wände zu einer Einheit zusammenzufassen.« Das ganze Gebäude besteht aus gegossenem Beton, der mit Ausnahme der Dachflächen sandgestrahlt wurde. Bei den komplizierten Schalungen wurde den Handwerkern das Äußerste abverlangt. Als Kontrast zum rauen Charakter der Räume wirken die farbenprächtigen Glasfenster, die Gottfried Böhm selbst entworfen hat. Der Mariendom verkörpert beispielhaft eine autonome Formensprache, die zwischen Tradition und Moderne vermittelt.

The interior also incorporates elements of a 'small town': the paving and street lamps of the pilgrims' way are continued into the central space, and side galleries and full-length wall niches housing altars and prayer chapels encourage the movement of pilgrims inside the building, which has seating for 800 and can hold 6,000 visitors overall. The upper church, veiled in mystical darkness, is arranged as a 'sacred marketplace'. As he did earlier at the parish centre of St Gertrude in Cologne (1961), Böhm created a monolithic concrete mass: 'I was inspired by the possibility of uniting ceilings and walls into a whole'. The entire building is made of cast concrete, which was sandblasted except for the roof surfaces. Extreme demands were made on the workers involved in the complicated formwork processes. The colourful stained-glass windows, designed by Böhm himself, provide a contrast to the raw character of the interior. In exemplary fashion, the cathedral represents the embodiment of an autonomous formal idiom that mediates between the traditional and the modern.

Die scharfkantigen Auffaltungen von Wand und Decke sollen an ein Zelt erinnern, das als Zeichen des Nicht-Sesshaften auch ein Symbol für die Pilgerschaft darstellt. Der Mariendom steht deshalb auf dem höchsten Punkt des Geländes.

The sharp-edged upward folds of wall and ceiling are intended to be reminiscent of a tent, which, as a symbol of those pursuing a non-settled way of life, is similarly a symbol of pilgrimage. This is why the cathedral stands at the highest point of the complex.

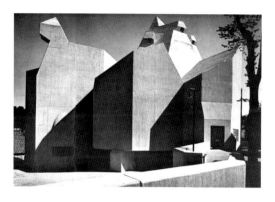

Carlo Scarpa

Friedhofskapelle
San Vito d'Altivole, Italien
1978

Cemetery Chapel
San Vito d'Altivole, Italy
1978

Lageplan
site plan

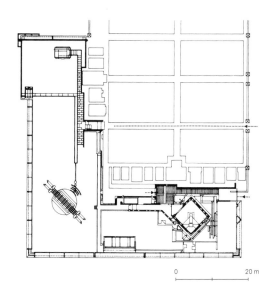

0   20 m

Carlo Scarpa (1906–1978) nimmt in der modernen Architektur eine einzigartige Stellung ein. Von Frank Lloyd Wright ebenso beeinflusst wie von der spielerischen Disziplin der Gruppe *De Stijl*, hat Scarpa dieses Erbe der Moderne zusammen mit der Tradition venezianischer Handwerkskunst in baumeisterliche Schöpfungen überführt, die völlig eigenständig sind. Besonders sein respektvoller Umgang mit alter Bausubstanz hat einigen Architekten als Vorbild gedient, etwa Guido Canali und Karljosef Schattner. Auch Scarpas letztes Werk von eigener Hand, der Privatfriedhof Brion, ist durch die Komposition der Anlage, die verfeinerte Materialbehandlung und die Kultivierung der Details ein ›Gesamtkunstwerk‹. Die Grabstätte für eine Fabrikantenfamilie liegt etwa zehn Kilometer nördlich von Castelfranco Veneto in flacher Landschaft und umschließt durch ihr erhöhtes, von Mauern gefasstes Niveau den Dorffriedhof von San Vito wie eine Bastion. Scarpas eigene Grabstelle befindet sich an der Grenze zwischen alter und neuer Anlage.

Carlo Scarpa (1906–78) occupies a unique position within modern architecture. Influenced as much by Frank Lloyd Wright as by the playful discipline of De Stijl, Scarpa carried this modernist legacy, together with the traditions of Venetian craftsmanship, through into architectural creations that are totally original. His respectful handling of old buildings, in particular, served as a model for such architects as Guido Canali and Karljosef Schattner. Scarpa's last work by his own hand, the Brion private cemetery, is similarly a Gesamtkunstwerk — a total work of art — owing to the composition, the sophisticated treatment of materials and the cultivation of detail. The funerary complex for a family of industrialists lies some 10 kilometres north of Castelfranco Veneto on the plain and, due to its elevated position enclosed by walls, it embraces the village cemetery of San Vito like a bastion. Scarpa's own grave is located on the boundary between the old and new complexes.

Die um 45 Grad zur Außenmauer gedrehte Kapelle lässt sich zu einem Wasserbecken hin öffnen. Scarpa: »Ich habe den natürlichen Sinn von Wasser und Erde ausdrücken wollen. Wasser ist die Quelle des Lebens.«

The chapel, set at an angle of 45 degrees to the outer wall, opens on to a pond. Scarpa: 'I wanted to express the natural meaning of water and earth — water is the source of life'.

Die öffentlich zugängliche Kapelle ist eines der fünf kleinen Gebäude, die Scarpa für den Privatfriedhof mit 2 200 Quadratmetern Fläche gestaltet hat. Der direkte Zugang zu ihr liegt am Parkplatz und wird durch einen Zypressenhain betont. Bei dem kleinen, quadratischen Gebäude mit sieben Metern Seitenlänge sind alle Motive des Friedhofs eindrucksvoll zusammengefasst: das kalkulierte Spiel der Öffnungen zwischen innen und außen, der ständige Wechsel von Enge und Weite, die Durchbildung aller Flächen und Wände mit Stufengesimsen und Abtreppungen, der Einsatz von baulichen Symbolen wie dem kreisförmigen Durchgang, die Bezüge zum Wasser. Der Sichtbeton als Grundmaterial wurde so unterschiedlich behandelt, dass er einerseits rau und abweisend wirkt, auf der anderen Seite fast zierlich und zerbrechlich. Bei seiner Gestaltung, die auch keine Kanten und Fugen ausließ, war der Architekt sicher genug, den Manierismus nicht zu übertreiben. Im Rahmen der weitläufigen Grabstätte, die eine Synthese von Scarpas Anschauungen darstellt, ist die Kapelle ein kostbarer ›Schrein‹ für Trauer und Andacht.

The chapel, which is open to the public, is one of five buildings that Scarpa designed for the private cemetery covering an area of 2,200 square metres. The chapel is accessed directly from the car park via an approach which is accentuated by a cypress grove. All the cemetery motifs are impressively summarised in the small, square building whose sides are 7 metres long: the calculated play on the apertures linking inside and outside; the constant alternations of narrowness and width; the styling of all surfaces and walls with stepped ledges and raking; the use of structural symbols such as the circular passageway; the references to water. The exposed concrete forming the basic material was treated so diversely that, on the one hand, it gives the impression of being rough and cold while, on the other, it seems almost delicate and fragile. In his styling, which extended even to the edges and joints, the architect had enough confidence not to exaggerate the mannerism. The chapel forms a precious 'shrine' for mourning and worship within the framework of the sprawling private cemetary, and represents a synthesis of Sarpa' ideas.

Unterschiedliche Texturen und sorg-
fältige Details lassen die einfachen
Materialien im Andachtsraum kostbar
erscheinen. Das gedämpfte Licht
trägt wesentlich zur Atmosphäre bei.

Varied textures and careful details
give a sumptuous look to the simple
materials used in the devotional
interior. The subdued lighting makes
a considerable contribution to the
atmosphere.

Alvar Aalto

Santa Maria Assunta
Riola di Vergato, Italien
1978

Santa Maria Assunta
Riola di Vergato, Italy
1978

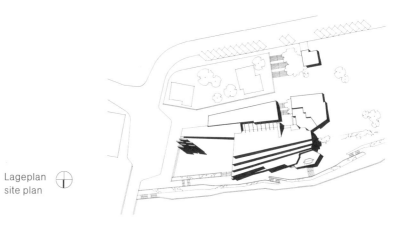

Lageplan
site plan

Der Turm aus fünf Betonscheiben
wurde erst 1994 unter Leitung von
Aaltos Witwe Elissa fertiggestellt.

Consisting of five slices of concrete,
the tower was completed only in 1994
under the direction of Aalto's widow,
Elissa.

Der damals schon weltberühmte Alvar Aalto (1898–1976) erhielt den Auftrag für Kirche und Gemeindezentrum in Riola von Giacomo Lercaro, dem ökumenisch ausgerichteten Kardinal von Bologna. Auch wegen finanzieller Probleme verzögerte sich die Ausführung des bereits 1966 vorgelegten Entwurfs um viele Jahre. Das Dorf Riola liegt mitten im Apennin, etwa 45 Kilometer südwestlich von Bologna an der Straße nach Pistoia. Die Kirche, deren Turm erst 1994 errichtet wurde, steht auf einer Terrasse zwischen dem Fluss Reno und einem sanft ansteigenden Hang. Vor der Eingangswand erstreckt sich nach Osten hin ein großer Platz, so dass sich die Gläubigen auch im Freien versammeln können. Die Kirche ist eine asymmetrische, keilförmig zulaufende Basilika mit einem asymmetrischen Gewölbe aus vorgefertigten, bis zu 25 Meter hohen Betonbögen, die das dreifach eingekerbte Dach tragen. Das Dach ist auch deshalb ungewöhnlich, weil es sich in Längsrichtung, zum Altar hin, deutlich absenkt. Das Gemeindezentrum und das Pfarrhaus liegen südlich der Kirche.

Alvar Aalto (1898–1976) was already world-famous when he was commissioned by the ecumenically minded Cardinal Giacomo Lercaro of Bologna to design a church and community centre in Riola. However, the design — submitted as early as 1966 — was not actually implemented for many years owing, among other factors, to financial problems. The village of Riola lies in the Apennines, about 45 kilometres south-west of Bologna, on the road to Pistoia. The church, whose tower was erected only in 1994, stands on a terrace between the River Reno and a gently rising slope. In front of the entrance wall, a large piazza extends towards the east so that the congregation can also assemble in the open air. The church is an asymmetrical basilica tapering into a wedge shape, with an asymmetrical vault of pre-cast concrete arches — up to 25 metres high — bearing the roof with its triple notch. The roof is also unusual in that it clearly descends longitudinally towards the altar. The community centre and presbytery lie to the south of the church.

Die Kirche mit dem markanten Dachprofil liegt außerhalb des Dorfzentrums am Ufer des Reno. Die langen Fensterbänder im Dach versorgen den Kirchenraum mit viel Tageslicht.

The church with its striking roof profile lies outside the village centre on the banks of the Reno. The long bands of windows in the roof provide the interior with plenty of daylight.

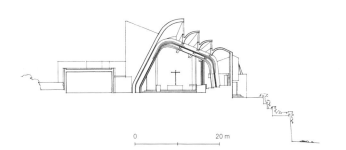

Querschnitt
cross section

0   20 m

Das Tageslicht, das von Nordwesten her durch die vertikalen Fensterbänder im eingekerbten Dach großzügig einfällt, moduliert die Wände und das Gewölbe im Kirchenraum.

The walls and vault of the interior are modulated by the daylight that pours in from the north-west through the vertical bands of windows in the notched roof.

Durch die enge Beziehung von Altar, Orgel, Chor und Baptisterium soll die Kirche die nachkonziliare Liturgie erfüllen. Der Taufraum (rechtes Foto) liegt neben dem Altar, hat eine Dachlaterne und ein Fenster mit Ausblick auf den Fluss. Die Sängerempore zieht sich stufenförmig in das Gewölbe hinein, während die 200 Sitzplätze konventionell in zwei Blöcken angeordnet sind. Den Hauptkirchenraum beherrschen die sieben asymmetrischen Stahlbetonbögen als sichtbar belassenes Tragwerk der Dachkonstruktion. Jeweils in drei Teilen vorgefertigt, wurden die Bögen auf der Baustelle zusammengesetzt und aufgerichtet. Innen sind die massiven Wände strahlend weiß gestrichen, außen mit einem hellen Naturstein verkleidet. Leider wurden mehrere von Aaltos Ideen während der langwierigen Ausführung aufgegeben, zum Beispiel die bewegliche Eingangswand, die den Kirchenraum an hohen Feiertagen zum großen Hof geöffnet hätte. Zu seinem 100. Geburtstag wurde Alvar Aalto von der Diözese mit einer Gedenktafel am Eingang zum Gemeindezentrum geehrt.

The church is intended to satisfy liturgical requirements following the Second Vatican Council by its close linking of altar, organ, choir and baptistry. Situated beside the altar, the baptistry (right) is provided with a roof lantern as well as a window looking out over the river. The singers' gallery is drawn stepwise into the vault, while the seating for 200 is arranged conventionally in two blocks. The seven asymmetrical reinforced-concrete arches dominate the main body of the church as a deliberately visible supporting framework for the roof. Each pre-cast in three parts, the arches were assembled and erected on site. The solid walls are painted brilliant white on the inside, whereas outside they are faced with a pale-coloured natural stone. Unfortunately, several of Aalto's ideas were abandoned during the lengthy construction process — for example the movable entrance wall, which would have opened up the interior to the large courtyard on special feast days. The diocese honoured the hundredth anniversary of Alvar Aalto's birth with a commemorative plaque, placed at the entrance to the community centre.

Wolfgang Pehnt

Im Zeichen der Liturgiereform
Neuer Kirchenbau im Rheinland

Den rheinischen Provinzen ist immer wieder besondere Produktivität im neueren Kirchenbau nachgesagt worden.[1] Den Zahlen nach ist die Bilanz der ersten Jahrzehnte nach 1945 ohnehin eindrucksvoll. Im Westen Deutschlands mit seinem hohen Zerstörungsgrad war der Bedarf an Wiederaufbau und Neubau besonders groß. Dazu kamen die Völkerwanderungen der Kriegs- und Nachkriegszeit, die Flüchtlingsströme aus den verlorenen Ostgebieten, die Wanderungsbewegungen zwischen altem Stadtkern und erweiterter Peripherie. Während für die Ruinen der Pfarr- und Stiftskirchen in den Innenstädten kaum noch Verwendung bestand, mussten in den neuen Großsiedlungen hunderte von Gemeindezentren errichtet werden – um der seelsorgerischen Aufgaben willen, aber auch um den gesichtslosen Agglomerationen sozialen Halt und wahrnehmbare Identität zu geben. In manchen Zeiten konnten die geistlichen Oberhirten jeden Sonntag an einer Kirchweihe teilnehmen. Die Frage »Sollen wir noch Kirchen bauen?«[2] kam erst in den späten sechziger Jahren auf, als der Bedarf gedeckt war, die Austritte aus den Kirchen sich mehrten, der sonntägliche Kirchenbesuch nachließ, aber auch der Gedanke an die Not in der Welt Bescheidenheit im eigenen Lande angeraten sein ließ.

Wegbereiter: Otto Bartning, Dominikus Böhm, Rudolf Schwarz

Das Bewusstsein für eine Hierarchie der Aufgaben, in der das sakrale Bauen obenan stand, war am Niederrhein seit je ausgeprägt. Die historische Bonner Stadtsilhouette war bis zum 20. Jahrhundert vom Münsterturm geprägt, die Kölner durch die romanischen Stiftskirchen und den Dom mit seinem 1880 vollendeten Turmpaar, dem seinerzeit höchsten Bauwerk der Welt. In Duisburg erhob sich lange vor Hochöfen und Fabrikschloten der ehemals höchste Kirchturm Norddeutschlands, der Turm von St. Salvator. Aus den aufbruchswilligen zwanziger und frühen dreißiger Jahren gab es im Westen Vorbilder, auf die man sich nach dem Zweiten Weltkrieg beziehen konnte. Auf protestantischer Seite hatten die Bauten Otto Bartnings in den zwanziger Jahren Zeichen gesetzt. Seine Kirche auf der Kölner Pressa-Ausstellung von 1928 war über parabolischem Grundriss errichtet. In der Durchlichtung und Entmaterialisierung konnte dieser Bau aus Stahl und Glas mit den gebauten Glasschreinen der Hochgotik wetteifern. Bei seiner Essener Rundkirche von 1929/30 übersetzte Bartning die Raumidee seines siebenzackigen, vierzehnteiligen Sternkirchen-Projekts von 1922 in die knappe Sprache der Moderne.

Auf katholischer Seite hatten Dominikus Böhm und Rudolf Schwarz Sakralbau und ›Neue Zeit‹ miteinander versöhnt. Böhm, der 1926 an die Kölner Werkschulen berufen worden war, realisierte mit St. Engelbert in Köln-Niehl (1930–32) einen seiner Lieblingsgedanken, den blütenförmigen, zentralisierenden Grundriss. Schwarz, von 1927 bis 1934 Direktor der Aachener Handwerker- und Kunstgewerbeschule, schuf für St. Fronleichnam in Aachen (1929–30) einen hohen, großartig kargen Raum, den ein einziges niedriges Seitenschiff begleitet. Die weiße Wand hinter dem Altarberg stellte für Schwarz nicht einen Raumabschluss dar, sondern eine ›Membran‹, durchlässig für eine Bewegung über jeden Raum hinaus. Beide Bauwerke waren der Amtskirche mühsam abgerungen, beide Baumeister sagten in der Folgezeit der reinen, strengen Geometrie ab – Schwarz schweren Herzens. Als Belegstücke radikalen Denkens standen diese Bauten, die den Krieg beschädigt überdauerten, gleichwohl zur Verfügung.

Dominikus Böhm
St. Engelbert / St Engelbert
Köln / Cologne, 1932

Under the Sign of Liturgical Reform
New Church Architecture in the Rhineland

The provinces of the Rhineland have a reputation for being un-usually productive when it comes to building new churches.[1]
In sheer number, the production during the first decades after 1945 is impressive in its own right. In western Germany, hard hit by destruction, the need for reconstruction and new building was especially high. This was compounded by the migrations of the war and post-war period, the stream of refugees from the lost regions to the East and the mass movement between ancient town core and expanding periphery. While there was little use for the ruins of parish and collegiate churches in the city centres, hundreds of community centres were required for the large new subdivisions — to provide pastoral care, naturally, but also to offer social support and a visible identity for these faceless agglomerations. For a while, the spiritual leaders could choose to attend the consecration of a church every single Sunday. It was only in the late 1960s that the question 'Should we still build churches?'[2] finally arose. The demand had been met, people were leaving the Church in droves and Sunday congregations dwindled. But a growing awareness of the poverty and misery elsewhere in the world also suggested a spirit of modesty in one's own country.

Forerunners: Otto Bartning, Dominikus Böhm, Rudolf Schwarz

The regions of the Lower Rhine had always been keenly aware of a hierarchy of tasks, in which sacred buildings occupied the very top. Until the 20th century, the historic town silhouette of Bonn was dominated by the cathedral tower, that of Cologne by Roman collegiate churches and by Cologne Cathedral with its twin towers completed in 1880, the tallest building on earth at the time. The highest church tower in northern Germany, the bell tower of St Salvator, rose into the sky in Duisburg, long before blast furnaces and factory stacks. The West was home to a number of precedent-setting models dating back to the adventurous spirit of the 1920s and early 1930s, and these served as reference models after the Second World War. On the Protestant side, Otto Bartning's buildings from the 1920s had set the tone. His church designed for the Pressa Exhibition in Cologne (1928) was raised on a parabolic plan. The steel and glass structure could easily compete with the High Gothic in terms of light-flooded and dematerialised space. In the round church in Essen from 1929 to 1930, Bartning translated his 1922 spatial concept of a heptagonal, fourteen-part star-shaped church project into the sparse language of Modernism.

On the Catholic side, Dominikus Böhm and Rudolf Schwarz had achieved a harmonious compromise of sacred building and 'new era'. Böhm, who had been called to the Werkschulen in Cologne in 1926, realised one of his favourite ideas with St Engelbert in Cologne-Niehl (1930–32): the flower-shaped, centralised plan. At St Fronleichnam in Aachen (1929–30), Schwarz, director of the Artisans- and Crafts School in Aachen from 1927 to 1934, created a tall, brilliantly spare space accompanied by a single, low, side aisle. To Schwarz, the white wall behind the altar mount was not a spatial completion but a 'membrane' permeable to movement beyond demarcated space. Both buildings had been wrested from the official Church with much debate, and both architects would turn away from pure, stringent geometry in the years that followed — Schwarz did so with a heavy heart. Nevertheless, these buildings, which were damaged but survived the war, were testaments to radical thinking.

Otto Bartning
Auferstehungskirche
round church
Essen, 1930

Zur Verfügung standen auch dieselben Baumeister. Aus Otto
Bartnings Programm der (ursprünglich) 48 Notkirchen – vorgefertigter, auf den Baustellen variierter Holzbinder-Konstruk-
tionen – wurden einige auch zwischen Aachen und Dortmund
realisiert. Als Patriarch des katholischen Kirchenbaus galt
Dominikus Böhm, bei Kriegsende 65-jährig. Seine Nachkriegs-
schöpfungen erreichten freilich nicht das Gewicht seiner Bauten aus den zwanziger und dreißiger Jahren. Manche wirkten
wie gedrungene, alte Dorfkirchen. Große Publizität erlangte
St. Maria Königin im Kölner Villenviertel Marienburg (1952 bis
54). Vom leichten, kinohaft geschwungenen Deckenspiegel
des Saals und der zum Park hin geöffneten Glaswand geht eine
Gelassenheit aus, die Böhm früher nicht gekannt hatte. Mit
dem Eintritt seines Sohnes Gottfried in die Werkstatt begannen
Gewebedecken und Dachfaltwerke aus Stahlbeton eine virtuose
Rolle zu spielen. Es war der Auftakt zu einem umfangreichen
Werk, das in seiner Plastizität und seinem Detailreichtum einen
Sonderweg in der deutschen Nachkriegsarchitektur einschlug.

Für Rudolf Schwarz, der nach der Aachener Fronleichnamskirche sich mit kleineren Aufträgen durch das Dritte Reich ge-
schlagen, allerdings während des Krieges im besetzten Lothrin-
gen auch Landesplanung großen Stils betrieben hatte, kam mit
dem Ende des Krieges überhaupt erst die große Zeit seines
Schaffens als Kirchenbauer. 24 Neu- und Wiederaufbauten zählt
das Werkverzeichnis zwischen 1945 und dem Jahr seines Todes
1961.[3] Zehn weitere Bauten wurden danach unter der Leitung
seiner Frau Maria vollendet. Fast immer sind es hohe, anspruchsvolle Figuren, gerichtete Räume, deren Bewegung nicht
an einem Zielpunkt endet, sondern über den Altar hinausführt.
Fast immer sind sie von einer Höhe und Weite, die den un-
mittelbaren Bedarf einer Gemeinde übersteigen. Seit St. Michael
in Frankfurt [Seite 38] erarbeitete sich Schwarz zu den Recht-
ecksälen, -hallen und -basiliken, den kreuz- oder T-förmigen
Räumen auch ein Repertoire der Kurvengeometrien, der Ellip-
sen und Parabeln. Zweimal, bei St. Ludger in Wuppertal-
Vohwinkel (1959–63) und St. Bonifatius in Wetzlar (1959 bis
64), entschied er, der das »Kapellchen von Corbusier« in
Ronchamp wenig schätzte,[4] sich sogar für fast freischwingende
Raummäntel.

Bei Böhm wie bei Schwarz sind die Wandflächen dieser Schöpfungen zumeist nicht mehr in abstraktem Weiß gehalten. Sie
lassen die Texturen und die Farbigkeit des jeweiligen Materials
zu ihrem Recht kommen, das Korn und den Ton des Bruch-
steins, Ziegels oder Sichtbetons. Der Zusammenarbeit mit den
bildenden Künstlern ist breiter Spielraum gegeben. Jetzt sind
es nicht mehr die wenigen erlesenen Akzente, ein schmales
Kruzifix, ein gezirkelter Taufstein, das asketische liturgische Ge-
rät, die das puristische Gehäuse umso puristischer erscheinen
lassen. Jetzt darf die Vitalität, die auch Krieg und Nachkriegs-
entbehrungen den rheinischen Künstlern nicht ausgetrieben
hatten, wieder zu Wort kommen, bei Schwarz und erst recht bei
den Böhms.

Liturgiereform und ›liturgischer Funktionalismus‹

Rudolf Schwarz war nicht nur durch seine Bauten einflussreich,
sondern ebenso durch seine Schriften. Von ihrer bildhaft-
anspruchsvollen Diktion ging eine eigene Suggestion aus. Sein
Buch *Vom Bau der Kirche*, 1938 in der ersten Auflage erschienen, kam 1947 ein zweites Mal heraus. Von einer Phänomeno-

Rudolf Schwarz
St. Fronleichnam
St Fronleichnam
Aachen, 1930

The same architects were also available after the war. Several of the 48 churches contained in Otto Bartning's emergency programme — prefabricated wooden truss structures, which could be modified on site — were realised in the region between Aachen and Dortmund. Dominikus Böhm, who was 65 years old at the end of the war, was widely regarded as the patriarch of Catholic church architecture. His post-war creations never reached the importance of his buildings from the 1920s and 1930s. Some have the appearance of stocky, old village churches. But St Maria Königin in Cologne's villa district (1952–54) received much publicity. The light, animated ceiling of the church hall and the glazed wall opening onto the adjacent park exude a composure previously unknown to Böhm. When his son Gottfried joined the workshop, woven ceilings and reinforced concrete roof folds began to play a virtuoso role. This was the prelude to an impressive *œuvre*, unique in Germany's post-war architecture for its plasticity and abundant detail.

After completing the Fronleichnamskirche in Aachen, Rudolf Schwarz had made ends meet during the Third Reich with smaller commissions, although he was also active in regional planning on a grand scale in occupied Lorraine. For Schwarz, the end of the war marked the beginning of his most active and successful period as a church architect. His catalogue includes 24 new and reconstructed projects between 1945 and 1961, the year of his death.[3] Ten additional projects were completed posthumously under the direction of his wife, Maria. Almost without exception, these buildings offer tall, exquisite spaces, whose movement does not come to rest at a specific terminal point but continues beyond the altar. Almost without exception, their height and width exceed the immediate demands of a community. After working on St Michael in Frankfurt [p. 38], Schwarz developed a repertoire of curved geometries, ellipses and parabolas in addition to the rectangular auditoria, halls and basilicas, the cruciform or T-shaped plans. Twice, at St Ludger in Wuppertal-Vohwinkel (1959–63) and at St Bonifatius in Wetzlar (1959–64), this architect, known for his rejection of 'Corbusier's little chapel' in Ronchamp[4], even created almost free-floating spatial envelopes.

In the case of Böhm as well as Schwarz, the wall surfaces of these creations are for the most part no longer kept in abstract white. They give proper due to the textures and colouring of the material in each instance, the grain and hue of ashlar, brick or fair-faced concrete. These designs allow ample room for collaboration with visual artists. The purist shell is rendered all the more purist no longer through a few exquisite accents, a slender crucifix, an encompassed baptismal font, or the ascetic liturgical instruments. The vitality, which even war and post-war austerity had been unable to diminish in the artists of the Rhine region, experienced a revival in the work of Schwarz and especially in that of Böhm.

Liturgical Reform and 'Liturgical Functionalism'

Rudolf Schwarz exerted considerable influence not only through his buildings but also in his writings, whose distinctive pictorial diction was highly suggestive. His book *Vom Bau der Kirche* [*On Church Building*], whose first edition was published in 1938, was released in a second edition in 1947. Based on a phenomenology of human behaviour, Schwarz developed seven church 'plans'. The author did not intend his catalogue of plans — rang-

Gottfried Böhm
im Atelier / in his studio
Köln / Cologne
um / c. 1982

logie menschlicher Verhaltensweisen ausgehend, entwickelte er darin sieben ›Pläne‹ des Kirchenbaus. Diesen Katalog, der vom »Heiligen Ring« bis zum »Dom aller Zeiten« reicht, wollte er nicht als Entwurfsanweisung verstanden wissen, sondern als »Samen von Dingen«[5], als Bildervorrat, der Konstanten des Menschlichen mit Formen der Gotteszuwendung verband.

Architektur, wo sie als Kunst auftrat, war für Schwarz nicht eine Funktion ihrer Nutzung, sondern eine Kategorie eigenen Rechts. Es war eine Überzeugung, die auch seine streitbaren Auseinandersetzungen mit dem Funktionalismus seiner Tage erklärt. Für Schwarz verband sich solches Zweckdenken mit dem Bauhaus – dem Bauhaus des Walter Gropius, nicht dem Bauhaus Mies van der Rohes – als seinem großem Feindbild. Doch auch den innerkirchlichen Dialog führte er ohne Scheu vor Konflikten. Das oft gehörte Wort von der Liturgie als Bauherr rief ihn auf den Plan. Ein Kirchenbau war für ihn keine »Liturgie-Maschine«, kein liturgisch gerechtfertigter Zweckbau, sondern eine künstlerisch autonome Gestalt, die den gottesdienstlichen Handlungen freies Spiel ließ.

Die kritische Auseinandersetzung mit dem, was Schwarz »liturgischen Funktionalismus« nannte, war umso aussagekräftiger, als die Reform der Liturgie dem neuen Kirchbau – auch dem von Schwarz – eine entscheidende Wende gegeben hatte. Mit Romano Guardini, einem charismatischen Fürsprecher der neuen Liturgie, war er eng befreundet. Belgische und nordfranzösische Reformklöster, die bereits im 19. Jahrhundert die Messfeier zu erneuern suchten, lagen dem Rheinland schon geografisch nahe. Mit dem Benediktinerkloster Maria Laach besaß die Region einen Vorort der Liturgiereform, in dem Gladbecker Krankenseelsorger Johannes van Acken einen beredten Wortführer.[6]

Lange vor dem Zweiten Vatikanum, das die Ziele der Liturgischen Bewegung bestätigte, praktizierten Kirchenbauer im Rheinland die Sichtbarkeit und den Zusammenhang der liturgischen Orte – alles unter einem Dach, unter einer durchgehenden Raumdecke – und unterstützten die gemeinsame Messfeier durch die räumliche Nähe von Gemeinde und Altar. Die kirchlichen Gremien segneten diese Schritte schon vor dem Konzil ab. Im Kölner Diözesanrecht, das auf einer Synode von 1954 neu formuliert wurde, hieß es, die enge Beziehung zwischen Priester und Gemeinde sei zu fördern und alles zu vermeiden, was eine Trennung von Gemeinde und Altar hervorrufe.[7] Auch die evangelischen Landeskirchen machten sich die Reform zu eigen, betonten neben der traditionellen Wortverkündigung nun die Abendmahlsfeier und suchten sie im »einhelligen Raum« (Otto Bartning) zu verwirklichen. »Dieses liturgische Handeln bedeutet für die Kraft des Kultus viel mehr als wir – gerade wir Evangelischen – wissen oder wissen wollen«, bekannte Bartning in einem posthum erschienenen Text.[8]

Vielfalt der Handschriften

Zur rheinischen Liberalität, aber auch zum Nachkriegskirchenbau überhaupt gehört, dass viele Handschriften statthaft waren. In der Erzdiözese Köln geht das Mitwirkungsrecht der Gemeinden weit, auch wenn die Vorschrift des *Codex Iuris Canonici* gilt, dass keine Kirche ohne Genehmigung des Diözesanbischofs errichtet werden darf. Das Generalvikariat achtet darauf, dass die Entscheidungen sachkundig gefällt werden und organisiert

Abtei Maria Laach
Maria Laach monastery
Krypta / crypt
1093 – 1130

ing from the 'sacred circle' to the 'cathedral for all times' — to be understood as a handbook for design. Rather, it should become a 'germ of all things',[5] a treasury of images linking the inherent and constant qualities of humankind to different forms of worship.

Schwarz maintained that architecture, where it appeared as an art form, was not a function of its purpose but a category in its own right. This conviction can help to explain the architect's passionate debates with the proponents of functionalism during his time. To Schwarz, such purpose-driven thinking was inextricably linked to his greatest foe — the Bauhaus of Walter Gropius not that of Mies van der Rohe. However, Schwarz was equally passionate, and fearless, in his debates with the ecclesiastical authorities. He was prompted to enter into the fray by the frequent references to the liturgy as a building manual. As far as Schwarz was concerned a church building was not a 'liturgical machine', not a building with a purpose underpinned by liturgical justification, but an autonomous artistic configuration that provided the freedom for liturgical services and practices to flourish.

The critical exploration of what Schwarz referred to as 'liturgical functionalism' was all the more meaningful for the sea change, which the liturgical reform had instigated in ecclesiastic architecture — including that of Schwarz, who was a close friend of Romano Guardini, a charismatic proponent of the new liturgy. Reform monasteries in Belgium and northern France, which had sought to renew the liturgy as early as the 19th century, were also in geographic proximity to the Rhineland. The region could look to the Benedictine monastery Maria Laach as a precursor of liturgical reform, and to Johannes van Acken, the pastor for the infirm in Gladbeck, as an eloquent spokesperson.[6]

Church architects in the Rhineland were committed to the visibility and contextual integration of liturgical sites — everything underneath one roof, beneath a single, continuous ceiling — long before the Second Vatican Council, which confirmed the goals of the liturgical movement, and supported the common celebration of the liturgy through the spatial proximity of congregation and altar. Ecclesiastic committees sanctioned these steps even prior to the Council. The Charter of Rights of the Diocese of Cologne, which was amended at a synod in 1954, emphasised the importance of establishing a close relationship between priest and congregation and condemned any separation of congregation and altar.[7] The Protestant Land churches also embraced the reform, putting additional emphasis on the celebration of the Communion as well as the traditional liturgy, hoping to breathe life into their plans by means of 'unanimous space' (Otto Bartning). In a text, published posthumously, Bartning declared: 'This liturgical act has far greater meaning for the power of worship than we — especially Protestants — know or want to know'.[8]

A Multiplicity of Signatures

The liberal spirit of the Rhineland, and post-war church architecture in general, allowed for a variety of signatures. The communities in the archdiocese of Cologne have far-reaching rights of participation, even though the provision that no church may be built without permission from the diocesan bishop (*Codex Iuris Canonici*) is strictly followed. The curacy ensures

Joachim und Margot Schürmann
Christkönig / Christ the King
Wuppertal, 1959

regelrechte Informationsreisen. Die Diözesanbaumeister hielten
sich mit eigenen Entwürfen zurück und betrachteten sich als
Sachwalter der freien Architekten, auch wenn sie in ihren Empfehlungen bestimmte Baumeister bevorzugten und andere
nicht. Im evangelischen Kirchenbau sind die Zuständigkeiten
vergleichbar geregelt. Bauherr ist die einzelne Kirchengemeinde,
Zustimmung gibt das Landeskirchenamt.

So entstanden gleichzeitig mit Bauten, die von der Ästhetik
handwerklicher Arbeit bestimmt sind, technisch anspruchsvolle Lösungen, die nur in der Zusammenarbeit mit bedeutenden
Bauingenieuren wie Josef Pirlet, Wilhelm Schorn oder Stefan
Polonyi möglich waren. In beiden Konfessionen gab es Architekten, die sich der neuen Tragwerke annahmen. Betonfaltwer-
ke, Stahlfachwerk oder Gitterschalen setzten sie für dynamische,
manchmal kristalline Gebilde und oftmals stützenfreie Räume
ein – so Josef Lehmbrock, Dieter Oesterlen [Seite 215] oder
Fritz Schaller. Oder entwickelten stille, disziplinierte, diaphane
Räume wie Joachim Schürmann in den frühen sechziger Jahren
[Seite 72]. Oder machten daraus auffällige Stadtzeichen wie
Paul Schneider-Esleben. Für St. Rochus in Düsseldorf-Pempelfort (1955) baute er über einem Dreipass-Grundriss, der an
Georg Dientzenhofers barocke Wallfahrtskirche Kappel bei
Waldsassen erinnert, übergangslose Wand- und Dachschalen
auf, die das Bild einer aufgeplatzten Fruchtkapsel assoziieren.

Fast alle größeren Architektenœuvres, die damals entstanden,
sind in sich selbst vielteilig und vielfältig. Gottfried Böhm
schlug im Abstand weniger Jahre unterschiedliche Richtungen
ein: verwegene Kraftakte wie St. Albert in Saarbrücken (1951
bis 53), die Karawansereien der späteren fünfziger Jahre mit
ihren Kegeldach-Türmen, die kristallinen Betonskulpturen, die
in der kathedralgroßen Wallfahrtskirche von Neviges [Seite 142]
kulminierten. Ihnen folgten zellenförmige Gruppenbildungen,
die sich in Wigratzbad (1972–76) oder Essen-Kettwig (1973
bis 83) zu wahren Zeltstädten addierten, Sinnbildern der Lebens-
pilgerschaft.

Wo aber wird in diesem Pluralismus der unverwechselbare
Lokalton vernehmbar? Rücksicht auf die regionale Besonderheit
ist immer wieder proklamiert worden. Der Kardinalserlass von
1912 legte den Baumeistern nachdrücklich die »herrlichen
Muster am Rheine« ans Herz, aber auch Moderne wie Rudolf
Schwarz wiesen auf die alten Vorbilder in der Nachbarschaft
hin. Mit der Vergangenheit mussten die Architekten ohnehin
viele Jahre lang zusammenarbeiten, bei der Auseinandersetzung mit dem ruinierten Bestand. Das Schicksal der romanischen Kirchen, die von Bonn bis Neuss fast alle im Krieg
schwer beschädigt waren, wurde ausgiebig diskutiert, am eindrucksvollsten in den Vorträgen, die im Winter 1947/48 in
der ungeheizten Aula der Kölner Universität stattfanden.[9] Der
Modus Vivendi zwischen Rekonstruktion und deutlich neuer
Ergänzung, der damals gefunden wurde, hielt nicht über die
Jahrzehnte hinweg, denn auch denkmalpflegerische Prinzipien
unterliegen dem Wandel. In den Nachkriegsjahren stand
an erster Stelle die purgierte, vereinfachte Wiederherstellung,
steinsichtig oder mit großen weißen Putzflächen, die den
historischen Bau auf einen idealtypischen Zustand reduzierte.
Diese Abstraktionen waren Leistungen eigenen Ranges. Der
nachfolgenden Generation galten sie als allzu frugal, asketisch,
unhistorisch und nicht schutzwürdig.

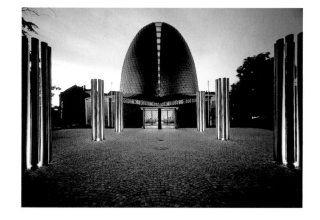

Paul Schneider-Esleben
St. Rochus / St Roch
Düsseldorf / Dusseldorf
1955

that decisions are based on sound knowledge, even going so far as to organise veritable fact-finding trips. The diocesan chief architects kept their own designs voluntarily in the background, seeing their role as champions of freelance architects, although their recommendations were often biased towards certain architects to the exclusion of others. The Protestant Church adopted a similar approach to decision-making in matters architectural: here the individual church congregation assumes the role of client, while the regional Church council grants permission.

The result was buildings, marked by the aesthetic of the craft, but also distinguished for technical solutions that were only feasible through collaboration with the leading structural engineers of the time such as Josef Pirlet, Wilhelm Schorn and Stefan Polonyi. A number of architects working for both denominations responded to the new load-bearing structures. Concrete foldwork, steel framework or grid formwork were employed to create dynamic, at times crystalline, constructs and often column-free spaces — for example by Josef Lembrock, Dieter Oesterlen [p. 215] and Fritz Schaller. Others such as Joachim Schürmann in the early 1960s developed tranquil, disciplined, diaphanous spaces [p. 72]. Some transformed churches into distinct urban landmarks, as Paul Schneider-Esleben did in the case of St Roch in Düsseldorf-Pempelfort (1955). The church features a trefoil-plan reminiscent of Georg Dienzenhofer's baroque pilgrimage chapel near Waldsassen, with seamlessly continuous wall- and roof sheathing, which suggests the image of an opening flower bud.

The major architectural *œuvres* of the period are multipartite and diverse in themselves, almost without exception. Thus Gottfried Böhm embarked on a variety of different directions within a few years: the daring *tour de force* of St Albert in Saarbrücken (1951–53); the caravanserai-inspired configurations of the late 1950s with their conical-roof topped towers; and the crystalline concrete sculptures, culminating in the pilgrimage church at Neviges [p. 142], cathedral-like in scale. These were followed by cellular ensembles that multiplied into veritable tent cities in Wigratzbad (1972–76) or Essen-Kettwig (1973–83), symbolising the pilgrimage of life.

But where is the distinctive local voice in this pluralist medley? The importance of regional character has been proclaimed again and again. The cardinal's edict from 1912 emphatically recommended that architects look to 'the glorious examples on the Rhine', but modernists such as Rudolf Schwarz also referred to traditional models in the region. Architects were compelled, at any rate, to collaborate with the past for many years through the task of having to work with a legacy that lay in ruins. The fate of the Romanesque churches — almost every single one from Bonn to Neuss had suffered severe damage in the war — was the subject of extensive discussions, most impressively during the lectures, which were presented in the winter of 1947/48 in the unheated auditorium at Cologne University.[9] A *modus vivendi* was developed during this period for coping with reconstruction versus distinctively new addition. It did not survive the subsequent decade, however, for the changes that followed were also founded on the principles of heritage protection. The principal focus in the post-war years was on clarifying, simplified reconstruction with fair-faced masonry or large white-rendered surfaces, which reduced the historic building to an idealised condition. These abstractions were unique achiev-

Gottfried Böhm
St. Albert / St Albert
Saarbrücken, 1953

Kirchen aus Trümmern

Was Chor und Apsis, Krypta und Baptisterium, Ambo und
Presbyterium bedeuteten, wurde den Architekten nicht nur bei
Studium und Lektüre deutlich, sondern bei der eigenen Res-
taurierungstätigkeit. Vielleicht haben sich die mächtigen
Apsiden, die Kleeblatt-Chöre, die Mauertiefe und -schwere im
Rheinischen länger gehalten als anderswo, weil sie zur alltäglichen Erfahrungswelt der Architekten gehörten. Vor allem
ist es der Umgang mit dem Material, der sich bei dieser Arbeit
formierte. Im Rheinland haben Architekten nicht nur beim
Wiederaufbau, sondern auch bei Neubauten Steine wie Reli-
quien behandelt. »Wir wollten sie in den neuen Bau wieder ver-
mauern, dass der geheiligte Stein Baustoff eines neuen Werks
werden konnte und das Alte im Neuen wieder auferstand«,
schrieb Schwarz über die aus Trümmersteinen neu errichtete
Kirche St. Anna in Düren (1951–56).[10] Hans Schilling, der
die lädierten Steine gleichfalls gern verwendete, wies auf die profane Seite der Sache hin: Sie kosteten nur einen Pfennig das
Stück. Über die Faszination des Materials hinaus ermöglichten
die Begegnungen mit dem zerstörten Alten eigenartige Syn-
thesen. Wie Gottfried Böhm seine viel geliebte Kapelle mit
der Trümmermadonna den Resten von St. Kolumba (1947–50)
einpflanzte oder Karl Band vier erhaltene Gewölbejoche von
St. Johann Baptist (1960–62) als hohen Schrein in einen
niedrigen neuen Raum setzte, das zeugte von Demut und Selbst-
bewusstsein zugleich.

Nicht nur die großen romanischen Kirchen, die vor dem
Einsturz bewahrt und zu neuem Leben erweckt werden mussten, wurden zu Lehrwerkstätten der Nachkriegsbaumeister.
In der ehemaligen Provinz Germania Inferior lag es nahe, vom
Romanischen aufs Römische zurückzugehen. In stadtrömi-
schen Bauten der ersten christlichen Jahrhunderte verband sich
das eine mit dem anderen: römischer Ziegelbau mit den Fröm-
migkeitsformen des spätantiken Christentums. So hatte sich
auch die Liturgische Bewegung auf frühchristliche Zelebrations-
formen bezogen: »Es gibt kaum eine Reform in der Kirche (...),
die nicht auf die altchristliche Basilika hingewiesen und sie,
wenn auch jeweils in der Sprache der Zeit, nachgeahmt hätte«,
schrieb Dom- und Diözesanbaumeister Weyres.[11] Die Ewige
Stadt wurde zu einem Bezugspunkt für viele rheinische Architekten, für die Böhms wie für Schwarz, für Oswald Mathias
Ungers wie für Emil Steffann oder Heinz Bienefeld. Die Ziegel-
techniken, die sich in Rom und auf rheinischem Ausgrabungs-
gelände lernen ließen, waren umso mehr willkommen, als
ihre Verwendung in christlichen Kultbauten an das Wort des
Apostel Paulus von den lebendigen Steinen der Gemeinde
erinnern konnte.[12]

Wendung zu Demut und Einfachheit

Der Gedanke an urchristliche Religiosität mag manchem Architekten beigestanden haben, als nach dem Zweiten Vatikanum
neben neuen liturgischen Formen eine veränderte Haltung
gefordert wurde. Nun war nicht mehr die *ecclesia triumphans*
verlangt, die ihre stolzen Zeichen in die neuen Stadtlandschaf-
ten setzte, sondern die demütige Kirche. Sie hatte ihrer Gemeinde nicht nur geistliche Dienste zu leisten, sondern ihr auch
ein mitfühlender Partner in weltlichen Freuden und Nöten zu
sein. Ihre Gehäuse setzten die Gläubigen nicht mehr den großen

Gottfried Böhm
Madonna in den Trümmern
St Columba
Köln / Cologne, 1950

ements. To the successor generation, they seemed all too frugal, ascetic and lacking in historic value, and therefore unworthy of heritage protection.

Churches from Rubble

Architects grew to understand the meaning of choir and apse, crypt and baptistery, *ambo* (or pulpit) and presbytery, not only at universities and lectures, but also from exposure to restoration tasks. Perhaps the massive apse, the trefoil choirs and massive walls have survived longer in the Rhineland than elsewhere because they were an integral part of the architects' day-to-day experience. But the most notable influence these experiences brought to bear was on material treatment. In the Rhineland, architects treated stones like relics, not only in reconstruction projects but also in new buildings. 'We wanted to integrate them into the masonry of the new building, so that the sacred stone might become the building material of a new work and the Old might be resurrected in the New', Schwarz wrote on the subject of the St Anna church in Düren (1951–56), which was built entirely from salvaged rubble.[10] Hans Schilling, who also liked to use reclaimed material, drew attention to the more profane aspect: these stones only cost a penny a piece. Beyond the fascination with the material as such, these encounters with damaged or destroyed historic substances made for some peculiar syntheses. Gottfried Böhm's installation of his beloved chapel with the *Trümmermadonna* ['rubble Madonna'] in the ruins of St Columba (1947–50), for example, or Karl Band's use of four preserved vault cross plates from St John the Baptist (1960–62) as a tall shrine in a low, new space — these gestures spoke simultaneously of humility and of self-confidence.

The large Romanesque churches, in need of being saved from collapsing and restoration to new life, were, however, not the only training grounds for post-war architects. A return from the Romanesque to the Roman seemed a natural step to take in the province formerly known as *Germania Inferior*. The urban Roman buildings of the first Christian centuries offered a marriage of both elements — Roman brick construction and the devout expression of Christianity in late Antiquity. Thus the liturgical movement also looked back to forms of worship dating back to early Christianity. As cathedral and diocesan architect Weyres put it: 'Nearly every church reform [...] has made a reference to the ancient Christian basilica, emulating it, albeit in a language appropriate to the relevant period'.[11] The Eternal City became a reference point for many architects from the Rhine, for Böhm and Schwarz, for Oswald Mathias Ungers as well as for Emil Steffan or Heinz Bienefeld. Brick masonry techniques, for which Rome and excavations sites in the Rhineland offered fertile training grounds, were all the more welcome as their application to new sacred buildings could be interpreted as a physical expression of the word on the living stones of the community, attributed to the apostle Paul.[12]

A Shift towards Humility and Simplicity

The thought of original Christian religiosity may have strengthened the resolve of many architects in the face of new demands in addition to the liturgical reform after the Second Vatican Council. Their brief was no longer to design the *ecclesia triumphans*, whose proud symbols would rise from the new urban landscapes, but a humble church. This new type of church

Karl Band
St. Johann Baptist / St John the Baptist
Köln / Cologne, 1962

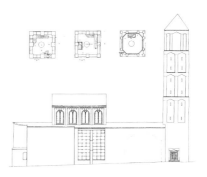

Weltgleichnissen aus, sondern boten Schutz in der modernen
Diaspora. Dabei bestärkte die Erinnerung an römisch-früh-
christliche Zentralbauten wie S. Costanza, S. Giovanni in Fonte
oder S. Stefano Rotondo zentralisierende Raumtendenzen, wie
sie sich in den fünfziger Jahren trotz der Warnungen der Kölner
Synode von 1954 andeuteten und nach dem Konzil durch-
setzten, mit polygonalen, kreisförmigen, quadratischen oder
unregelmäßigen Grundrissen.

Emil Steffann, der am Ende seines Lebens jahrelang, wenn auch
ergebnislos, für S. Stefano Rotondo in Rom geplant hat, ist
ein Architekt dieser Wendung zu Demut und Einfachheit geworden. Die zeittypische Neigung zu verwandelbaren, vielseitig
nutzbaren Mehrzweckbauten machte er nicht mit. Steffann, der
aus Lübeck stammte, aber in Assisi und Rom zur Architektur
fand und seit den fünfziger Jahren im Rheinland praktizierte,
schuf eine Architektur der Geborgenheit, in der sich der Einzelne aufgenommen fühlt. Es sind feste Häuser, in denen Werte
der Tradition überliefert und weitergeführt wurden, oft auch
mit antiken Bautypen wie Vorhalle und Atrium. Die zeitgenössischen Stätten der Andacht und des Gebets waren für Steffann
so etwas wie die neuen Katakomben. In den Bauten seines eins-
tigen Mitarbeiters Heinz Bienefeld erhielt sich diese Haltung
bis in unsere Tage, auch wenn bei Bienefeld größere Material-
farbigkeit und ornamentale Wandtextur hinzukamen. Sein
Gemeindezentrum in Köln-Blumenberg, in dem die Prinzipalstücke der Glaubensausübung wie an einem Wegrand aufgestellt scheinen, wird erst nach dem Tod des Architekten vollendet – einer der selten gewordenen Kirchenbauten dieser Jahre.

1
Richard Biedrzynski, *Kirchen unserer Zeit*, München 1958, S. 46;
Barbara Kahle, *Rheinische Kirchen des 20. Jahrhunderts*, Landes-
konservator Rheinland Arbeitsheft 39, Köln 1985, S. 7; Willy Weyres,
Neue Kirchen im Erzbistum 1945–56, Düsseldorf 1957, S. 14.
2
Motto einer Kölner Kirchenbautagung von 1969.
3
Wolfgang Pehnt, *Rudolf Schwarz 1897–1961. Architekt einer anderen
Moderne*, Werkverzeichnis von Hilde Strohl, Ostfildern 1997.
4
Rudolf Schwarz, *Brief über Ronchamp*, in: *Baukunst und Werkform*,
1956/9, S. 117 f.
5
Rudolf Schwarz, *Kirchenbau. Welt vor der Schwelle*, Heidelberg 1960,
S. 151.
6
Johannes van Acken, *Christozentrische Kirchenkunst*, Gladbeck 1923[2].
7
Erzbischöfliches Generalvikariat (Hg.), *Kölner Diözesansynode 1954*,
Köln 1954, Absatz 802.
8
Otto Bartning, *Vom neuen Kirchbau*, in: Bund Deutscher Architekten u. a.
(Hg.), *Planen und Bauen im neuen Deutschland*, Köln, Opladen 1960,
S. 158.
9
*Kirchen in Trümmern. Zwölf Vorträge zum Thema ›Was wird aus den
Kölner Kirchen‹*, Köln 1948.
10
Rudolf Schwarz, *Kirchenbau*, a.a.O., S. 223.
11
Willy Weyres, *Geschichtliche Grundlagen*, in: Willy Weyres, Otto Bartning
(Hg.), *Kirchen. Handbuch für den Kirchenbau*, München 1959, S. 35.
12
Rudolf Schwarz, *Kirchenbau*, a.a.O., S. 224.

Emil Steffann
St. Matthias / St Matthew
Euskirchen, 1966

not only had to provide spiritual services for the community, but also act as an empathetic partner in all worldly joys and challenges. The dwellings of this new church no longer exposed their faithful to the great parables of the world, but offered shelter amidst the modern Diaspora. The memory of early Christian buildings from the Roman period, such as S. Costanza, S. Giovanni in Fonte and S. Stefano Rotondo inspired the type of centralised spatial plan that began to appear in the 1950s despite the cautions issued at the Cologne synod of 1954. After the Second Vatican Council, these tendencies successfully established themselves through polygonal, circular, square or irregular plans.

Emil Steffann, who spent the last years of his life planning for S. Stefano Rotondo in Rome, albeit without results, was one architect who adopted this shift towards humility and simplicity. He never subscribed to the trend towards flexible, multi-purpose buildings suitable for a variety of uses that was typical of the time. Steffann, originally from Lübeck, had discovered his own path to architecture in Assisi and Rome. Practising in the Rhineland since the 1950s, his architecture offered shelter, embracing the individual. These are solid buildings that preserve and perpetuate traditional values, frequently with typological elements borrowed from Antiquity such as porch and atrium. For Steffann, contemporary sites of meditation and prayer were akin to modern-day catacombs. This attitude has survived into the present day in the buildings of his former staff member, Heinz Bienefeld, albeit with a more varied colour scale in the materials and ornamental wall texture. Steffann's community centre in Cologne-Blumenberg was completed after the architect's death. In this, one of the rare new church buildings of the period, the principal elements of the practice of faith seem to be arranged as if lined up on either side of a path.

1
Richard Biedrzynski, Kirchen unserer Zeit, Munich, 1958, p. 46;
Barbara Kahle, 'Rheinische Kirchen des 20. Jahrhunderts', *Landeskonservator Rheinland*, journal no. 39, Cologne, 1985, p. 7; Willy Weyres, *Neue Kirchen im Erzbistum 1945–56*, Düsseldorf, 1957, p. 14.
2
Theme of a church architecture conference in Cologne in 1969.
3
Wolfgang Pehnt, *Rudolf Schwarz. 1897–1961. Architekt einer anderen Moderne*, catalogue by Hilde Strohl, Ostfildern, 1997.
4
Rudolf Schwarz, 'Brief über Ronchamp', in *Baukunst und Werkform*, 1956/9, pp. 117ff.
5
Rudolf Schwarz, *Kirchenbau. Welt vor der Schwelle*, Heidelberg, 1960, p. 151.
6
Johannes van Acken, *Christozentrische Kirchenkunst*, Gladbeck, 1923 (second edition).
7
Erzbischöfliches Generalvikariat (ed.), *Kölner Diozesansynpode 1954*, Cologne, 1954, paragraph 802.
8
Otto Bartning, 'Vom neuen Kirchbau', in Bund Deutscher Architekten u.a. (eds.), *Planen und Bauen im neuen Deutschland*, Cologne, Opladen, 1960, p. 158.
9
Kirchen in Trümmern. Zwölf Vorträge zum Thema ›Was wird aus den Kölner Kirchen‹, Cologne, 1948.
10
Rudolf Schwarz, *Kirchenbau*, op. cit. p. 223.
11
Willy Weyres, 'Geschichtliche Grundlagen', in Willy Weyres and Otto Bartning (eds.), *Kirchen. Handbuch für den Kirchenbau*, Munich, 1959, p. 35.
12
Rudolf Schwarz, *Kirchenbau*, op. cit. p. 234.

Heinz Bienefeld
St. Bonifatius / St Boniface
Wildbergerhütte, 1981

Heinz Bienefeld

St. Bonifatius
Wildbergerhütte, Deutschland
1981

St Boniface
Wildbergerhütte, Germany
1981

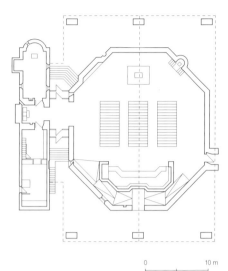

Grundriss
floor plan

0   10 m

Einfache, ruhige Formen: Das auf den
Giebelseiten weit vorgezogene Satteldach liegt auf archaisch wirkenden
Außenpfeilern. In die Kirche fällt nur
gedämpftes Licht ein.

Simple, tranquil forms: the double-
pitched roof drawn far forward on the
gable ends rests on external pillars
that give an archaic effect. The
interior receives only subdued light.

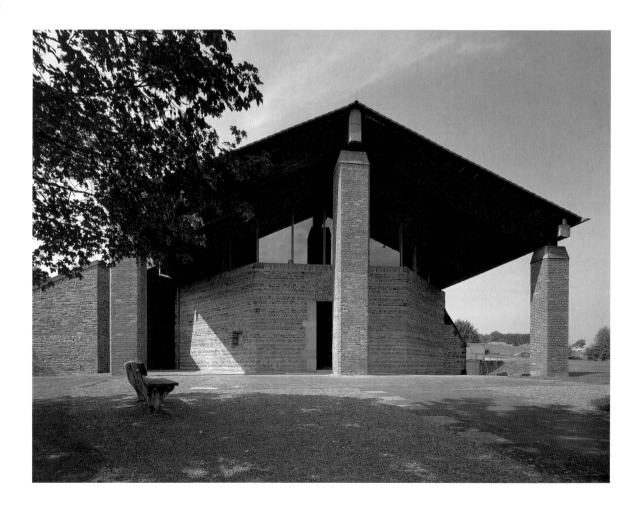

Im Werk des großen Baumeisters Heinz Bienefeld (1926–1995) nehmen die wenigen Sakralbauten eine wichtige Rolle ein, weil sie über seine sonst vorherrschende ›Architektur des Privaten‹ hinausgehen. Diese Kirche steht in einem abgelegenen Dorf nordwestlich der Stadt Siegen und bildet zusammen mit dem Pfarrhaus den Mittelpunkt eines neuen Wohngebiets. Der Bau beeindruckt durch seine ruhigen Formen. Über dem achteckigen Zentralraum erhebt sich ein mächtiges Satteldach, das auf den Giebelseiten vorgezogen ist. Es wird von drei langen Leimbindern getragen, die auf den sechs mächtigen Außenpfeilern ruhen. Weil die gemauerten Wände nicht belastet sind, konnten sie vom Dach durch ein Glasband getrennt werden. Bienefelds bevorzugtes Material war unverputzter Ziegelstein, dessen farblichen und formalen Reichtum er durch seine handwerkliche Gestaltung steigerte: durch Fischgrätmuster, Netzverband oder Rundbogen. Hier sind die nahezu geschlossenen Wände durch kunstvoll gelegte Schichten aus Naturstein und Ziegel lebendig gegliedert. Der ganze Bau lässt die Orientierung an klassisch-antiken Vorbildern spüren.

The few religious buildings in the œuvre of the great architect Heinz Bienefeld (1926–95) are particularly important since they go beyond his otherwise predominantly private architecture. Located in a remote village north-west of Siegen, this church — together with the presbytery — forms the central focus of a new residential area. The structure is impressive because of its tranquil forms. Above the octagonal central space rises a massive double-pitched roof, drawn forward at the gable ends. Its weight is borne by three long cement trusses which rest on six thick external pillars. As the masonry walls are not load-bearing, it was possible to separate them from the roof by a band of glazing. Bienefeld's preferred material was raw brick. He accentuated its richness of colour and form through hand-crafted configurations: herringbone pattern, reticulated bond, semicircular arch. The almost totally closed walls are broken up in a lively manner by the artistic layering of natural stone and brick. Throughout the structure one senses the influence of models from the Classical period and Antiquity.

Karljosef Schattner

Kapelle im Priesterseminar
Eichstätt, Deutschland
1984

Seminary Chapel
Eichstätt, Germany
1984

Der Innenhof des Anbaus wird durch
flächenhafte Wände geprägt. Die fast
geschlossene Hauskapelle ist durch
einen schmalen Graben von der Kies-
fläche des Hofs getrennt.

The inner courtyard of the extension
is characterised by extensive wall surfaces. A narrow trench separates the
almost completely closed private
chapel from the gravel surface of the
courtyard.

»Die Gegenwart leugnen hieße die Geschichte leugnen« – unter diesem einleuchtenden Motto hat der Diözesanbaumeister Karljosef Schattner den vom Barock geprägten bayerischen Bischofssitz Eichstätt um herausragende Architektur der Moderne bereichert. Schattner, der sein Amt von 1957 bis 1992 ausübte, hat in der Kleinstadt aber nicht nur Neues geschaffen, sondern mit gleichem Engagement auch historische Gebäude vor dem Abriss bewahrt. Sein Grundsatz, die zeitgenössischen Umbauten oder Erweiterungen im Dialog mit der alten Substanz zu entwerfen, kommt auch bei dem spannungsreichen Ensemble des Priesterseminars zum Ausdruck, das vom Turm der Jesuitenkirche überragt wird. Schattners flacherer Anbau bezieht sich axial auf den Südtrakt des Seminars aus dem späten 17. Jahrhundert und schließt zugleich den Komplex zur Talaue hin ab. Drei Flügel mit Einzelzimmern rahmen einen Hof, in dessen Mitte die um 45 Grad gedrehte Hauskapelle des Seminars liegt. Aufgrund eines fachpolitischen Votums mussten die neuen Trakte anstelle von Flachdächern mit Pultdächern versehen werden, was den erwünschten Kontrast zu den historischen Bauten erschwert.

'To deny the present would be to deny history.' This was the enlightening motto under which the diocesan architect Karljosef Schattner brought outstanding works of modern architecture to the Bavarian episcopal seat of Eichstätt, which was strongly baroque in character. Schattner, who held office from 1957 to 1992, not only created new buildings in the small town, however; with the same passion he also saved historic buildings from demolition. His principle of designing contemporary conversions or extensions in relation to existing structures is demonstrated in this exciting seminary ensemble which is overshadowed by the tower of the Jesuit church. Schattner's flatter extension refers axially to the southern wing of the seminary, which dates from the late 17th century, while at the same time closing off the complex on the side towards the river meadow. Three wings containing single rooms surround a courtyard, in the middle of which the private chapel of the seminary is set at an angle of 45 degrees. As a result of an expert policy decision new wings had to be provided with pent roofs instead of flat roofs, making the desired contrast to the old buildings more difficult to achieve.

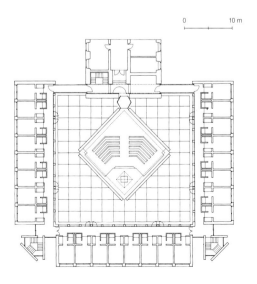

0   10 m

 Grundriss
floor plan

Die disziplinierte Formensprache
zeigt sich auch im korrespondierenden
Fugenbild von Fußboden und Kassettendecke. Das Glasfenster in der Ecke
hat Jürgen Hafner entworfen.

The disciplined formal idiom is likewise evident in the corresponding
jointing of floor and coffered ceiling.
The glass window in the corner was
designed by Jürgen Hafner.

Die im Grundriss quadratische Hauskapelle berührt mit ihrer nördlichen Spitze den langen Barocktrakt des Priesterseminars. Weil aber der auf sie zulaufende Flur des Altbaus nicht mittig angeordnet ist, musste Schattner beim Eingang zur Kapelle einen Kunstgriff anwenden: Eine zweiflügelige Tür führt durch einen perspektivisch geschnittenen Zugang in den sechseckigen Vorraum, vom dem aus erst die Kapelle betreten wird (rechtes Foto). Die beiden Bankreihen knicken zu dem diagonal gestellten Altar hin ab. Den streng gezeichneten und schlicht möblierten Raum überspannt eine Kassettendecke aus Sichtbeton. Zu den Wänden hin lässt die Decke schmale Streifen frei, die von Glasbändern auf dem Dach belichtet werden. Ein weiteres Oberlicht ist über dem Altar angebracht. Außerdem sind die Raumecken durch vertikale Lichtschlitze geöffnet. Die Glasfenster in der Kapelle wurden nach Entwürfen von Jürgen Hafner ausgeführt. Durch die zurückhaltende Formensprache sowie durch die wenigen, gut aufeinander abgestimmten Materialien hat der kleine Andachtsraum eine angenehme, fast noble Atmosphäre.

Square in ground plan, the private chapel meets the seminary's long baroque wing at its northern tip. But because the corridor of the old building that runs towards it is not centred, Schattner had to employ a trick at the entrance to the chapel: a double door leads through a perspectively divided access into the hexagonal ante-room, and it is only from there that one actually enters the chapel (right). The two rows of pews bend towards the diagonally positioned altar. A coffered ceiling of exposed concrete spans the interior, which is characterised by austere lines and simple furnishings. Towards the walls, narrow strips in the ceiling are left free and provide light via bands of glazing in the roof. A further skylight is positioned above the altar, and the corners of the interior are also opened up by vertical slits. The glass windows in the chapel were based on designs by Jürgen Hafner. The small devotional space has a pleasant, almost noble atmosphere as a result of the muted formal idiom and the use of a few, well-harmonised materials.

Hans van der Laan

Abtei St. Benediktusberg
Vaals, Niederlande
1986

St Benedictusberg Abbey
Vaals, The Netherlands
1986

Die Westansicht zeigt die burgartige
Erweiterung des Klosters durch Hans
van der Laan. Die Krypta wird durch
liegende Fenster belichtet, die Kirche
durch Obergaden.

A westerly view shows Hans van
der Laan's castle-like extension to
the abbey complex. The crypt is
lit by horizontal windows, the church
by clerestorys.

Grundriss
floor plan

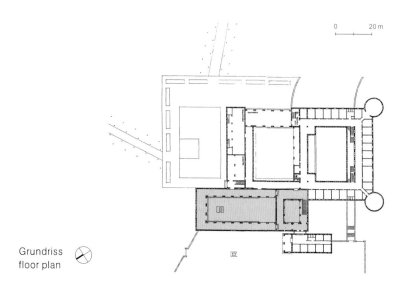

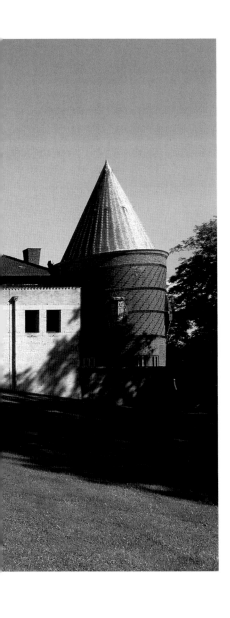

Bei dem über sechs Jahrzehnte währenden Bau der Benediktinerabtei, die an der Straße von Aachen nach Maastricht in einem bewaldeten Südhang liegt, haben zwei Architekten ihre Handschrift hinterlassen. Der ältere, zum Tal hin orientierte Bereich des Klosters wurde 1922 von dem berühmten Kirchenbaumeister Dominikus Böhm (1880–1955) entworfen: Zwei mächtige runde Ecktürme flankieren die Südfassade des Gebäudes, das aus besonders großen, unverputzten Backsteinen gemauert ist. Die gereihten Fenster der Mönchszellen und die im Innenhof vorspringenden Erker erinnern an Klosterbauten auf dem Berg Athos in Griechenland. Nachdem die Abtei die Wirren der Nachkriegszeit überstanden hatte, wurde in den fünfziger Jahren der Architekt und Benediktinermönch Hans van der Laan (1904–1991) mit ihrer Erweiterung beauftragt, vor allem mit dem Bau der noch fehlenden Klosterkirche. Van der Laan setzte die bestehende Anlage in mehreren Bauabschnitten nach Norden hin fort: 1962 wurde die Krypta fertiggestellt, sechs Jahre später die Kirche, 1986 schließlich Sakristei und Bibliothek an einem weiteren Innenhof.

Two architects left their mark in the construction of this Benedictine abbey situated on a wooded, south-facing slope on the road from Aachen to Maastricht — a process that took more than 60 years. The older section, on the valley side, was designed in 1922 by the famous church architect Dominikus Böhm (1880–1955). Two massive round corner towers flank the southern façade of the building, whose walls are constructed in particularly large, raw bricks. The rows of windows of the monks' cells and the jutting oriel in the inner courtyard are reminiscent of the monastery buildings on Mount Athos in Greece. After the abbey had survived the turmoil of the post-war period, in the 1950s the architect and Benedictine monk Hans van der Laan (1904–91) was given the task of extending it, in particular by adding a church. Van der Laan extended the existing complex towards the north in several phases: in 1962 the crypt was completed, six years later the church, then finally in 1986 the sacristy and library, which were set in an additional inner courtyard.

Hans van der Laans Bauten und Räume strahlen eine nüchterne Schönheit und die Atmosphäre von Zeitlosigkeit aus. Besonders die große Krypta hat einen archaischen Charakter.

Hans van der Laan's buildings and interiors radiate a sober beauty and an atmosphere of timelessness. The large crypt, in particular, is archaic in character.

Hans van der Laan hatte den Ehrgeiz, eigene Gestaltungsprinzipien zu entwickeln. Davon sind auch seine drei Klosterbauten geprägt. Neben einem Kloster in Belgien (1975) und einem in Schweden (1996) war die Abtei St. Benediktusberg seine bedeutendste Bauaufgabe. Hier kommen seine Entwurfsregeln auch besonders rein zum Ausdruck: die klar gezeichneten Kubaturen, die baumeisterlichen Fügungen, das sichtbare Mauerwerk, der Rhythmus regelmäßiger Wandöffnungen. Zwei Vorhöfe trennen das Kloster und die Kirche von der Außenwelt. Durch die Pforte betritt man den ersten Innenhof (Foto links unten). Dort führt eine breite Treppe über eine Galerie in die Abteikirche, die der Heiligen Jungfrau Maria gewidmet ist. Der schlichte Raum entspricht genau den Bedürfnissen des Klosters und lässt sich mit einem römischen Haus vergleichen. Völlig geschlossene Seitenschiffe umgeben das mittlere Schiff, in dessen Obergaden ringsum ein Fensterband zur Belichtung der Kirche eingeschnitten ist. Die Ziegelwände tragen einen dünnen Überzug aus grauem Zementputz. Van der Laan hat auch alle Einbauten und Möbel entworfen.

Hans van der Laan's ambition was to develop his own design principles, and this is evident in his three monastic works. Apart from a monastery in Belgium (1975) and one in Sweden (1996), this abbey in Vaals was his most important architectural commission. Here too his design rules are expressed in an especially pure manner: the cleanly drawn cubatures, the masterful jointing, the exposed masonry, the rhythm of the regular apertures in the walls. Two forecourts separate the abbey complex and church from the outside world. One gains access to the first inner courtyard through a gate (photo at bottom left). Broad steps then lead via a gallery into the abbey church dedicated to the Holy Virgin Mary. The simple interior is a perfect match for the monastery's requirements and can be compared to a Roman house. Completely closed side aisles flank the central nave, into whose clerestory a band of windows is inserted all around to let in light. The brick walls are faced with a thin layer of grey cement. Van der Laan also designed all the fittings and furniture.

St. Magnus
Lillestrøm, Norwegen
1988

St Magnus
Lillestrøm, Norway
1988

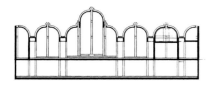

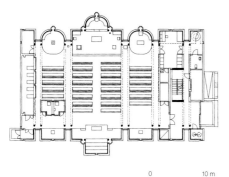

Grundriss und Längsschnitt
floor plan and
longitudinal section

0   10 m

Lillestrøm ist ein gepflegtes Land-städtchen östlich von Oslo. Die Kirche wirkt aufgrund ihrer maßvollen Höhe sowie ihrer Gliederung in mehrere ›Häuser‹ fast zierlich und fällt deshalb im durchgrünten Wohngebiet wenig auf. Im Unterschied zu der introvertierten Kirche St. Hallvard in Oslo [Seite 104] haben Kjell Lund und Nils Slaatto den Außenbau von St. Magnus markant gestaltet. Das Dachprofil der Südfassade bestimmen die jeweils durch ein Oberlicht geteilten Gewölbe. Der Hauptkirchenraum zeichnet sich nach außen durch ein hohes, basilikales Gewölbe ab. Die in einer Viertelkreisform präzis vorgefertigten Betonelemente der Decke tragen ihre Last auf lange Querbalken ab, die auf Rundstützen liegen. Obwohl alle Elemente des Tragwerks hellweiß gestrichen sind, lässt sich die Konstruktion ablesen. Der Grundriss zeigt das additive Prinzip von gereihten Raumeinheiten. Die Kirche ist aber keine neutrale Hülle: Drei Schiffe mit drei Apsiden charakterisieren ihre Bestimmung. Das Licht fällt vor allem durch die Oberlichter in die Kirche ein. Verglaste Schlitze in den Wänden öffnen den hellen, freundlichen Raum dezent zu seiner Umgebung.

Lillestrøm is a well-cared-for small country town to the east of Oslo. The church gives an impression almost of fragility as a result of its moderate height and its arrangement into a number of 'houses', and thus does not stand out much amid the pervasive greenery of the residential area. Unlike the introverted church of St Hallvard in Oslo [p. 104], however, Kjell Lund and Nils Slaatto gave St Magnus's exterior a striking appearance. The roof profile of the southern façade is determined by vaults, each divided by a skylight. The main body of the church is marked on the outside by a high basilican vault. The weight of the concrete components of the ceiling, pre-cast precisely in quarter-circle form, is borne by long transverse beams resting on round pillars. Although all the elements of the supporting framework are painted a bright white, it is still possible to discern the construction. The ground plan displays the additional principle of spatial units arranged in rows. However the church is no neutral shell: three aisles with three apses characterise its purpose. Light enters the interior chiefly through the skylights, but glazed slits in the walls of the bright, friendly church provide discreet glimpses of its surroundings.

Auch im Schiff der Taufkapelle bildet das Holz der Bänke und Einbauten einen schönen Kontrast zu dem weiß gestrichenen Tragwerk aus Beton.

In the baptismal chapel, too, the wood used for pews and fittings presents a pleasing contrast to the white-painted concrete of the supporting frame-work.

Peter Zumthor

Kapelle Sogn Benedtg   Sogn Benedtg Chapel
Somvix, Schweiz   Somvix, Switzerland
1988   1988

Wie eine ›Arche‹ liegt die mit Schin-
deln verkleidete Kapelle an einem
Bergweg im Steilhang. Der frei stehende, hölzerne Glockenträger erinnert
an eine ›Himmelsleiter‹.

Like an ark, the shingle-covered
chapel lies beside a mountain path
on a steep slope. The free-standing
wooden bell-stand recalls a 'ladder
to Heaven'.

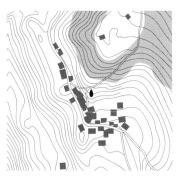

Das kleine Dorf Somvix liegt im schweizerischen Kanton Graubünden, nur wenig entfernt vom berühmten Kloster Disentis. Das ursprünglich gotische, dann barock überformte Kirchlein des Ortes wurde im Winter 1984 durch eine Lawine zerstört. Die neue, aus einem Wettbewerb hervorgegangene Kapelle steht deshalb an einer geschützteren Stelle oberhalb des Dorfes. Wie bei seinen anderen Projekten hat sich Peter Zumthor mit dem »konkreten Ort« auseinander gesetzt, um dann einen »in sich ruhenden« Baukörper zu entwerfen. In Anlehnung an historische Kapellen wächst das turmartige Bauwerk ohne Sockel aus dem Steilhang heraus – nur ein abgeschrägter Fußpunkt trennt die Verkleidung aus Schindelholz vom Boden. Die Gestalt der Kapelle, das in einer Spitze zulaufende Oval, soll an eine bergende Weiblichkeit erinnern. Das Tragwerk ist eine Holzkonstruktion: Die 37 frei stehenden Stützen bilden mit der gekrümmten Pfette und den Sparren ein Skelett. Ein umlaufendes Lichtband trennt die Wand vom Dach. Der einfache Holzboden wurde zwischen den Stützen eingelegt und die Innenwand silberfarbig gestrichen. In der Kapelle verbindet sich die typologische Eigenständigkeit mit einer sinnlichen Präsenz des Materials.

Somvix is a small village in the Swiss canton of Graubünden (Grisons), not far from the celebrated monastery at Disentis. Its little church, originally Gothic but with a baroque overlay, was destroyed by an avalanche in 1984. Consequently the new chapel, resulting from a competition, has been placed in a more sheltered position above the village. As with his other projects, Peter Zumthor involved himself with the 'very place' in order to design a building that is 'at peace with itself'. In imitation of historic chapels, the tower-like structure rises — without any substructure — from the steep slope; only a sloping base separates the shingle cladding from the ground. The shape of the chapel, an oval tapering to a point, is intended to be a reminder of protective femininity. The supporting framework is made of timber: 37 free-standing supports form a skeleton together with the curved purlin and the rafters. A band of windows all around separates the wall from the roof. The simple wooden floor was laid between the supports and the silver-painted interior wall. Typological originality and the sensuous presence of materials are combined in the chapel.

Licht und Schatten spielen auf den
silberfarbig gestrichenen Wänden.
Der Altar ist nach Osten ausgerichtet.
Der Raum wirkt trotz der einfachen
Materialien stimmungsvoll.

Light and shadow play on the silvery
walls. The altar is aligned to the
east. Despite the simple materials,
the interior is full of atmosphere.

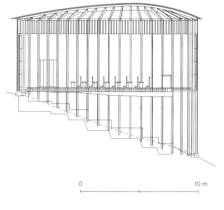

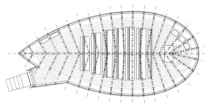

Grundriss
und Längsschnitt
floor plan and
longitudinal section

Fabrizio Brentini

Vom neuen Grundriss zum Gesamtkunstwerk
Kirchenbau in der Schweiz nach dem Zweiten Weltkrieg

Es gibt in der Schweiz schon vor dem Zweiten Weltkrieg einzelne Versuche, die Längsgerichtetheit im Grundriss aufzugeben, aber erst mit den Lösungen von Fritz Metzger für die katholischen Kirchen in Riehen und Zürich findet der entscheidende Quantensprung zu einer größeren Flexibilität statt. Zwar können die Kirchen erst 1949/50 vollendet werden, doch werden die Pläne schon 1947 veröffentlicht und als wesentliche Fortschritte im katholischen Kirchenbau international gewürdigt.

Die Frage nach dem liturgiegerechten Grundriss

St. Franziskus in Riehen besteht aus einem Trapez für das Schiff und einem Oval für den Chor. Die Trennung von Gemeinderaum und Presbyterium bleibt zwar erhalten, doch wird die Teilnahme der Besucher am Geschehen im Chor dadurch erleichtert, dass für die gleiche Anzahl Besucher die maximale Distanz zwischen Altar und den hintersten Bankreihen durch die Entfaltung in die Breite entscheidend verringert wird. Im Grunde findet hier eine Angleichung an den Theaterraum statt. Metzger verzichtet trotz des bescheidenen Hauptgebäudes keineswegs auf kirchenaffirmierende Elemente. Der frei stehende Turm ist ein unübersehbares Wahrzeichen des ganzen Quartiers. Typologisch wird er zum Vorbild für unzählige Nachahmungen bis zur Mitte der sechziger Jahre. Die Zürcher Kirche Felix und Regula [Seite 34] muss mit Ausnahme des aufdringlichen Turmes als eine der reifsten europäischen Kirchen des 20. Jahrhunderts bewertet werden. Dem großen Queroval für die Gemeinde fügt Metzger je ein Rechteck für den Chor- und den Eingangsbereich an. Erstaunlich ist die Materialwahl: Asphalt für den Boden, Beton für die Decke und die Stützen, Zementsteine für die Wände. Einzig die Fenster von Ferdinand Gehr im schmalen Lichtband verleihen dem Raum einen farblichen Akzent. Magistral wölbt sich die flache Kalotte über das ganze Oval. Nach Emil Schubiger, der als Ingenieur die Statik der Wölbung aufgrund von Modellstudien berechnet hat, ist diese Kalotte mit dem maximalen Durchmesser von 24 Metern und einer Stichhöhe von lediglich 1,60 Metern die flachste, die bis dahin ausgeführt wurde.

Fast gleichzeitig mit den Kirchen in Riehen und Zürich bauen Max Ernst Haefeli, Rudolf Steiger und Werner M. Moser (der Sohn von Karl, der 1925–30 mit Robert Curjel die berühmte Betonkirche St. Antonius in Basel verwirklicht hat) die neuapostolische Kirche in Genf, bei der die Hauptausrichtung in der Diagonale des Quadrats verläuft. Diese viel beachtete Lösung wird wenig später auch im katholischen Kirchenbau verwendet, so besonders von Hermann Baur bei der Bruder-Klaus-Kirche in Biel (1957/58).

Ronchamp und die Folgen

1955 wird auf einem Hügel über Ronchamp die Kapelle Notre-Dame-du-Haut von Le Corbusier [Seite 55] eingeweiht. Der Meister der rationalen Architektur lässt sich hier von den sanften Wellen der Landschaft inspirieren und modelliert eine Hülle, deren Hauptmerkmal das Fehlen des rechten Winkels ist. Zu den fleißigsten Pilgern nach Ronchamp zählen die Schweizer, welche die Sprache der Kapelle in devoter Abhängigkeit bis zum Exzess umsetzen. Viele Theologen begrüßen die plastische Bauweise, wohl auch deswegen, weil sie aus der Hülle und dem Raumeindruck unzählige religiöse Symbole herauszulesen vermögen. Hermann Baur, der bis dahin erstaunlich lang dem Longitudinalgrundriss die Treue gehalten hat, ist von

Fritz Metzger
St. Franziskus / St Franziskus
Riehen, 1950

Fabrizio Brentini

From New Floor Plan to Total Work of Art
Swiss Church Architecture after the Second World War

Even prior to the Second World War, there were isolated attempts in Switzerland to abandon the longitudinal focus of the church ground plan but it would take Fritz Metzger's solutions for the Catholic churches in Riehen and Zurich to inspire a decisive shift towards greater flexibility. Although the churches were only completed in 1949/50, the plans were published as early as 1947 and were internationally recognised as important signs of progress in Catholic church architecture.

The Relationship between Ground Plan and Liturgy

St Franziskus in Riehen is composed of a trapezoidal aisle and an oval choir. While congregation and presbytery are still separated, the public is drawn into the activities of the choir section by the fact that the maximum distance between altar and the last pew is considerably diminished and the width is increased, thus accommodating the same number of visitors. One could say that the plan adopts the principles of a theatrical space. Yet despite the modest principal structure, Metzger has by no means abandoned elements which underline its ecclesiastical nature. The free-standing tower is a distinctive landmark of the entire district. Typologically, it would become the model for countless imitations until the mid-1960s. The church of Saints Felix and Regula [p. 34] in Zurich must be seen as one of the most accomplished European church buildings of the 20th century, its somewhat obtrusive tower aside. Metzger adds a rectangle for both the choir and the entrance area, respectively, to the large horizontal oval reserved for the congregation. The choice in materials comes as a surprise: asphalt for the floor, concrete for the ceiling and the columns, concrete blocks for the walls. The only colour accent in the interior is provided by the narrow band of stained glass windows by Ferdinand Gehr. The shallow calotte spans the entire oval in an imperious arc. Emil Schubiger, the engineer who calculated the statics of the arc in model studies, maintains that this calotte, with a maximum span of 24 metres and a mere 1.6-metre rise, was the flattest arc that had ever been built up to that time.

Almost concurrent with the churches in Riehen and Zurich, Max Ernst Haefeli, Rudolf Steiger and Werner M. Moser (son of Karl Moser, who had realised the famous concrete church St Anthony in Basle together with Robert Curjel in 1925–30) erected the New Apostolic church in Geneva, whose principal axis follows the diagonal of the square. This widely discussed solution was soon after adopted for Catholic church buildings, especially by Hermann Baur in the Bruder-Klaus Church in Biel (1957/58).

Ronchamp and its Consequences

In 1955, the chapel of Notre-Dame-du-Haut by Le Corbusier [p. 57] was inaugurated on a hill above Ronchamp. The master of rational architecture sought inspiration in the gently undulating landscape, modelling a skin whose chief characteristic is the absence of right angles. The Swiss are among the most eager pilgrims to Ronchamp, transforming the language of the chapel into devout dependence in the extreme. Many theologians welcome the plastic form — perhaps because the skin and the impression of space are evocative of countless religious symbols. Hermann Baur, who had remained astonishingly loyal to the longitudinal ground plan, was so enchanted with Ronchamp that he seized the first opportunity to render his own interpretation

Fritz Metzger
St. Franziskus / St Franziskus
Riehen, 1950

Ronchamp derart begeistert, dass er bei der ersten möglichen
Gelegenheit seine Interpretation der plastischen Architektur
präsentiert. Die katholische Kirche in Birsfelden (1958/59),
deren Wegführung vom Vorplatz über den seitlichen Eingang
zum Mittelgang einem U folgt, kopiert in einigen Belangen
Ronchamp sehr genau. Die Perforierung der rechten Seiten-
wand ist eine Paraphrase der Südwand von Ronchamp, die indirekte Lichtführung des überhöhten Chores wiederholt das
System der halbrunden Turmschächte. Ernest Brantschen seiner-
seits übernimmt den Raumeindruck der Decke durch die
manieristische Dachschale der Kirche in St. Gallen-Winkeln
(1958/59) – von der Seite betrachtet, hat man den Eindruck
eines Auseinanderbrechens. Auch seine Kirche in Sulgen (1959
bis 61) erinnert nicht nur von Ferne an die Südwand von
Ronchamp. Schließlich ist auch die vielgelobte Kollegiumskirche in Sarnen von Ernst Studer (1964–66) von der Sprache
Le Corbusiers abhängig. Der Grundriss basiert auf der Lösung
von Metzger in Zürich, die Disposition der Decke ebenfalls,
nur dass Studer kein Betongewölbe konstruiert, sondern eine
verkleidete Stahlstützenkonstruktion gewählt hat.

Die folgende Phase in der Schweizer Kirchenarchitektur ist nur
schwer zu überblicken. Sämtliche Grundrisstypen, sämtliche
Varianten bei der Gestaltung des Äußeren, sämtliche Möglichkeiten der Innenraumdisposition werden durchgespielt. Das
gilt nicht nur für die katholische Konfession, welche die spekta-
kuläreren Bauten realisiert, sondern auch für die evanglisch-
reformierte. Deren qualitätvollste Bauten stammen von Benedikt Huber, etwa die Thomaskirche (1958) und die Tituskirche
(1963–65) in Basel sowie seine Kirche in Rotkreuz (1966),
daneben von Werner Küenzi, zum Beispiel die Bethlehemkirche
in Bern (1960) und die Kirche in Zäziwil (1963/64), und
nicht zuletzt von Ernst Gisel, darunter seine Kirchen in Effretikon (1961) und in Reinach (1961).

Franz Füeg und Walter M. Förderer

Aus der Masse des Gebauten ragen vor allem die Werke zweier
Architekten heraus. Franz Füeg, der sich architektonisch an
der Schule Mies van der Rohes orientiert, konstruiert 1964–66
mit St. Pius in Meggen [Seite 108] einen hohen Kasten in
Montagebauweise. Die Doppel-T-Stahlträger setzt er in einem
strengen Raster von 1,68 Metern und facht sie mit durchschei-
nenden Marmorplatten aus. Die dünne Haut zeigt lediglich
den Raum für die Versammlung der Gemeinde an. Das Mobiliar
folgt ebenfalls einem auf das Nötigste reduzierten Vokabular.
Füeg nennt als Quelle die klassizistische Solothurner Kathedrale. Diese zunächst verblüffende Aussage bestätigt sich bei genauer Analyse. Die Wirkung von Weiß verbindet Meggen ebenso mit Solothurn wie die Anlage der Treppe, die Disposition
des Turmes und die Anordnung der Eingänge. St. Pius wirkt
allerdings wenig nach. Fritz Metzger findet in seinen späten Kirchenbauten wie in Oberengstringen (1963/64) und in Allschwil
(1966/67) zu einer Bauweise, die wenigstens gesinnungsmäßig
mit Meggen verglichen werden kann. Das beste Zeugnis der
modularen Bauweise neben Meggen steht in Luterbach bei
Solothurn (1965/66). Der klare, evangelisch-reformierte Kult-
bau von Hans R. Bader, der den verglasten Innenraum mit einer
durch vier Eckstützen unterfangenen Betondecke umrahmt,
lässt sich in die so genannte Solothurner Schule einordnen, die
in den sechziger Jahren in der Schweiz zum wichtigsten Gefäß
für die Rezeption der Architektur von Mies van der Rohe wird.

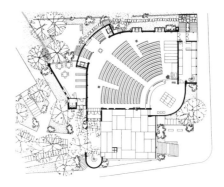

Hermann Baur
Kirche / church
Basel / Basle, 1959

Ernst Studer
Kollegiumskirche
collegiate church
Sarnen, 1966

of sculptural architecture. The Catholic church in Birsfelden (1958/59), whose *promenade architecturale* describes a U-shape from the forecourt via the entrance at the side to the centre aisle, is an exact copy of Ronchamp in several regards. The perforation on the right-hand wall is a paraphrase of the south wall at Ronchamp, and the indirect lighting strategy of the elevated choir reprises the system of the semicircular tower shafts. Ernest Brantschen, in turn, adopted the spatial impression of the ceiling in his Mannerist ceiling sheath in the church of St Gallen-Winkeln (1958/59) — seen from the side, one has the impression of a form breaking apart. His church in Sulgen (1959 – 61), too, is reminiscent of the south wall at Ronchamp, and not only from a distance. And finally, the much-praised collegiate church in Sarnen by Ernst Studer (1964 – 66) is also founded on the language of Le Corbusier. The ground plan is based on Metzger's solution in Zurich, as is the disposition of the ceiling, only here Studer chose a clad steel-column structure instead of a concrete vault.

The subsequent phase in Swiss church architecture is difficult to summarise. All types of ground plans, all variations in the design of the exterior, every possible option in the disposition of the interior are played out. This is not only true for the Catholic denomination, for which truly spectacular buildings are realised during this period, but also for the reformed Protestant Church. The most impressive buildings for the latter were the work of Benedikt Huber, for example the Thomaskirche (1958) and the Tituskirche (1963 – 65) in Basle, as well as his church in Rotkreuz (1966). Other examples are the work of Werner Küenzi, for example the Bethlehemkirche in Bern (1960) and the church in Zäziwil (1963/64), and last but not least the work of Ernst Gisel and his churches in Effretikon (1961) and Reinach (1961) among others.

Franz Füeg and Walter M. Förderer

The work of two architects in particular stands out from the mass of built projects. Franz Füeg, whose architecture is in the tradition of Mies van der Rohe, erected a tall box in modular construction at St Pius in Meggen (1964 – 66; p. 108). Füeg arranged the H-beams in a rigorous 1.60-metre grid and used translucent marble panels as infill. The thin skin merely sketches the outline of the space for the gathering of the congregation. The vocabulary of the furnishings, too, is reduced to the absolute minimum. Füeg points to the classicistic Cathedral in Solothurn as his source of inspiration and upon closer analysis this somewhat puzzling comparison is indeed confirmed. The church in Meggen is related to the model in Solothurn through the effect of white and the design of the staircase, the disposition of the tower and the placement of the entrances. But St Pius did not have a lasting impact. In his later church buildings, at Oberengstringen (1963/64) and at Allschwil (1966/67), for example, Fritz Metzger developed a style that relates to Meggen at least in spirit. Aside from Meggen, the most impressive exponent of the modular building method is found in Luterbach near Solothurn (1965/66). The clean, reformed Protestant place of worship by Hans R. Bader, framing the glazed interior with a concrete ceiling supported on four corner pillars, belongs in the tradition of the so-called Solothurn School, which became the most important vessel for the reception of Mies van der Rohe's architecture in Switzerland in the 1960s.

Ernst Gisel
Kirche / church
Effretikon, 1961

Ernst Studer
Kollegiumskirche
collegiate church
Sarnen, 1966

Innerhalb kürzester Zeit gewinnt Walter M. Förderer nach dem Erfolg im Wettbewerb für die neue Hochschule in St. Gallen nicht weniger als sieben Konkurrenzen für kirchliche Zentren, die alle zwischen 1966 und 1971 realisiert werden. Die Bauten kann man im Gegensatz zu Meggen kaum beschreiben. Förderer geht beim Planen auch anders vor. Jeder Entwicklungsschritt wird am Modell ausgelöst. Der Architekturplan ist eine Übertragung des Modells auf das Papier. Die Modelle im Maßstab 1:20 dienen auf der Baustelle zudem als Orientierungshilfen. Förderers Kirchen sind Großplastiken mit unzähligen Kanten, Durchbrechungen, Kammern und Höfen. Der Turm mit der monumentalen Kreuzplastik fungiert einerseits als eine Art Wahrzeichen und andererseits als zusätzliches Gefäß für kleinere Gruppenräume. Der Weg zu den Eingängen führt fast überall über verschiedene Hohlräume und Verwinkelungen zu einem Innenhof als Sammelbecken und Vorbereitungszone. Die Kirchenräume sind ausgesprochen dunkel. Ein niedriger Umgang lässt den Raum ringförmig erfassen. Es besteht keine Trennung zwischen Chor und Gemeindesektor. Die liturgischen Zeichen bilden zusammen ein skulpturales Ambiente. Hauptmerkmal der Bauten ist die fast exhibitionistische Zurschaustellung des rohen Betons, der für Förderer die angenehme Eigenschaft der beliebigen Formbarkeit besitzt – der Rohbau ist bereits der vollendete Bau.

Förderer wehrt sich in seinen zahlreichen Schriften immer wieder gegen die Beanspruchung der räumlichen Mitte durch die Institution Kirche. 1964 schlägt er denn auch intime und dezentrale Kirchenräume in Hochhäusern vor. Die von ihm gewünschten Gebilde notwendiger Zwecklosigkeit darf man nicht mit seinen Kirchen gleichsetzen. Trotzdem belegen seine Zentren die Mitte, ganz eklatant in Hérémence [Seite 138]. Ein Widerspruch? Nur scheinbar. Die Kirchen von Förderer dienen nur bedingt der Liturgie. In erster Linie sind es seine Denkmäler. Sie sollen seine bildhauerische Botschaft verkünden und in diesem Sinne sollen sie auch Mitte sein. Mit anderen Worten: Die Aufgabe Kirche gibt ihm die größten Freiheiten, um seine plastischen Vorstellungen großräumlich zu verwirklichen. Nach 1975 nimmt er Abschied von der Architektur und konstruiert von da an seine so genannten Raumkästen.

Ein solitäres Werk, wenngleich in letzter Zeit immer stärker rezipiert, ist der von Mirco Ravanne 1965–68 erfolgte Umbau des Kapuzinerklosters Sion, bei dem er, an seinen Lehrmeister Jean Prouvé anknüpfend, durch die aus gefalteten Flächen komponierte Fassade des Zellentraktes und die spitzig aufgebrochenen Oberlichter der Sakristei dem Ensemble eine der alpinen Welt nachempfundene Splissigkeit verleiht.

Das Zeitalter der Multifunktionalität

Die Wogen der Studentenunruhen mit den gesellschaftspolitischen Diskursen betreffen auch die Kirche als Gebäude, bei dem nun kirchenaffirmierende Elemente abgelehnt werden. Das hat zur Konsequenz, dass der Einraum für die kultische Gemeinde diversifiziert wird. Man baut demnach eine Zone, die für die verschiedensten Lebensformen einer Pfarrei dienlich sein kann: für die Liturgie, für ein Fest, für eine Versammlung, für einen Vortrag. Im Äußeren gleicht man die Zentren der Bebauungsweise der Quartiere an. Man verzichtet auf Türme, auf Wahrzeichen, auf Höhe. Als extremes Beispiel sei das katholische Zentrum Winterthur-Seen von Benito Davi aus dem Jahr 1974

Hans R. Bader
Kirche / church
Luterbach, 1966

Mirco Ravanne
Kloster / monastery
Sion, 1968

Following his success in the competition for the new college in St. Gallen, Walter M. Förderer won no less than seven competitions in rapid succession for ecclesiastical centres, which were all realised between 1966 and 1971. By contrast with Meggen, these buildings almost defy description. Förderer also proceeds in an entirely different manner during the planning phase. Each step is the result of work on the model, and the architectural plan is a transfer of the model onto paper. The models, on a scale of 1:20, also serve as orientation guides on site. Förderer's churches are monumental sculptures with countless edges, penetrations, compartments and courtyards. The tower with the monumental cross sculpture acts as a kind of landmark and doubles as an additional container for smaller group rooms. The route to the entrances leads almost invariably through a variety of hollow spaces and mazes into a courtyard that serves as a gathering place and preparation zone. The church spaces are extremely dark. The space is encircled by a low ambulatory. There is no separation between choir and community sector. The liturgical symbols provide a sculptural ambience. The chief characteristic of the buildings is an almost exhibitionist focus on natural concrete, which, to Förderer, has the agreeable quality of being suitable to any form — thus the skeleton construction is already the finished building.

In his numerous writings, Förderer repeatedly rejects the institutional demand that churches must have a spatial centre. In 1964 he therefore proposes intimate and decentralised church spaces in high-rise blocks. These structures of necessary purposelessness, which he advocates, should not be equated with his churches. Nevertheless, his centres feature a distinct middle, most notably in Hérémence [p. 138]. A contradiction? Only on the surface. Förderer's churches are only partly in the service of the liturgy. They are personal monuments, first and foremost, intended to proclaim his sculptural message and, in this sense, they are also central. In other words: the task of building a church affords him the greatest freedom for realising his sculptural ideas on a large scale. Förderer resigned from architecture after 1975 and dedicated himself to constructing his so-called spatial boxes.

Mirco Ravanne's conversion of the Capuchin monastery Sion (1965–68) is a singular work, although it has been more favourably received in recent years. In the vein of his master Jean Prouvé, Ravanne invests the ensemble, which takes it inspi-ration from the Alpine surroundings, with a spliced quality by means of the façade on the dormitory wings, which is composed of folded surfaces, and the articulated skylights in the sacristy.

The Age of Multifunctionality

The era of student unrest saw socio-political debates which also addressed the church as a building, but rejected its ecclesiastical elements. The direct consequence was the diversification of the single space for the community of worshippers. This means building a zone that can serve the wide variety of social life in a parish: the liturgy, a party, a public meeting or a lecture. Externally, these 'centres' are adapted to the existing building style of the relevant district. Towers, landmarks, height — these aspects are relinquished. It is worth noting the Catholic centre in Winterthur-Seen by Benito Davi from 1974 as an extreme exponent of this trend. The square principal space can be divided into nine smaller squares with the help of sliding walls,

Walter M. Förderer
Heiligkreuzkirche
Church of the Holy Cross
Chur, 1969

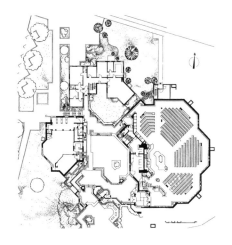

erwähnt. Der quadratische Hauptraum kann dank den Schiebe-
wänden in neun kleinere Quadrate, die miteinander beliebig
kombinierbar sind, unterteilt werden. Die Fragmentierung des
Grundrisses hat zur Folge, dass im Raum selber auf die architektonische Gewichtung eines Elements, oder besser: auf eine
Regie, gänzlich verzichtet wird. Die Idee der so genannten multifunktionalen Zentren scheitert. Selbst Förderer, der entschie-
denste Verfechter dieses Konzepts, beweist mit St. Konrad in
Schaffhausen (1969–71), dass das Verschmelzen der Funktionen bei der Ausgestaltung der Hülle keine Veränderung nach
sich ziehen muss. Der Kirchenraum wird statt mit Bänken
mit Stühlen möbliert, ansonsten ist gegenüber seinen früheren
Kirchen mit Ausnahme des Wegfalls des Turmes kein Bruch
zu erkennen.

Ein spezieller Bereich sind die wenigen ökumenischen Zentren,
die in den beiden von Manuel Pauli entworfenen Kirchen von
Langendorf (1970/71) auf identischem Grundriss und mit
einem gemeinsamen Glockenträger einen wichtigen Vorläufer
besitzen. Benedikt Huber entwirft 1975/76 das unprätentiöse
Zentrum in Kehrsatz, und Ernst Gisel 1979–81 das breite, einen
intimen Platz eingrenzende Zentrum von Steinhausen. Den
insofern ehrlichsten Bau konzipiert Gisel 1967/68 für das Pestalozzidorf in Trogen. Der kleine unscheinbare Holzpavillon
beherbergt im Inneren arenaförmige Sitzstufen um eine runde
Mitte, in der alle Konfessionen ihren Kult ausüben können.

Der Hang zum Gesamtkunstwerk

Mario Botta entfacht 1986 mit seinem Projekt für Mogno im
Kanton Tessin einen überraschenden Aufruhr. Dies ist umso
erstaunlicher, als seine 1996 eingeweihte Kirche im Grunde an
die forcierte Zeichenhaftigkeit der sechziger Jahre anschließt.
Sie ist wieder ein Kultraum, der mit vielen Effekten, mit einer
raffinierten Lichtführung und einem geometrischen Symbolismus
aufgeladen wird. Das Oval wird so abgeschnitten, dass die Be-
dachung einen Kreis bildet. Das Positive von Mogno ist aber,
dass die Aufgabe Kirchenbau von der ersten Garde der Architekten neu entdeckt wird. Zudem wird der kreisförmige Grundriss
zu einer Art Kanon für die nachfolgenden Kirchenbauten. Der
Kreis provoziert offensichtlich gewisse Assoziationen: die Kirche
als Mutter, der Raum als Mutterschoß, das Weibliche in der
Religion im Sinne des Bergenden, Schützenden und Tragenden.
Bottas jüngstes Werk weist in eine ähnliche Richtung, ja kann
als Höhepunkt einer Gesamtinszenierung betrachtet werden.
Auf dem Monte Tamaro führt eine lange Brücke zu einer luftigen
Kanzel, von der man einen herrlichen Panoramablick auf die
Tessiner Alpen genießen kann. Die ganze Landschaft wird sa-
kralisiert, die Naturbetrachtung ist die eigentliche Liturgie. Das
kommt einem impliziten Pantheismus recht nahe.

Ein Gesamtkunstwerk eigener Art ist die Kapelle in Giova von
Mario Campi und Franco Pessina (1988). Der Bau ist nur bedingt eine Kapelle als Ort des Gebets und der kleinen Messen.
Er ist bewusst im Dialog mit der überragenden Landschaft komponiert. Zudem ist er gleichsam physisch erfahrbar. Eine Treppe
führt zum Umgang auf dem Dach des Würfels. Der Kegel, der
im Inneren durch kreisförmig angeordnete Säulen ausgezeichnet
ist, ahmt architektonisch die Welt der Berggipfel nach.

Die 1988 errichtete Holzkapelle von Peter Zumthor in Sogn
Benedtg [Seite 178] ist zur Inkunabel der Deutschschweizer

Ernst Gisel
Holzpavillon / wood pavilion
Pestalozzidorf / Pestalozzi village
Trogen, 1968

which can be used in a variety of combinations. The consequence of this fragmented plan is the complete absence of architectural emphasis on one element in the space itself or, more precisely, a complete absence of staging. The idea of the so-called multifunctional centres failed. Even Förderer, the most determined advocate of this concept, proved with St Konrad in Schaffhausen (1969–71), that a fusion of functions need not translate into changes in the design of the envelope. The church space is furnished with chairs instead of benches; otherwise there is no evidence of a break with his earlier church design, with the exception of the absence of a tower.

The few ecumenical centres occupy an outsider position, for which the two churches in Langendorf designed by Manuel Pauli (1970/71) serve as important predecessors. Pauli raised them on an identical ground plan and with a shared bell tower. In 1975/76 Benedikt Huber designed the unpretentious centre in Kehrsatz, followed in 1979/81 by Ernst Gisel's broad centre in Steinhausen surrounding an intimate space. The most honest building in this regard is Gisel's structure for the Pestalozzi village in Trogen from 1967 to 1968. The interior of the small, inconspicuous wood pavilion features seating steps arranged like an arena around a circular middle, where all denominations can practice their faith.

The Tendency towards *Gesamtkunstwerk*

In 1986 Mario Botta unleashed an unexpected storm of contention with his project for Mogno in the canton of Ticino. The reaction was all the more surprising since his church, consecrated in 1996, represented basically a straightforward continuation of the intensified symbolism of the 1960s. Once again, this is a space for worship laden with special effects, with a clever lighting strategy and geometric symbolism. The oval is truncated in such a manner that the roofing forms a circle. The positive aspect in Mogno, however, is that the task of church building was rediscovered by top-notch architects. Moreover, the circular ground plan became a kind of canon for subsequent church buildings. Obviously the circle evokes certain associations: the church as mother, the space as a maternal womb, the feminine in religion in the sense of shelter, protection and support. Botta's most recent work points in a similar direction, indeed it can be understood as the highlight in an ensemble. On the Monte Tamaro a long bridge leads to a lofty pulpit, from which one can enjoy a glorious panoramic view of the Ticino Alps. The landscape as a whole is made sacred, and looking at nature becomes the true expression of the liturgy. The result is not unlike an implicit expression of pantheism.

The chapel in Giova by Mario Campi and Franco Pessina (1988) is a *Gesamtkunstwerk* of a very unique kind. The structure is only partly a chapel as a site for prayer and services for small groups. It enters into a deliberate dialogue with the overpowering landscape. And this dialogue can be physically experienced as it were. Stairs lead up to the observation platform on the roof of the ambulatory. The cone, whose interior is distinguished by columns in a circular arrangement, is an architectural imitation of the world of mountain peaks that surrounds it.

The timber chapel by Peter Zumthor (1988) in Sogn Benedtg [p. 178] has become the undisputed birthplace of Swiss German 'New Simplicity'. The simple wood structure rising from a leaf-

Mario Botta
Kirche / church
Mogno, 1996

›Neuen Einfachheit‹ schlechthin geworden. Der sich über einem blattförmigen Grundriss erhebende, schlichte Holzbau besitzt eine unglaublich starke Präsenz, während das Innere durch die Geschlossenheit der Hülle und durch einen irritierend silbernen Anstrich eine ähnliche Würde ausstrahlt wie die Kirchen von Rudolf Schwarz, der in Sogn Benedtg explizit Pate stand. In der Folge bietet Zumthor bei anderen Bauaufgaben Innenräume an, die gern mit Stimmungen in Sakralräumen verglichen werden, besonders beim Thermalbad in Vals.

Damit stehen wir womöglich vor einer neuen Schwelle, jenseits der keine reinen Kirchenbauten mehr vorzufinden sind, weil deren Aufgabe von anderen Typen übernommen werden. Und zurück bleibt die Erinnerung, wie im Falle der Betonkapelle von Christian Kerez in Oberrealta im Bündnerland (1992/93), die nur noch ein leeres Zeichen ist. Oder man schafft konfessionsunabhängige Zellen für das Bedürfnis nach Stille, wie dies im Fall der 1998/99 realisierten Besinnungstätte von Pascale Guignard und Stefan Saner an der Gotthard-Autobahn im Kanton Uri geschehen ist [Seite 306]. Die spezielle Stimmung in diesem ansonsten leeren Raum rührt von zerbrochenem Flaschenglas her, das in die vitrinenähnlichen Kästen gefüllt ist, welche zwei Drittel der Wände besetzen – damit haben die Architekten das Postulat von Walter M. Förderer nach Gebilden von notwendiger Zwecklosigkeit auf eine überraschende Weise umgesetzt.

Weiterführende Literatur:
Fabrizio Brentini, *Bauen für die Kirche. Katholischer Kirchenbau des 20. Jahrhunderts in der Schweiz*, Luzern 1994.

Mario Campi · Franco Pessina
Kapelle / chapel
Giova, 1988

Christian Kerez
Kapelle / chapel
Oberrealta, 1993

shaped plan has a stunning presence, while the unbroken skin and somewhat irritating silvery paint finish of the interior exude a dignity similar to the churches by Rudolf Schwarz, whose work clearly provided the inspiration. Subsequently Zumthor frequently created interior spaces for other building tasks, which are often compared to sacred spaces in atmosphere, especially in the case of the thermal baths in Vals.

We have, perhaps, reached a new threshold, beyond which pure church architecture no longer exists because this task has been assumed by other building types. What remains is a memory, as in the case of the concrete chapel by Christian Kerez in Ober-realta in the Bündner Region (1992/93), which is no more than a vacuous symbol. Or non-denominational cells to satisfy the yearning for silence, as is the case of the meditation space by Pascale Guignard and Stefan Saner on the St Gotthard *autobahn* in the Canton of Uri (1998/99; p. 306). The unique ambience in this otherwise empty space is the result of broken bottle glass, which is gathered in vitrine-like boxes and occupies two thirds of the walls — a surprising response by the architects to Walter M. Förderer's call for structures of necessary purposelessness.

Recommended reading:
Fabrizio Brentini, *Bauen für die Kirche. Katholischer Kirchenbau des 20. Jahrhunderts in der Schweiz*, Lucerne, 1994.

Peter Zumthor
Kapelle / chapel Sogn Benedtg
Somvix, 1988

Ottokar Uhl

St. Judas Thaddäus
Karlsruhe, Deutschland
1989

St Judas Thaddeus
Karlsruhe, Germany
1989

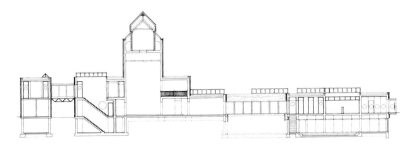

0   10 m

Längsschnitt
longitudinal section

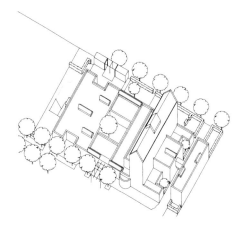

Seit mehr als vier Jahrzehnten setzt sich der österreichische Architekt Ottokar Uhl für einen Gemeinschaft stiftenden Kirchenbau ein. Sein Engagement begann 1958 mit der katholischen Studentenkapelle in Wien [Seite 89]. Eine Pionierleistung stellt auch dieses Gemeindezentrum dar, das aus einem Wettbewerb hervorging. Neureut ist ein Stadtteil im Norden von Karlsruhe, der an Alexander Mitscherlichs Wort von der »Unwirtlichkeit« neuer Siedlungen erinnert. Einziger Ruhepunkt in dem formal aufgeregten Stadtviertel ist das Gemeindezentrum am Marktplatz. Der Entwurf von Uhl bestand darin, »auf die schwierige städtische Randlage in einfacher, zurückhaltender Form zu reagieren«. Eine schlichte Hülle gibt dem dreistufig ansteigenden Bauwerk mit Kirche, Pfarrbüro, Pfarrwohnung, Mehrzweckraum und Kindergarten eine prägnante Gestalt. Drei Elemente tragen dazu bei: die mit geometrischen Formen rhythmisierten Fassaden, die Wände aus hellem Betonstein (ein ›maßstäbliches‹ Material), der hohe Kirchenbau als Blickpunkt im zergliederten Stadtviertel. Vorbild für ihn waren die regionaltypischen Tabakspeicher.

For more than four decades the Austrian architect Ottokar Uhl has been advocating the building of churches that foster a sense of community. His involvement began in 1958 with the Roman Catholic students' chapel in Vienna [p. 89]. The present community centre, the product of a competition, also represents a pioneering achievement. Neureut is an urban district in the northern part of Karlsruhe that evokes Alexander Mitscherlich's words about the 'inhospitableness' of new settlements. The only calm point within the district is the community centre on the Marktplatz. Uhl's design brief was to 'react to the difficult location on the edge of the city in a simple, restrained form'. A simple shell gives a concise shape to the building on three levels incorporating church, parish office, presbytery, multi-purpose room and kindergarten. Three elements contribute to this: the facades, punctuated rhythmically by geometric forms; the walls of light concrete blocks (a true-to-scale' material); and the tall church, as a visual focus within the disjointed urban area. The model for this unusual building was the tobacco stores that are typical of the region.

Im Gegensatz zu den »Wohn-Klötzen« im Stadtviertel soll die Kirche ein vertrautes »Haus« mit Satteldach signalisieren. Bei der Gestalt bezog sich Ottokar Uhl auf die alten Tabakspeicher in der Rheinebene, deren weitgehend geschlossene Baukörper einen Dachaufsatz tragen.

In contrast to the district's residential blocks, the church is intended to signal a familiar 'house' with double pitched roof. Ottokar Uhl based its design on the old tobacco stores of the Rhine plain — largely closed structures topped by a roof.

Der offene Grundriss des Kirchenraums ist eine Herausforderung für
das Gemeindeleben. Der Altar ist
ein einfacher Holztisch, statt Bänken
gibt es loses Gestühl. Ottokar Uhl:
»Entscheidend wird sein, ob dieser
Raum auf eine Gemeinde trifft, die
zu neuen Erfahrungen bereit ist.«

The open ground plan of the interior
represents a challenge for the life of
the community. The altar is a simple
wooden table, and there is moveable
seating instead of pews. Ottokar Uhl:
'The decisive factor will be is whether
this space encounters a congregation
that is ready for new experiences'.

aOttokar Uhl hat stets für eine »Kirche in dieser Welt« plädiert. Der Sakralbau soll mit dem alltäglichen Leben verbunden sein – keine Räume für Repräsentation, sondern räumliche Angebote für ein aktives Gemeindeleben. Deshalb ist der schmucklose Kirchenraum mit einem beweglichen Altar nach mehreren Seiten hin erweiterbar. Uhl verwendet für ihn den Begriff der »verfremdeten Basilika«. Der Raum ist zwar dreischiffig, aber quer orientiert, und zudem sind die beiden Seitenschiffe breiter als das Mittelschiff. Eines der Seitenschiffe ist die höchste Raumstufe und wird durch eine rund sechs Meter breite und 28 Meter lange Lichtdecke unter dem verglasten Satteldach belichtet. Der Eingang zur Kirche liegt nicht axial, sondern seitlich, so dass der Besucher durch seine Bewegung den Raum erkunden kann. Der offene Grundriss ermöglicht unterschiedliche liturgische Nutzungen, für die kleine Werktagsgemeinde ebenso wie für die sonntägliche Feier: »Die Kirche will in Dienst genommen, sie will als Instrument behandelt werden.« (Uhl) Auf diese Weise gestalten die Aktivitäten der Gemeinde den angebotenen Freiraum. Adresse: Karlsruhe-Neureut.

Ottokar Uhl has always pleaded for a 'Church in this world'. Even religious architecture should be linked as closely as possible with everyday life: not interiors designed with a view to prestige, but spaces offered for an active community life. This is why the plain church interior with a movable altar is extendable on several sides. Uhl uses the term 'defamiliarised basilica'. Although the interior has a nave and two side aisles, it is orientated on the diagonal and the side aisles are both wider than the nave. One of the aisles forms the highest level of the interior and is lit by a light ceiling, around 6 metres wide and 28 metres long, which is positioned below the glazed double-pitched roof. The entrance to the church is deliberately placed not axially, but laterally, so that the visitor can discover the interior through his or her movements. The open ground plan makes a variety of liturgical uses possible, whether for the small workday congregation or for the major Sunday services: 'The church wants to be put to use, it wants to be treated as an instrument' (Uhl). The congregation's activities consequently shape the free space that is offered. Address: Neureut, Karlsruhe.

Andrés Perea

Santa Teresa de Jesús
Madrid, Spanien
1991

Santa Teresa de Jesús
Madrid, Spain
1991

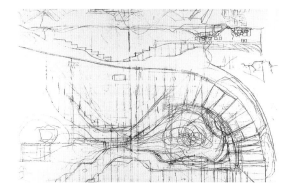

Entwurfsskizze
outline sketch

Madrid ist von einem Gürtel großer Wohnsiedlungen umgeben. Im Norden liegt der Bezirk Tres Cantos, dessen Tristesse das Pfarrzentrum mildern soll. Andrés Perea hat die Anlage im Kontrast zur Wohnbebauung gestaltet – sie erscheint wie eine Mulde in der Silhouette der Vorstadt. Nach drei Seiten hin grenzt eine Mauer das Pfarrzentrum wie ein Mantel von der Umgebung ab. Im Nordosten, wo auch der Haupteingang liegt, öffnet sich das Bauwerk durch Glaswände zu einem erhöhten Platz. Einprägsam ist vor allem sein wellenförmig verlaufendes Dach, das im Hinblick auf die höheren Wohnblöcke als ›fünfte Fassade‹ gestaltet ist. Es ruht auf einer Stahlkonstruktion und fällt zum Platz hin in Stufen ab. Von dort aus gesehen befindet sich links der Kirchenraum, betont durch einen Glasfirst auf der Außenmauer, und rechts der Gemeindesaal. Dazwischen liegt ein Wandelgang, der sich im Gebäude zu einem ›Kreuzgang‹ vor den Nebenräumen des Pfarrzentrums weitet. Adresse: Madrid-Tres Cantos, Avenida de la Vega.

Madrid is surrounded by a belt of large housing settlements. To the north lies the outer district of Tres Cantos, whose dreariness the parish centre is intended to alleviate. Andrés Perea favours a figurative rationalism, and he designed the complex as a contrast to the dense housing: it appears like a hollow in the silhouette of the suburb. On three sides a wall shields the gleaming white parish centre from its surroundings. To the north-east, which is also where the main entrance is located, the building opens up via glass walls on to a raised square. Particularly eye-catching is its undulating roof, which is designed as a 'fifth façade' from the perspective of the higher blocks of flats. It rests on a steel structure and descends in graduated stages to the square. Viewed from the square, the church itself is on the left, emphasised by a glass ridge on the outer wall, while on the right is the community hall. Between them lies a covered walk, which widens out deep inside the building in front of the side rooms of the parish centre to form a sort of cloister. Address: Avenida de la Vega, Tres Cantos, Madrid.

Der Wandelgang führt in die Tiefe des Gebäudes, wo an einem zweiten Eingang die Nebenräume des Pfarrzentrums liegen. In der Kirche fällt das Licht durch eine verglaste Dachzone auf den Altarbereich.

The wide covered walk leads into the depths of the building, where the side rooms of the parish centre are situated off a second entrance. In the church, light falls through a glazed roof zone on to the altar area.

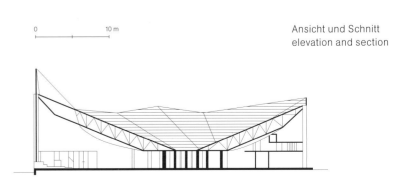

0   10 m

Ansicht und Schnitt
elevation and section

Mario Botta

Kathedrale
Evry, Frankreich
1995

Cathedral
Evry, France
1995

Der Haupteingang zur Kathedrale liegt südöstlich in einem Flachbau. Die Großform des abgeschnittenen Zylinders erinnert an Le Corbusiers Entwurf für die Torso gebliebene Kirche in Firminy bei Saint-Etienne.

The cathedral's main entrance lies to the south-east in a flat building. The overall form of the cut-off cylinder is reminiscent of Le Corbusier's design for the church at Firminy, near Saint-Etienne, which has never progressed beyond the skeleton stage.

0   50 m

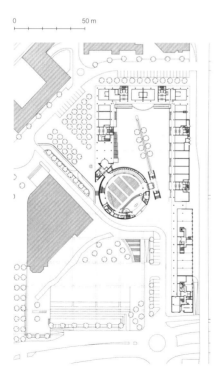

Lageplan
site plan

Dieser spektakuläre Rundbau ist die erste Kathedrale, die in Frankreich seit der Revolution von 1789 gebaut wurde. Sie steht in einer ›Ville nouvelle‹ südlich von Paris, die überwiegend in den siebziger Jahren erbaut wurde. Zusammen mit dem Rathaus begrenzt sie nach Süden den zentralen ›Platz der Menschenrechte‹. Die Großform der Kathedrale ist ein schräg abgeschnittener Zylinder von 17 bis 34 Metern Höhe, auf dessen Dachrand ein Kranz von Laubbäumen gesetzt wurde. Diese manierierte Geste steht im Widerspruch zum Bauwerk, das Mario Bottas Vorlieben für Geometrie und Symmetrie verkörpert. Mit Ausnahme des südöstlich in einen Flachbau integrierten Haupteingangs sind die Regeln außen wie innen streng eingehalten. Der Grundriss zeigt zwei massive Mauerschalen in Kreisform, deren Zwischenraum auch für ein Museum sakraler Kunst genutzt wird. Im Kirchenraum mit 1300 Plätzen weist ein dreieckiges Gewölbe auf das dahinter liegende Museum hin. Anfangs als Zentralraum geplant, wurde die von oben belichtete Kirche konventionell eingerichtet. Bottas Gesamtplanung für das Areal ist nur teilweise ausgeführt.

This spectacular round building is the first cathedral to be built in France since the Revolution of 1789. It is situated in a new town to the south of Paris that for the most part dates from the 1970s. Together with the town hall it forms the southern boundary of the central square, the Place des Droits Humains. The cathedral is shaped overall like an obliquely cut-off cylinder, 17 to 34 metres in height, with a crown of deciduous trees set around its roof edge. This mannered gesture is inconsistent with the building, which embodies Mario Botta's special liking for geometry and symmetry. With the exception of the main entrance, integrated into a flat building to the south-east, the rules are observed strictly both inside and out. The ground plan reveals two solid wall shells in a circular form, the space between them being used, among other things, to house a museum of sacred art. In the interior of the cathedral, which can seat 1,300 people, a triangular vault acts as a pointer to the museum lying beyond. Initially planned with a central focus, the church which is lit from above was then laid out in a conventional manner. Botta's overall plan for the area has only partially been realised.

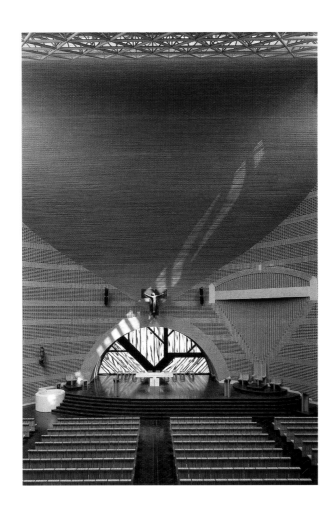

Álvaro Siza

Santa Maria
Marco de Canaveses, Portugal
1995

Santa Maria
Marco de Canaveses, Portugal
1995

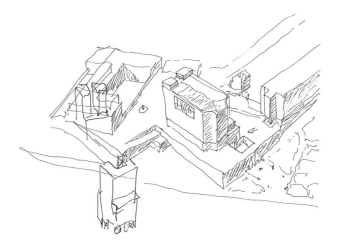

Skizze Gesamtplanung
sketch of overall plan

Weil das Land über ein reiches Erbe sakraler Bauwerke verfügt (auch eine Folge aus der Hochzeit des Kolonialismus), werden in Portugal selten neue Kirchen gebaut. In Marco de Canaveses hingegen, einer sprunghaft bis chaotisch gewachsenen Stadt 60 Kilometer östlich von Porto, gab es zuvor nur eine Kapelle. Álvaro Siza lehnte seine Gesamtplanung an das Vorbild portugiesischer Kirchenplätze an: Kirche, Gemeindezentrum und Haus des Priesters sollen im Endausbau einen ›Adro‹ (Vorplatz) rahmen. Zu einem Drittel aus EU-Zuschüssen finanziert, ist bislang nur die Kirche errichtet. Das durch seine verputzten Mauern hell strahlende Gebäude sitzt in einem Hang, wobei es seine Rückseite einer Ortsstraße zuwendet. Siza hat zusammen mit Edite Rosa die Typologie im Sinne einer geometrischen Abstraktion neu interpretiert. An der südlichen Eingangsfassade erinnern die seitlich vorspringenden Volumen an Türme, obwohl sie die Dachkante nicht überragen. Die Rückseite dagegen ist durch zwei in den Baukörper eingezogene Apsiden geprägt, weshalb das Bauwerk hier wie eine ›Bastion‹ erscheint.

Since Portugal has a rich heritage of religious buildings (including a number from the heyday of colonialism), new churches are rarely constructed there. However Marco de Canaveses, a town 60 kilometres east of Porto which has undergone rapid — not to say chaotic — expansion, had previously only had a chapel. Álvaro Siza's overall plan was based on the model of Portuguese church squares: church, community centre and priest's house should eventually, when completed, frame an *adro* (front courtyard). Financed roughly equally by EU grants, by the town and by the congregation, the church is all that has been built of this complex to date. Its plastered walls shining brightly, it lies on a slope with its rear turned to a local street. Together with Edite Rosa, Siza reinterpreted the typology in the sense of geometric abstraction. The masses projecting at the sides on the southern entrance façade remind one of towers, although they do not rise above the edge of the roof. The rear, on the contrary, is marked by two apses that are drawn into the body of the building, giving it something of the look of a 'bastion' at this point.

Zwei vorspringende Bauteile flankieren den zehn Meter hohen Haupteingang. Das linke Volumen enthält
das hohe Baptisterium, das rechte
die Empore und den Glockenträger.

Two projecting elements flank the
10-metre-high main entrance. The
mass on the left holds the high
baptistry, the one on the right the
gallery and belfry.

Grundriss
floor plan

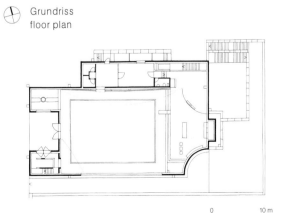

0   10 m

Während der auf einem Granitsockel stehende Außenbau Ruhe und Erhabenheit ausstrahlt, wirkt der im Grundriss rechtwinklige Innenraum dynamisch. Die Wegkirche ist auf den Altarbereich ausgerichtet, der jedoch durch die beiden ›negativen‹ Apsiden verengt und zugleich gesteigert wird. Für räumliche Bewegung sorgt vor allem die um einen Meter eingewölbte Westwand, wo drei Fenster in tiefen Leibungen sitzen. Die Massivität der konvexen Wand ist nur vorgetäuscht, da eine Gipskartonschale vorgeblendet wurde. Siza bezeichnet das Tageslicht als »Protagonisten des Raumes, der die Stimmung schafft«. Im Kirchenraum hat er alle Möglichkeiten der Lichtführung genutzt. Das direkte Licht aus den Fenstern gleitet zugleich als Streiflicht über die Wände, das aus einem Schacht hinter dem Altar kommende indirekte Licht beleuchtet die beiden Blendfenster mit Streulicht. Bis auf einen 16 Meter langen Sehschlitz in der Ostwand, der Ausblicke in die zersiedelte Landschaft gewährt, ist der Raum im unteren Bereich völlig geschlossen, wobei die Außenwände mit einem 1,50 Meter hohen Streifen aus hellgelben, handgearbeiteten ›Azulejos‹ (Fliesen) verkleidet sind.

Whereas the exterior set on a granite base radiates a sense of calm and solemnity, the interior, rectangular in ground plan, is dynamic in its impact. The church based on the processional plan is aligned towards the altar zone, which however is narrowed and simultaneously emphasised by the two 'negative' apses. Spatial movement is assured primarily by the west wall, over-arched by around one metre, where three windows sit in deep soffits. The solidity of the convex wall is purely illusory, since a shell of gypsum plasterboard was inserted as a blind. Siza describes daylight as 'the protagonist of the space, which creates the atmosphere'. He has used every possibility of introducing light into the interior. While the direct light from the windows simultaneously produces light glancing off the walls, the indirect light emanating from a shaft behind the altar illuminates the two blind windows with diffused light. The lower zone of the interior is entirely sealed, except for a 16-metre-long slit in the east wall that gives a view of the largely overdeveloped landscape. The outer walls are faced with a 1.5-metre-high strip of bright yellow, hand-made *azulejos* (tiles).

Das Hauptportal wird nur bei kirchlichen Zeremonien geöffnet. Die Rückfront erhebt sich auf einem hohen Sockel, in dem der Vorhof zur Kapelle liegt.

The main portal is only opened on special ecclesiastical occasions. The rear front rises up on a high base, which incorporates the forecourt to the chapel.

Allmann, Sattler, Wappner

Herz-Jesu-Kirche
München, Deutschland
2000

Church of the Sacred Heart
Munich, Germany
2000

Die Tore wurden mit dem Künstler Alexander Beleschenko entwickelt. Die blauen Glasscheiben tragen kleine Schriftzeichen in Nagelform. Bei geöffneten Toren prallt der Blick an der inneren Holzwand ab.

The gates were developed in conjunction with the artist Alexander Beleschenko. The blue panes of glass bear small characters in the form of nails. When the gates are open, one's gaze bounces off the inner wooden wall.

0   20 m

Grundriss
floor plan

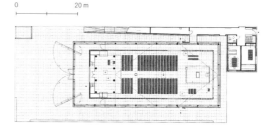

Als Ersatz für eine abgebrannte Holz-kirche ist der kubische Bau aus einem Wettbewerb hervorgegangen. Der siegreiche Entwurf ist zwar architektonisch bemerkenswert, liturgisch jedoch ein Rückschritt, weil die Gemeinde in Anlehnung an den Vorgängerbau eine Wegkirche ge-fordert hatte. Eine liturgisch innova-tive Lösung wäre der Entwurf von Friedrich Kurrent mit einer räumlich-funktionalen Trennung von ›Wort‹ und ›Mahl‹ gewesen. Die drei jungen Architekten haben eine Raum-im-Raum-Idee verfolgt. Die äußere Hülle ist eine Stahl-Glas-Konstruktion mit bündigen Flächen, so dass der Ein-druck einer gespannten Haut ent-steht. Der Eingang ist in zwei 14 Meter hohe Tore eingeschnitten, die sich hydraulisch bewegen lassen. Die innere Hülle besteht aus einer Holz-konstruktion mit Lamellen aus unbehandeltem Ahornholz, die sich zum Altarbereich hin zunehmend öffnen und dadurch die Lichtinsze-nierung wirkungsvoll unterstützen. Zwischen beiden Hüllen liegt ein Umgang mit einer Darstellung des Kreuzwegs. In den metallenen Wandvorhang hinter dem Altar ist ein großes Kreuz eingewebt. Adresse: München-Neuhausen, Lachnerstraße.

This cubical building was the result of a competition to replace a wooden church that had burned down. But although the winning design is a remarkable achievement architec-turally, in liturgical terms it is a back-ward step because the community requested a church with a traditional processional layout like that of its predecessor. One liturgically inno-vative solution would have been Friedrich Kurrent's design, with a spa-tial–functional separation of 'Word' and 'Communion'. Instead the three young architects pursued the idea of a space within a space. The outer shell is a steel and glass construction with surfaces set flush so that the impression created is of a stretched skin. The entrance is cut into two 14-metre-high gates which can be moved hydraulically. The inner shell consists of a wooden structure with maple slats that are increasingly open towards the altar region and in this way effectively assist in the manipu-lation of light. Between the two shells lies an ambulatory with a represen-tation of the Stations of the Cross. A large cross is woven into the metallic hanging behind the altar. Address: Lachnerstrasse, Neuhausen, Munich.

St. Franziskus
Steyr, Österreich
2001

St Francis
Steyr, Austria
2001

Keith Sonnier hat mit farbigen Leucht-
stoffbändern seine erste Arbeit
im sakralen Raum geschaffen. Die
Formen sollen an Fische erinnern –
eine urchristliche Symbolik.

Keith Sonnier created his first oeuvre
in the religious sphere from coloured
fluorescent strips. The shapes are
intended to be reminiscent of fishes
— a traditional Christian symbol.

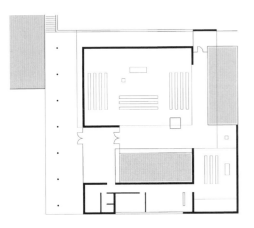

Grundriss
floor plan

0   10 m

Durch diese Kirche hat der Stadtteil Resthof im Norden von Steyr erstmals eine Mitte erhalten. Von gleichförmigen Wohnbauten aus den frühen siebziger Jahren gerahmt, bildet die aus kubischen Formen komponierte Kirche das städtebauliche wie auch das ideelle Zentrum des Wohnquartiers. Der in einem kleinen Wettbewerb erfolgreiche Entwurf von Peter und Gabriele Riepl öffnet den Kirchenbau einladend zu einem größeren Platz, wobei ein langes, von Rundstützen getragenes Vordach den voll verglasten Eingang schützt. Sowohl durch seine klare Gestalt als auch durch den monolithisch verwendeten, olivgrün durchgefärbten Beton unterscheidet sich der Kirchenbau von seiner uninspiriert geplanten Umgebung. Peter Riepl kam es auf ein lebendiges Gebäude an: »Die Kirche ist erdacht als poröser Körper, in dem die Fülle des Lebens Platz und Nischen findet. Das Haus dient dazu in fester und bestimmter Weise, verzichtet aber auf beherrschende Symbolik und bedrängende Botschaften. Der eigentliche Akteur ist das Leben selbst.« Geradezu ein Wahrzeichen des Stadtteils ist der Glaskubus an der Südostecke, aus dem bei Dunkelheit die Lichtinstallation von Keith Sonnier leuchtet.

This new church provided Resthof, an area in the northern part of the town of Steyr, with a centre for the very first time. Enclosed by uniform residential buildings dating from the early 1970s, the building composed of cube shapes forms the residential district's spiritual centre as well as its central focus in terms of urban development. The design by Peter and Gabriele Riepl means that the church opens invitingly on to a fairly large square, whereby a long canopy on round supports shields the totally glazed entrance. The church stands out from the uninspired planning of its surroundings because of its clear form and also because of the olive-green concrete which is used in a monolithic fashion. Peter Riepl's concern was to produce a living building: 'The church is devised as a porous body in which there are spaces and niches for the full richness of life. For this the house serves in a firm and determined manner but foregoes dominant symbolism and oppressive statements. The actual protagonist is life itself'. The elevated glass cube on the south-eastern corner from which Keith Sonnier's light installation glows at night has become a veritable symbol of the district.

Nach dem Entwurf der Architekten beherbergt das Gebäude sowohl Mensch, Pflanze und Erde als auch Stein, Wasser und Licht. Vom Eingang aus erblickt man zunächst einen erhöht liegenden und nach innen verglasten Innenhof, der japanisch gestaltet ist. Eine Konzentration auf wenige Elemente und Materialien zeichnet auch den rechteckigen, wohl proportionierten Kirchenraum aus. Der Boden ist mit Schieferplatten aus Portugal belegt, die Wände sind mit hellem Birkenholz ausgekleidet. Im Zentrum steht der Altarblock aus rot gebeiztem Holz, um den sich die Gemeinde auf drei Bankgruppen versammelt. Die 150 Sitzplätze lassen sich durch loses Gestühl in dem offen gegliederten Haus erweitern. Durch ein verglastes Band im Dach kann wechselndes Tageslicht auf die Altarwand fallen. Außerdem sind nach Norden und Westen die Wände vom Boden durch ein kniehohes Unterlicht getrennt. Jenseits der verglasten Ostwand liegt ein Wasserbecken. Die benachbarte Taufkapelle öffnet sich nach oben in den Glaskubus, den das Lichtkunstwerk ausfüllt.

In line with the architects' design, the building accommodates humankind, plants and earth as well as stone, water and light. From the entrance one initially glimpses a Japanese-style inner courtyard, elevated and glazed on the inside. A concentration on just a few elements and materials is also a feature of the rectangular, well-proportioned church interior. The floor is laid with slabs of slate from Portugal, and the walls are lined with light birch. In the centre stands the altar block, made of wood which is stained red, and around which the congregation gathers in three groups of pews. The seating capacity of 150 can be augmented by adding loose chairs in the open-plan space. The fluctuating daylight falls on to the altar wall through a band of glazing in the roof. In addition, to north and west the walls are separated from the floor by low-level lighting at knee height. On the other side of the glazed east wall lies a pond. The adjacent baptismal chapel opens upwards into the glass cube filled with the artistic light installation.

Vor allem das helle Birkenholz der Wandverkleidungen verleiht dem Kirchenraum einen ruhigen Charakter. Im Zentrum steht der Altarblock aus rot gebeiztem Holz.

In particular, it is the pale birch lining the walls that gives the interior its friendly, peaceful character. In the centre stands the altar block of wood which is stained red.

224 Egon Eiermann
Matthäuskirche
Pforzheim, Deutschland
St Matthew's
Pforzheim, Germany
1953

228 Heikki und Kaija Siren
Studentenkapelle
Espoo, Finnland
Students' chapel
Espoo, Finland
1957

230 Olaf Andreas Gulbransson
Friedenskirche
Manching, Deutschland
Peace Church
Manching, Germany
1958

232 Alvar Aalto
Vuoksenniska Kirche
Imatra, Finnland
Vuoksenniska Church
Imatra, Finland
1958

246 Peter Celsing
St. Thomas
Stockholm, Schweden
St Thomas
Stockholm, Sweden
1960

248 Sir Basil Spence
Kathedrale
Coventry, Großbritannien
Cathedral
Coventry, Great Britain
1962

252 Egon Eiermann
Kaiser-Wilhelm-Gedächtniskirche
Berlin, Deutschland
Kaiser Wilhelm Memorial Church
Berlin, Germany
1963

254 Werner Max Moser
Kornfeldkirche
Riehen, Schweiz
Kornfeld Church
Riehen, Switzerland
1964

256 Aarno Ruusuvuori
Tapiola Kirche
Espoo, Finnland
Tapiola Church
Espoo, Finland
1965

260 Raili und Reima Pietilä
Kaleva Kirche
Tampere, Finnland
Kaleva Church
Tampere, Finland
1966

262 Helmut Striffler
Versöhnungskirche
Dachau, Deutschland
Church of Reconciliation
Dachau, Germany
1967

276 Sigurd Lewerentz
St. Petrus
Klippan, Schweden
St Peter
Klippan, Sweden
1967

280 Timo und Tuomo Suomalainen
Temppeliaukio Kirche
Helsinki, Finnland
Temppeliaukio Church
Helsinki, Finland
1969

282 Jørn Utzon
Kirche und Gemeindezentrum
Bagsværd, Dänemark
Church and Community Centre
Bagsværd, Denmark
1976

286 Juha Leiviskä
Myyrmäki Kirche
Vantaa, Finnland
Myyrmäki Church
Vantaa, Finland
1984

290 Richard MacCormac
Kapelle im Fitzwilliam College
Cambridge, Großbritannien
Fitzwilliam College Chapel
Cambridge, Great Britain
1991

294 Heinz Tesar
Evangelische Kirche
Klosterneuburg, Österreich
Protestant Church
Klosterneuburg, Austria
1995

298 Reitermann / Sassenroth
Kapelle der Versöhnung
Berlin, Deutschland
Chapel of Reconciliation
Berlin, Germany
2000

302 Meinhard von Gerkan
Christus-Pavillon
Volkenroda, Deutschland
Christus-Pavillon
Volkenroda, Germany
2000/2001

Horst Schwebel

Eine Scheu vor großen Gesten
Protestantischer Kirchenbau aus theologisch-liturgischer Sicht

Die Konzentration auf Deutschland bei der Behandlung des evangelischen Kirchenbaus in der zweiten Hälfte des 20. Jahrhunderts hängt mit dem kaum mehr vorstellbaren Ausmaß der Zerstörungen nach dem Zweiten Weltkrieg zusammen. Die Nullpunkt-Situation barg die Chance eines Neuanfangs. Man traf sich zunächst in Baracken und behelfsmäßigen Gebäuden. Eine gewisse Berühmtheit erhielten die 48 Notkirchen von Otto Bartning (1947–49). Bartning hatte vier Typen von Notkirchen entworfen. Durch die Stiftung des Weltrats der Kirchen und vor allem amerikanischer Kirchen wurden Holzbinder mit einer Dachkonstruktion aufgestellt, deren Umschließung durch Mauerwerk von den Gemeinden selbst bewerkstelligt wurde; Steine gab es ohnehin genug. Bartning sprach von der »gültigen Gestalt aus der Kraft der Not heraus«.[1]

Rolle der Kirchbautage

1947 lud Gerhard Kunze zum ersten Kirchbautag nach Hannover ein, dem unter dem neuen Vorsitzenden Oskar Söhngen 1948 der Evangelische Kirchbautag in Berlin und dann 23 weitere Kirchbautage bis 2002 in Leipzig folgten. Anhand der Publikation der Vorträge und Diskussionen und der 1957 gegründeten Zeitschrift *Kunst und Kirche* lässt sich die Kirchbauentwicklung verfolgen. 1951 verabschiedete der Evangelische Kirchbautag in Rummelsberg das *Rummelsberger Programm*.[2] Ein wichtiger Programmpunkt ist die Ablehnung eines so genannten christlichen Baustils. Man wendet sich gegen das Eisenacher Regulativ, worin es heißt: »Die Würde des christlichen Kirchenbaues fordert Anschluß an einen der geschichtlich entwickelten christlichen Baustile und empfiehlt in der Grundform des länglichen Vierecks neben der altchristlichen Basilika und der sogenannten romanischen (vorgothischen) Bauart vorzugsweise den sogenannten germanischen (gothischen) Styl.«[3]

Eine solche Stilpräferenz kann es nach Meinung von Rummelsberg nicht mehr geben. Vielmehr gilt, dass jede Zeit ihre eigenen Formen finden muss, in denen der christliche Gehalt zum Ausdruck gebracht werden soll. Die innere Orientierung des Kirchengebäudes ist auf den Gottesdienst ausgerichtet: »Der gottesdienstliche Bau und Raum soll sich um seines Zweckes willen klar unterscheiden von Bauten und Räumen, die profanen Aufgaben dienen. Aber zugleich wächst er über jede rationale Zweckbestimmung hinaus, da er mit seiner Gestalt gleichnishaft Zeugnis von dem geben soll, was sich in und unter der gottesdienstlich versammelten Gemeinde begibt: nämlich die Begegnung mit dem gnadenhaft in Wort und Sakrament gegenwärtigen heiligen Gott.« Dadurch erfolgt eine Abgrenzung gegenüber einem ausschließlich profanen Raum. Mit dem Bezug auf den Gottesdienst knüpft man an Cornelius Gurlitt an, der 1906 auf dem 2. Kirchbaukongress in Dresden den Kirchenbau als »gebaute Liturgie« verstand. Otto Bartning forderte, dass die architektonische Spannung des Raumes der liturgischen Spannung entsprechen solle. Der Raum selbst, den Rummelsberg 1951 vorsah, ist ein gerichteter Raum mit einer Altarbühne, an deren Übergang zum Hauptraum die Kanzel als Ort der Predigt seitlich ihren Platz findet. Die Baustoffe sollen natürliche Materialien sein; Kunststoffe werden abgelehnt, darunter Eternit, Sperrholz und Beton.

Nach der Zeit der Provisorien wollte man wieder eine richtige Kirche mit moderner Ausstattung haben. Einen nicht unbeträchtlichen Einfluss auf die Kirchenraumgestaltung hatte die

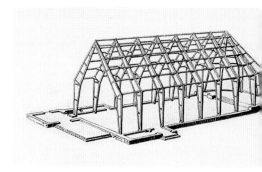

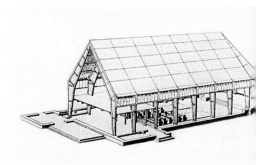

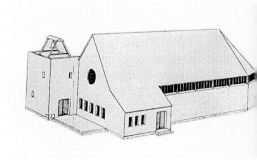

Otto Bartning
Notkirche Typ B / type B
emergency church
1947–1949

Horst Schwebel

An Aversion to Grand Gestures
Theological and Liturgical Perspectives on Protestant
Church Architecture

The focus on Germany in any exploration of Protestant church
architecture in the second half of the 20th century is linked
to the destruction after the Second World War, whose scale has
become almost unimaginable. This 'ground-zero' situation contained an opportunity for a new beginning. To begin with
people congregated in barracks and temporary buildings. Otto
Bartning's 48 emergency churches (1947– 49) gained some
fame. Bartning had designed four types of temporary church.
Simple timber girders topped by a roof structure were erected
with the help of the Foundation of the World Council of
Churches and above all American church organisations; it was
then left to each community to fill in the walls — after all,
there was no lack of rubble. Bartning spoke of the 'valid form
born from the power of need'.[1]

The Role of Congresses on Church Architecture

In 1947, Gerhard Kunze issued the invitation to the first Congress on Church Architecture in Hanover, followed by the
Protestant Congress on Church Architecture in 1948 led by the
new chairman Oskar Söhngen in Berlin and then 23 further
congresses culminating in Leipzig in 2002. The evolution of
church architecture is chronicled in the published lectures and
discussions at the congresses and the journal *Kunst und Kirche*,
founded in 1957. In 1951, the Protestant Congress on Church
Architecture ratified the Rummelsberg Programme.[2] The rejection of a so-called *Christian* style of building is an important
element of the programme. It is in opposition to the Eisenach
Regulation which states: 'The dignity of Christian church
architecture lies in perpetuating one of the historically evolved
Christian building styles; the recommendation is to favour the
basic form of the elongated rectangle, especially in the so-called
Germanic (Gothic) style in addition to the ancient Christian
basilica and the so-called Romanesque (early Gothic) style'.[3]

The Rummelsberg Programme overthrew the validity of this
kind of stylistic preference, stating that each era must discover
its own particular formal expression of Christian content. The
internal orientation of the church building must be centred
on the mass: 'The building or space dedicated to celebrating the
mass must be distinct according to its purpose from buildings
or spaces that serve for profane tasks. At the same time, however,
it [the sacred space] explodes the boundaries of rational definition of purpose since its form must at the same time be an allegory of the events that take place within and among the community gathered to celebrate mass: namely, the encounter with
the benevolent presence of God in word and sacrament'. This
creates a clear distinction between sacred and exclusively secular
spaces. With regard to the mass, the delegates returned to the
idea initially formulated by Cornelius Gurlit at the Second Congress on Church Architecture in Dresden (1906) of church architecture as 'built liturgy'. Otto Bartning demanded that the
architectonic power of the space should correspond to the power
of the liturgy. The space itself, according to the vision formulated
at Rummelsberg in 1951, was marked by a clear orientation
toward an altar positioned on a stage and a pulpit to one side of
this stage for delivering the sermon. The programme also expressed a preference for natural materials and a rejection of artificial
materials, among them asbestos cement, plywood and concrete.

Having passed through a period of making do with provisional
solutions, there was a desire to create true church buildings with

Otto Bartning
Notkirche Typ B / type B
emergency church
1947–1949

liturgische Bewegung in Gestalt der aus der Berneuchner Bewegung hervorgegangenen Michaelsbruderschaft. Ihr Ziel war die Schaffung einer symbolisch-liturgischen Kultur mit einer Orientierung an der katholischen Messfeier. Zu den Forderungen gehört die Ostung des Kirchenraums wie auch der räumlich hervorgehobene Altar als »Grenzstein der irdischen Welt« (Karl Bernhard Ritter); dahinter ist der Bereich der Eschatologie, des wiederkommenden Christus.[4] Für die Taufe ist ein eigener Taufort (Taufkapelle) am Eingang des Kirchenraums vorgesehen, so dass der Gläubige symbolisch den Weg von der Taufe zum Altar als Grenze zur Ewigkeit geht. Der Idealtyp dieses Modells ist in St. Michael in Nienburg (1957) von Peter Hübotter verwirklicht. Obgleich die Michaelsbruderschaft in Bezug auf die Innenraumgestaltung des evangelischen Kirchenraums großen Einfluss hatte, vermochte sich das Konzept, die Taufe im Eingangsbereich anzusiedeln, nicht durchzusetzen. Da man in den Agendenreformen die Taufe als gemeindliche Kasualhandlung aufwertete und in den Hauptgottesdienst aufnahm, wurde der Taufstein neben Altar und Kanzel zum dritten Prinzipalstück, das in die Sichtweite des Gottesdienstbesuchers tritt. In der Johanneskirche in Taufkirchen von Andreas Olaf Gulbransson steht der Taufstein sogar im Zentrum des Raumes, fächerförmig umgeben von drei Bankblöcken und in Korrespondenz zur Altar-Kanzel-Zone.

Bis auf wenige Ausnahmen – etwa die Kirchen von Gulbransson – sind evangelische Kirchen der fünfziger Jahre auf die Prinzipalstücke Altar, Kanzel, Taufe orientierte, längs gerichtete Räume. Sofern man nicht an der reformierten Bildlosigkeit festhält, gibt es Kruzifixe, Glasfenster, Paramente mit christlicher Symbolik. Während in der europäischen Kunstszene die abstrakte Malerei auf dem Vormarsch ist, bleiben die Glasfenster und die vereinzelten Deckenmalereien bibelbezogen. Helle, klare Flächen und der Verzicht auf weiteres Ornament lassen die Räume puristisch erscheinen. In den sechziger Jahren werden die Grundrisse reicher, wenn man sich von den Möglichkeiten der Geometrie anregen lässt, und der Turm steht meist frei neben dem Kirchenschiff.

Kirche und Kunst

Ein wichtiger Impuls, der den Kirchenbau und die kirchliche Kunst nachhaltig veränderte, ging von Frankreich aus. Dort hatte der Dominikanerpater Alain Couturier prominente Künstler aufgefordert, in der Kirche tätig zu werden. Matisse, Chagall, Rouault, Bonnard und andere waren seinem Ruf gefolgt. In der Kirche Sacré Cœur in Audincourt hatte Fernand Léger ein umlaufendes Glasband aus Betonglas geschaffen, Bazaine hatte den Zylinder einer Taufkapelle ebenfalls mit Betonglas umhüllt, von Manessier kann man in der Dorfkirche von Les Bréseux (Jura) abstrakte Glasfenster bewundern. Für Künstler und Architekten wurden diese nahe an der deutschen Grenze gelegenen Orte zu ›Wallfahrtsorten‹. Dies betraf das Betonglas, dessen Leuchtkraft einen jeglichen Raum in ein Lichterlebnis zu verwandeln vermochte, ebenso wie die abstrakte Malerei, die – vor allem in ihrer geometrischen Spielart – mit der Architektur korrespondiert, und vor allem den Beton, einen Baustoff, mit dem sich auch plastisch formen ließ. In der Christuskirche in Bochum und bei anderen Kirchen von Dieter Oesterlen schuf Helmut Lander expressiv-dynamische Betonglaswände mit den Farben Gelb, Weiß, Blau. In der Kaiser-Wilhelm-Gedächtniskirche in Berlin von Egon Eiermann

Peter Hübotter, Bert Ledeboer,
Rolf Romero
St. Michael / St Michael
Nienburg, 1957

Andreas Olaf Gulbransson
Johanneskirche
Taufkirchen, 1956

modern interiors. The design of the interior was greatly influenced, among other things, by the liturgical movement initiated by the Michaelsbruderschaft (Brotherhood of St Michael) — a splinter group from the Berneuchner movement. The chief goal of the group was to create a symbolic liturgical culture that would echo the traditional Catholic mass. The stipulations called for an east-facing sanctuary and an altar that would be spatially emphasised as a 'stone marking the boundary to the earthly world' (Karl Bernhard Ritter); beyond this boundary lay the eschatological sphere of Christ Incarnate.[4] A separate baptismal zone (baptismal chapel) was set aside near the entrance for the baptismal sacrament, creating a symbolic path for the faithful from the baptismal font to the altar, the latter representing the threshold to eternity. This model was ideally realised at St Michael in Nienburg (1957) by Peter Hübotter. Although the Brotherhood of St Michael exerted tremendous influence on the interior design of Protestant churches, the concept of placing the baptismal font at the entrance did not take hold. In the agenda reforms, baptism had been elevated to the status of a communal occasional act integrated into the mass, thereby making the baptismal font the third principal element in the congregation's field of vision in addition to altar and pulpit. In Andreas Olaf Gulbransson's Johanneskirche in Taufkirchen, the baptismal font occupies the very centre of the space, surrounded as if by an unfurling fan by three blocks of pews and establishing an immediate correspondence to the zone formed by the altar and the pulpit.

With few exceptions — for example, Gulbransson's churches — most Protestant churches of the 1950s are longitudinal spaces that are clearly oriented toward the principal elements of altar, pulpit and baptismal font. The absence of imagery in keeping with the reform movement is only relieved here and there with crosses, stained glass windows and paraments (vestments or tapestries) decorated with Christian symbols. While abstract painting conquered the European art scene, the stained glass windows and isolated ceiling murals remained steeped in biblical imagery. Bright, clear areas and the absence of further ornamentation give these spaces a purist air. In the 1960s the plans became more varied whenever architects found inspiration in the abundance of geometry, and the bell tower was generally realised as a detached structure.

Church and Art

An important impulse, which would have a lasting influence on church architecture and sacred art, originated in France, where the Dominican priest Alain Couturier had invited prominent artists to create works for the church. Matisse, Chagall, Rouault, Bonnard and others answered his call. Fernand Léger created a continuous ribbon of structural glass for the Sacré Cœur in Audincourt; Bazaine, too, enveloped the cylinder of a baptismal chapel in structural glass; and visitors to the village church at Les Bréseux (in the Jura Mountains) can still admire abstract stained glass windows by Manessier. For artists and architects, these sites, so close to the German border, became veritable 'pilgrimage sites'. This was due to the use of structural glass, whose luminous intensity transformed every space into an experience of light, and also in response to the abstract art, which corresponded to the architecture especially in instances where it toyed with geometry, and above all in admiration of concrete, a building material that opened possibilities for sculp-

Dieter Oesterlen
Christuskirche / Christ church
Bochum, 1960
Glasfenster / stained-glass windows
von / by Helmut Lander

wurde das Oktogon mit einem Vorhang aus Betonformsteinen ummantelt, in die kleinteilige Betonglasteile auf dem Grundton Blau eingelegt sind. Im Kirchenraum, im Inneren des Oktogons, ist der Besucher allseitig von blauem Licht umgeben, in dem violette, rote, gelbe und grüne Farbnester leuchten.

Die Möglichkeit, mit Beton plastische Körper zu formen, wurde auch von evangelischen Baumeistern – trotz des Verdikts von Rummelsberg – wahrgenommen. Helmut Striffler schuf mit der Versöhnungskirche auf dem ehemaligen KZ-Gelände in Dachau ein eindrucksvolles Raumgebilde, bei dem er den rechten Winkel – typisch für die KZ-Architektur – bewusst vermied. Lothar Kallmeyer sprach von »neuer Plastizität« und davon, »dass die Architektur derzeit eine vorher nicht ausgetragene Stilform nachholt: nämlich den Expressionismus«.[5]

Europäische Impulse

Finnland nimmt in der Kirchenarchitektur des 20. Jahrhunderts einen Spitzenplatz ein. Der wichtigste Vertreter ist Alvar Aalto mit seiner Organik, den Schalendächern und die jeden Sonnenstrahl einfangende Lichtführung. Die Kapelle in Otaniemi von Kaija und Heikki Siren (1957) war das erste Kirchengebäude mit einer Altarwand aus Glas, die den Blick über ein frei stehendes Kreuz hinweg in den Wald einräumte. Diese Aussicht nach draußen wurde in Berlin von Peter Lehrecke bei der Kirche Zur Heimat und von Paul Baumgarten bei der Kirche am Lietzensee übernommen. Bei der Pfingstbergkirche von Carlfried Mutschler in Mannheim sind sogar alle vier Wände in Glas aufgelöst. In Finnland ist mit dem Blick in die Natur eine Art Schöpfungstheologie verbunden, wobei auch Pflanzen und Bäume in den Kirchenraum einbezogen werden. Dass man die Tempelkirche in Helsinki in einen ›Steinbruch‹ eingrub, entspricht ebenfalls dem theologisch begründeten Schöpfungsbezug.

Zu den Bauten der reformierten Kirche war im Rummelsberger Programm zu lesen: »Der Versammlungsraum soll die einfache und schlichte Gestalt der ›nach Gottes Wort reformierten‹ Gemeinde sein. Seine Schönheit liegt nicht im Schmuck, sondern im reinen Verhältnis der Maße, des Lichtes und der Tönung.«[6] Eine Gleichnishaftigkeit des Raums zum gottesdienstlichen Geschehen wird von dem reformierten Architekten und Theoretiker Otto Senn abgelehnt.[7] Seine Modellentwürfe für die christliche Gemeinde wurden nur zum Teil verwirklicht. In der Thomaskirche in Basel (1956) sind fünf Bankblöcke – der fünf Seiten des Pentagons – auf den fast zentral stehenden Tisch und die Kanzel ausgerichtet. Auch die um Tisch und Kanzel im Winkel angeordneten Bankreihen der Tituskirche von Benedikt Huber (1964) zeigen ein Gemeinschaftsmodell, das sich gegenüber dem auf den Altarbezirk ausgerichteten Raum positiv abhebt. Senn knüpft bewusst an die Zentralraumidee an, an den reformierten ›Tempel‹ von Lyon (1567), an die Idealentwürfe von Leonhardt Christoph Sturm (1712) und vor allem an Bartnings Sternkirche (1922).

In den Niederlanden konnte der Architekt Karel L. Sijmons zusammen mit dem Theologen W. G. Overbosch neue Raumgedanken verwirklichen. Schon in der Adventskirche in Den Haag (1957) hatte Sijmons den Predigtraum klar vom Abendmahlsraum, in dem an Tischen das Mahl gefeiert wird, abgetrennt. Die Thomaskirche in Amsterdam-Süd (1967) stellt ein geschachteltes Raumgefüge mit deutlicher Trennung der ver-

Egon Eiermann
Kaiser-Wilhelm-Gedächtniskirche
Kaiser Wilhelm Memorial church
Berlin, 1963

Peter Lehrecke
Kirche zur Heimat
'Zur Heimat' church
Berlin, 1957

Carlfried Mutschler
Pfingstbergkirche
Pfingstberg church
Mannheim, 1962

tural form. Helmut Lander created expressive, dynamic structural glass walls in yellow, white and blue for the Christuskirche in Bochum and for other churches designed by Dieter Oesterlen. In Egon Eiermann's Kaiser Wilhelm Memorial church in Berlin the octagon was wrapped in a curtain of concrete mould blocks set into small structural glass components on a blue background. In the church interior, inside the octagon, visitors are surrounded by blue light on all sides, enlivened with violet, yellow and green colour accents.

Protestant architects also seized upon the opportunity of creating sculptural forms with concrete — despite the interdiction in the Rummelsberg Programme. With the Church of Reconciliation (Versöhnungskirche) on the former concentration camp site at Dachau, Helmut Striffler achieved an impressive spatial construct that deliberately avoids the use of the right angle, so typical of concentration camp architecture. Lothar Kallmeyer spoke of a 'new plasticity' and of the fact that 'architecture is catching up with a previously unexplored style — Expressionism'.[5]

Helmut Striffler
Versöhnungskirche
Church of Reconciliation
Dachau, 1967

European Impulses

Finland is a leader in 20th-century church architecture, represented first and foremost by Alvar Aalto who was noted for his organic approach, his shell roofs and his lighting strategies that capture each and every ray of sun. The chapel in Otaniemi by Kaija and Heikki Siren (1957) was the first church building to feature a fully transparent altar wall offering a view past a free-standing cross into the forest beyond. This view of the outside was adopted in Berlin by Peter Lehrecke in the church Zur Heimat and by Paul Baumgarten in the Church on the Lietzensee. Carlfried Mutschler even dissolved all four walls into glass in his design for the Pfingstberg church in Mannheim. In Finland, the view of and into nature is linked to a kind of Creation theology that introduces plants and trees in the church interior. The decision to carve the Temple church in Helsinki out of a 'quarry' also speaks of a reference to creation founded in theology.

The Rummelsberg Programme offered the following comments on the buildings of the reformed church: 'The communal space should be the plain and simple expression of the community "reformed in the image of God's Word". Its beauty does not lie in ornamentation but in the pure relationship of dimension, light and colour'.[6] The reformed architect and theoretician Otto Senn rejected the idea of interpreting the physical space as a visual allegory of the spiritual act of celebrating the mass.[7] His model designs for the Christian community were only partially realised. In the St Thomas church in Basel (1956), five blocks of pews — the five sides of a pentagon — are oriented toward the almost central altar and the pulpit. And the pews surrounding the altar and pulpit in the St Titus church by Benedikt Huber (1964) represent yet another communitarian model of a positive alternative to the altar-focussed space. Senn establishes a deliberate link to the idea of the centralised space, to the reformed 'temples' of Lyon (1567), the idealised designs by Leonhardt Christoph Sturm (1712) and above all Bartning's Sternkirche (1922).

In the Netherlands, the architect Karel L. Sijmons joined forces with the theologian W. G. Overbosch to realise new spatial

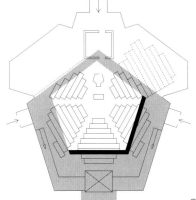

Otto H. Senn
Wettbewerbsentwurf
competition entry
Thomaskirche / St Thomas
Basel, 1955

schiedenen Funktionen dar. Von dem mehrfach gewinkelten Predigtraum schreitet man in einer Prozession in den angrenzenden Abendmahlsraum, um dort stehend das Mahl in Empfang zu nehmen. Es handelt sich um einen Betonbau mit vielen anregenden ›Raumbildern‹. Aus Holland kam auch der Agora-Gedanke in die Bundesrepublik. Die bei den neuen Stadtgründungen des Flevoland-Polders geschaffenen überdachten ›Marktplätze‹ (die ›Agoren‹ in Dronten und Lelystadt) gewannen symbolische Funktion. Kirche als Agora bedeutet, dass die Kirche in den neu gebauten Stadtvierteln ein Raumangebot für zwischenmenschliche Kommunikation anbietet, ein Stück ›Freiraum‹ in einer technokratisch verwalteten Welt.[8]

Kirchliche Gemeindezentren

Mitte der sechziger Jahre verlagerte sich die Entwicklung auf das Gemeindezentrum. Stand bis dahin der Kirchenbau im Mittelpunkt des Interesses, so wird beim Begriff ›Gemeindezentrum‹ deutlich, dass kirchliches Handeln vielgestaltig ist und die gottesdienstliche Funktion lediglich *eine* unter mehreren Formen kirchlicher Präsenz darstellt. Mit diesem Programm verbunden war der Abbau von ›Schwellenangst‹, die Betonung des Foyers als Einladung an alle, die Bereitstellung vielfach zu nutzender Räume für mannigfache Kommunikation und damit die Abkehr von einer betont kirchlichen Präsentationsweise. Dem zuletzt genannten Grund sind als erstes die Türme zum Opfer gefallen. Umstritten blieb, inwieweit der dem Gottesdienst vorbehaltene Raum sich dem Stil des Gemeindezentrums anpassen oder ob er ein eigenes, im traditionellen Sinn ›kirchliches Gepräge‹ beibehalten solle. Gutes Beispiel für eine konsequente Lösung ist das Gemeindezentrum St. Paulus in Burgdorf von Paul Posenenske (1973). Es handelt sich um ein Gemeindezentrum unter einem Dach, dessen Mittelpunkt ein zentraler, den übrigen Räumen gegenüber überhöhter Raum ist. Für einen großen Gottesdienst lassen sich alle Räume zusammenschließen, durch ein Schiebewandsystem aber auch in sieben Bereiche gliedern, die zugleich miteinander verbunden werden können. Jeder Raum ist mit dem angrenzenden kombinierbar. Das trifft auch auf den zentralen, für den Gottesdienst vorgesehenen Raum zu, dessen Prinzipalstücke (Altar, Kanzel, Taufe) verändert aufgestellt oder weggenommen werden können. Eine derartige multifunktionale Nutzung birgt freilich auch Probleme. Das Institut für Kirchenbau und kirchliche Kunst der Gegenwart an der Marburger Universität konnte in einer mehrjährigen Untersuchung[9] von 17 Gemeindezentren mit Mehrzweckraum feststellen, dass sich in allen Gemeindezentren die Tendenz bemerkbar machte, den zentralen Mehrzweckraum auf *eine* Funktion – nämlich den sonntäglichen Gottesdienst – zu reduzieren und den Raum formal zu ›resakralisieren‹.

Der Verzicht auf Selbstdarstellung wurde theologisch mit dem »Kirche-Sein für andere« begründet, wobei man für die wertneutrale Erscheinung der Kirche und die Mobilität von Gestühl und Prinzipalstücken ethisch argumentierte. Auf der Kirchbautagung in Bad Boll (1965) ging es einmal um die Erweiterung des Gottesdienstbegriffs im Anschluss an Röm 12,1.2 (ff) und 1. Petr 2,8 – 3,9. Der Begriff ›Gottesdienst‹ wurde mit dem Begriff ›Alltag‹ eng verbunden, so Eduard Schweizer: »Nichts ist im Neuen Testament heilig im Gegensatz zu einem profanen Bezirk beziehungsweise besser gesagt, alles ist heilig, nichts ist mehr profan, weil Gott die Welt gehört und weil die Welt der Ort ist, an dem man Gott preisen und Gott Dank erweisen soll.«[10]

Karel L. Sijmons
Thomaskirche / St Thomas
Amsterdam, 1966

concepts. As early as 1957, Sijmons had created a clear separation between preaching area and sacrament area in the Advent church in The Hague, where the sacrament is celebrated at communal tables. The St Thomas church in south Amsterdam (1967) is a complex, compartmentalised spatial construct with clear, functional divisions. From the sermon area with multiple angles, the congregation passes through a processional transition into the adjacent sacrament area where they stand to receive the sacrament. This is a concrete structure with many animating 'spatial images'. The idea of the *agora* also came to Germany from Holland. The roofed 'market squares' (the *agoras* in Dronten and Lelystadt) built in the process of new town developments in Flevoland-Polders assumed a symbolic function. The church as an *agora* signifies that the church provides a space for interpersonal communication in newly developed urban districts, a 'free space' in a world dominated by technocracy.[8]

Community Centres

In the mid-1960s, the development shifted toward community centres. Where church architecture had been the centre of focus, the shift toward creating a 'centre for the community' was a clear expression of the variety of ecclesiastic activity and that the mass was but *one* among many forms of ecclesiastical presence. This approach also aimed at overcoming the 'threshold fear', emphasising the foyer as an open invitation to all, offering spaces amenable to a variety of uses for a wide range of communication and hence abandoning the emphatically ecclesiastical manner of presentation. The bell towers were the first item to be eliminated as a reflection of this new 'worldly' presentation. The issue of how much the sanctuary itself should be adapted to the style of the community centre or whether it should preserve its own 'ecclesiastical character' in the traditional sense, remained contentious. The community centre of St Paul in Burgdorf by Paul Posenenske (1973) offers a good example of a rigorous solution. The structure is a community centre under one roof, whose focal point is a central space elevated from the surrounding rooms. All rooms can be joined into a single large space for the purpose of celebrating a large service by means of a system of sliding walls; conversely, the interior can also be divided into seven areas that are nevertheless interconnected. Each room can be combined with the adjacent room. This also applies to the central room, the actual 'sanctuary' whose principal elements (altar, pulpit and baptismal font) can be moved to different positions or even removed altogether. Of course, a multi-functional use of this kind also presents some problems. The Institute for Church Architecture and Contemporary Ecclesiastic Art at the University of Marburg carried out a study over several years[9] at 17 community centres with multi-purpose spaces, and discovered a common tendency in all centres to reducing the central multifunctional space to *one* function — Sunday mass — thus formally 'resanctifying' the space.

The voluntary relinquishment of self-representation was based theologically on the intent of 'being a church for others', with ethical arguments being put forth to justify the neutral appearance of the church building and the mobility of the seating arrangements and of the principal elements. The agenda of the Congress on Church Architecture in Bad Boll (1965) focussed on two principal issues. Firstly, the expansion of the concept of the mass in the sense of Romans 12, 1.2 ff. and 1 Peter, 2.8–3.9, wherein the term 'mass' was closely linked to the term

Paul Posenenske
Paulusgemeinde / community centre of St Paul
Burgdorf, 1973
Grundrisse mit Nutzungsvarianten
Floor plan with different uses

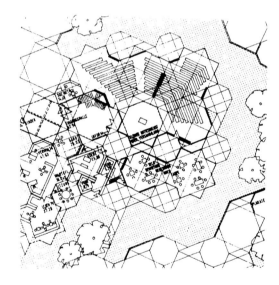

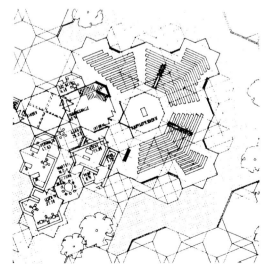

Die zweite Argumentationsreihe ging vom Auftrag als »Teilnahme an der Mission Gottes« als »dienende Präsenz (serving presence)« aus, Werner Simpfendörfer forderte das »bauliche Provisorium«. Der Begriff ›Gottesdienst‹ wird in Richtung Welt erweitert, ohne dass er in seiner Tiefendimension erschlossen würde. Das Warum und Wozu des Dienstes wird von den jeweiligen Bedürfnissen, Nöten und Erwartungshaltungen der Menschen abgeleitet. Funktionsfähige Räume zu bauen, um den vielfältigen Anforderungen zu genügen, war die Aufgabe, der Raum wurde als ›Instrument‹ begriffen. Auf dem Kirchbautag in Darmstadt (1969), mitten in den Studentenunruhen, forderte die Evangelische Jugend das »Ende des Kirchenbaus« zugunsten der Verwendung der finanziellen Mittel für Sozialleistungen und für die Dritte Welt.[11]

Die Herausforderung solcher Gedanken, deren ethischer Ernst nach wie vor unbestritten ist, wirkte sich auf das Schaffen von Räumen und das künstlerische Gestalten ausgesprochen negativ aus. Kreativität stand unter dem Verdacht des Verrats an sozialer Verantwortung für das Ganze. Der Mehrzweckraum-Gedanke scheiterte nicht an mangelnder theologischer Reflexion, sondern an einer falschen Einschätzung anthropologischer Gegebenheiten. Bei dem Gebäude, das als Kirche angesprochen werden soll, in dem man Gottesdienst feiert und betet, besteht offensichtlich ein Bedürfnis nach Identifikation, das sich durch einen Mehrzweckraum nicht befriedigen lässt.

Heutige Aufgaben

Seit den achtziger Jahren hat sich das Problem dahin gehend verlagert, dass nicht mehr neue Kirchen im Zentrum des Interesses stehen, sondern die Frage, wie die überkommene Bausubstanz genutzt und erhalten werden kann. Die Abwanderung der Bevölkerung in die Randbezirke reduzierte die Zahl der innerstädtischen Gemeindeglieder in drastischer Weise, während der Gebäudebestand gleich blieb. In Frankfurt am Main ist die Zahl der Evangelischen von 400 000 Personen am Anfang der sechziger Jahre bis auf 155 000 geschrumpft. Berechnungen haben ergeben, dass sich die Kirche in Frankfurt von 40 Prozent ihres Baubestandes trennen müsste. Da man aber eher ein Gemeindehaus als eine Kirche aufgibt, müssten über den Gottesdienst hinausgehende gemeindliche Funktionen in die bisherige Kirche verlagert werden. Bei der Heilig-Kreuz-Kirche in Berlin wurde beispielhaft demonstriert, wie durch räumliche Veränderungen und Einbauten auf verschiedenen Ebenen ein attraktives Gemeindezentrum geschaffen werden kann. In den ostdeutschen Landeskirchen ist der Bestand an Bauten schwerlich zu halten. In Mecklenburg sind über 40 Kirchen akut bedroht. In der Kirchenprovinz Sachsen entfallen auf knapp 600 000 Evangelische mehr als 2 200 historische Kirchen.

Dem Problem zu großer und zum Teil leer stehender Kirchen begegnet man in allen europäischen Großstädten. Sofern es gelingt, eine Kirche zur Ausstellungs- oder Konzertkirche umzuwidmen, wird man dies begrüßen. Aus den Niederlanden und aus Großbritannien sind allerdings Umwidmungen bekannt, die den Kirchencharakter des Gebäudes nicht mehr erkennen lassen: die Kirche als Restaurant, Diskothek, Wohnhaus, Kaufhaus, Parkhaus, Hotel, Tanzstudio, Radiostation.

Obwohl die Bauetats der Landeskirchen durch die Erhaltung der Substanz belastet sind, gibt es auch Neubauten. Im ländli-

Architekten am Spreewaldplatz
Heilig-Kreuz-Kirche, Umbau
Church of the Holy Cross, reconstruction
Berlin, 1995

'everyday'. As Eduard Schweizer put it: 'There is nothing in the New Testament that is holy or sacred in contrast to the realm of the profane, or, more precisely, everything is sacred, nothing is profane because the world belongs to God and because the world is the place where we praise and give thanks to God'.[10]

The second argument was based on the challenge of 'participating in God's mission as a serving presence', interpreted by Werner Simpfendörfer as a challenge to create a 'provisional architecture'. The term 'service' [in German: *Gottesdienst*, lit. 'service of God'] is expanded in a worldly sense without truly exploring the full depth of its meaning. The whys and wherefores of the service are based on the relevant needs, yearnings and expectations of human beings. The task was to build functional spaces that would answer to the wide variety of requirements; the space was understood as an 'instrument'. At the Congress on Church Architecture in Darmstadt (1969), in the midst of student unrest, the Protestant Youth Council called for an 'end to church architecture' in order to divert those funds earmarked for building into social services and aid for the Third World.[11]

The challenge posed by these ideas, whose ethical integrity remains uncontested, had a powerful negative impact on the creation of spaces and on artistic invention. Creativity had become suspect as undermining social responsibility for all. The idea of the multi-purpose space did not fail owing to a lack of theological reflection, but as a result of misjudging anthropological realities. A building that is defined as a church, where people go to celebrate mass and to pray, obviously gives rise to a need for identification, which cannot be satisfied by a multi-purpose space.

Current Tasks

Since the 1980s the challenge has shifted yet again, in that the focus is no longer on new churches but on utilising and preserving existing, traditional or historical structures. As populations shifted toward the periphery, inner-city communities dwindled drastically while the existing building substance remained the same. In Frankfurt am Main, the number of Protestants has shrunk from 400,000 at the beginning of the 1960s to 155,000. Calculations suggest that the Church administration should let go of some forty per cent of its current buildings in Frankfurt. However, since it is much preferable to sell a community building than a church, community functions that go beyond celebrating the mass would have to be incorporated into hitherto exclusively ecclesiastical buildings. The conversion of the Church of the Holy Cross (Heilig-Kreuz) in Berlin is an ideal example of how spatial alterations and internal additions on various levels can be used to create an attractive community centre. The inventory of existing church buildings is especially threatened in the former East German states. Over forty churches are at acute risk in Mecklenburg alone. And the church district of Saxony boasts over 2,200 historic churches for a Protestant community of no more than 600,000.

The problem of churches that are too large or vacant is a reality in all major European cities. Where churches can be successfully converted into exhibition or concert halls, this may be a reality to be embraced. However, some conversions in the Netherlands and in Great Britain have virtually obliterated the church char-

Meinhard von Gerkan
Christus-Pavillon
Hannover / Hanover, Expo 2000
Eingang / entrance

chen Raum wurden Kirchen vergrößert und durch Gemeindesäle und Gruppenräume ergänzt. In ehemals katholischen
Gebieten, in denen der Anteil der Evangelischen gestiegen ist,
wurden neue Kirchen gebaut. Auch Betriebsansiedlungen,
der Bau eines Flughafens oder die Ansiedlung von Russland-
deutschen machten Kirchenneubauten erforderlich. Kommt es
dazu, wollen die Gemeinden *richtige* Kirchen haben und keine
Mehrzweckräume. Die Prinzipalstücke – Altar, Kanzel, Taufe –
werden wieder fixiert, statt losem Gestühl werden Bänke be-
vorzugt. Anstelle des lang gestreckten Rechtecks findet man oft
Grundrissformen, welche die Gemeinde um eine reale oder
gedachte Mitte kreisen lassen. Ein Beispiel dafür ist die Segenskirche in Aschheim bei München von Friedrich Kurrent (1996).
Neue Bauaufgaben sind auch Kapellen in Krankenhäusern,
Haftanstalten, Friedhöfen oder an Autobahnen.

Zu den wichtigsten Beiträgen heutigen kirchlichen Bauens gehört der Christuspavillon von Meinhard von Gerkan auf der
Expo 2000 in Hannover. Der Besucher wurde an der Plaza über
ein Gewässer, ein Atrium und einen Kreuzgang in einen würfel-
förmigen Raum geführt, der über weiße Marmorwände und
neun Lichtluken – an der Verbindung der Stahlsäulen mit dem
Dach – sein Licht empfängt. Dieser Raum, dem Expo-Betrieb
bewusst entgegen gestellt, strahlte Stille und Geborgenheit aus
und erwies sich gleichwohl als Ort von Gottesdienst und Kommunikation. Eine Krypta mit Sandfußboden und Meditations-
bild ermöglichte private Andacht und innere Einkehr. Ob die
jetzige Nachnutzung im Kloster Volkenroda (Thüringen) eine
sinnvolle Entscheidung war, wird sich noch erweisen müssen.

Im Unterschied zum katholischen Sakralbau ist der evangelische
Kirchenbau weniger spektakulär. Das liegt an einer gewissen
Scheu vor dem imperialen Gestus, an der Betonung der *theo-
logia crucis* vor der *theologia gloriae*. Für einige sind Bartnings
Notkirchen das heimliche protestantische Ideal geblieben.
Angesichts der Diskussion über den Mehrzweckraum konnte
man aber feststellen, wie ernst es der Kirche war, bis hin zur
Preisgabe ihres Kirche-Seins. Um so stärker ist seitdem das Bedürf-
nis nach einem künstlerisch gestalteten Raum, einem Ort
der gottesdienstlichen Feier, der Stille und der Identifikation.

1
Zit.: Stephan Hirzel, Gespräch mit Otto Bartning, *Die Stahlkirche und
die Notkirchen-Aktion,* in: *Kunst und Kirche* 1 (1958), S. 26.
2
Evangelische Kirchbautagung Rummelsberg, 1951, Hg. Arbeitsausschuss
des Evangelischen Kirchbautags, Berlin 1951, S. 159–164.
3
Gerhard Langmaack, *Evangelischer Kirchenbau im 19. und 20. Jahrhundert,* Kassel 1971, S. 272.
4
Karl Bernhard Ritter, *Kirchenbau als Symbol,* in: *Kunst und Kirche*
1 (1960), S. 3–11.
5
Lothar Kallmeyer, *Neue Tendenzen im Kirchenbau,* in: *Tradition und
Aufbruch im evangelischen Kirchenbau.* Evangelische Kirchbautagung in
Hannover 1966, Hamburg 1967, S. 102–116, hier S. 115.
6
Rummelsberger Programm (s. Anm. 2), S. 163.
7
Otto Senn, *Evangelischer Kirchenbau im ökumenischen Kontext. Identität
und Variabilität – Tradition und Freiheit,* Basel–Boston–Stuttgart 1983.
8
H. R. Blankesteijn, *Kirche in der Mitte. Versuche in den Niederlanden,*
in: *Kunst und Kirche* 1 (1969), S. 2–13.
9
Martin Görbing, Hans Graß, Horst Schwebel, *Planen–Bauen–Nutzen.
Erfahrungen mit Gemeindezentren,* Giessen 1981.
10
Görbing, Graß, Schwebel (s. Anm. 9), S. 132 f., auch folgende Zitate.
11
Bauen für die Gemeinde von morgen. Evangelische Kirchbautagung in
Darmstadt 1969, Hamburg 1969, S. 157f.

acter of the building: the church has become restaurant, discotheque, housing project, department store, hotel, dance studio or radio station.

Although the building budgets of the state churches are weighed down by the burden of preserving existing structures, there are some new building projects. In rural areas, churches have been enlarged and expanded with the addition of community halls and group rooms. In formerly Catholic regions, where the number of Protestants has grown, new churches have been erected. Corporate housing schemes, the construction of a new airport or settlement of Russian Germans have also contributed to the need for new church buildings. Whenever this is the case, the communities in question want to have *real* churches, not multi-purpose spaces. The principal elements — altar, pulpit and baptismal font — are once again fixed in place, solid pews are preferred to folding chairs. The elongated rectangle is often abandoned in favour of ground plans that allow the community to form a circle around a real or imagined centre, for example in the Segenskirche in Aschheim near Munich, designed by Friedrich Kurrent (1996). Chapels in hospitals, penitentiary institutions and cemeteries or along highways also represent new building tasks.

One of the most important contributions to contemporary church architecture was the Christus-Pavillon by Meinhard von Gerkan for Expo 2000 in Hanover. Visitors were led from the plaza across a water feature, an atrium and a cloister into a cube-shaped room lit by white marble walls and nine skylights at the junction of steel columns and roof. In deliberate contrast to the hustle and bustle of the World's Fair, this room exuded an air of tranquillity and shelter — a place for worship and for communication. A crypt with a sand floor and a meditation image allowed for private prayer and contemplation. Whether the current use of the pavilion as part of the monastery at Volkenroda (Thuringia) was a sensible decision remains to be seen.

Protestant sacred buildings are less spectacular than their Catholic counterparts. This is borne out of a certain aversion to grand gestures, an emphasis on the *theologia crucis* rather than the *theologia gloriae*. Some continue to regard Bartning's emergency churches as the secret ideal of Protestant churches. The debate on the multi-purpose room, however, demonstrated the seriousness of the Church in realising its new goals, even to the point of abandoning its being-as-church. Ever since, the desire for an artistically created space, for a site dedicated to celebrating the mass, to silence and identification, has grown all the more.

Friedrich Kurrent
Segenskirche
Aschheim, 1996
Linke Seite: Dachkonstruktion
Left: roof construction

1
Stephan Hirzel in conversation with Otto Bartning, 'Die Stahlkirche und die Notkirchen-Aktion' in *Kunst und Kirche* 1 (1958), p. 26.
2
Protestant Congress on Church Architecture, Rummelsberg, 1951, ed. Arbeitsausschuss des Evangelischen Kirchbautags, Berlin 1951, pp. 159–64.
3
Gerhard Langmaack, *Evangelischer Kirchenbau im 19. und 20. Jahrhundert*, Kassel 1971, p. 272.
4
Karl Bernhard Ritter, 'Kirchenbau als Symbol' in *Kunst und Kirche* 1 (1960), pp. 3–11.
5
Lothar Kallmeyer, 'Neue Tendenzen im Kirchenbau' in *Tradition und Aufbruch im evangelischen Kirchenbau. Evangelische Kirchenbautagung in Hannover 1966*, Hamburg 1967, pp. 102–16, p. 115.
6
Rummelsberg Programme (see note 2), p. 163.
7
Otto Senn, *Evangelischer Kirchenbau im ökumenischen Kontext. Identität und Variabilität – Tradition und Freiheit*, Basle–Boston–Stuttgart 1983.
8
H. R. Blankesteijn, 'Kirche in der Mitte. Versuche in den Niederlanden' in *Kunst und Kirche* 1 (1969), pp. 2–13.
9
Martin Görbing, Hans Graß, Horst Schwebel, *Planen–Bauen–Nutzen. Erfahrungen mit Gemeindezentren*, Giessen 1981.
10
Ibid., pp. 132ff., also for subsequent quotations.
11
Bauen für die Gemeinde von morgen. Evangelical conference on church architecture in Darmstadt 1969, Hamburg 1969, pp. 157ff.

Egon Eiermann

Matthäuskirche
Pforzheim, Deutschland
1953

St Matthew's
Pforzheim, Germany
1953

Egon Eiermann (1904–1970) zählte in der westdeutschen Nachkriegszeit zu den wenigen herausragenden Architekten, die zugleich über Einfluss verfügten. Auch international bekannt wurde er vor allem durch seine zumeist in präziser Stahlbauweise konstruierten öffentlichen Gebäude und Verwaltungsbauten. Bei seiner bedeutenden Kirche in Pforzheim verwendete er hingegen Beton, den er ansonsten wegen seiner beliebigen Formbarkeit als »charakterlos« ablehnte. Allerdings diente der Beton rein konstruktiven und nicht plastischen Zwecken. Die Pfarrkirche wurde in einer westlich gelegenen Gartenvorstadt auf einem nach Osten abfallenden Gelände errichtet. Im Sockel des Gebäudes befinden sich die von Süden her voll belichteten Gemeinderäume, darüber erhebt sich der in Wandfelder gegliederte Saalbau der Kirche. Die Felder zwischen den Stützen sind rasterartig mit Betonformsteinen aus Trümmersplit ausgefacht, in deren achteckigen Öffnungen verschiedenfarbige Gläser sitzen. Der Turm ist mit der Kirche verbunden.

During the post-war period in West Germany, Egon Eiermann (1904–70) was considered to be one of the few outstanding architects who also wielded some influence. On the international stage, too, he was famous primarily for his public and office buildings, mostly employing precise steel construction methods. In the case of his important church in Pforzheim, on the other hand, he used concrete, which he otherwise rejected as 'lacking character' because of its arbitrary malleability. Even so, the concrete here served purely constructional and not sculptural purposes. The parish church was erected in a garden suburb west of the town on a plot that slopes down towards the east. In the basement are the community rooms, fully exposed to light from the south, while above is the single-nave church, organised into wall sections. The sections between the supports are infilled in a grid-like manner with moulded concrete bricks made from crushed rubble in which there are octagonal apertures containing glass of different colours. The tower is connected to the church.

Die in verschiedenen Farben leuchtenden Gläser in den ziegelroten oder weißen Betonformsteinen verleihen dem längs gerichteten Kirchenraum eine eindrucksvolle Atmosphäre.

The multicoloured panes of glass gleaming in the brick-red or white moulded concrete bricks lend an impressive atmosphere to the longitudinally organised interior.

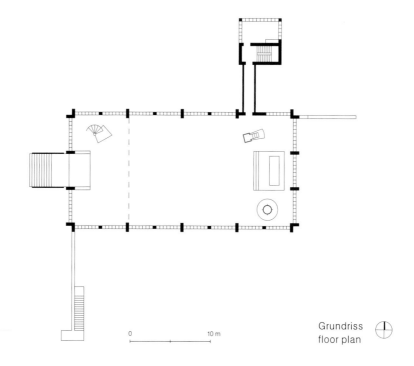

0   10 m

Grundriss
floor plan

Auf einer Tafel neben dem Eingang wird auf die Bedeutung des Gebäudes hingewiesen: »Neuartige Verwendung von Stahlbeton und Glas im Kirchenbau.«

The building's importance is indicated by a plaque next to the entrance shielded by a canopy: 'Innovative use of reinforced concrete and glass in a religious edifice'.

Hier wie auch später bei der Gedächtniskirche in Berlin [Seite 252] hat Eiermann für den modernen Industriebau typische Werkstoffe und Gestaltqualitäten auf neuartige Weise in den Sakralbau eingeführt. Deshalb wurde die Matthäuskirche seinerzeit als ›Fanal‹ verstanden. Das Skelett aus Stahlbeton trägt durch fünf Binder das flach geneigte Satteldach. So nüchtern der Außenbau erscheint, so poetisch vermittelt sich dem Besucher der Kirchenraum. Die über 2000 verschiedenfarbigen Gläser tauchen den Raum in ein diffus gefiltertes, mit dem Tageslauf der Sonne wechselndes Licht. Nachts strahlt das Licht in die Umgebung, »so dass der Bau wie ein leuchtender Schrein in der Landschaft steht« (Eiermann). Das vom Architekten bis hin zum losen Gestühl der Kirche durchgestaltete Gebäude hat durch eine Betonsanierung sowie durch neue Fensterelemente im Sockelgeschoss leider an Charakter eingebüßt. Adresse: Pforzheim-Arlinger, Hochkopfstraße.

Here, as later also at the Kaiser-Wilhelm-Gedächtniskirche in Berlin [p. 252], Eiermann introduced materials and design qualities typical of modern industrial building methods into a religious building in a manner that was totally novel. This is why the Matthäuskirche was regarded as a 'beacon' at that time. The reinforced-concrete skeleton bears the shallow incline of the double-pitched roof by means of five principal beams. As sober as the exterior may appear, the interior of the church turns out to be a poetical experience for the visitor. More than 2,000 different-coloured glass panes bathe the space in diffusely filtered light that changes during the day with the course of the sun. At night, light radiates out into the surrounding area 'so that the building stands like a glowing shrine in the landscape' (Eiermann). Styled by the architect down to the moveable seating in the church, the building has unfortunately lost some of its character through renovation of the concrete as well as through addition of new window elements in the basement. Address: Hochkopfstrasse, Arlinger, Pforzheim.

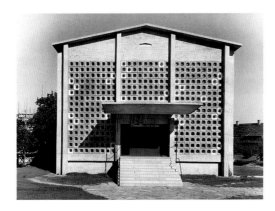

Heikki und Kaija Siren

Studentenkapelle	Students' chapel
Espoo, Finnland	Espoo, Finland
1957	1957

Diese Kapelle hat Schule gemacht. Ihre verglaste Altarwand war unter anderem das Vorbild für die Kirche Zur Heimat in Berlin [Seite 216]. In der finnischen Architektur der fünfziger Jahre nimmt sie durch den programmatischen Bezug zu Landschaft und Natur die Rolle eines Schlüsselwerks ein. Heikki Siren und seine Frau Kaija (1920–2001) hatten 1953 den Wettbewerb für das Gebäude im Studentendorf der neuen Technischen Universität in Otaniemi gewonnen. Ihr Entwurf unter dem Motto ›Alttari‹ (Altar) orientierte sich völlig an der örtlichen Situation, einem bewaldeten Grundstück oberhalb eines Meeresarms. Durch ihre Gliederung wie auch durch die durchgängig verwendeten Materialien erinnert die Kapelle an historische finnische Holzkirchen. Ausgehend von einem umzäunten Hof entwickelt sich der Baukörper zwischen zwei Längswänden aus rotem Sichtmauerwerk. Auf den niedrigen Eingang und mehrere Nebenräume folgt der Kultraum, der besonders durch die sichtbare Dachkonstruktion bestimmt ist. Das Pultdach fällt von der nach Süden hoch liegenden Glaswand steil zur Altarwand hin ab, die völlig in Glas aufgelöst ist, so dass die Natur im Raum stets anwesend ist.
Adresse: Otaniemi, Jämeräntaival.

This chapel set a precedent: among other things, its glazed altar wall was the model for the Zur Heimat church in Berlin [p. 216]. It is considered a key work in Finnish architecture of the 1950s because of its programmatic association with landscape and nature. Heikki Siren and his wife Kaija (1920–2001) won the competition for the building in the student village of the new Technical University at Otaniemi in 1953. Under the motto 'Alttari' (altar), their design was completely orientated to the local situation — a wooded site above a sea inlet. Its organisation and the materials used throughout make the chapel reminiscent of historical Finnish wooden churches. Starting from the fenced courtyard, the building unfolds between two longitudinal walls of exposed red masonry. The low entrance and the side rooms are followed by the space for worship — the chapel proper — which is defined by the visible roof construction in particular. From the glass wall high up on the south side the pent roof falls steeply down towards the altar wall, built entirely of glass, so that nature is always present in the interior.
Address: Jämeräntaival, Otaniemi.

Schnitt
section

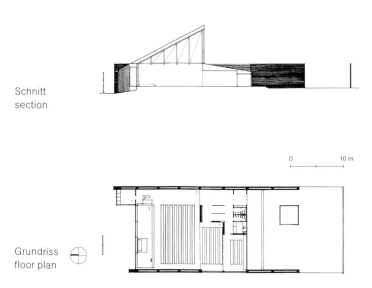

0   10 m

Grundriss
floor plan

228

Besonders die sichtbare Holzkonstruktion des zum Altar hin steil abfallenden Pultdachs prägt den Kultraum
mit 180 Sitzplätzen. Werden die
Sakristei und der Clubraum zugeschaltet, erhöht sich die Kapazität auf
300 Plätze. Das wohl proportionierte
Stahlkreuz steht hinter der völlig verglasten Altarwand im Außenraum.

The exposed wooden construction
of the pent roof sloping steeply down
to the altar gives a particular character to the chapel, which has seating
for 180. If the sacristy and club room
are added, the capacity increases
to 300. The well-proportioned steel
cross stands outside, behind the completely glazed altar wall.

Olaf Andreas Gulbransson

Friedenskirche
Manching, Deutschland
1958

Peace Church
Manching, Germany
1958

Die Steine für das lebendig wirkende Mauerwerk der kleinen Kirche bei Ingolstadt wurden durch teilweises Abtragen der alten Festungsmauer gewonnen. Die Natursteinwände sind durch Ziegelbänder gegliedert.

The stone used to produce the lively look of the masonry of this small church near Ingolstadt was obtained by partially dismantling an old fortress wall. The natural stone walls are divided up by bands of brick.

Grundriss
floor plan

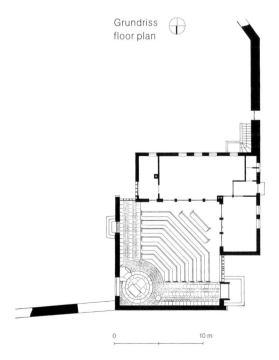

0   10 m

In den fünfziger Jahren wird im deutschen wie im schweizerischen Kirchenbau häufig die Sonderform des diagonal ausgerichteten Quadratraums verwendet. Der Münchner Baumeister Olaf Andreas Gulbransson (1916–1961) verwirklicht diesen architektonischen und liturgischen Typus bei insgesamt acht Kirchen. Die kleine Friedenskirche in Manching bei Ingolstadt, außerhalb des Ortes auf dem flachen Gelände einer früheren Festungsanlage errichtet, auf dem während der späten Kriegsjahre fahnenflüchtige Soldaten hingerichtet wurden, ist ein besonders eigenständiges Werk. Durch das teilweise Abtragen einer Vorwerksmauer nutzte Gulbransson das ursprünglich militärischen Zwecken dienende Material für den Bau dieser dem Frieden gewidmeten Kirche aus Naturstein und gliedernden Sichtziegeln. Die beiden großen Dreiecksflächen des Dachs steigen zur höchsten Raumecke hin an, unter der mit dem Altarbereich das liturgische Zentrum liegt. Altar und Kanzel sind im Sinne der Einheit von Wort und Sakrament eng miteinander verbunden. Um die Gemeinde auf den Altar hin zu konzentrieren, ist das feste Gestühl zweimal abgeknickt. Das schmückende Fenster über dem Altar hat die Form eines russischen Kreuzes.

In the 1950s, the special form of the diagonally laid-out square space was frequently used in both German and Swiss religious architecture. The Munich architect Olaf Andreas Gulbransson (1916–61) implemented this architectural and liturgical type in a total of eight churches. The small Friedenskirche in Manching, near Ingolstadt, is a particularly original work; it was built outside the village on the flat site of earlier fortifications on which, during the latter years of the war, military deserters were executed. Through partial dismantling of an outworks wall Gulbransson was able to use material that had originally served military purposes to construct this church — dedicated to peace — from natural stone and bands of exposed brickwork. The two large triangular surfaces of the roof swoop up to the highest corner of the church interior, below which lies the liturgical centre with the altar zone. Altar and pulpit are closely connected, in the sense of the unity of word and sacrament. The fixed seating bends round in two places in order to focus the congregation on the altar. The decorative window above the altar takes the form of a Russian cross.

Alvar Aalto

Vuoksenniska Kirche
Imatra, Finnland
1958

Vuoksenniska Church
Imatra, Finland
1958

Alvar Aalto (1898–1976), einer der
fünf Großmeister der modernen Architektur, hat während seiner Laufbahn
mehr als 20 Kirchen entworfen. Er
schätzte diese Aufträge sehr, weil er
im Sakralbau seine Raumvorstellun-
gen freier entwickeln konnte. Die
große Kirche von Vuoksenniska, einem Ortsteil der Industriestadt Imatra
an der Grenze zu Russland, die auch
als Kirche der drei Kreuze bezeichnet
wird, ist sein organischstes Werk.
Der Entwurf ging zum einen von den
akustischen Anforderungen im Sinne
der lutheranischen Liturgie aus: Der
mehrfach gewölbte und zur schmalen
Nordwand hin ansteigende Kirchensaal unterstützt die Schallführung
von Wort und Orgel. Die asymmetrische Raumfigur bildet sich im Außenbau ab, der nur bei einem Rund-
gang erfasst werden kann. Auf der
Ostseite des Gebäudes drücken
sich die drei ›Häuser‹ in großen Fenstergruppen aus. Zum Zweiten dient
das Bauwerk nicht nur kirchlichen, sondern auch sozialen Aktivitäten. Deshalb lässt sich der Saal mehrfach
unterteilen, wobei insgesamt sechs
Eingänge die Erschließung über-
nehmen.

Alvar Aalto (1898–1976), one of the
five grand masters of modern architecture, designed more than twenty
churches during the course of his
career. He was very appreciative of
such commissions because, in religious architecture, he was able to
develop his spatial concepts more
freely. The large church — also known
as the Church of the Three Crosses
— in Vuoksenniska, a district of the
industrial town of Imatra, near the
Russian border, is his most organic
work. For example, the design was
based on the acoustic requirements
of the Lutheran liturgy: the multi-
vaulted church rising towards the
narrow north wall supports the sound
conduction of voices and organ.
The asymmetrical shape of the interior
is reflected in the exterior, which
can only be understood by walking
round the building. On the eastern
side the three 'houses', or sections,
are expressed in large groups of
windows. Secondly, the building is
used not just for ecclesiastical but
also for social activities. The interior
space can therefore be subdivided
in many ways, with a total of six entrances providing access.

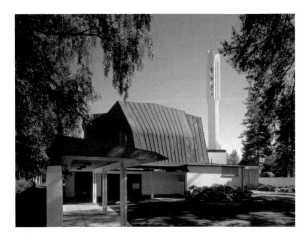

Weil in der Umgebung mehrere Fabrik-
schlote stehen, ist die Spitze des
34 Meter hohen Kirchturms plastisch
gestaltet. Kirchengebäude und
Pfarrhaus liegen in einem Waldstück.

Since there are several factory chim-
neys in the neighbourhood, the top of
the 34-metre-high tower is shaped
three-dimensionally. The church and
vicarage are set on a wooded site.

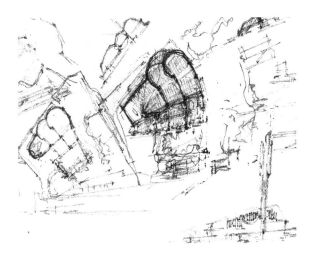

Der Kirchensaal umfasst im Ganzen 800 Plätze auf losem Gestühl. Durch schallschluckende Schiebewände, die zum Teil in den beiden mittig stehenden Betonpfeilern des Tragwerks untergebracht sind, lässt sich der Raum für kleinere Kirchenfeiern oder für gleichzeitige Aktivitäten mehrfach unterteilen. Außerdem kann ein weiterer Raum auf der Westseite zugeschaltet werden. Während der nördlich angeordnete Altarbereich mit Kanzel und Orgel durch ein großes, nach Süden gerichtetes Dachfenster belichtet wird, erhält der tiefere Raum durch drei große, in der Ostfassade erhöht liegende Fenstergruppen ausreichendes Tageslicht. Unter den insgesamt 103 verglasten Öffnungen haben nur zwei dasselbe Format. Das mit Kupfer überzogene Dach folgt den gewölbten Decken des Innenraums. Durch eine lange Betonmauer ist der wie eine weiße Skulptur im Wald liegende Kirchenbau mit dem flachen Nebengebäude verbunden, das auch mehrere Wohnungen enthält.

The hall-like interior has room for a total of 800 people on moveable seating. The space can be divided up in many ways for smaller church ceremonies or for simultaneous activities by means of sliding sound-proof partitions, some of which are housed in the two central concrete pillars of the supporting framework. A further space on the west side can also be added. While the altar zone with pulpit and organ, arranged on the north side, is lit via a large roof window open to the south, the space deeper within the church receives adequate daylight through the three large groups of windows lying high up on the eastern façade. Of the altogether 103 glazed apertures, only two have the same format. The copper-clad roof follows the shape of the vaulted ceilings of the interior. The church, lying like a white sculpture in the wood, is connected via a long concrete wall with the flat side-building, which also contains several apartments.

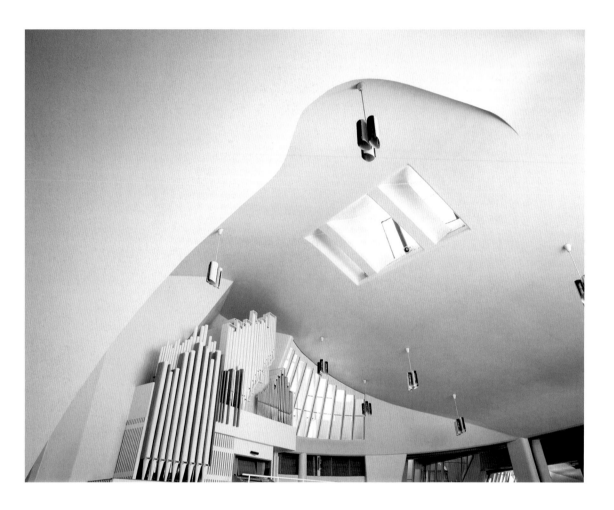

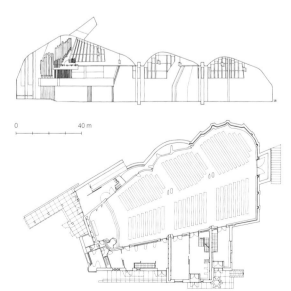

0   40 m

Grundriss und Schnitt
floor plan and
longitudinal section

Schallschluckende Schiebewände,
die zum Teil in den mächtigen, mittig
stehenden Betonpfeilern des Tragwerks untergebracht sind, machen es
möglich, den Kirchensaal mehrfach
zu unterteilen. In der Ostfassade liegen die drei Fenstergruppen.

Sound-proof sliding walls, some of
which are housed in the massive,
central concrete pillars of the supporting framework, make it possible
to divide the large interior space in
numerous ways. The three groups of
windows are located on the eastern
façade.

Bauen für die Staatskirche
Kirchenarchitektur in Finnland 1950–2000

Anspruchsvolle moderne Kirchenarchitektur lässt sich aus vielen Perspektiven bewundern. Streng genommen handelt es sich auch bei ihr um ein Paradoxon, warnt doch die christliche Lehre vor weltlicher Prachtentfaltung – »Mein Wort ist nicht von dieser Welt«. Hätte sich die christliche Kirche nicht innerhalb der römischen Kultur entwickelt, wäre kaum die Tradition einer ihre Botschaft verkündenden Architektur entstanden. Von den frühchristlichen Basiliken an hat die Kirche in allen Phasen ihrer Geschichte ihre sakralen Stätten im Einklang mit den jeweils geltenden Stilen so groß und so schön wie möglich gestaltet. Der Durchbruch der Moderne in den späten zwanziger Jahren war gleichbedeutend mit der Ablehnung historischer Werturteile; er stellte den Versuch dar, der Architektur zu einer von Tradition und Ornament befreiten, reinen neuen Ästhetik zu verhelfen. Dass es der Kirche selbst angesichts dieser Revolution gelang, ihre Position an der Spitze der Architektur beizubehalten, ist hinsichtlich der Kulturgeschichte als wahrhaft interessantes Phänomen zu betrachten.

Historischer Hintergrund

Auch in Finnland fanden die hitzigsten Debatten über Stilfragen in der Architektur seit dem Ende der zwanziger Jahre bei Wettbewerben für Kirchenbauten statt. Junge Architekten reichten Beiträge ein, bei denen sie sämtliche Hauptmerkmale der deutsch-holländisch-französischen Moderne verwendeten. Die bekannteste Auseinandersetzung spielte sich in den Jahren 1930–32 im Zusammenhang mit dem Projekt für eine Kirche im Tehtaanpuisto Park im Süden von Helsinki ab. Obwohl die Jury anfänglich funktionalistische Entwürfe auszeichnete, führte der Gegenschlag der alten Generation zu einer zweiten Phase des Wettbewerbs und einer Ausschreibung, die dezidiert zur Verwendung traditioneller Formen aufrief. Dem entsprechend ging das Projekt an den alternden Meisterarchitekten Lars Sonck, und die rote Backsteinkirche wurde nach seinem Entwurf 1935 fertig gestellt.

Im Laufe der zwanziger Jahre entstanden in der jungen Republik Finnland, die 1917 ihre nationale Unabhängigkeit erklärt hatte, Dutzende eindrucksvoller Kirchenbauten. Ungeachtet der formal herrschenden Religionsfreiheit räumten die 1919 erlassene Verfassung sowie das Kirchengesetz der evangelisch-lutherischen Kirche von Finnland eine Sonderstellung als Staatskirche ein. Dank ihres Rechts, Steuern zu erheben, war die Kirche in der Lage, Bautätigkeiten in großem Maßstab durchzuführen. In lokalpatriotischem Geist wurden selbst in kleinen Ortschaften spektakuläre Kirchenbauten errichtet.

Bei den Kirchen der zwanziger Jahre handelt es sich um historistische Bauten, deren räumliche und formale Gestaltung vor allem auf der Architektur des 17. und 18. Jahrhunderts basierte, einer Zeit, in der Finnland unter dem Einfluss Schwedens stand. Architekturstudenten fertigten maßstabsgerechte Zeichnungen der in diesen Jahrhunderten entstandenen Holzkirchen an, und es herrschte ein stark romantisch geprägtes Nationalgefühl vor. Die ›zeitlose‹ Architektursprache des nordischen Klassizismus eignete sich in jeder Hinsicht für den kirchlichen Gebrauch. Der am meisten verbreitete Typus zeichnete sich durch ein lang gestrecktes Kirchenschiff mit einem Turm aus, dem in Städten, kleineren Gemeinden und auf dem Lande eine dominierende Stellung zukam. Gegen Ende des Jahrzehnts

Erik Bryggman
Tehtaanpuisto Kirche / church
Helsinki, 1930
Wettbewerbsmodell
competition model

Alvar Aalto
Kirche / church
Muurame, 1929

Riitta Nikula

Building for the State Church
Church Architecture in Finland 1950–2000

Ambitious modern church architecture can be admired from many perspectives. Seriously speaking, the whole tradition of church architecture is a paradox, for Christian teaching advises against worldly ostentation — 'My Word is not of this world'. If the Christian Church had not emerged within mainstream Roman culture, the heritage of an architecture proclaiming its message would hardly have come about. Ever since the Early Christian basilicas, the Church has in all stages of its history made its sacral venues as large and as beautiful as possible in keeping with contemporary ideals of style. The breakthrough of Modernism in the late 1920s marked a rejection of historical value judgements; it was an attempt to provide architecture with a pure, new aesthetic, free of tradition and ornament. The fact that even in this revolution the Church managed to maintain its role in the lead of architecture is a truly interesting phenomenon in terms of cultural history.

Historical Background

In Finland, too, the most heated debates on style in architecture took place around the turn of the 1920s and 1930s in connection with architectural competitions for the design of churches. Young architects would submit competition entries employing all the main features of German-Dutch-French Modernism. The most prominent conflict of opinion took place in 1930–32 in connection with the project for a church in Tehtaanpuisto park in south Helsinki. At first, a competition jury rewarded functionalist designs but the counter-attack of the old generation led to a second stage in the competition and a brief expressly calling for the use of traditional forms. Accordingly, the project went to the ageing master architect Lars Sonck , and the red-brick church of his design was completed in 1935.

During the 1920s dozens of impressive churches were built in the young republic of Finland, which had gained national independence in 1917. Despite formal freedom of religion, the constitution of 1919 and the Church Act gave the Evangelical-Lutheran Church of Finland special status as the state church. Through its right to levy taxes, the church was able to conduct construction activities on a broad scale. Impressive churches were erected even in small localities in a spirit of local patriotism.

The churches of the 1920s were historicist works of architecture, whose spatial and formal design was based above all on the architecture of the 17th and 18th centuries, a period when Finland belonged to the Swedish realm. Students of architecture would make measured drawings of the wooden churches of those centuries, and there was a strong romantic national sentiment. The timeless architectural language of ascetic Nordic Classicism was in all ways suited to ecclesiastical use. The most popular type of church was a long-nave space designed with a tower at one end, which was given a dominant position in towns, smaller communities and in the rural context. Towards the end of the decade young architects introduced a variant that made reference to village churches sketched on visits to Italy. Here, the tower is a separate campanile standing next to the main section. Muurame Church, from 1929, by Alvar Aalto is one of the most sensitive works executed along these lines. It reveals how Aalto saw his home region as the Tuscany of Finland.

Lars Sonck
Tehtaanpuisto Kirche / church
Helsinki, 1935

führten junge Architekten eine Variante ein, die Bezug nahm auf Dorfkirchen, deren Skizzen auf Italienreisen entstanden waren. Hier nimmt der Turm die Form eines Campanile an, der neben dem Hauptbau zu stehen kommt. Bei der 1929 entstandenen Muurame Kirche von Alvar Aalto handelt es sich um einen der stilvollsten Bauten dieser Art. Er offenbart, wie sehr Aalto seinen heimatlichen Landstrich als die Toskana Finnlands verstand.

Kirchenarchitektur und Moderne

Im Jahr 1930 errichtete man neben der mittelalterlichen grauen Steinkirche von Parainen eine kleine Friedhofskapelle. Der Architekt der Kapelle, Erik Bryggman, hatte seit der Zeit um 1910 in zahlreichen Wettbewerbsbeiträgen einfühlsame sakrale Motive entwickelt. In der Kapelle von Parainen sind diese Motive weitestgehend reduziert: ein asketischer, weißer Kubus, ein sanft geneigtes Satteldach und ein Interieur, das beherrscht wird von dem seitlich einfallenden Tageslicht. Die 1941 errichtete Auferstehungskapelle in Turku stellt eine ausgereifte Synthese von Bryggmans Architekturmotiven dar. Diese wunderbar zeitlose Kapelle steht in enger Verbindung zu dem umgebenden Waldfriedhof. Im Schiff verschmilzt die Mystik der Natur mit christlicher Symbolik.

P.E. Blomstedt und Erkki Huttunen führten einen Funktionalismus reinsten Wassers in den finnischen Kirchenbau ein. Im Jahr 1932 begann Blomstedt mit dem Entwurf einer modernen Kirche in Kannonkoski. Die Masse des Baukörpers erhebt sich vom Altar hin zur hoch aufragenden Vorderfassade mit ihrem massiven Turm und der außen liegenden Kanzel. 1937 entstand in der Industriestadt Nakkila eine von Erkki Huttunen entworfene, aus massiven Formen zusammengesetzte Kirche. Ihr hoher Turm beherrscht eine weit ausgebreitete Landschaft.

Während der von begrenzten Ressourcen geprägten, entbehrungsreichen Nachkriegsjahre legte der Nationale Kirchenrat den Gemeinden nahe, ihre Anstrengungen auf den Wohnungsbau zu konzentrieren und ihre eigenen Aktivitäten auf einfache Gemeindesäle zu beschränken. Spenden aus dem Ausland ermöglichten es jedoch, in Lappland sowie in der nordostfinnischen Region Kainuu einige Kirchen zu errichten, um die im Krieg zerstörten zu ersetzen. Die 1950 in Kemijärvi und Rovaniemi und 1951 in Kuusamo erbauten Kirchen waren Entwürfe Bertel Liljeqvists, die das Erbe der zwanziger Jahre aufgriffen.

Bei seinem Entwurf für die Kirche der Drei Kreuze in Vuoksenniska wandte sich Alvar Aalto von sämtlichen traditionellen Lösungen ab. Dieses 1957/58 in einem Kiefernwäldchen errichtete skulpturale Gebäude [Seite 232] ist von einem freien Rhythmus bestimmt; sein Innenraum lässt sich in drei Abteilungen gliedern. In all seinen Variationen verhilft dieser asymmetrische Raum zu lyrischen Erfahrungen. Somit ist es kaum verständlich, weshalb besonders diese Kirche auf heftigen Widerstand stieß. Der Volksmund nannte sie einen »Anti-Teufelsbunker«.

Während des folgenden Jahrzehnts setzte sich in der finnischen Kirchenarchitektur eine strenge Moderne durch, die sich geometrischer Grundformen bediente und Romantik sowie Individualismus vermied. Die 1960 errichtete Vatiala Friedhofskapelle von Viljo Revell weist ein Kirchenschiff auf, das sich als para-

Erik Bryggman
Auferstehungskapelle
Ressurrection chapel
Turku, 1941

In 1930 a small funeral chapel was built next to the medieval
grey stone Church of Parainen. Since the 1910s, the architect
of the chapel, Erik Bryggman, had developed sensitive sacral
themes in many competition entries. In the Parainen chapel,
the themes are at their most reduced: an ascetic white cube,
a gently sloping saddleback roof and an interior dominated by
daylight from one side in the choir. The Resurrection Chapel
in Turku, built in 1941, was a mature synthesis of Erik Bryggman's architectural themes. This wonderfully timeless chapel is
closely connected to the surrounding forested cemetery of the
site. In the nave, the mysticism of nature blends with Christian
symbolism.

P. E. Blomstedt and Erkki Huttunen introduced pure-bred functionalism into Finnish church architecture. In 1932, Blomstedt,
began to design a modern church at Kannonkoski. The mass
of this building rises from the altar towards the high main façade,
with its solid tower and outdoor pulpit. In 1937 a church of
solid forms, designed by Erkki Huttunen, was built for the industrial community of Nakkila. Its high tower dominates a wide
historic landscape.

During the post-war years of limited resources and austerity,
the National Church Board encouraged the local congregations
to focus their efforts on constructing housing and to restrict
their own operations to modest parish halls. Donations from
abroad, however, made it possible to build a few churches in
Lapland and the Kainuu region of north-eastern Finland to
replace ones that had been destroyed in the war. The churches
built at Kemijärvi and Rovaniemi in 1950 and in Kuusamo
in 1951 were designed by Bertel Liljeqvist in keeping with the
heritage of the 1920s.

In his design of the Church of the Three Crosses at Vuoksenniska
[p. 232], Alvar Aalto turned his back on all old, standard solutions. Built in 1957–58 in a stand of pines, this sculptural
building has a free rhythm; its interior can be partitioned into
three parts. In all its different variations, this asymmetric space
presents lyrical experiences. It is hard to understand why this
church, in particular, provoked strong opposition: the general
public called it an 'anti-devil bunker'.

During the following decade, a strict Modernism employing
basic geometric shapes and eschewing Romanticism and indi-
vidualism gained ground in Finnish church architecture. The
Vatiala funeral chapel (1960) by Viljo Revell has a nave rising in
the form of a parabolic concrete shell from the low horizontal
of auxiliary space and rooms. In the Church of Lauritsala
(1968, competition held in 1958) Toivo Korhonen and Jaakko
Laapotti designed a dramatically asymmetrical mass. The
triangular church has a concrete roof rising into a tower at one
corner. In 1958–61 Aarno Ruusuvuori developed a tetrahe-
dral monumental design for Hyvinkää Church, towering over
its surrounding community like a pyramid. In Huutoniemi
Church in Vaasa (1964), the building's mainly rectangular concrete forms and glass express an idiom that elsewhere and in
less sacral connections would be described with the originally
English term 'Brutalist'. In 1967 a second funeral chapel
was built in the large cemetery of Turku. The spacious horizontal levels of Holy Cross chapel by Pekka Pitkänen assemble

Viljo Revell
Friedhofskapelle / funeral chapel
Vatiala, 1960

belförmige Betonschale über die niedrigen Nebenräume erhebt.
Mit der Kirche von Lauritsala (1968, der Wettbewerb fand
bereits 1958 statt) schufen Toivo Korhonen und Jaakko Laapotti
einen spektakulär asymmetrischen Baukörper. Die dreieckige
Kirche verfügt über ein Betondach, das sich an einer Ecke zum
Turm erhebt. In den Jahren 1958 bis 1961 entwickelte Aarno
Ruusuvuori für die Hyvinkää Kirche ein monumentales, tetra-
edrisches Konzept, das sich einer Pyramide gleich über die
umgebende Ortschaft erhebt. Im Falle der Huutoniemi Kirche
in Vaasa (1964) zeigen die überwiegend rechteckigen Bauteile
aus Beton und Glas eine Formensprache, die andernorts und in
weniger sakralem Zusammenhang mit dem ursprünglich engli-
schen Ausdruck »brutalistisch« bezeichnet würde. 1967 entstand dann auf dem ausgedehnten Friedhof von Turku eine
zweite Friedhofskapelle. Die geräumigen horizontalen Ebenen
der Heilig-Kreuz-Kapelle von Pekka Pitkänen konzentrieren
die dort offene Landschaft in einer einzigen Komposition. Die
extrem asketische Betonarchitektur der Kapelle verströmt ein
unverfälschtes Gefühl des Friedens.

Wohngebiete und Vororte

Nach dem Zweiten Weltkrieg entstand in den neuen Wohnge-
bieten der finnischen Städte eine große Zahl von Kirchen. Die
Region um Helsinki erlebte mehrere nationale Migrationswellen
und reagierte auf den gravierenden Wohnungsmangel mit der
fortlaufenden Entwicklung neuer Gebiete innerhalb eines Net-
zes aus Eisenbahnlinien und Autostraßen. In den Städten
Helsinki, Vantaa, Espoo und Kauniainen, welche die ›Metropolitan Area‹ von Helsinki ausmachen, lässt sich die Vielfalt moderner Kirchenarchitektur bestens studieren.

Der erste Abschnitt (1950–54) des Wohngebiets der Technischen Universität in Otaniemi war Finnlands erste Studenten-
gemeinde. Die Technische Universität selbst zog erst in den
sechziger Jahren von Helsinki auf den Campus von Otaniemi.
Der von Alvar Aalto konzipierte Bebauungsplan folgt den vor-
gegebenen Höhenlinien des Geländes; die Wohnheime aus
rotem Backstein stehen in lockerer Anordnung auf dem bewaldeten Terrain, und die Kapelle besetzt einen ruhig gelegenen
Standort in seinem Zentrum. Den 1954 ausgeschriebenen
Wettbewerb für die Kapelle von Otaniemi gewannen Kaija und
Heikki Sirén. Die Kapelle [Seite 228] verkörpert die extreme
Ausprägung einer für lutherisch gehaltenen Askese, die zugleich
einen modernen Pantheismus vertreten sollte. Auch hier sind
die Wände des rechteckigen Hauptraums aus gewöhnlichem
rotem Backstein gemauert. Die Aufmerksamkeit des Besuchers
wird auf die völlig verglaste Altarwand gelenkt, und die natürliche Umgebung liefert den ständig wechselnden Altarschmuck.

1965 wurde in der Gartenstadt Tapiola eine Kirche erbaut,
deren minimalistische Architektur stets höchst umstritten war,
und zwar schon seit Aarno Ruusuvuori 1961 den Wettbewerb
für sich entschieden hatte. Die Kirche [Seite 256], die neben
dem Einkaufszentrum an der wichtigsten Fußgängerachse von
Tapiola erbaut wurde, wendet dem geschäftigen Treiben bewusst
ihre Rückseite zu. Der hohe Raum des Kirchenschiffs erhebt
sich in der Form eines präzis umschriebenen Kubus über eine
rhythmische Anordnung niedriger Zäune, Vorgärten und
Gemeindeeinrichtungen. Das Grau der Betonflächen ist nicht
kaschiert.

Pekka Pitkänen
Heilig-Kreuz-Kapelle
Holy Cross chapel
Turku, 1967

the wide-open landscape of the site into a single composition. The chapel's extremely ascetic concrete architecture exudes a barren feeling of peace.

Housing Areas and Suburbs

After the Second World War, a great number of churches were built in the new housing areas of Finland's towns and cities. The Helsinki region has received several waves of internal migration and has responded to a severe housing shortage by continually developing new residential areas in its surrounding network of railways and motorways. The diversity of modern church architecture can well be studied in the cities of Helsinki, Vantaa, Espoo and Kauniainen, which form the Helsinki Metropolitan Area.

The first stage (1950–54) of the University of Technology housing area at Otaniemi in Espoo was Finland's first student town. The Helsinki University of Technology did not move to the Otaniemi campus until the 1960s. The Otaniemi plan, by Alvar Aalto, follows the natural elevation contours of the site; the red-brick dormitories were placed sparsely in the forest setting, and the chapel was given a quiet location in the middle of the area. The architectural competition held in 1954 for the Otaniemi Chapel was won by Kaija and Heikki Siren. The chapel [p. 228] is an extreme expression of an asceticism regarded as Lutheran and modern pantheist. The walls of the rectangular main space are of ordinary red brick. The visitor's attention is drawn to the altar wall, which is all glass. The natural setting is a continuously changing altarpiece.

In 1965 a church was built in the garden city of Tapiola, whose minimalist architecture has been a subject of contention ever since Aarno Ruusuvuori won the architectural competition for the project in 1961. Situated next to the commercial centre and built on the main pedestrian axis of the area, the church [p. 256] turns its back, with determination, on the bustle of its surroundings. The high nave space rises in the form of a strictly defined cube from a rhythmic array of low fences, front yards and parish facilities. The grey of the concrete surfaces has not been masked.

West of Tapiola is the residential area of Olari. Its church, built in 1981, was designed by Käpy and Simo Paavilainen to avoid visual clutter. The red-brick walls of the church rise high above the nearby busy thoroughfare and a chaos of different commercial buildings. Behind them is the tranquillity of a historical manor courtyard. The main space and its two wings encircle the old manor yard. Inside the church, the soft daylight is complemented by decorative electric lamps. Malmi Church was also built in 1981. Here, Kristian Gullichsen also attached the historical ambience of an old courtyard to a new church of red brick. Moreover, Gullichsen employed quotes from medieval churches and the architecture of Alvar Aalto. The controlled result is convincingly unique. In Kauniainen Church (1983) Gullichsen continued to use quotes, subtly associating them with traditional religious motives. The designs were a source of surprise and fascination for many; this strict modernist had broken the taboos of several decades.

At the Itäkeskus commercial centre in eastern Helsinki, St Matthew's Church and cultural centre (1979–84) are an

Käpy und / and Simo Paavilainen
Kirche / church
Olari, 1983

Kristian Gullichsen
Kirche / church
Kauniainen, 1983

Westlich von Tapiola befindet sich das Wohngebiet von Olari. Seine 1981 erbaute Kirche wurde von Käpy und Simo Paavilainen in der Absicht entworfen, ein visuelles Durcheinander zu vermeiden. Die hohen roten Backsteinmauern der Kirche überragen die nahe gelegene, stark befahrene Durchgangsstraße und eine Ansammlung verschiedener Geschäftsbauten. Hinter den Mauern empfängt einen die beschauliche Ruhe eines historischen Innenhofs. Der Hauptraum und seine beiden Flügel umgeben den Hof des alten Herrenhauses. Im Inneren der Kirche wird das sanfte Tageslicht durch dekorative elektrische Lampen ergänzt. Auch die Kirche von Malmi wurde 1981 errichtet. Kristian Gulllichsen verbindet hier ebenfalls das historische Ambiente eines Hofs mit einer neuen Kirche aus rotem Backstein. Außerdem verwendet er Zitate aus mittelalterlichen Kirchen und der Architektur Alvar Aaltos. Das kalkulierte Ergebnis überzeugt durch seine Einzigartigkeit. Bei der Kirche von Kauniainen (1983) setzt Gullichsen wiederum Zitate ein; hier verknüpft er sie subtil mit traditionellen religiösen Motiven. Die Entwürfe überraschten und faszinierten viele, hatte doch dieser konsequent moderne Architekt die Tabus mehrerer Dekaden verletzt.

Die St. Matthäuskirche mit dem angegliederten Kulturzentrum (1979–84), neben dem größten Einkaufszentrum der nordischen Länder im Osten von Helsinki gelegen, gleicht einer Insel des Friedens. Die in kleinem Maßstab konzipierten Bauteile aus rotem Backstein wurden von Björn Krogius und Veli-Pekka Tuominen in schwungvoller Manier gestaltet und angeordnet. In Verbindung mit der kleinen Kirche vervollständigen die komfortablen, wohnraumähnlichen Versammlungsräume die warme, einladende Atmosphäre einer modernen Dorfkirche.

Unter den Meistern der modernen finnischen Architektur war es Juha Leiviskä, der sich am stärksten auf den Kirchenbau konzentrierte. Seine Kirchen gleichen rhythmischen Abfolgen von Räumen unterschiedlicher Höhe. Die Puolivälinkangas-Kirche in Oulu wurde 1975 fertig gestellt, die Myyrmäki-Kirche mit Gemeindezentrum in Vantaa im Jahr 1984 und die St. Johannes-Kirche in Männistö bei Kuopio im Jahr 1993. Die Myyrmäki-Kirche [Seite 286] wendet einer Eisenbahnlinie ihre Rückseite zu und öffnet sich statt dessen zu einem lichten Birkenwäldchen. Der Rhythmus ansteigender, räumlicher Abfolgen verbindet sich mit überströmendem Tageslicht, mit Gruppen kleiner Beleuchtungskörper und Raumtextilien. Bei der Kirche in Männistö werden Farbflächen in schmalen Vertikalen als immaterielle Farbe im Raum reflektiert: Kunst und Architektur bilden eine Einheit. Leiviskä selbst unterstreicht den Einfluss barocker Architektur sowie der Umgebung, und er spricht häufig von den Parallelen zwischen Architektur und Musik.

Eine neue Monumentalität

Das von Alvar Aalto geplante Zentrum von Seinäjoki zeigt, wie die traditionelle europäische Stadtmitte mit modernen Mitteln geschaffen werden kann. Stadtregierung, kulturelle Einrichtungen und die Kirche verfügen sämtlich über Gebäude mit ausgeprägtem Charakter, die zusammen mit geschickt proportionierten Plätzen der Stadt zu einer ausgeprägten Individualität verhelfen. Der Wettbewerb für die Kirche wurde bereits 1952 ausgeschrieben, die als ›Lakeuden Risti‹ (Kreuz der Ebenen) bekannte Kirche im Jahr 1960 vollendet. Das angegliederte Gemeindezentrum entstand 1966. Der Kirchturm, der sich über

islet of peace next to the largest shopping mall in the Nordic countries. The red-brick buildings of small scale were designed and composed in a vivid manner by Björn Krogius and Veli-Pekka Tuominen. The comfortable, home-like meeting areas in connection with the small church are an addition to the warm and welcoming mood of a modern village church.

Of the masters of modern Finnish architecture, Juha Leiviskä has concentrated the most on church architecture. His churches are rhythmic series of spaces of differing heights. Puolivälinkangas Church in Oulu was completed in 1975, Myyrmäki Church [p. 286] and Parish Centre in Vantaa in 1984, and St John's Church in Männistö, Kuopio, in 1993. Myyrmäki church turns its back on the railway and opens instead on to a slender birch coppice. The rhythm of rising spatial sequences is finished off by spilling-over daylight, groups of small lamps and spatial textiles. In Männistö Church, colour surfaces are reflected in narrow verticals as immaterial colour in space. Art and architecture are one. Leiviskä himself emphasizes the influence of baroque architecture and the environment, and he always speaks of the parallels between architecture and music.

A New Monumentality

The centre of the city of Seinäjoki, planned by Alvar Aalto, shows how the traditional European city centre can be created with modern means. Local government, cultural affairs and the church all have buildings of distinct character, which, together with skilfully dimensioned squares and piazzas give the city a strong personal identity. The architectural competition for the church was already held in 1952, and the church, known as Lakeuden Risti [Cross of the Plains] was completed in 1960. The surrounding parish centre was built in 1966. Rising above the South Ostrobothnian plains, the church tower is a landmark for the whole city. Inside the church there is a mood of serious tranquillity characteristic of the province.

The solid vertical volume of Kaleva Church [p. 260], designed by Raili and Reima Pietilä and built in 1966, assembled a diverse array of post-war housing areas in Tampere. The individualistic architecture of the Pietiläs is hard to explain within any particular context. The skilful concrete structures create a dramatic mood. The space within the church, delimited by convex verticals, has understandably been compared to Gothic cathedrals. The floor plan has been interpreted as a fish design, the symbol of the Early Christian congregation. In 1979, the Pietiläs planned a centre for Hervanta, Tampere's satellite town. Here, the spaces and facilities for cultural services, health care, commerce and the church form an expressive red-brick composition, in Reima Pietilä's terms 'a red belt' which brings together the elements of a bleak and gloomy environment. The parish centre, built in 1979, hardly distinguishes itself from the other facilities. As professor of architecture at the University of Oulu, Reima Pietilä broke down the monolithic façade of Finnish modernism. His students and pupils (the so-called 'Oulu School') discovered regionalism and post-modernism. The Myllyoja Parish Centre (1983) by Juha Pasanen and Lasse Vahtera combines solemnity with cosiness in an interesting manner.

In 1960 the architects Timo and Tuomo Suomalainen won a competition for a church in the Töölö section of Helsinki, a dense urban fabric from the 1920s. The new church was to be

Alvar Aalto
Kirche und Gemeindezentrum
church and parish centre
Seinajöki, 1960–1966

die Ebene des südlichen Österbotten erhebt, gilt als Wahrzeichen der ganzen Stadt. Im Inneren der Kirche herrscht eine Stimmung ernsthafter Gelassenheit, einer für die ganze Gegend typischen Haltung.

Der massive, vertikale Baukörper der Kaleva Kirche, ein 1966 ausgeführter Entwurf von Raili und Reima Pietilä, fungiert als Klammer für mehrere uneinheitliche Wohngebiete aus der Nachkriegszeit in Tampere [Seite 260]. Die individualistische Architektur der Pietiläs lässt sich nur schwer in einen gestalterischen Kontext einordnen. Die kunstgerechte Betonkonstruktion erzeugt eine dramatische Anmutung. Der Vergleich des von konvexen Vertikalen gegliederten Kirchenraums mit gotischen Kathedralen erscheint nahe liegend. Der Grundriss gleicht einer Fischform, dem Symbol der frühchristlichen Gemeinden. Im Jahr 1979 planten die Pietiläs dann ein Zentrum für Hervanta, eine Satellitenstadt von Tampere. Hier bilden die Räume und Einrichtungen für kulturelle Institutionen, Gesundheitsdienste, Läden und die Kirche eine expressive Anlage aus rotem Backstein, in den Worten Reima Pietiläs »einen roten Gürtel«, der eine triste Umgebung zusammenfasst. Das Gemeindezentrum unterscheidet sich kaum von den übrigen Einrichtungen. Reima Pietilä, der an der Universität von Oulu eine Professur für Architektur innehatte, zerlegte die monolithischen Fassaden der finnischen Moderne. Seine Studenten und Schüler (die so genannte Oulu-Schule) entdeckten für sich regionale Bezüge sowie die Postmoderne. Das 1983 entstandene Myllyoja-Gemeindezentrum von Juha Pasanen und Lasse Vahtera vereint auf reizvolle Weise feierlichen Ernst mit Behaglichkeit.

Im Jahr 1960 gewannen die Architekten Timo und Tuomo Suomalainen den Wettbewerb für eine Kirche in Helsinkis Stadtteil Töölö, einem dicht bebauten Gebiet aus den zwanziger Jahren. Die neue Kirche sollte an einer im Stadtplan reservierten Stelle entstehen. Den Suomalainens gelang es, zwei gegensätzliche Ziele zu vereinen – den Standort als offenes Parkgelände zu erhalten und gleichwohl dort einen ›Tempel‹ zu schaffen. Die nach etlichen Problemen 1969 vollendete Temppeliaukio Kirche [Seite 280] wurde in den felsigen Untergrund hineingebaut. Der unter einer flachen Kuppel gelegene Hauptraum erhebt sich nur wenig über den höchsten Punkt des Geländes. Man betritt die Kirche durch einen tunnelartigen Eingang. Das kunstvoll grobe Mauerwerk, der sorgfältig ausgeführte Beton sowie die markante Kupferverkleidung der Decke umgrenzen einen Raum, in den das Tageslicht durch die Öffnungen zwischen den die Kuppel tragenden Balken fällt. Die schroffe Anmutung dieser versteckt liegenden Kathedrale spricht Besucher aus sämtlichen Kulturkreisen an. Im Jahr 2000 erwies sich die Kirche als eines der vier beliebtesten Touristenziele in ganz Finnland.

Der moderne Sakralbau umfasst erhabene Monumente ebenso wie kleine Gemeindezentren. Schon in den zwanziger Jahren des 19. Jahrhunderts wurden Gemeindesäle in das Raumprogramm aufgenommen. Jetzt, zu Beginn des dritten Jahrtausends, scheint es, als seien auch Finnlands Kathedralen errichtet und als wären Gemeindezentren, Tagesstätten und Versammlungsräume in Verbindung mit den alten Kirchen aktueller geworden. Gleichwohl bleibt die evangelisch-lutherische Kirche Finnlands weiterhin auf vielfältige Weise an der baulichen Entwicklung des finnischen Alltags beteiligt. Zumindest Tagesstätten für Kinder, Friedhofkapellen und Friedhöfe spielen im Leben der meisten Bürger eine Rolle. Bei der Planung von Bauten dieser

Art fühlen sich die Architekten mit einem großen Erbe verbunden – selbst weniger wichtige Ausschreibungen auf diesem Gebiet ziehen zahlreiche Bewerber an.

Weiterführende Literatur:
20th century Architecture. Finland. Hrsg. v. Marja-Riitta Norri, Elina Standertskjöld und Wilfried Wang, München 2000. *Ars Sacra Fennica. Aikamme taide taide kirkossa. Vår tids kyrkokonst. Sacral art in our times,* Helsinki 1987. Riitta Nikula, *Bebaute Landschaft. Finnlands Architektur im Überblick*, Helsinki 1993.

Timo und / and Tuomo Suomalainen
Temppeliaukio Kirche / church
Helsinki, 1969
Längsschnitt / longitudinal section

at a site originally reserved in the town plan. The Suomalainens succeeded in combining two opposite goals — to preserve the site as an open park while also creating a temple. Completed in 1969 after various difficulties, Temppeliaukio Church [p. 280] was quarried in the bedrock of the site. Its main space is under a low dome barely rising above the highest point of the rocky site. The church has a tunnel-like entrance. The studied coarse masonry, the careful concrete work, and the expressive copper of the interior demarcate a space which receives daylight from openings between the beams supporting the dome. The bare and rugged spirit of this hidden cathedral appeals to visitors of all cultures. In the year 2000, Temppeliaukio Church was one of Finland's four most popular tourist attractions.

Modern sacral architecture includes solemn monuments and small parish centres. Parish halls were already included in the accommodation of space in the 1920s. Now at the beginning of the third millennium, it seems also that Finland's cathedrals have been built, and that the parish centres, meeting rooms and day-care facilities in connection with the old churches have become more topical. The Evangelical-Lutheran Church of Finland, however, is in many ways continually involved in building and developing the Finnish milieu. At least children's day-care facilities, funeral chapels and cemeteries are at some stage timely in the lives of most citizens. In planning them, architects feel that they are in contact with traditions and heritage of long standing; even minor architectural competitions in this area receive a great many entries.

Further reading:
Marja-Riitta Norri, Elina Standertskjöld and Wilfried Wang (eds.), *20th-Century Architecture. Finland*, Munich, 2000.
Ars Sacra Fennica. *Aikamme taide taide kirkossa. Vår tids kyrkokonst. Sacral art in our times*, Helsinki, 1987.
Riitta Nikula, *Architecture and Landscape, the Building of Finland*, Helsinki, 1993.

Timo und / and Tuomo Suomalainen
Temppeliaukio Kirche / church
Helsinki, 1969

Peter Celsing

St. Thomas
Stockholm, Schweden
1960

St Thomas
Stockholm, Sweden
1960

Die Trabantenstadt Vällingby nordwestlich von Stockholm ist ein
Vorzeigeobjekt für den ambitionierten
schwedischen Städtebau der fünfziger Jahre. Das Zentrum der Wohn-
und Geschäftsstadt bildet ein riesiges
Einkaufszentrum, das über der Metro-
station errichtet wurde und eine Seite
des Stadtplatzes einfasst. Schräg
gegenüber, somit ein unmittelbarer
Nachbar von Handel und Verkehr, liegt
in einem flachen Hang die Thomaskirche, zu deren Entwurf Peter Celsing
äußerte: »Wesentlich war, dass die
Kirche diese materielle Welt respek-
tierte, statt mit ihr in Wettbewerb
treten zu wollen.« Durch ihre kubische
Baugestalt schließt sie sich wie eine
Bastion weitgehend von der Außenwelt ab. Für die tragenden Wände wurden außen und innen rote Sichtziegel
verwendet, die Deckenträger bestehen aus vorgespanntem Beton. Der
Kirchenraum liegt im Norden des
Gevierts und öffnet sich durch eine
Fensterwand zu einem Gartenhof. Der
auf den Altar längs gerichtete Raum
wirkt ernst und würdevoll. Vor der
Fensterwand steht ein großes Taufbecken mit ständig fließendem Wasser als Sinnbild des Lebens.

The satellite town of Vällingby, north-
west of Stockholm, is a showpiece
for the ambitious Swedish urban developments of the 1950s. The heart
of the residential and commercial
town is a huge shopping centre built
above the underground station and
flanking one side of the town's square.
Diagonally opposite — and thus a
close neighbour of trade and traffic
— on a slight slope lies the church
of St Thomas, regarding the design of
which Peter Celsing said: 'It was
essential that the church respected
this material world, instead of trying to
compete with it'. As a consequence
of its cubical form the church is shut
off from the outside world to a large
extent, like a bulwark. Exposed red
bricks were used for the load-bearing
walls both inside and outside, while
the ceiling beams are of pre-stressed
concrete. The church space lies in
the northern part of the square and
opens on to a courtyard garden via
a wall of glazing. The interior, aligned
longitudinally towards the altar, creates a solemn and dignified impression. In front of the glazed wall stands
a large baptismal font with constantly
flowing water as a symbol of life.

Vor der im Hang stehenden Westfassade erhebt sich der markant gestaltete Glockenturm. Lange Fensterbänder weisen in den Ziegelwänden auf die zahlreichen Nebenräume der Kirche und die Räume des Gemeindeamts hin.

The strikingly shaped bell tower rises in front of the western façade, built on the slope. The long bands of windows in the brick walls indicate the church's numerous side rooms and the offices of the local authority.

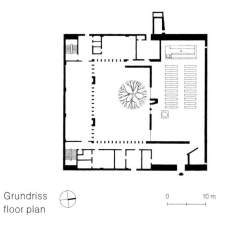

Grundriss
floor plan

0   10 m

Sir Basil Spence

Kathedrale
Coventry, Großbritannien
1962

Cathedral
Coventry, Great Britain
1962

Als Mahnmal gegen den Krieg markieren die Ruinen der im November
1940 zerstörten spätgotischen
Kathedrale den Umriss des früheren
Kirchenschiffs. Die Fläche ist gartenartig gestaltet. Im Hintergrund erhebt sich das monumentale Eingangs-
portal der neuen Kathedrale, die
aus einem offenen Wettbewerb hervorging.

The ruins of the late Gothic cathedral
destroyed in November 1940 preserve the outline of the earlier nave as
a reminder of the horrors of war. The
site has been landscaped. The monumental portal of the new cathedral,
which was the result of an open competition, looms in the background.

Im November 1940 bombardierte die deutsche Luftwaffe die englische Industriestadt Coventry und zerstörte sie in weiten Teilen, darunter auch die spätgotische Kathedrale, von der nur der Turm erhalten blieb. Auf Befehl Hitlers sollten die britischen Städte »ausradiert« werden. Der Bau der neuen Kathedrale, der ersten modernen, begann 1951 mit einem Wettbewerb, an dem 219 Architekten teilnahmen. Gewinner wurde Sir Basil Spence (1907–1976) mit seinem Vorschlag, die Ruinen des Gotteshauses in die Neuplanung einzubeziehen. Getrennt durch einen Vorhof, stehen sich der rund 90 Meter lange Neubau und die Reste des gotischen Gebäudes fast rechtwinklig gegenüber, wobei die Fläche des früheren Kirchenschiffs gartenartig gestaltet ist. Obwohl von der ›Avantgarde‹ nicht geschätzt, demonstrierte die neue Kathedrale eine Abwendung der anglikanischen Staatskirche von ihren bis dahin konservativen Bauvorstellungen. Insofern stellt sie ein wichtiges Zeugnis der modernen britischen Architektur dar. Aufgrund der in Zickzacklinien verlaufenden Längswände aus massiv verwendetem Sandstein ist der durch zwei Kapellen erweiterte Außenbau unverwechselbar.

In November 1940 the Luftwaffe bombed the English industrial city of Coventry and destroyed large parts of it, including the late Gothic cathedral, of which only the tower survived. On Hitler's orders British towns and cities were to be 'wiped out'. The construction of a new cathedral, the first modern one, began in 1951 following a competition in which 219 architects took part. The eventual winner was Sir Basil Spence (1907–76) with his proposal to incorporate the ruins in the new plan. The new building, about 90 metres long, and the remains of the Gothic building stand practically at right angles to one another, separated by a forecourt, whereby the area once occupied by the earlier nave is laid out as a garden. Although not appreciated by the avant-garde, the new cathedral demonstrated the Church of England's move away from its previously conservative architectural concepts. To this extent the cathedral is an important testament to modern British architecture. The exterior, made wider by the addition of two chapels, is unmistakable because of the zigzag lines of the solid sandstone longitudinal walls.

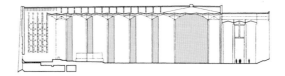

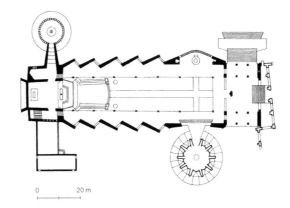

Grundriss und Längsschnitt
floor plan and
longitudinal section

0   20 m

Der längs gerichtete Kirchenraum kann rund 2 000 Gläubige auf beweglichem Gestühl aufnehmen. Die zunehmende Entfernung vom Hochaltar vor der Nordwand ist allerdings liturgisch von Nachteil. Überdeckt wird der dreischiffige Raum von einem Stahlbetongewölbe, dessen Maße und gliedernder Rhythmus von der alten Kathedrale übernommen sind. Die neue Konstruktion ist einem spätgotischen Netzgewölbe nachempfunden. Zwei Reihen sehr schlanker, nach unten verjüngter, vorgefertigter Betonstützen tragen das Gewölbe. Weil die Stützen auf dünnen Stahlkernen stehen, scheint die von Ove Arup entwickelte Konstruktion über dem Boden zu schweben. Im Gegensatz zum gotischen Bauprinzip ist das Gewölbe vom massiven Außenbau getrennt. Die schräg gestellten Mauerpfeiler der Außenwände bilden kleine Nischen aus, die raumhoch verglast sind. Die Ostwand ist beim Eingang für das Taufbecken nach außen gewölbt, gegenüber liegt der Zugang zur polygonalen Chapel of Unity. Über dem Altar hängt der 24 Meter hohe Wandteppich von Graham Sutherland mit einer Darstellung des triumphierenden Christus.

The longitudinally laid-out interior can accommodate 2,000 churchgoers on movable seating. The increasing distance from the high altar positioned in front of the north wall is however a disadvantage in liturgical terms. The space, consisting of a nave and two side aisles, is topped by a reinforced-concrete vault, the dimensions and structural rhythms of which were copied from those of the old cathedral. The new structure is an adaptation of a late-Gothic fan vault. Two rows of extremely slender prefabricated concrete pillars, tapering towards the base, support the vault. Since the pillars stand on thin steel cores, the structure, developed by Ove Arup, appears to float above the ground. In contrast to Gothic building principles, the vault is separate from the solid exterior. The piers of the outer walls, set at a slant, form small niches which are glazed full-length. At the entrance, the eastern wall curves outwards to hold the baptismal font, while the entrance to the polygonal Chapel of Unity lies opposite. Above the altar hangs Graham Sutherland's 24-metre-high tapestry of Christ in Glory.

Auch die neue Kathedrale will ein Hort der Künste sein. Die vielen Werke, hier die Dornenkrone über dem Chorgestühl, sorgen aber für Unruhe.

The new cathedral also wishes to be regarded as a treasury of the arts. However, the many works — here the Crown of Thorns over the choir stalls — also introduce an element of restlessness.

Egon Eiermann

Kaiser-Wilhelm-Gedächtniskirche
Berlin, Deutschland
1963

Kaiser Wilhelm Memorial Church
Berlin, Germany
1963

Der oktogonale Kirchenraum wird vom
blauen Licht der Glaswände erfüllt.
In das Wabenraster sind rote, gold-
farbige und grüne Flecken eingesetzt,
um den Eindruck zu steigern.

The octagonal church interior is filled
with blue light from the glass walls.
Red, gold and green specks are
inserted into the honeycomb grid in
order to enhance the effect.

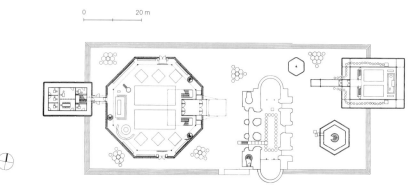

0   20 m

Grundriss
floor plan

1895 als ehrendes Denkmal für
Kaiser Wilhelm I. eingeweiht, wurde
die Kirche im November 1943 bei
einem alliierten Luftangriff zerstört.
Die für eine Ausstellung genutzte
Turmruine ist ein Mahnmal gegen den
Krieg und mit dem Nagelkreuz aus
Coventry zugleich eine Stätte der
Versöhnung. Der Neubau, der in Gestalt von vier Baukörpern die Ruine
flankiert, ist das Ergebnis eines Wettbewerbs. Egon Eiermann (1904 bis
1970) musste aufgrund von öffentlichen Protesten die Turmruine erhalten. Westlich von ihr stehen die neue
Kirche als geschlossenes Oktogon
und das flache ›Foyer‹ mit den Gemeinderäumen, auf ihrer Ostseite das
Sechseckprisma des neuen Turms
und die Kapelle. Eine gemeinsame
Plattform fasst die neuen Bauten
zusammen, die nach einem einheitli-
chen System errichtet wurden. Das
überall sichtbare Stahlskelett ist mit
Betonelementen ausgefacht, die
kassettenartig aufgelöst sind und in
Kirche, Turm und Kapelle farbige
Gläser nach einem künstlerischen
Entwurf von Gabriel Loire aus Chartres tragen.

Officially opened in 1895 as a memorial in honour of Emperor Wilhelm I,
the church was destroyed in an Allied
air attack in November 1943. The ruins
of the tower — used for an exhibition
— are a reminder of the horrors of war
and at the same time, with the Cross
of nails from Coventry, a place of reconciliation. The new four-block structure which flanks the ruins resulted
from a competition. Egon Eiermann
(1904–70) was forced to retain the
ruined tower following public protests.
To its west stand the new church in
the shape of a closed octagon and
the flat foyer with community rooms,
while to its east are the hexagonal
prism of the new tower and the chapel. A common platform unites these
new buildings, which were erected
according to a uniform system. The
steel skeleton, visible from all sides,
is infilled with concrete elements
which have a broken, compartmentalised surface appearance and, in
the church, tower and chapel, hold
coloured glass panes based on
an artistic design by Gabriel Loire of
Chartres.

Werner Max Moser

Kornfeldkirche
Riehen, Schweiz
1964

Kornfeld Church
Riehen, Switzerland
1964

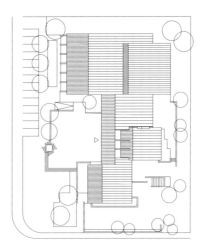

 Lageplan
site plan

0   20 m

Die plastisch ausgebildete Turm-
spitze erinnert an den Glockenturm der Vuoksenniska Kirche von
Alvar Aalto [Seite 232]. Auf dem
rechten Foto ist die geschützte
Vorhalle zu sehen.

The three-dimensionally built-up
top of the tower is reminiscent of
the bell tower of Alvar Aalto's
church at Vuoksenniska [p. 232].
The covered portico can be seen
in the photo on the right.

Werner Max Moser (1896–1970), Sohn des berühmten Architekten Karl Moser, gehört zu den wichtigen Vertretern der Schweizer Moderne. 1928 ein Gründungsmitglied der CIAM (Congrès Internationaux d'Architecture Moderne), war er unter anderem an der Planung der Werkbundsiedlung Neubühl in Zürich beteiligt. Seine Beschäftigung mit dem Kirchenbau begann bereits in den zwanziger Jahren. Die Kornfeldkirche in Riehen bei Basel, eines seiner Spätwerke, ist ein vorzügliches Beispiel für die ›sanfte Schweizermoderne‹ der Nachkriegszeit. Die unter asymmetrischen Satteldächern zusammengefasste Baugruppe fügt sich maßstäblich gut in das ruhige Wohnviertel ein. Als äußeres Zeichen dient der hohe Glockenturm mit seiner plastischen Krone. Die um einen Hof angeordnete Anlage ist zurückhaltend, aber einladend. Eine überdachte Vorhalle führt zum Kirchenfoyer als ›Ort der Begegnung‹. Auch der Kirchenraum ist durch die dominante Verwendung von Holz wohnlich gestaltet. Die in der Ostecke stehende Kanzel schließt den Kreis der feiernden Gemeinde, die Sitzreihen in L-Form treppen sich zum Abendmahltisch hin ab. Der erweiterbare Kirchenraum wirkt würdevoll, aber nicht ›sakral‹.

Werner Max Moser (1896–1970), son of the celebrated architect Karl Moser, was among the important representatives of Swiss Modernism. A founding member of CIAM (Congrès Internationaux d'Architecture Moderne) in 1928, he participated among other things in the planning of the Werkbund's Neubühl housing scheme in Zurich. His involvement with churchbuilding had begun as early as the 1920s. The Reformed Kornfeldkirche at Riehen, near Basle, one of his late works, is a superb example of the 'gentle Swiss Modernism' of the postwar period. The group of buildings drawn together under large, asymmetrical double-pitched roofs fits true to scale into the peaceful residential neighbourhood. The tall bell tower, with its sculpted top acts as an external sign. The complex arranged around a courtyard is restrained, but welcoming. A covered portico leads into the foyer as a 'place of meeting'. The interior layout too has a homely feel as a result of the dominant use of wood. The pulpit positioned in the eastern corner closes the circle of the celebrating congregation. The extendable interior space gives the impression of being dignified, but not 'sacred'.

Werner Max Moser hat den fast quadratischen Kirchenraum mit 350 Sitzplätzen als »Wohnstube« bezeichnet. Durch eine bewegliche Wand lässt sich der Gemeindesaal zuschalten.

Werner Max Moser described the near-square church interior with seating for 350 as a 'living-room'. The space occupied by the community hall can also be added in, if required, by means of a movable partition.

Aarno Ruusuvuori

Tapiola Kirche
Espoo, Finnland
1965

Tapiola Church
Espoo, Finland
1965

Der lichte Birkenwald, der große Bereiche von Tapiola durchzieht, reicht
bis zur Kirche. Bei diesem Blick
auf die fast geschlossene Nordwand
ist rechts das Pfarrhaus zu sehen.

The light birch woods which thread
through large areas of Tapiola extends right up to the church. In this
view, looking towards the almost
closed north wall, the presbytery is
visible on the right.

Tapiola, die in den frühen fünfziger Jahren gegründete ›Stadt im Wald‹ westlich von Helsinki, genießt als eine modellhafte Neuplanung seit langem Weltruhm. Im Geist der Nachkriegszeit nach Funktionen angelegt, ordnet sich dieser heutige Stadtteil von Espoo in ausgedehnte Wohnviertel um ein Geschäfts- und Einkaufszentrum. Östlich des Zentrums, in direkter Nachbarschaft zu einem Hotel und einer Schwimmhalle, wurde die Kirche mit Gemeindezentrum errichtet. Aarno Ruusuvuori (1925–1992), der zuvor die ebenso bedeutenden Betonkirchen in Hyvinkää und Vaasa geschaffen hatte, entwarf die Anlage in Abgrenzung zur geschäftigen Umgebung als eine Welt für sich. Westlich der Kirche liegen an begrünten Innenhöfen die flachen Gebäude der Gemeindeeinrichtungen, die durch eine Mauer vom Fußweg abgeschirmt sind. Den Außenbau des hoch aufragenden, fast burgartigen Kirchenkubus prägen abgewinkelte Betontafeln, welche die Fassaden vertikal gliedern. Die Kirche hat keinen Turm, sondern am Eingang einen niedrigen Glockenträger.

As a planned new model town Tapiola, the 'town in the woods' founded to the west of Helsinki in the early 1950s, has enjoyed international fame for a long time now. Laid out functionally in the spirit of the post-war period, Tapiola — today part of Espoo — is arranged as widely spaced residential districts surrounding a business and shopping centre. The church together with parish centre was erected east of the central zone in the direct vicinity of a hotel and an indoor swimming pool. Aarno Ruusuvuori (1925–92), who had previously created the equally important concrete churches at Hyvinkää and Vaasa, designed the complex as distinct from its bustling environment, in a world of its own. Located to the west of the church in grassy inner courtyards, the flat buildings of the parish offices are shielded from a footpath by a wall. Angled concrete slabs that organise the façades vertically mark the exterior of the high, almost fortress-like cube of the church. The church has no tower, but there is a low bell-stand at the entrance.

Grundriss
floor plan

0   20 m

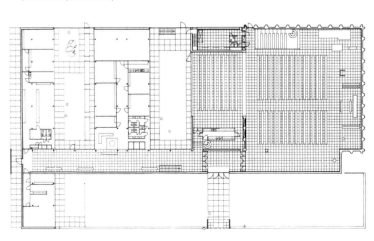

Auf den Kircheneingang folgt zunächst ein niedriges Seitenfoyer, damit der anschließende Saal umso intensiver erlebt werden kann. Wie bei seinen anderen Kirchenbauten ist Ruusuvuori auch hier ein Raum von großer Klarheit und Eindringlichkeit geglückt. Aus akustischen Gründen wurde den massiven Stahlbetonwänden eine innere Schale aus graubraunen Betonsteinen vorgemauert. Der bis auf die Prinzipalstücke fast schmucklose Raum wird durch das nordische Licht ›beseelt‹, das vor allem aus der nach Westen hoch gelegenen Glaswand einfällt. Um das Tageslicht zu filtern und zugleich auf den Chor vor der Ostwand zu konzentrieren, wurde auf der Innenseite der Glaswand ein tiefes Gitter aus Betontafeln eingebaut. Außerdem gibt es Öffnungen in der Dachhaut. Ruusuvuori, der seit den sechziger Jahren zu den großen finnischen Architekten einer gestrafften Moderne zählte, stellte seine Arbeit unter das Motto: »Die Struktur ist der Schlüssel zur Schönheit.« Dieser Ansatz ist nicht immer verstanden worden. Seit dem Wettbewerb von 1961 umstritten, wird die Tapiola Kirche von Kritikern bis heute als ›Beton-Bunker‹ bezeichnet. Adresse: Espoo-Tapiola.

The entrance to the church is followed initially by a low side foyer so that the visitor experiences the adjoining single-nave space all the more intensely. As with his other churches, here again Ruusuvuori succeeded in creating a space of great clarity and impact. An inner shell of grey-brown concrete blocks was constructed within the solid reinforced-concrete walls for acoustic reasons. The interior, almost devoid of decoration except for the principal elements, is enlivened by the Nordic light which enters principally from the glass wall set high up towards the west. In order to filter the daylight and at the same time concentrate attention on the chancel in front of the eastern wall, a deep grid of concrete slabs was inserted on the inner side of the glass wall. There are additional apertures in the skin of the roof. Ruusuvuori, who was regarded as one of the great Finnish architects of a streamlined form of Modernism from the 1960s onwards, worked with his credo: 'Structure is the key to beauty'. This approach was not always understood. Controversial ever since the competition of 1961, the Tapiola Church is still described by critics today as a 'concrete bunker'. Address: Tapiola, Espoo.

Durch seine asketische Einfachheit wirkt der hohe Kirchenraum erhaben. Im Verlauf des Tages ändert sich das Spiel von Licht und Schatten auf den grau-braunen Betonsteinwänden.

The high church interior gives an impression of solemnity as a result of its ascetic simplicity. The interplay of light and shadows on the grey-brown concrete-block walls changes over the course of the day.

Raili und Reima Pietilä

Kaleva Kirche
Tampere, Finnland
1966

Kaleva Church
Tampere, Finland
1966

Die Industriestadt Tampere wird auch »skandinavisches Manchester« genannt. In den fünfziger Jahren nahm die Bevölkerung derart zu, dass mehrere neue Wohnquartiere errichtet werden mussten. Eines dieser großen, aber gesichtslosen Viertel sollte durch einen Kirchenbau seine Mitte und damit seine Identität erhalten. Deshalb wurde im Wettbewerb von 1959 eine monumentale Lösung gefordert. Reima Pietilä (1923–1993) und seine Frau Raili entwarfen für das Bauwerk auf einem Hügel eine skulpturale Gestalt von 30 Metern Höhe. Die konvexen oder konkaven Bauteile aus Stahlbeton, die sich allesamt unterscheiden, wurden in einer aus dem Industriebau übernommenen Gleitschalung ausgeführt. Ur-sprünglich in Sichtbeton geplant, sind die organoid wirkenden Wände mit hellgelben Platten verkleidet. Zwischen ihnen öffnen sich insgesamt 18 schmale Fensterschlitze, die vom Bo-den bis zum Flachdach reichen. Der Außenbau spiegelt sich im Innenraum mit 1120 Sitzplätzen. Mit ihm hat Reima Pietilä, lange Jahre der Antipode von Alvar Aalto, einen der eindrucksvollsten modernen Innenräume in Finnland geschaffen. Adresse: Tampere-Kaleva, Kaupinkatu.

The industrial city of Tampere is also known as 'the Scandinavian Manchester'. In the 1950s the population increased to such an extent that several new residential zones had to be built. The intention was to give one of these large, but faceless districts a centre — and thus an identity — by building a church. The competition of 1959 consequently demanded a monumental solution. Reima Pietilä (1923–93) and his wife Raili designed a sculptural shape, 30 metres in height, for the construction on a flat-topped hill. The convex or concave reinforced-concrete building elements, all different from one another, were executed in a slipform technique copied from industrial construction methods. Originally planned to be made of exposed concrete, the organoid-effect walls are faced with bright yellow slabs. Between these are a total of 18 narrow window slits extending from the ground to the flat roof. The powerful exterior is mirrored in the interior, which has seating for 1,120. It appears foreshortened because its maximum width is roughly half its length. Here Reima Pietilä, for many years the antithesis of Alvar Aalto, created one of the most impressive modern interiors in Finland. Address: Kaupinkatu, Kaleva, Tampere.

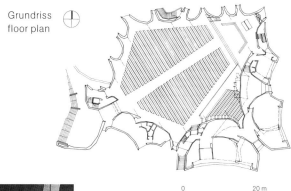

0   20 m

Eng auf den Altarbereich zulaufend,
soll der Kirchenraum eine ›gotische
Atmosphäre‹ vermitteln. Reima Pietilä
hat auch die zweifach geknickte Altar-
skulptur mit dem Titel *Gebrochenes
Rohr* entworfen. Die aus der massiven
Betonwand vorspringende Kanzel
wird außerdem durch eine muschel-
förmige Skulptur betont.

Narrowing towards the altar zone,
the interior is intended to convey
a 'Gothic atmosphere'. Reima Pietilä
also designed the altar sculpture
with a double bend entitled *Broken
Reed*. The pulpit jutting out from
the solid concrete wall is given additional emphasis through the shell-
shaped sculpture.

Helmut Striffler

Versöhnungskirche
Dachau, Deutschland
1967

Church of Reconciliation
Dachau, Germany
1967

Diese Kirche auf dem Gelände des
ehemaligen Konzentrationslagers
(KZ) in Dachau bei München war eine
der großen Herausforderungen im
Sakralbau des 20. Jahrhunderts. Angeregt wurde sie von ausländischen
Protestanten, die teilweise selbst
im Lager gelitten hatten. Im März
1933 eingerichtet, war Dachau das
erste KZ der Nationalsozialisten. Hier
wurden vor allem politische Gefange-
ne inhaftiert, darunter viele Pfarrer
und Geistliche. Seit 1965 ist das KZ-
Gelände eine Gedenkstätte, die alljährlich von zahllosen Menschen aus
vielen Nationen aufgesucht wird.
In welcher Gestalt aber kann eine der
Versöhnung gewidmete Kirche an
staatlichen Terror und persönliches
Leid erinnern? Der im Wettbewerb
erfolgreiche Mannheimer Architekt
Helmut Striffler entwarf einen plastisch durchgebildeten ›Gegenort‹ zum
Rechteck-Schema der KZ-Planung.
In ein Kiesbett eingegraben, hat der
Neubau nirgends einen rechten Winkel – auch die Böden und Decken
sind schräg. Die ganze Anlage besteht aus einem angenehm patinier-
ten Sichtbeton.

This church in the grounds of the
former concentration camp at Dachau,
near Munich, presented one of the
great challenges of 20th-century religious architecture. Its creation was
prompted by foreign Protestants,
some of whom had themselves suffered in the camp. Set up in March
1933, Dachau was the Nazis' first
concentration camp. It held mainly
political prisoners, including many
clergymen and priests. Since 1965
the site has been a memorial, visited
every year by countless people
from many nations. But in what form
can a church dedicated to reconciliation also act as a reminder of state-
organised terror and personal suffering? The winner of the competition,
Mannheim based architect Helmut
Striffler, designed a three-dimensionally modelled 'counter-place' to the
rectangular layout of the concentration camp. Sunk below a layer of
gravel, the new building does not
contain a single right angle: even the
floors and ceilings are set on the
slant. The entire complex is built of
well-patinated exposed concrete.

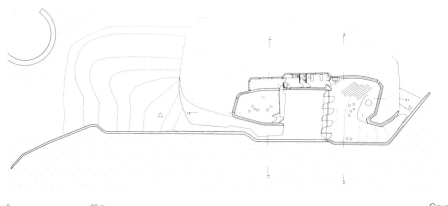

0   20 m

Grundriss
floor plan

Die Kirche mit einem separaten Leseraum ist als ›Weg‹ angelegt: Er führt
von der terrassierten Freitreppe hinab
in einen intimen Hof und aus der Kirche wieder hinauf zum Licht.

The church with its separate reading
room is laid out as a 'path': from
the terraced flight of steps the visitor
goes down into an intimate courtyard,
and then from the church back up
into the light.

Die Bronzestatue *Drei Männer im Feuerofen* wurde von holländischen Protestanten gestiftet. Carel Kneulman nennt sein Werk im Leseraum »ein Sinnbild des Vertrauens auf Errettung«.

The bronze statue *Three Men in the Fiery Furnace* was donated by Dutch Protestants. Carel Kneulman calls his work in the reading room 'a symbol of trust in salvation'.

Helmut Striffler hat seine Versöhnungskirche selbst charakterisiert: »Sie ist als lebendige Spur in die unbarmherzige Fläche des Lagers eingegraben, als eine bergende Furche gegen das unmenschliche Ausgesetztsein, das man auch heute immer wieder spürt, wenn man durch das Lager geht.« Der Weg durch das Gebäude führt von der Freitreppe aus zunächst durch einen dunklen Gang, der sich zu einem Innenhof öffnet. An ihm liegen der kleinere Leseraum und die sich aufgipfelnde Kirche gegenüber, wobei die Räume durch Glaswände aufeinander bezogen sind. Der fast schmucklose Kultraum mit einer Deckenkonstruktion aus Stahl und Holz unterteilt sich in einen intimen Andachtsbereich und einen ansteigenden Weg zum Ausgang im Kiesbett. In den scheinbar frei fließenden Betonkörper sind mehrere Kunstwerke integriert, etwa Reliefs mit Darstellungen leidender Häftlinge von Hubertus von Pilgrim, die zusammen mit der Außenwand gegossen wurden (rechts oben). Das schwenkbare Stahltor zum Hof hat Fritz Kühn mit einem Text in vier Sprachen gestaltet. Folgende Bibelworte sind in die harte Oberfläche geätzt: »Zuflucht ist unter dem Schatten deiner Flügel.«

Helmut Striffler himself characterised his church of reconciliation thus: 'It is sunk into the pitiless surface of the camp as a living trace, as a sheltering furrow against the inhuman state of exposure that one still senses today, again and again, when walking through the camp'. The path through the building initially leads from the steps through a dark passageway which opens out into an inner courtyard. Opposite lie the smaller reading room and the church rising up to a peak, the spaces being interconnected via glass walls. The almost entirely plain place of worship with a steel-and-wood ceiling is divided into an intimate zone for prayer and an ascending path that leads up to the exit in the gravel under-layer. Several works of art are integrated into the seemingly free-flowing concrete masses: for example reliefs depicting suffering prisoners by Hubertus von Pilgrim, cast at the same time as the outer wall (top right). The swivelling steel gate into the courtyard with a text in four languages was fashioned by Fritz Kühn. The following words from the Bible are etched into the hard surface: 'Refuge is in the shadow of your wings'.

Gabriele Schickel

Abschied von der Wegkirche
Süddeutscher Kirchenbau nach dem Zweiten Weltkrieg

Nach Kriegsende galten die ersten Bemühungen der Sicherung und Wiederherstellung ruinöser Sakralbauten. Ein Wiederaufbau, der die Kriegsschäden unsichtbar machen sollte, fand in der Bevölkerung große Zustimmung, weil er dem Wunsch nach der Rückkehr zu einem scheinbar unversehrten und im weiteren Sinne unschuldigen Zustand entsprach. In Süddeutschland jedoch steht im Gegensatz dazu der Name von Hans Döllgast in herausragender Weise für einen dokumentarischen Umgang mit den architektonischen Wunden des Krieges, welcher die Haltung des Un-Geschehen-Machens verweigert.

Beim Wiederaufbau der benediktinischen Abteikirche St. Bonifaz in München 1949/50 schuf er aus den neoromanischen Basilikaruinen einen modernen Sakralraum, in dessen Gestaltung sowohl der Vorgängerbau als auch die Spuren der gewaltsamen jüngsten Vergangenheit einbezogen wurden. Obwohl dadurch nur ein verkürzter, eher breiter als langer Kirchenraum entstand, beschränkte sich Döllgast bei der Neuerrichtung der Kirche auf die Ausdehnung der erhaltenen, südlichen Langhausmauern, die er mit einer Nordwand aus Trümmerziegeln schloss. Beschädigte Sockel, Säulen und Kapitelle wurden durch klar abgesetzte Betonformen ergänzt, das Dach mit offenem Tragwerk war in der Untersicht mit unbehandeltem Heraklith verschalt. Döllgasts Absicht war es, durch die Unterscheidung in Material und Form die Nahtstellen zwischen originalen Gebäudeteilen und Ergänzungen sichtbar werden zu lassen und damit gleichsam die geschichtlichen Schichten des Gebäudes zu dokumentieren. Deshalb sollten auch die Ziegelwände unverputzt bleiben. Diese Vorstellung stieß jedoch bei den Auftraggebern auf Widerspruch, so dass der Kirchenraum schon bei seiner Vollendung weiß getüncht und 1971 erneut entscheidend umgestaltet wurde.

Orientierung an der Vorkriegsmoderne

Als eigentlicher Neubeginn des Kirchenbaus nach der Wiederaufbauphase galt in Süddeutschland die 1955 geweihte evangelische Matthäuskirche in München. Um die gesellschaftliche Umorientierung als tief greifende Wandlung auch im kirchlichen Bereich sichtbar zu machen, griff man gerade in der evangelischen Kirche auf Positionen der Vorkriegsmoderne in Bezug auf die Verwendung neuer Materialien und Grundrisse zurück. So schloss Gustav Gsaenger bei der Planung von St. Matthäus an parabelförmige Kirchengrundrisse an, wie sie schon Otto Bartning oder Dominikus Böhm verwendet hatten. Durch konkav und konvex geführte Außenwände entwickelte er jedoch die geometrische Bestimmtheit der Parabel zu einem freien, organisch geschwungenen Grundriss weiter.

Der Kirchenraum selbst ist mit Ausnahme der Apsis und einem Teil der Nordwand von gangartigen Nebenräumen sowie dem im Westen nierenförmig quer gelagerten Gemeindesaal umgeben. Auch im Aufriss sind die geschwungenen Linien beibehalten, so dass das dünne Betondach in einer Kurve über die Altarzone emporsteigt. Erscheint der Baukörper von drei Seiten entsprechend den außen liegenden Gemeinderäumen mit vertikaler Aufglasung wie ein profaner Hallen- oder Saalbau der fünfziger Jahre, so hat Gsaenger an der Ostseite mit der geschlossenen Apsiswand und einem mächtigen, quadratischen Turm das Kirchengebäude doch in einem traditionell-monumentalen Sinne charakterisiert. Im Inneren zeigt der um sieben Stufen erhöhte Altarraum in der Parabelspitze, auf den drei zusammen-

Gustav Gsaenger
Matthäuskirche / St Matthew
München / Munich, 1955

Gabriele Schickel

Farewell to the Processional Church
South German Church Architecture after the Second World War

At the end of the war, early efforts were aimed at securing and restoring sacred buildings that lay in ruins. Reconstruction, which would erase the ravages of war, found widespread support among the public as it corresponded with the desire to return to seemingly undisturbed and, in a broader sense, innocent living conditions. In southern Germany, however, Hans Döllgast's approach provided a counterpoint in that his documentary treatment of the architectural wounds inflicted by the war rejected this attitude of undoing all that had occurred.

During the reconstruction of the Benedictine abbey St Boniface in Munich (1949/50), Döllgast transformed the neo-Romanesque ruins of the basilica into a modern sacred space whose design incorporated both its historic predecessor and the traces of the violent recent past. The architect restricted his reconstruction efforts to expanding the surviving walls of the main aisle on the south side and erecting a north wall constructed with reclaimed bricks as a termination, even though this approach resulted in a shortened space that is wide rather than elongated. Damaged plinths, columns and capitals were reinforced with distinctly different concrete moulds and the exposed roof truss was clad in untreated Heraklith insulating boards. Döllgast aimed to make visible the seams where original building components and new completion met by differentiating between material and form, thereby documenting the historic layers of the building. The same logic lay behind the proposal to use exposed brick walls on the interior, an idea that met with strong opposition from his clients. Consequently, the interior walls were immediately whitewashed upon completion and completely refurbished in 1971.

Finding Inspiration in Pre-war Modernism

In 1955, the consecration of the Protestant church of St Matthew in Munich marked a new stage in church architecture after the reconstruction phase in southern Germany. The Protestant Church, especially, looked to pre-war modernism for inspiration with regard to new materials and plans as an external expression of the profound impact of societal changes in the Church. In designing St Matthew's, Gustav Gsaenger returned to the idea of parabolic church plans previously employed by Otto Bartning and Dominikus Böhm. Yet Gsaenger translated the severe geometry of the parabola into a free, organically curved plan by plotting the exterior walls in concave and convex lines.

With the exception of the apse and one section of the north wall, the church space itself is surrounding by corridor-like ancillary spaces and the kidney-shaped transverse community hall at the western end. The curved theme is carried through to the vertical plane where the thin concrete roof rises in a curve above the altar zone. While the fabric appears like a typical 1950s secular hall structure on three sides by virtue of the vertical glazing of the attached community space, Gsaenger nevertheless invested the church with a traditional, monumental character on the east face where he created a solid, unbroken apse wall and added a massive, square tower. In the interior, the altar space, which is raised by seven steps and to which three converging rows of pews lead, marks a distinct transverse axis at the tip of the parabola where the altar is framed by two of a total of six black columns and the floor-to-ceiling wall mosaic in the background. The column on the south side supports the elevated chancel with acoustic canopy. To the west, the space is divided from the

Hans Döllgast
St. Bonifaz / St Boniface
München / Munich, 1950

laufende Bankreihen hinführen, eine klare Querachse, in der zwei von insgesamt sechs schwarzen Säulen den Altar und das dahinter liegende raumhohe Wandmosaik rahmen. Die südliche Säule trägt die erhöhte Kanzel mit Schalldeckel. Im Westen ist der Raum durch Glaswände und Türen gegen den bei Bedarf zu öffnenden Gemeindesaal abgetrennt. Durch eine weit vorgezogene, tief liegende Empore versuchte Gsaenger die unklare Grenzsituation für den Sakralraum zu lösen. Die in St. Matthäus sichtbare architektonische Ambivalenz zwischen sakral und profan, traditionell und modern spiegelt eine bis heute virulente Problematik im Kirchenbau.

Dagegen kann die ebenfalls 1955 geweihte katholische Klosterkirche Herz Jesu in München, ein Werk der Architekten Alexander von Branca und Herbert Groethuysen, als erste Neuinterpretation eines Sakralraums nach dem Krieg gelten, bei dem Stahlbetonkonstruktion und Raumgefüge als kongruent zur religiösen Funktion erlebt werden. Mit der nördlichen Längswand fügt sich die Kirche in die geschlossene Wohnbebauung eines städtischen Straßenraums ein und schließt das den Klosterhof umgebende Geviert aus Wohn- und Wirtschaftsgebäuden nach vorne ab. Schon von außen wird der Aufbau des Raumes im Dach mit einer von vier Quertonnen durchschnittenen Längstonne thematisiert. Der rechteckige, hohe Innenraum mit Altar und Haupteingang in der zur Klosterpforte orientierten Längsachse zeigt eine Einbeziehung der Konstruktion in die Raumgestaltung. Hier ist das strenge Betonraster gegen die weiß ge-schlemmte Ziegelausfachung der Wandflächen sichtbar und trägt neben den schlanken, kantigen Betonpfeilern, die im Rhythmus der Quertonnen des Daches die beiden Bankreihen im Kirchenschiff begleiten, zur Raumordnung bei. Beidseitig engen Querwände den Chor auf den erhöhten Altarraum hin ein und schaffen dahinter liegende separate Andachtsräume für die Klosterschwestern. Der Altarraum selbst endet in einer hohen geraden Betonwand mit dem Tabernakel und einem Kreuz und wird von flachbogigen Betonlamellen überfangen, durch die das Hauptlicht des Raumes auf den Altarbereich konzentriert wird.

Eine ähnlich dichte Verschränkung von traditionsgebundener Raumauffassung und moderner Gestaltung zeigt die 1962 fertig gestellte evangelische Erlöserkirche in Erding-Klettham (Oberbayern). Hans-Busso von Busse führte das auf einem organischen Architekturverständnis basierende Projekt zusammen mit Roland Büch durch. Die Kirche liegt zwischen einem Vorhof mit Glockenträger und der Pfarrwohnung mit Gemeindesaal in einer Flucht mit den Ziegelmauern der längsrechteckigen, geschlossenen Anlage. Ihr schiefergedecktes, geschwungenes Zeltdach wird von einer bemerkenswerten Holzleimkonstruktion getragen, die im Inneren Raumform, Raumaufteilung und -stimmung herstellt. Sie besteht aus mächtigen Bindern, die im Mittelschiff spitzbogenartig zum Dach hochsteigen und flachbogig über die Seitenschiffe ausschwingen. Licht erhält der Raum durch ein umlaufendes Fensterband, den verglasten Windfang unter der Empore im Westen und die vollverglaste Abschlusswand im Osten, vor der die längsrechteckige, ziegelgemauerte Altarwand mit einfachem hölzernem Altartisch, Lesepult und Kreuz steht. Die Bänke sind in dem längs gerichteten Raum als geschlossener Block im Mittelschiff angeordnet.

Alexander von Branca · Herbert Groethuysen
Klosterkirche Herz Jesu
nunnery church of the Sacred Heart
München / Munich, 1955

community hall by glass walls and doors, which can be opened when needed. Gsaenger sought to relieve the somewhat vague peripheral position of the sanctuary by adding a low, cantilevered gallery. The architectonic ambivalence between the sacred and the profane, tradition and modernity, so evident in St Matthew, is a reflection of a virulent problem that continues to plague church architecture to this day.

Conversely, Alexander von Branca's and Herbert Groethuysen's Catholic nunnery church of the Sacred Heart (Herz Jesu) in Munich can be justly seen as the first new post-war interpretation of a sacred space, where reinforced steel structure and spatial construct are experienced congruently with the religious function. The longitudinal north wall integrates the church into the dense housing environment of an urban quarter, forming the frontal completion to the quadrangle of residential and commercial buildings around the monastery courtyard. The internal structure of the space is visible even from the outside in the shape of the roof: a longitudinal barrel crossed by four shorter barrels at right angles. The high rectangular interior with altar and main entrance aligned to the longitudinal axis, which is oriented toward the monastery portal, reflects how the construction is integrated into the design of the interior space. The severe concrete grid is clearly discernible in the whitewashed brick infill of the wall surfaces. The grid contributes to the internal order in combination with the slender, angular concrete columns accompanying the two sets of pews in the apse in synch with the rhythm established by the crosswise roof barrels. Transverse walls on both sides attenuate the choir in the direction of the raised altar space, creating separate prayer rooms for the sisters behind it. The altar space itself terminates in a tall straight concrete wall with the tabernacle and a cross. Shallow concrete louvres direct most of the light penetrating into the space on the altar.

A similarly close integration of traditional spatial ideas and modern design is found in the Protestant Church of the Redeemer (Erlöserkirche) in Erding-Klettham (Upper Bavaria), completed in 1962. Hans-Busso von Busse executed the project, which was based on an organic reading of architecture, in collaboration with Roland Büch. The church is situated between a forecourt with bell tower and the vicarage with community hall in alignment with the brick walls of the enclosed rectangular complex. The slate-covered curved tent roof is supported by a striking bonded wood structure, which determines the form, divisions and mood of the interior space. It is comprised of massive girders that rise steeply toward the roof above the nave-like lancet arches and settle into shallow arches above the aisles. Light penetrates into the space through the continuous window ribbon, the glass-enclosed porch beneath the western gallery and the fully glazed end wall to the east. The latter is preceded by the rectangular altar wall in brickwork, as well as the altar, lectern and cross, all in plain wood. The pews are arranged in a solid block formation set into the nave of the longitudinally oriented space.

From Processional Church to Parish Centre

In South Germany, church architecture did not become fully emancipated from traditional references, especially the processional church, until the late 1960s, when new themes espoused by theologians and communities alike were translated into

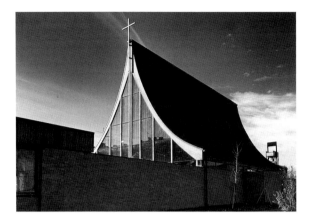

Hans-Busso von Busse
Erlöserkirche
Church of the Redeemer
Erding, 1962

Von der Wegkirche zum Gemeindezentrum

Erst Ende der sechziger Jahre hat sich der Kirchenbau in Süddeutschland vollends von traditionellen Bezügen, besonders
der Wegkirche, emanzipiert und sowohl auf evangelischer wie
katholischer Seite neue, von Theologen und Gemeinden ge-
wünschte Inhalte architektonisch formuliert. Zum Hauptthe-
ma entwickelte sich neben der Zentralkirche der Bau von
Gemeindezentren, in denen der Stellenwert des Kirchengebäudes unter-schiedliche Interpretationen erfuhr. Grundsätzlich
waren durch die Einführung kleinerer Gemeinden auch kleinere
Räume erforderlich. Die Motivationen der einzelnen Pfarreien
reichten jedoch von dem Ziel, alle gemeindlichen Belange in
einer Bauanlage zu konzentrieren, um einen engeren Zusammenhang zwischen Kirche und Leben zu schaffen, über Sparsam-
keit bis hin zu dem Verlangen nach intimeren, auf die Anzahl
der Gemeindemitglieder zugeschnittenen Gebetsräumen. Gemeindezentren waren und sind aber auch eine mögliche kirchliche und architektonische Antwort auf die geänderten äußeren
Bedingungen für den Kirchenbau.

Ohne auf die Problematik näher einzugehen, fällt auf, dass die
Mehrzahl der Kirchen seit den sechziger Jahren isoliert in einem
städtebaulich undifferenzierten Umfeld, oft zwischen Wohn-
blockzeilen, in einer Einfamilienhaussiedlung oder zwischen
Hochhäusern ihren Platz finden musste. Die strukturelle Schwie-
rigkeit dieser Standorte wurde von der Gebäudekonzeption
her durch die Weglassung des Kirchturms, der Ostung und eines
architektonisch deutlich akzentuierten Haupteingangs verstärkt, so dass bei Kirchenbauten von einem symptomatischen
Verzicht nicht nur auf Repräsentation, sondern auch auf eine
ordnende Wirkung nach außen und von einer Konzentration
auf das Innere gesprochen werden kann. Dennoch wurden oft
auch bei den Innenräumen selbst geringe Bindungen an eine
christliche Architektursprache durch die Verwendung profaner
Grundrisse und Formen aufgegeben und durch die Reduktion
auf bloße Gebrauchszwecke ersetzt.

Am konsequentesten ging im süddeutschen Raum Kurt Ackermann bei der Planung evangelischer Gemeindezentren in einem
geometrisch-funktionalen Stil mit diesen, zeitweise auch vom
Selbstverständnis der Institution Kirche her begründeten Vor-
gaben um. Die 1971 geweihte Friedenskirche in Gundelfingen
an der Donau, nahe am Stadtzentrum zwischen der Haupt-
durchgangsstraße, dem Parkplatz eines Supermarktes und einem
Wohngebiet mit Einfamilienhäusern situiert, liegt an einem abgesenkten Hof und bildet mit den im rechten Winkel ange-
schlossenen, niedrigeren Gemeinderäumen eine Baugruppe. Die
Kirche ist als kubischer Baukörper mit einem offenen, in das
Bauwerk integriertem Glockenträger errichtet. Von dem gedeck-
ten Verbindungsgang zwischen Kirche und Gemeindezentrum
aus betritt man einen Vorraum, der seitlich in den eigentlichen
Sakralraum führt. Wie der Außenbau besteht dieser hohe,
fast quadratische Raum aus weiß geschlemmtem Ziegelmauerwerk. Die Decke wird von verleimten schwarzen, quadratischen
Holzbindern getragen, der Fußboden besteht aus roten Ton-
fliesen. Licht erhält der Raum durch eine Laterne über dem
Altar sowie je ein Fenster an der Rückwand und in der Orgelni-
sche gegenüber dem Eingang. Der einfache hölzerne Altartisch
war nach dem Konzept des Architekten von zwei Seiten mit
im rechten Winkel zueinander stehenden Stuhlreihen umgeben,
die heute halbkreisförmig angeordnet sind.

Kurt Ackermann
Friedenskirche / Peace church
Gundelfingen, 1971

architectonic form in Protestant and Catholic parishes. In addition to the centralised church plan, the building of community centres where the status of the 'church' or sanctuary proper was interpreted in a variety of ways soon emerged as a principal theme. A common premise was that smaller congregations also required smaller rooms. Yet the individual parishes were motivated by a wide range of interests from aiming to concentrate communal services in a single complex to achieving a closer integration of church and everyday life, to economising or fulfilling a desire for more intimate prayer rooms designed for the size of a particular congregation. Parish centres were and are, however, also a possible ecclesiastic and architectonic response to the changed external conditions for church architecture.

Without exploring the issue in detail, it is nevertheless worth noting that since the 1960s most churches had to make do with anonymous urban surroundings, frequently situated between housing blocks, single-family estates or high-rise developments. The structural challenge posed by these locations was emphasised by the absence of church tower, eastward orientation and distinct main entrance. In short, one can speak of a symptomatic relinquishment in church buildings not only of forms of representation, but also of external order in favour of a focus on the interior. Even in the interior, however, the last vestiges of adherence to a Christian architectural vocabulary were often abandoned by the employment of secular ground-floor plans and forms and the reduction to a pure utilitarianism.

The most rigorous implementation of these characteristics, which were partially founded in the Church's new self image, are found in Kurt Ackermann's Protestant parish centres in the southern Germany, realised in a functional, geometric style. The Peace church in Gundelfingen on the Danube, consecrated in 1971, is located near the town centre between the main traffic artery, a supermarket car park and a single-family housing estate. It lies in a sunken courtyard and forms a cohesive ensemble together with the lower community rooms connected to the main building at right angles. The church is cubical, with an open bell tower integrated into the principal structure. Visitors step from the covered walkway between church and community centre into an ante-chamber that leads into the actual sanctuary from the side. Like the exterior, this tall, nearly square space is realised in whitewashed brickwork. The ceiling is supported by square, black, bonded timber girders and the floor is covered in red terracotta tiles.

A lantern suspended above the altar and two windows — one set into the rear wall and one in the organ niche across from the entrance — allow light to penetrate into the interior. The simple wooden altar was initially surrounded on two sides by rows of chairs set at right angles, in keeping with the architect's vision; today, they are arranged in a semicircle. In Gundelfingen, the church still stands as an independent building with some concessions to established traditions. On the other hand in his design for the Protestant Christ church in Bad Füssing (Lower Bavaria; consecrated in 1972), the architect subsumed the specific task of creating a church space wholly under his rigorous architectural concept based on the right angle, interpreting it merely as one functional space among others. The community centre sits at the top of a slope and presents a hermetic, elongated rectangular fair-faced concrete visage to the chaotic development of its surroundings. The church, em-

Kurt Ackermann
Friedenskirche / Peace church
Gundelfingen, 1971

Während in Gundelfingen die Kirche noch als eigenständiger Baukörper erscheint und gewisse Konzessionen gegenüber dem Kultus gemacht wurden, unterwarf der Architekt in der 1972 geweihten evangelischen Christuskirche in Bad Füssing (Niederbayern) die spezifische Aufgabe Kirchenraum völlig seinem strikten, auf dem rechten Winkel basierenden Architekturkonzept und fasste ihn als einen Funktionsraum unter anderen auf. Das Gemeindezentrum liegt auf einer Anböschung und begegnet der chaotischen Bebauung des Umfelds mit einem hermetischen, längsrechteckigen Sichtbetonbau. Die Kirche, am Außenbau durch einen offenen Glockenträger hervorgehoben, ist im Inneren auf einen schmucklosen Gebetsraum reduziert. Die Wände des relativ niedrigen, nahezu quadratischen Raumes mit einem Fußboden aus naturfarbenem Kokosteppich und einer Decke aus quadratischen weißen Holzbindern sind in Sichtbeton belassen. Licht erhält der Raum von der Rückwand zum Innenhof her. In der originalen Anordnung ist eine kleine halbrunde Nische neben dem Altartisch für das Taufbecken vorgesehen, während die Orgel schräg in einer vorderen Raumecke platziert ist. Der ursprünglich völlig puristische Raum mit im rechten Winkel zueinander stehenden Stuhlreihen, wurde 1994 mit großformatigen Gemälden ausgestattet. Zugleich wurde die Anordnung von Altar und Taufbecken verändert.

Aus einer völlig gegenteiligen Auffassung heraus entstand die 1979 geweihte katholische Kirche St. Ignatius in München-Kleinhadern. Der Architekt Josef Wiedemann verstand die Kirche mit Gemeindezentrum als Oase in einer unpersönlichen Neubausiedlung mit mehrgeschossigen Wohnblocks und legte die niedrige Bebauung ringförmig um das zentrale Kirchengebäude. Der durch ein Fensterband sehr helle, zwölfeckige Kirchenraum mit Ziegelwand wird von einem Zeltdach mit frei stehendem, hölzernem Dachstuhl aus geschälten Baumstämmen überdeckt. Der steinerne, auf einem Podest stehende sechseckige Altar ist etwas aus der Raummitte gerückt und auf allen Seiten von den Gemeindebänken und der Sedilienbank umgeben. Wiedemann bezog sich bei dieser Konzeption auf die mit den Zentralkirchen verbundene Vorstellung von der um den Opfertisch versammelten Gemeinde und versuchte dem Raum durch die Absenkung zur Mitte mit dem Grundstein hin sowie durch die 12-Zahl der Stützen, durch Ährenmuster in den Ziegelwänden und andere Details eine christlich-tradierte, symbolische Dimension zu geben.

Neue Kirchen am Millennium

Auch bei den jüngsten, in den Jahren 2000 und 2001 geweihten süddeutschen Kirchenbauten lässt sich eine Tendenz zu monolithischen Gebäudeformen und asketischer Raumbildung feststellen. Großer Wert wird in diesen Neubauten jedoch auf eine sakrale oder meditative Raumstimmung gelegt, die aus dem verwendeten Material und der Lichtführung hervorgehen soll. Die ökumenische Kapelle des BRK-Seniorenzentrums in Tirschenreuth (Oberpfalz) von Brückner & Brückner etwa ist als hohes kubisches Gebäude errichtet, dessen Außenwände den gleichmäßigen Wechsel von Pfeilern in Ziegelmauerwerk und vertikalen Fensterschlitzen zeigen. Im Inneren wird die Altarwand von Lichtstreifen gerahmt, der Längsraum durch das einfallende Seitenlicht rhythmisiert.

Eine komplizierte Lichtinszenierung bestimmt die katholische Kirche St. Jakobus und Bruder Konrad mit einem Gemeinde-

Kurt Ackermann
Christuskirche / Christ church
Bad Füssing, 1972
unten / below:
Innenraum / interior

phasised on the exterior by an open bell tower, is reduced to an unadorned prayer room on the inside. The walls of the fairly low, nearly square space with natural coconut matting as floor covering and a ceiling of white, square timber girders are executed in fair-faced concrete. Light penetrates into the space through the rear wall overlooking the courtyard. The original scheme envisioned a small, semicircular niche next to the altar for the baptismal font, while the organ was placed on a diagonal projecting into the corner at the front of the room. In 1994 large-scale paintings were added to the initially unrelieved purist space with rows of chairs placed at right angles. The arrangement of altar and baptismal font was changed at the same time.

The concept for St Ignatius, a Catholic church in Munich-Kleinhadern, consecrated in 1979, was based on a completely different premise. To architect Josef Wiedemann, the church with community centre represented an oasis in an impersonal new housing scheme and he arranged the low complex in a ring around the central church building. The dodecagonal, brick-walled church, bathed in light that falls into the space through a ribbon window, is covered by a tent roof with an open timber roof truss composed of stripped logs. The hexagonal stone altar is raised on a platform and slightly off centre. It is surrounded on all sides by the pews and the sedilia. With this concept Wiedemann established a link to the image of the congregation gathered around the offering which is associated with centralised churches. He added a symbolic dimension in the Christian tradition by lowering the keystone at the centre of the space, using 12 columns, laying the brick walls in a wheat spike pattern and other details.

New Churches at the Millennium

Even the most recent church buildings in southern Germany, those consecrated in 2000 and 2001, are characterised by a penchant for monolithic form and ascetic spatial design. At the same time, one has a clear sense of the value attached to creating a sacred or meditative ambience in these new buildings, largely by means of materials and lighting strategies. The ecumenical chapel at the BRK-retirement home in Tirschenreuth (Upper Palatinate) by Brückner & Brückner, for example, is a tall cubical structure whose exterior walls reveal a balanced alternation between posts in the brickwork and vertical window slits. In the interior the altar wall is framed by strips of light, while light from the sides provides a rhythm in the longitudinal room.

St Jacob and Friar Konrad, a Catholic church with community centre in Frankfurt-Nierderlenbach designed by architect Günter Pfeifer, is most notable for its complex lighting scheme. The church is part of an autonomous, enclosed ensemble with community rooms, constructed with reinforced concrete and in part with timber, whose individual spaces rise to different heights. The east-facing church space terminates in a rectangular apse that lies directly across from the entrance. The altar is surrounded by benches on three sides and stands almost in the centre of the nearly square space. The nave is bordered on both sides by chapels dedicated to the Virgin Mary and a baptismal chapel respectively, as well as a separate tabernacle room. To the east, the interior is illuminated by daylight from a cross cut into the apse wall and a window in the tabernacle room. The west side features large skylights, whose quintuple division using different light filters casts a veil of light across the entire space.

Josef Wiedemann
St. Ignatius / St Ignatius
München / Munich, 1979

Brückner & Brückner
Kapelle / chapel
Tirschenreuth, 2000

273

zentrum in Frankfurt-Niedererlenbach von Günter Pfeifer. Die Kirche gehört zu einem geschlossenen Geviert mit Gemeinderäumen in Stahlbeton- und teilweiser Holzkonstruktion, das sich aus Baukörpern unterschiedlicher Höhe zusammensetzt. Der geostete Kirchenraum endet in einer dem Eingang gegenüber liegenden, rechteckigen Apsis. Nahezu in der Mitte des fast quadratischen Raumes steht der Altartisch, der an drei Seiten von Bänken umgeben wird. Parallel zum Kirchenschiff liegen auf beiden Seiten eine Marien- und eine Taufkapelle sowie ein eigener Tabernakelraum. Im Osten wird die Kirche durch ein in die Apsiswand eingeschittenes Kreuz und durch eine Öffnung im Tabernakelraum belichtet. Nach Westen hin sind große Oberlichteinbauten angebracht, die durch eine fünffache Zonierung verschiedener Lichtfilter den gesamten Raum mit einem Lichtnetz überziehen.

Im Jahr 2001 wurde das katholische Gemeindezentrum Herz Jesu in Völklingen (Saarland) eingeweiht, ein Werk der Architekten Lamott. Das Gemeindezentrum befindet sich an der Peripherie des Ortsteiles Ludweile in einer heterogenen Umgebung. Deshalb beschlossen die Architekten, die Anlage um einen Hof zu ordnen und das Zentrum mit Sichtbetonscheiben nach außen hin abzuschließen. Das Kirchengebäude ist durch Material und Form, besonders durch eine hohe, in einem Wasserbecken stehende Sichtbetonwand an der Eingangsseite und Cor-Ten-Stahlplatten unter einem überkragenden Dach hervorgehoben. Dieser Außenbau enthält erst den eigentlichen, abgesenkten, gläsernen Kirchenraum mit einer ausgegrenzten Apsis mit vergoldeten Kreuz im Zwischenraum zwischen Glasfassade und davor stehender Cor-Ten-Stahlplatte. Das von den Architekten in diesem Gebäude mehrfach formulierte Thema ist die Ausgrenzung des Sakralraums aus der profanen Welt, das sie als inhaltlichen Ansatz sehen, wie sich Kirche heute in der Gesellschaft darstellen könnte. Diese architektonische Ausbildung des Gegensatzes von sakral und profan stellt im Dickicht der Meinungen, wie eine Kirche aussehen solle, erstmals wieder grundsätzliche Bedeutungen klar, von denen aus eine Neuinterpretation der Bauaufgabe möglich scheint.

Lamott Architekten
Gemeindezentrum Herz Jesu
parish centre of the Sacred Heart
Völklingen, 2001

The Catholic community centre of the Sacred Heart (Herz Jesu) in Völklingen (Saarland) by Lamott architects was consecrated in 2001. The community centre is located on the periphery of the Ludweile district in a heterogeneous environment. The architects decided to arrange the complex around a courtyard and to screen the centre from its surroundings with fair-faced concrete panels. Within this complex, the church is singled out in material and form, especially by a tall fair-faced concrete wall rising out of a reflecting pool on the entrance side and by a Cor-Ten steel panel beneath the cantilevered roof. This external structure serves as a quasi-shell surrounding the actual sanctuary or church, a lowered, glazed space whose apse projects beyond the plan with a gilded cross set into the cavity between glass façade and Cor-Ten steel panel. The central theme in this building, which the architects reprised in several variations, is the distinction between the sacred space and the profane world in the context of how the Church could represent itself in contemporary society. This architectonic development of the contrast between the sacred and the profane brings a new clarity of fundamental meaning to the thicket of opinions as to what a church building should look like. From this, a new interpretation of this particular building task seems possible.

Günter Pfeifer
St. Jakobus / St Jacob
Frankfurt am Main, 2000

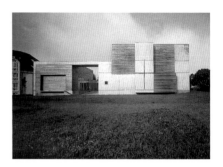

Sigurd Lewerentz

St. Petrus
Klippan, Schweden
1967

St Peter
Klippan, Sweden
1967

Sigurd Lewerentz (1885–1975) zählt
in der schwedischen Architektur
des 20. Jahrhunderts zu den großen
Einzelgängern. Nach dem Studium
hatte er auch bei Theodor Fischer und
Richard Riemerschmid in München
gearbeitet, dann orientierte er sich
am nordischen Neoklassizismus.
Bekannt wurde er 1915 durch den zusammen mit Gunnar Asplund gewon-
nenen Wettbewerb für den Waldfriedhof in Stockholm. Dennoch erhielt
Lewerentz erst in hohem Alter die
gebührende Anerkennung. Sein Werk
ist überschaubar, obwohl er uner-
müdlich arbeitete. Der jeweils lange
Entwurfsprozess strapazierte seine
Bauherren und Mitarbeiter auch deshalb, weil Lewerentz die Lösungen
bis zuletzt offen halten wollte und oftmals erst auf der Baustelle entschied.
Wesentlich zu seinem späten Ruhm
haben die Kirchen St. Markus in einem Stockholmer Vorort (1960) und
St. Petrus in der kleinen Gemeinde
Klippan in Schonen beigetragen. Bei
der zweiten Kirche kommt das Stre-
ben nach einer reduzierten Gestaltung bis hin zum Detail noch stärker
zum Ausdruck.

Sigurd Lewerentz (1885–1975) is
considered as one of the great loners
of 20th-century Swedish architecture. After completing his studies he
worked, among others, with Theodor
Fischer and Richard Riemerschmid
in Munich, subsequently taking inspiration from Scandinavian Neo-
Classicism. He became well known
in 1915 through the competition for
the Woodland Cemetery in Stockholm,
which he won jointly with Gunnar
Asplund. Yet Lewerentz only received
due recognition when already well
advanced in years. His work is easily
summed up, although he worked
tirelessly. The design process, always
lengthy, was hard on both his clients
and colleagues because he insisted
on keeping solutions open until the
very last minute and often only reached a decision on the building site.
The churches of St Mark (1960) in a
Stockholm suburb and St Peter in the
small community of Klippan in the
Skåne region made vital contributions
to his eventual late fame. Lewerentz's
striving for a reduction in form, even
in the smallest details, is expressed
even more strongly in the second of
these churches.

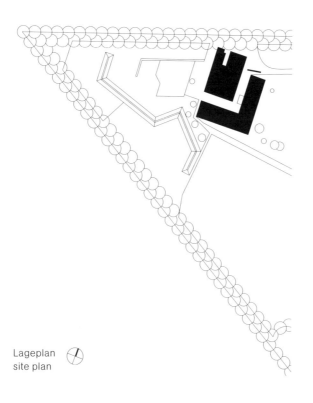

Lageplan
site plan

Der Kirchenbau (links) und das Gebäude für die Gemeinderäume liegen
auf einem dreieckigen Grundstück.
Das ganze Ensemble spiegelt sich in
einer Wasserfläche.

The church (left) and the building
housing the community rooms
lie amid trees on a triangular plot.
The whole complex is reflected in
a pond.

Lewerentz kam es auf eine ganzheitliche Durchbildung des Gebäudes an. In Kontrast zum handwerklich verarbeiteten Backstein wurde Stahl als modernes Material eingesetzt.

Lewerentz was concerned with the design of a building as an integrated whole. Steel, as a modern material, was used as a contrast to the handcrafted bricks.

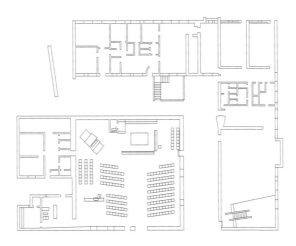

Grundriss
floor plan

Typisch für Lewerentz ist die funktionale Gliederung der Anlage: Hier
umschließt der flachere Trakt der Gemeinderäume L-förmig die Kirche.
Zwischen beiden Bauten verläuft eine
breite Passage. Die Wände der Kirche sind aus dunklem Helsingborger
Backstein. Im freien Laufverband
massiv gemauert, verleiht er ihnen
durch die breiten Mörtelfugen einen
rauen Charakter. Zugleich wirken sie
lebendig, weil Steine in unterschiedlichen Farbtönen verwendet wurden.
Auch im Kirchenraum erweist sich
eine virtuose Materialbehandlung.
Der archaische Raum ist fast dunkel,
nur durch kleine Öffnungen kann
Tageslicht eindringen. Auf der Außen-
seite der dicken Wände sind sie
durch Isolierglasscheiben geschlossen, die von Klammern gehalten werden. Das Dach, dessen Form sich
am Außenbau abbildet, besteht aus
einem flachen, ziegelgemauerten
Gewölbe, das auf zwei Stahlträgern
ruht. Diese wiederum werden von
einem T-förmigen Stahlpfeiler ge-
stützt, der etwas exzentrisch im Raum
steht. Wie alle Elemente des Bauwerks von Lewerentz bis ins Detail
behandelt, hebt und senkt sich
der Boden mit einem Belag aus unterschiedlichen Klinkern und Kacheln.

The functional layout of the complex
is typical of Lewerentz's work. Here
the flatter wing holding the community rooms encloses the church in
an L-shape. A broad passage runs between the two buildings. The walls
of the church are built of dark Helsing-
borg bricks. Solidly worked in a free
course, these give the walls a rough
character because of the wide mortar
joints. At the same time they impart
a feeling of animation due to the use
of varying shades of bricks. In the
interior, too, there is evidence of vir-
tuosity in the handling of the materials. The archaic space is almost dark;
daylight enters only through small
apertures which, on the outer surface
of the thick walls, are shut by means
of insulating glass panes held by
clamps. The roof, the form of which is
reproduced on the exterior, consists
of a shallow brickwork vault resting
on two steel girders. These in turn are
supported by a T-shaped steel pier,
positioned slightly off-centre within
the space. The floor — like every other
element in Klewerentz's buildings
processed down to the last detail —
rises and falls, with a covering of different types of tiles and clinker bricks.

Timo und Tuomo Suomalainen

Temppeliaukio Kirche
Helsinki, Finnland
1969

Temppeliaukio Church
Helsinki, Finland
1969

Die Kirche mit 1000 Sitzplätzen zählt
in Finnland zu den meist besuchten
Touristenzielen. Außerdem ist der mit
einer Galerie ausgestattete Raum ein
beliebter Konzertsaal.

Seating 1,000 people, the church is
among Finland's most-visited tourist attractions. The interior with its gallery is
also popular as a concert hall.

Seit 1906 war das Grundstück im
bürgerlichen Stadtteil Töölö für eine
Kirche freigehalten worden. Nach
zwei ergebnislosen Wettbewerben in
den dreißiger Jahren brachte erst
ein dritter 1961 die Entscheidung. Ihn
gewannen die Brüder Suomalainen
mit einem Entwurf, dessen Dramatik
im finnischen Kirchenbau eine Ausnahme darstellt. Wegen Änderungen
im Raumprogramm wurde die Fertigstellung bis 1969 verzögert. Weil
das Volumen des Rundbaus aus dem
Granit herausgebrochen wurde, blieb
der Charakter des felsigen Hügels
weitgehend erhalten. Die Kuppel mit
ihrem Durchmesser von 24 Metern,
die von vorgefertigten, radial angeordneten Betonstreben getragen wird,
ragt nur wenig über das Gelände
hinaus. Im Außenraum ist sie durch
eine unregelmäßige Mauer aus Bruchstein geschützt. Innen liegt zwischen
der Kuppel und den Wänden aus
Natur- und Bruchstein ein umlaufendes Glasband, durch welches das
Licht spektakulär einfällt. Die Decke
des Kirchenraums ist ein dichtes Ge-
flecht aus Kupferdrähten.

The plot of land in the middle-class
district of Töölö had been reserved for
a church ever since 1906. Following
two unproductive competitions in the
1930s it was only a third, held in 1961,
that proved decisive. It was won by
the Suomalainen brothers with a dramatic design that is exceptional within the field of Finnish church-building.
Completion was delayed until 1969
owing to changes in the spatial programme. The character of the rocky
hill was largely preserved, since the
volume of the round structure was
dug out from the granite. The dome,
24 metres in diameter, its weight
borne by prefabricated concrete stanchions arranged radially, protrudes
only slightly above the ground. On the
outside it is protected by an irregular
wall of rubble. On the inside, between
the dome and the walls built from
natural stone and rubble, there is a
surrounding band of glazing through
which light enters in a spectacular
fashion. The ceiling of the interior is
formed by a dense mesh of copper
wire.

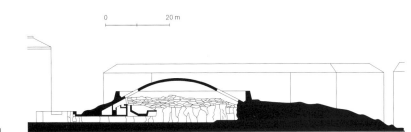

Längsschnitt
longitudinal section

Jørn Utzon

Kirche und Gemeindezentrum
Bagsværd, Dänemark
1976

Church and Community Centre
Bagsværd, Denmark
1976

Die Gestalt der lebhaft aufgestaffelten Kirchenanlage soll an ein landwirtschaftliches Gebäude erinnern. Durch die neu gepflanzten Bäume ist sie in die Umgebung eingebunden.

The shape of the church complex, built up in an animated manner, is intended to be reminiscent of an agricultural building. The newly planted trees integrate it into its surroundings.

Die Kirche in einer Vorortgemeinde von Kopenhagen wirkt nicht nur nach Meinung ihrer Kritiker wie ein »Getreidespeicher«. Tatsächlich war diese Erscheinung ein wichtiger Ansatz für Jørn Utzons Entwurf. Zum einen spielt die Gestalt auf das klassische Bild der ›heiligen Scheune‹ an, zum anderen verweist sie auf die landwirtschaftliche Vergangenheit des Ortes. Dabei verhüllt der kubisch aufgestaffelte Außenbau den zur Decke hin dynamisch gestalteten Kirchenraum. Im Tragrahmen aus Stahlbeton haben die vier parallelen Stützenreihen unterschiedliche Funktionen: Die beiden äußeren dienen in ihrer ganzen Höhe als vertikale Träger, während die beiden inneren oberhalb der Empore in einem zusammen mit ihnen gegossenen Querträger münden. Dieser Wechsel vom Tragrahmen zum monolithischen Querträger bildet das statische System für die Schalengewölbe aus Stahlbeton. Die durch Betonfertigteile geschlossenen Außenwände sind teils unbehandelt, teils mit Keramik verkleidet, die Pultdächer mit Welleternit gedeckt.

It is not just its critics who think that the church in a Copenhagen suburb looks like a 'grain silo'. In fact this look formed an important starting point for Jørn Utzon's design. On the one hand, the shape plays on the classical image of the 'holy cattle shed', on the other it is a reference to the agricultural past of the locality. The exterior, a pile of graduated cubes, conceals an interior which rises up in dynamic shapes to the ceiling. The four parallel rows of supports in the reinforced-concrete framework have differing functions: the two outer ones act throughout their height as vertical supports, while the two inner ones above the gallery lead into a transverse beam that was cast simultaneously with them. This change from supporting frame to monolithic transverse beam forms the static system for the reinforced-concrete shell vaults. The outer walls, filled with pre-cast concrete elements, are partly left untreated and partly given a ceramic facing, while the pent roofs are covered with corrugated metal.

Längsschnitt
longitudinal section

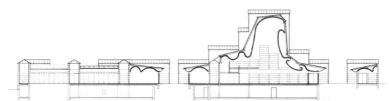

Die ebenfalls sehr sorgfältig gestaltete Sakristei liegt auf der Rückseite der breiten Altarwand. Die textile Ausstattung aller Räume hat Utzons Tochter Lin entworfen.

The sacristy, likewise designed with great care, lies to the rear of the wide altar wall. The textiles used throughout the interior were designed by Utzon's daughter, Lin.

Jørn Utzon hat die eindrucksvolle Gestalt des Kirchenraums erläutert: »Das bekannte Problem, einen großen Raum zu überspannen, ist hier in einer zeitgemäßen Form gelöst. Inspiriert von den Wolken habe ich einen Raum gestaltet, der nach oben hin verschwindet. Er ist nicht dunkel, nicht auf eine Bühne oder einen Hochaltar ausgerichtet, sondern ein Raum, in dem man Gemeinsamkeit sucht und findet.« Die Schalengewölbe überspannen das 20 Meter breite Hauptvolumen und fallen wellenförmig zu den Seiten hin ab, was für eine gute Akustik sorgt. Für ihren Bau wurde Spezialbeton auf eine Drahtmattenbewehrung gespritzt. Während des Gießens verwendete man eine Rauschalung, deren Struktur auf den Gewölben sichtbar ist. Das von oben einfallende Tageslicht moduliert die Schalen in unzähligen Weißtönen – von strahlender Helligkeit im hohen Bereich bis hin zu Schattenbildungen über dem Eingang. Zur künstlichen Beleuchtung dienen weiße, auf langen Metallrohren gereihte Glühbirnen, die für eine festliche Atmosphäre sorgen. Die Wand hinter dem betonierten Altar ist als Ziegelgitter gestaltet, die einfachen Bänke bestehen aus gefärbtem Kiefernholz.

Jørn Utzon has explained the imposing design of the church's interior in the following terms: 'Here the well-known problem of spanning a large space is solved in an up-to-date form. Inspired by clouds, I have designed a space that vanishes upwards. It is not dark, not directed towards a stage or a high altar, but a space in which one seeks common ground and finds it'. The shell vaults span the 20-metre-wide main volume of the church and fall in undulating folds at the sides, ensuring that the acoustics are good. To construct them, special concrete was sprayed on to an armature of wire matting. During the casting process a rough mould was used, the structure of which can be seen on the vaults. Daylight falling in from above modulates the shells in countless shades of white – from radiant brightness in the upper regions down to shadow formations above the entrance. White light bulbs lined up on long metal tubes serve as artificial lighting and produce a ceremonial atmosphere. The wall behind the concrete altar is shaped like a brick screen, and the simple pews are of dyed pinewood.

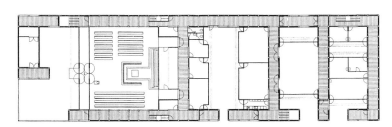

Juha Leiviskä

Myyrmäki Kirche
Vantaa, Finnland
1984

Myyrmäki Church
Vantaa, Finland
1984

Juha Leiviskä beschäftigt sich seit über 30 Jahren mit Kirchenbau. Dabei hat er zu einem unverwechselbaren Ausdruck gefunden. Seine nach immer den gleichen Grundprinzipien entworfenen Kirchen stehen in mehreren Regionen Finnlands. Als sein wichtigstes »Baumaterial« bezeichnet Leiviskä das Tageslicht. Dieser Ansatz bestimmt auch die Kirche mit Gemeindezentrum von Myyrmäki in Vantaa, einer Großstadt in der Region Helsinki. Um das schwierige Grundstück, das zwischen einer Bahnlinie und einem Park liegt, optimal zu nutzen, hat Leiviskä die ebenso lange wie schmale Baugruppe hart an den Bahnkörper gesetzt. Aus zwei Richtungen staffeln sich die kubischen Baukörper bis zur Südwestecke mit dem plastisch gestalteten Glockenturm hin auf. Der Kirchenraum richtet sich nach Westen, die Altarwand erscheint als ein von Licht belebtes Relief.

Juha Leiviskä has been involved in the building of churches for over thirty years and has found a way of expressing himself in a distinctive fashion. His churches, always based on the same design principles, can be seen in several regions of Finland. Leiviskä names daylight as the most important 'building material'. This also formed his starting point for the church and community centre of Myyrmäki in Vantaa, a large town in the Helsinki region. In order to make optimal use of the difficult location between a railway line and a park, Leiviskä placed the long, narrow building ensemble hard up against the railway track. From two directions the graduated cubical buildings are built up towards the south-western corner with the three-dimensionally formed bell tower. The church interior is aligned towards the west; the altar wall has the effect of a relief animated by the light.

0   50 m

Lageplan mit Grundriss
site with floor plan

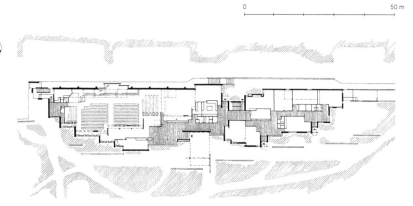

Durch die Positionierung des Bauwerks blieb nach Osten hin der Park mit seinem alten Birkenbestand erhalten. Auf dieser Seite öffnet sich die Kirchenanlage durch ihre Eingänge in den niedrigen Vorbauten. Die mit gelben Ziegelsteinen verkleideten Fassaden sind durch vorspringende Mauerscheiben markant gefasst. Im Kontrast zu den dämmrigen, versetzt angeordneten Vorhallen überrascht der hohe und weite Kirchenraum durch seine helle, einzigartige Atmosphäre. Juha Leiviskä spricht von einem Lichtschleier: »Das Licht zeichnet und verwischt die Konturen, es untermalt die reiche Ausstattung und bringt alles zum Klingen.« Hoch über der Altarwand, die indirekt, nämlich seitlich und von oben belichtet wird, hängt die mehrteilige Textilarbeit von Kristiina Nyrhinen. Von unten wirken die Bahnen des Kunstwerks wie lichtdurchlässige Wolken. Die Lampen mit einem gelblichen Kunstlicht setzen ›Lichtpunkte‹ im weißen bis zartfarbigen Raum. Adresse: Vantaa, Bahnstation Louhela.

Owing to the positioning of the construction, it was possible to retain the park to the east with its old birch trees. On this side the church complex is opened up via the entrances into the low ante-rooms. The façades, faced with yellow bricks, are strikingly framed by projecting wall slabs. In contrast to the dimly lit, staggered entrance zones, the high, wide interior comes as a surprise because of its bright, unique atmosphere. Juha Leiviskä speaks of a veil of light: 'The light delineates and blurs the contours, it accentuates the rich furnishings and makes everything ring out'. High above the altar wall, lit indirectly from the side and from overhead, hangs a multi-part textile work by Kristiina Nyrhinen. Viewed from below, the panels of the work of art give the impression of transparent clouds. The lamps with their yellowish artificial light set points of light within the white to pastel-toned space. Address: Louhela Railway Station, Vantaa.

Richard MacCormac

Kapelle im Fitzwilliam College
Cambridge, Großbritannien
1991

Fitzwilliam College Chapel
Cambridge, Great Britain
1991

Das Fitzwilliam College, das nördlich des Stadtzentrums von Cambridge liegt, erhielt seinen Status erst im Jahr 1966. Damals bezog es neue Gebäude, die der bekannte britische Architekt Denys Lasdun etwas schematisch geplant hatte. Zwei Jahrzehnte später wurde das College von Richard MacCormac durch einen ebenfalls dreigeschossigen Flügel erweitert. Die anschließende Planung der Kapelle mehr als 20 Jahre nach den ersten Bauten (auch an diesem College sind die Gläubigen eine Minderheit) war für MacCormac eine so undankbare wie reizvolle Aufgabe. Undankbar deshalb, weil die Kapelle an den spröden, unvollendeten Ostflügel von Lasdun angehängt ist. Aber auch reizvoll: Die von zwei gerundeten Mauerschalen gefasste Kapelle stellt nunmehr einen markanten ›Kopf‹ im großen Innenhof dar. Die zweifache Bänderung im Mauerwerk aus schwarzem Backstein setzt die Betonstürze von Lasduns Gebäude bildlich fort, ansonsten hat MacCormac ein eigenständiges Bauwerk geschaffen.

Fitzwilliam College, which lies to the north of Cambridge's town centre, only attained college status in 1966. At that time it moved into new buildings which had been planned rather schematically by the well-known British architect Denys Lasdun. Two decades later, the college was extended with the addition of another three-storeyed wing by Richard MacCormac. The subsequent planning of the chapel (more than 20 years after the first buildings — in this college, too, the faithful are in a minority) was for MacCormac a task as thankless as it was attractive. Thankless, because the chapel is tacked on to Lasdun's brittle, unfinished east wing, but also attractive: the chapel, framed by two rounded wall shells, now forms a striking 'head' to the large inner courtyard. The double banding within the dark brickwork is a visual continuation of the concrete supports of Lasdun's structure, but otherwise MacCormac has created an independent building.

Sprengaxonometrie
exploded axonometric
projection

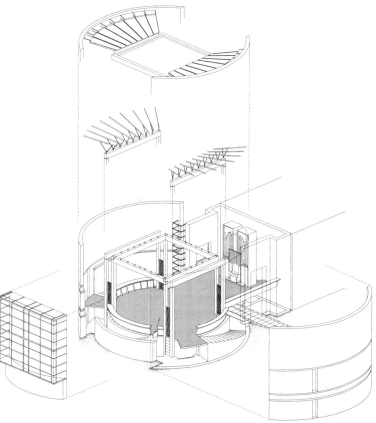

Richard MacCormac vergleicht seine Kapelle mit einer »Arche«, dem mittelalterlichen Symbol für den Weg zum Heil. Die Treppenaufgänge werden durch hohe Glashäuser belichtet.

Richard MacCormac likens his chapel to an ark, the medieval symbol for the path to salvation. The stairways are lit by means of high glass housings.

Vertikale Glashäuser lassen das
Tageslicht bis ins Erdgeschoss fallen,
wo der Eingang zur Kapelle liegt.
Das Kreuz in der Glaswand ist eines
der wenigen christlichen Symbole.

Vertical glass housings allow daylight in right down to the ground floor,
where the entrance to the chapel is
situated. The Cross in the glass wall is
one of the few Christian symbols.

Durch die funktionale Schichtung des Bauwerks (unten die Krypta als Begegnungsraum, oben die Kapelle) wurde sowohl ein kompaktes Volumen als auch die notwendige Höhe erreicht. Im Andachtsraum setzt ein von vier Pfeilerpaaren getragener Betonrahmen die orthogonale Struktur von Lasduns College fort. Als quadratischer Raum im Raum wird der Rahmen von einer konzentrischen Kreisform umhüllt, wobei zwischen beiden die gerundeten Treppenaufgänge liegen. Die Orgel steht im tieferen Bereich der Kapelle, gegenüber liegt der Altar vor der völlig verglasten Ostwand. Konstruktiv sind die äußeren Mauerschalen und das Betontragwerk voneinander getrennt. Das Dach, eine in zwei Flügeln ausschwingende Holzkonstruktion, ruht auf dem Betonrahmen. Die Unterseite des Kapellenbodens ist durch ihre beplankte Wölbung wie ein Schiff ausgebildet, so dass im Schnitt die Kapelle an eine ›Arche‹ erinnert. Adresse: Cambridge, Huntingdon Road.

A compact volume, as well as the necessary height, was achieved through functional layering of the building (the crypt below as a meeting area, the chapel above). In the place of worship a concrete frame, its weight borne by four pairs of pillars, continues the orthogonal structure of Lasdun's college. As a square space within the space, this frame is hidden by a concentric circle, whereby the rounded stairways lie between the two. The organ stands deeper within the chapel; the altar is opposite, in front of the completely glazed east wall. In constructional terms, the outer wall shells and the concrete supporting framework are separate. The roof — a wooden structure terminating in two wings — rests on the concrete frame. The underside of the chapel floor is shaped like a ship as a result of its planked curvature, so that in section the chapel reminds one of an 'ark'. Address: Huntingdon Road, Cambridge.

Heinz Tesar

Evangelische Kirche
Klosterneuburg, Österreich
1995

Protestant Church
Klosterneuburg, Austria
1995

Der an ein Schiff gemahnende Baukörper ragt aus dem parkartigen
Hang. Das ebenso schlanke wie hohe
Stahlkreuz vor der Apsis wurde
aus minimierten Profilen konstruiert.

The body of the building, which puts
one in mind of a ship, looms up
from the park-like slope. The steel
cross, slender and tall, in front of
the apse was constructed from mini-
mised sections.

Wie Sigurd Lewerentz [Seite 276] ist auch der drei Generationen jüngere Heinz Tesar ein Einzelgänger. Seine gerade im Kirchenbau eigenwilligen Raumschöpfungen, lassen sich nicht ›einordnen‹. Charakteristisch für ihn sind zwei Ansatzpunkte: der Ort und das Licht. Klosterneuburg ist eine kleine Stadt an der Donau nordwestlich von Wien. Weit oberhalb der Uferstraße liegt die Kirche in einem parkartigen Hang. Von seinen ersten poetischen Skizzen an ließ sich Tesar von der Idee einer »Kirche im Hügel« leiten. Die kleine evangelische Gemeinde selbst wünschte sich einen »gemeinschaftsbildenden Raum«. Der markante Baukörper vereint beide Vorstellungen: Von der Ortsstraße aus gesehen ragt der gerundete Kirchenbau wie ein angedocktes Schiff aus dem Gelände, der ovale Grundriss wiederum führt die Gläubigen eng zusammen. Die Gestalt des Gebäudes wird nicht gestört, weil der Glockenträger im benachbarten alten Pfarrhaus verblieben ist. Unverwechselbar ist die auf einem Betonsockel stehende Außenwand mit ihrem Muster aus quadratischen Fenstern, die zum östlich gelegenen Altarbereich hin aufsteigen. Das Tageslicht fällt außerdem durch 25 Kuppeln auf dem bewachsenen Dach in den Raum ein.

Although three generations younger than Sigurd Lewentz [p. 276] Heinz Tesar is also a loner. His spatial creations, particularly unconventional in the context of religious architecture, are impossible to categorise. Two starting points — location and light — are characteristic of his work. Klosterneuburg is a small town on the River Danube, north-west of Vienna. The church lies high above the riverside road on a park-like slope. From his first poetic sketches onwards Tesar let himself be guided by the idea of a 'church on the hill'. The small Protestant congregation itself wanted a 'community-forming space'. Both these concepts are combined in the imposing body of the building: seen from the Ortsstrasse, the rounded church looms up above the ground like a docked ship, the oval ground plan in turn bringing the faithful close together. There is nothing to disrupt the shape of the building since the bell holder has been kept in the neighbouring old vicarage. The outer wall set on a concrete plinth, with its pattern of square windows rising towards the altar zone to the east, is very distinctive. In addition, daylight enters the church through the 25 domes on the overgrown roof.

Längsschnitt
longitudinal section

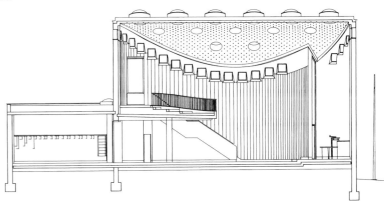

0   10 m

Grundriss
floor plan

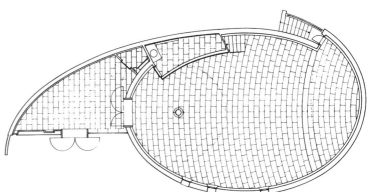

Lageplan ⊕
site plan

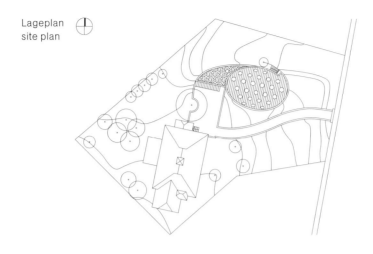

Der Eingang zur Kirche liegt auf der Südseite in einem niedrigen Anbau, der organisch aus dem ovalen Baukörper entwickelt ist. Alle tragenden Wände wurden aus ›Mantelbeton‹ errichtet und sind außen wie innen weiß verputzt. Die Decke des Kirchenraums wölbt sich als organoide Schale entsprechend der Dachhaut nach oben. Durch 25 Öffnungen fällt das Tageslicht von oben in den Raum ein, der von »armen Materialien, aber reichen Formen« geprägt ist. Die entscheidende Rolle übernimmt dabei das Licht, wie Tesar betont: »Das Licht im Raum ist der Beginn der Architektur. Der Raum wird aus dem Licht geboren und spiegelt eine breite Palette von Farbe, Intensität, Bewegung und von Tag und Nacht.« Gerade unter dem Aspekt der Lichtdramaturgie zeigt sich, dass Tesar eine barocke Raumauffassung pflegt, wobei sie hier paradoxerweise eine evangelische Gemeinde zufrieden stellt. So lässt auch eine kleine, kreisrunde Öffnung in der Altarwand und im Altarbild von Hubert Scheibl einen Lichtstrahl nach innen dringen. Der protestantischen Liturgie folgt die prominente Stellung der Kanzel als Ort der Wortverkündigung. Der Raum wird auch für Kirchenmusik genutzt.

The entrance to the church lies on the south side in a low annexe which develops organically out of the oval mass. All the load-bearing walls were constructed using pre-cast concrete, and are plastered white both outside and inside. The ceiling of the interior arches upwards in the form of an organoid shell, or skin, corresponding to the skin of the roof. Daylight penetrates through 25 apertures from above into the interior which is characterised by 'poor materials, but rich forms'. Light plays the decisive role in this, as Tesar emphasises: 'The light in the space is where architecture begins. The space is born from the light and reflects a broad palette of colour, intensity, movement, of day and night'. It is evident, particularly from the aspect of dramatic lighting effects, that Tesar favours a baroque perception of space, whereas here, paradoxically, it satisfies a Protestant congregation. Thus a small, circular opening in the altar wall and in Hubert Scheibl's altarpiece allows a ray of light to pierce the interior as well. The prominent position of the pulpit, as the place for proclamation of the Word, follows the Protestant liturgy. The interior is also used for church music.

Die Öffnungen in der Betondecke
lassen das Licht auf dem weißen Putz
spielen. Für die künstliche Beleuchtung wurden dezente, in den Wänden
befestigte Stablampen entwickelt.

The openings in the concrete ceiling
permit light to play on the white
plaster. Discreet wall-mounted flash-
lights were developed as artificial
lighting.

Kapelle der Versöhnung
Berlin, Deutschland
2000

Chapel of Reconciliation
Berlin, Germany
2000

Dieses kleine Bauwerk und seine Umgebung spiegeln die wechselvolle
Berliner Geschichte der letzten vier
Jahrzehnte. Es steht genau dort,
wo seit dem Bau der ›Mauer‹ im Jahr
1961 die frühere Versöhnungskirche stand: noch im Ostteil der Stadt,
aber im ›toten Streifen‹ zwischen
dem inneren und äußeren Mauerring.
Weil sie den Patrouillen im Wege
stand, wurde die historistische Kirche
1985 von den DDR-Grenztruppen
gesprengt. Als die Gemeinde 1995,
sechs Jahre nach dem Fall der Mauer,
das Grundstück zurück erhielt, wollte sie am gleichen Platz wieder ein
Gotteshaus errichten. Aus einem kleinen Wettbewerb gingen dann die jungen Architekten Rudolf Reitermann
und Peter Sassenroth als Sieger hervor. Der Grundriss der neuen Kapelle
der Versöhnung ist ein Oval, in das
zwei Rechtecke für den Eingang und
die Altarnische eingeschnitten sind.
Mit unterschiedlichem Abstand zur
Kapelle bildet die Eiform einer lichtdurchlässigen Holzkonstruktion die
äußere Hülle. Das Kreuz wurde in die
hellen Lamellen eingebeizt.

This small building and its surroundings reflect Berlin's varied history over
the last forty years. It stands where
an earlier Church of Reconciliation
(Versöhnungskirche) had stood since
the erection of the Wall in 1961 — still
in the eastern sector of the city, but
in the no man's land between the
Wall's inner and outer rings. The historic church was blown up by East
German border troops in 1985 because it got in the way of the patrols.
When in 1995, six years after the
fall of the Wall, the plot of land was
returned to the congregation, they
wished to erect another place of
worship on the very same spot. The
young architects Rudolf Reitermann
and Peter Sassenroth emerged vic-
torious from the small competition.
The ground plan of the new chapel
of reconciliation is an oval into which
two rectangles are cut for the entrance and the altar niche. Varying in
distance from the chapel, a translucent wooden structure in an egg
shape forms the outer shell. The cross
was etched into the light-coloured
slats.

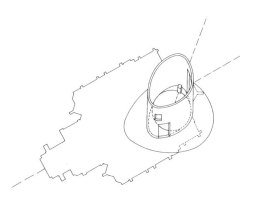

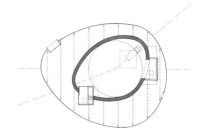

Grundriss
floor plan

0   10 m

Die Geschichte ist im Gelände bewahrt: Ein Kiesbett symbolisiert den
Ort der gesprengåten Kirche, die
Betonplatten erinnern an den Verlauf
des früheren Patrouillenwegs.

History is preserved on the site: a
bed of gravel symbolises the location
of the demolished church and the
concrete slabs remind people of the
route taken by the border patrols.

Aus dem Vorgängerbau wurde der
Altaraufsatz gerettet, der in einer
Wandnische hängt. Der neue, nach
Osten gerichtete Altar ist ebenso wie
Boden und Wand eine Lehmarbeit
von Martin Rauch.

The altarpiece rescued from the earlier
church now hangs in a wall niche. The
new altar, orientated towards the east,
was — like floor and wall — executed in
cobwork by Martin Rauch.

Der ovale Andachtsraum ist eine ungewöhnliche Konstruktion. Anstelle des von den Architekten vorgeschlagenen Materials Beton, das an die abgebrochene ›Mauer‹ erinnert hätte, entschied sich der Bauherr schließlich für Stampflehm, aus dem der Boden und die 60 Zentimeter dicke Wand bestehen. Diese Konstruktion, die auch der franziskanisch-ökologischen Absicht des Auftraggebers entsprach, wurde nach alter Tradition vom österreichischen Lehmbauer Martin Rauch ausgeführt. Dabei wurden in die schichtenweise gepressten Lehmringe sowohl Ziegelsplitter der zerstörten Kirche als auch verbindende Flachsfasern eingegeben. Auf dem gelb-braunen Wandoval changiert das von oben einfallende Licht, so dass der körnige Charakter des Baustoffs markant in Erscheinung tritt. Der aus dem Vorgängerbau gerettete Altaraufsatz hängt in einer 11 Meter hohen Nische, während sich der neue Altar nach Osten orientiert. Mit Gussasphalt ausgelegt, dient der unterschiedlich breite Bereich zwischen den beiden Wandschalen als Wandelgang und Versammlungsraum. Durch die vertikalen Holzlamellen dringt das Licht gefiltert ein. Adresse: Berlin-Mitte, Bernauer Straße.

The oval devotional space is an unusual structure. Instead of the material proposed by the architects — concrete — which would have served as a reminder of the torn-down Wall, the client eventually decided to use rammed earth, or cob, from which the floor and the 60-centimetre-thick walls are made. This construction, which also accorded with the end user's Franciscan and/or ecological intentions, was executed by the Austrian cob-builder Martin Rauch according to traditional methods. During the process, fragments of brick from the earlier church and flax fibres for binding were added to the rings of earth, compressed layer by layer. When light entering from above flickers on the yellowish-brown oval of the wall, the grainy character of the building material is very evident. The altarpiece rescued from the church hangs in a niche 11 metres high, while the new altar is orientated towards the east. Laid with poured asphalt, the area — varying in width — between the two wall shells is used as a covered walk and assembly area. Light is filtered through the vertical wooden slats. Address: Bernauer Strasse, Central Berlin.

Meinhard von Gerkan

Christus-Pavillon
Volkenroda, Deutschland
2000/2001

Christus-Pavillon
Volkenroda, Germany
2000/2001

Längsschnitt
longitudinal section

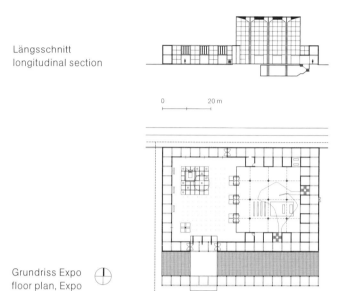

0   20 m

Nach seiner Nutzung auf der Expo
in Hannover wurde der Stahl-Pavillon
demontiert und im Kloster Volkenroda in Thüringen neu aufgebaut,
allerdings ohne Turm und Krypta.

After the Hannover Expo the steel
pavilion was dismantled and reass-
embled at the monastery of Volkenroda in Thuringia, though without its
tower and crypt.

Grundriss Expo
floor plan, Expo

Im Gegensatz zum mediokren Deutschen Pavillon auf der Expo 2000 in Hannover war der aus einem Wettbewerb hervorgegangene Christus-Pavillon ein architektonisches Ereignis. Im Auftrag der Evangelischen Kirche in Deutschland hatte Meinhard von Gerkan eine neu interpretierte Klosteranlage entworfen, um »einen Ort der Kontemplation auf diesem Jahrmarkt der Eitelkeiten« zu schaffen. Schon bei der Planung des zerlegbaren Pavillons stand fest, dass er nach der temporären Nutzung auf der Expo seinen endgültigen Standort auf dem Klostergelände von Volkenroda in Thüringen erhalten sollte. Im August 2001 dort neu eingeweiht, erfüllt das Gebäude auch die von der Expo geforderte ›Nachhaltigkeit‹. Das Tragwerk des Pavillons ist ein Stahlskelett mit einem räumlichen Grundraster von 3,40 Metern. Das Skelett ist ganz unterschiedlich geschlossen: durch transparente oder opake Glasflächen, durch transluzente Marmortafeln sowie durch gefüllte Glasfelder in den zweischaligen Bereichen. Im Unterschied zu einer historischen Klosteranlage umschließt der Kreuzgang als hohes und schmales Bauteil sowohl den großen Innenhof als auch den quadratischen ›Christus-Raum‹.

In comparison with the mediocre German Pavilion, the Christus Pavillon — the outcome of a competition — proved to be a real architectural event at Expo 2000 in Hannover. The Protestant Church in Germany had commissioned Meinhard von Gerkan to design a new interpretation of a monastery in order to create 'a place of contemplation at this fair of the vanities'. It was already clear during the planning of the dismantleable pavilion that, after its temporary use at the fair, its definitive location should be the monastery of Volkenroda in Thuringia. Reconsecrated there in August 2001, the building also satisfies the 'lasting' quality demanded at Expo 2000. The pavilion's supporting framework is a steel skeleton with a basic spatial grid of 3.4 metres. The skeleton is filled in a variety of ways: with transparent or opaque glass areas, with translucent marble slabs and, in the double-skinned sections, with filled glass zones. Unlike the situation in a historic monastery, the cloister in the form of a tall, narrow element encloses both the large inner courtyard and the square 'Christ space'.

Der 18 Meter hohe ›Christus-Raum‹ erhebt sich auf einer quadratischen Grundfläche mit 25 Metern Seitenlänge. Das Tragwerk ist als Tisch ausgebildet, wobei die Köpfe der neun hohen Kreuzstützen durch quadratische Oberlichter betont werden. Zusätzliches Licht fällt durch die transluzenten Wandfelder ein, die aus Glastafeln mit aufgeklebtem hellen Marmor bestehen. Dadurch entsteht im Raum, dessen Boden mit sauber verarbeiteten Sichtbetonplatten belegt ist, eine würdevolle Atmosphäre. Die äußeren Glaswände des Kreuzgangs sind zweischalig konstruiert und mit unterschiedlichen Materialien gefüllt, darunter Holzstücke, Wegwerfbestecke, Muscheln und Einwegfeuerzeuge. Diese natürlichen oder technischen Objekte bilden einen variantenreichen Lichtfilter, der im Kreuzgang wechselnde Stimmungen entstehen lässt. Die hohen Eingänge zum Andachtsraum sind schwellenlos gestaltet. Adresse: Körner-Volkenroda bei Mühlhausen in Thüringen.

The 18-metre-high Christus-Pavillon stands on a square plot with side dimensions of around 25 metres in length. The supporting framework is built up like a table, whereby the tops of the nine high crosspieces are emphasised by square skylights. Additional light enters through translucent wall sections consisting of glass plates with pale marble bonded on. This gives the interior, the floor of which is laid with cleanly finished slabs of exposed concrete, a dignified atmosphere. The cloister's outer glass walls are constructed as a double skin and filled with diverse materials, including pieces of wood, shells, disposable cutlery and throwaway cigarette lighters. These natural or technical objects form a highly varied filter for light which produces changing moods in the cloister. The tall entrances to the devotional space are designed without a sill. Address: Volkenroda, Körner, near Mühlhausen in Thuringia.

Die Glasfelder im Kreuzgang sind mit
44 verschiedenen Stoffen gefüllt.
Die natürlichen Materialien und technischen Produkte stellen Bezüge
zur Außenwelt her.

The double-skinned glass sections in
the cloister are filled with 44 different
materials. The natural materials and
technical products create links to the
outside world.

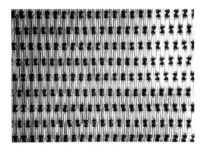   

Das Kloster Volkenroda wird von der
Jesus-Bruderschaft geführt, einer
evangelischen Lebensgemeinschaft
mit ökumenischer Ausrichtung.

The monastery of Volkenroda is run
by the Brotherhood of Jesus, a Protestant community with an ecumenical
slant.

Expo Hannover / Hanover Expo, 2000
Haupteingang / main entrance

Wolfgang Jean Stock

Ein sakraler Meilenstein
Kapelle der Weltreligionen am Gotthardpass

Zunächst gibt das Gebäude ein Rätsel auf. Wer auf der schweizerischen Gotthardpass-Autobahn nach Norden hinunter fährt, erblickt in einer lang gezogenen Rechtskurve zwischen den Ausfahrten Erstfeld und Altdorf ein Bauwerk, das sich nicht von selbst erklärt. Ist der Kubus mit den quadratischen Öffnungen im Betonskelett ein technisches Gebäude? Oder handelt es sich, worauf die grünlich schimmernden Fensterfelder hindeuten könnten, um ein Denkmal? Vielleicht ist der Bau aber auch nur ein Teil der benachbarten Raststätte. Jedenfalls wurde die Neugier geweckt – und am Parkplatz folgt die Aufklärung: Das Gebäude ist eine ökumenische Kapelle und trägt den Namen *Ort der Besinnung an der Autobahn in Uri.* Dass seine Anlage wie auch seine Gestalt der Aufgabe in überzeugender Weise gerecht werden, kann jeder erfahren, der sich auf diese ungewöhnliche Architektur einlässt.

Autobahnkirchen

Von vielen werden die ›Wegkapellen‹ an den europäischen Autobahnen als liebenswertes, aber längst überholtes Beiwerk belächelt. Manche können sich gar nicht vorstellen, dass solche Orte einem Bedürfnis entsprechen. Dies ist jedoch eine große Täuschung. Schon allein die über zwanzig Kirchen und Kapellen an den deutschen Autobahnen (katholisch, evangelisch oder ökumenisch) werden im Jahr von insgesamt mehreren Millionen Menschen aufgesucht. Zu den Spitzenreitern gehört die Kirche St. Christophorus an der Autobahn von Karlsruhe nach Basel, ein Bau des Architekten Friedrich Zwingmann in markanter, pyramidaler Zeltform, der 1978 am Rand der Raststätte Baden-Baden vollendet wurde. In ihrer Ausstattung verkörpert die Kirche eine zeittypische Abkehr von den zuvor meist schmucklosen Sakralräumen. Vermutlich tragen neben den spektakulären, turmhohen Bildwerken von Emil Wachter im weitläufigen Außenbereich auch seine innenräumlich dominierenden Betonreliefs dazu bei, dass hier alljährlich rund 300 000 Besucher gezählt werden. Sie stört nicht, dass in Kirche und Krypta die Wände, Brüstungen, Bänke und Decken wie überkrustet wirken, sondern lassen sich von den erzählenden Darstellungen einnehmen. Besonders Esoteriker, so berichtet der Pfarrer, seien derart fasziniert, dass sie die Anlage für Meditationen nutzen würden.

Bauwerk mit Fernwirkung

Zu St. Christophorus mit seiner populär-christlichen Bildkunst stellt die zwanzig Jahre später, 1998, fertig gestellte Autobahnkapelle am Gotthardpass eine klare Alternative dar. Hier wird man nicht von gestalterischer Opulenz überwältigt, sondern von einer reduzierten Formensprache überrascht. Die beiden jungen Zürcher Architekten Pascale Guignard und Stefan Saner, die sich beim Wettbewerb für diese Aufgabe gegen 363 Mitbewerber durchsetzen konnten, haben bei ihrem Entwurf auf das »Urmaterial« von Architektur vertraut, um einen sinnfälligen Begriff des frühmodernen deutschen Baumeisters Fritz Schumacher zu zitieren – auf Raum und Licht.

Ausgangspunkt für den Entwurf war die prominente Lage der Kapelle zwischen der Autobahn und dem Fluss Reuss. Weil sie ein einprägsamer ›Meilenstein‹ für die Autofahrer werden sollte, haben Guignard und Saner das Gebäude auf seine Fernwirkung hin konzipiert. Ein Element ist seine strenge kubische Gestalt mit dem regelmäßigen Fassadenbild, ein zweites das wechselnde

Guignard & Saner
Kapelle der Weltreligionen
chapel of World Religions
Gotthardpass / St Gotthard Pass, 1998

Friedrich Zwingmann
St. Christophorus / St Christophorus
Baden-Baden, 1978
Krypta / crypt

Wolfgang Jean Stock

A Sacred Milestone
Chapel of World Religions at the St Gotthard Pass

At first, the building presents a puzzle. Travellers on the Swiss highway across the St. Gotthard Pass suddenly catch a glimpse of a building that is difficult to read as they navigate a long right bend between the Erstfeld and Altdorf exits. Is the cube with its square openings punctured into the concrete skeleton a technical facility? Or is it a monument, as the greenish sheen in the windows may suggest? Perhaps the building is simply part of the adjacent highway stop and restaurant. At any rate, people are intrigued — and their questions are answered as soon as they pull into the car park: the building is an ecumenical chapel, christened 'Site of Contemplation on the Highway at Uri'. Anyone, who approaches this unusual architecture with an open mind will experience how convincingly the layout and design of the structure answer to the particular task.

Roadside Chapels

Many deride the 'roadside chapels' on European highways as an endearing but superannuated accessory. Some cannot even imagine that such locales may fulfil a need. They could hardly be more wrong. The more than twenty churches and chapels on the German highways alone (Catholic, Protestant or ecumenical) are visited by several million people each year. St Christophorus on the route from Karlsruhe to Basel on the edge of the Baden-Baden rest stop is a prime example. Designed by architect Friedrich Zwingmann in a distinctive, pyramidal tent form, it was completed in 1978. Its interior embodies the rejection of adornment in sacred spaces that is typical of the time. No doubt Emil Wachter's stunning monumental works on the exterior and his concrete bas-reliefs, which dominate the interior, play an important role in attracting the estimated 300,000 visitors each year. They are obviously unperturbed by the 'encrusted' appearance of the walls, sills, pews and ceilings in the church and crypt and allow themselves to be captivated by the narrative depictions. The esoterically inclined, especially, as the priest remarks, are fascinated to such a degree that they use the site for meditation.

Impact from a Distance

Completed twenty years later, in 1998, the highway chapel on the St Gotthard Pass stands in stark contrast to St Christophorus. Far from overwhelming with aesthetic opulence, its refreshing appeal lies in its reduced formal language. Two young Zurich architects Pascale Guignard and Stefan Saner won the competition for this project against a field of 363 participants. Their proposal paid homage to the 'primeval material' of architecture, to use an apposite phrase coined by Fritz Schumacher, a master of early German Modernism. In other words, the architects relied on space and light.

The initial impulse for the design was inspired by the prominent location of the chapel between the highway and the River Reuss. The brief called for a memorable 'milestone' for the drivers passing on the highway; to this end, Guignard and Saner conceived the building with a view to the impact it would have when seen from a distance. The first conceptual element is the severe cubic form itself in combination with the balanced façade image. Secondly, there is the changing play of light in the box-type windows filled with greenish glass shards: by day the square openings reflect the sunlight, by night the glazing, lit from the inside, transforms the structure into a mysterious illumi-

Friedrich Zwingmann
St. Christophorus / St Christophorus
Baden-Baden, 1978

Lichtspiel in den mit grünlichen Glasscherben gefüllten Kasten-
fenstern: Tagsüber reflektieren die quadratischen Öffnungen das
Sonnenlicht, bei Dunkelheit erzeugt die von innen illuminierte
Verglasung einen geheimnisvollen Leuchtkörper. Drittens heben
die Architekten ihre Materialwahl hervor: »Die Verwendung
von Ortbeton, Glas und Aluminium verleiht der Kapelle die nö-
tige Rauheit, um sich in dieser Berg- und Autobahnlandschaft
zu behaupten. Durch seine Stofflichkeit entspricht der Beton
auch dem Standort am Ufer der Reuss. Seine Oberflächen werden sich im Laufe der Zeit verändern, die Patina wird eine Spur
der Himmelsrichtungen und der Jahreszeiten hinterlassen.«

Kapelle der Weltreligionen

Auf dem Weg zum Andachtsraum gelangt man zunächst in einen Hof, der von einer hohen Betonmauer mit integrierten
Sitzbänken eingefasst ist, um den Verkehrslärm abzuhalten. So
kann sich der Besucher bereits hier auf die besondere Situation
einstimmen, wobei sein Blick über die Mauer hinweg immer
wieder in die großartige Alpenlandschaft gelenkt wird. Den
ökumenischen Grundgedanken der Kapelle unterstützt die sensible ›Kunst am Bau‹ von Clara Saner und Selma Weber. Wie
scheinbar vergessene Ritualgegenstände hängen über der Hof-
mauer übergroße Gebetsketten und -riemen, die gleichzeitig
mit der Mauer in Gestalt von Halbreliefs gegossen wurden. Die
fünf ›versteinerten‹ Objekte stehen für das Christentum, den
Islam, den Buddhismus und den Hinduismus sowie für den
jüdischen Glauben. Ergänzt wird die künstlerische Arbeit durch
eine Schrifttafel mit Zitaten aus den Büchern der Weltreligionen.

Guignard & Saner
Kapelle der Weltreligionen
chapel of World Religions
Gotthardpass / St Gotthard Pass, 1998
Innenraum / interior

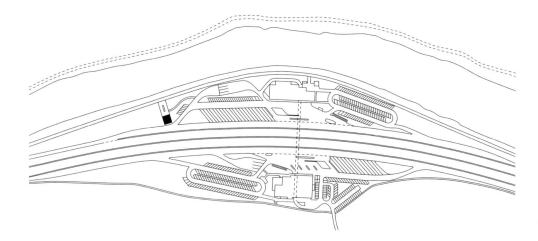

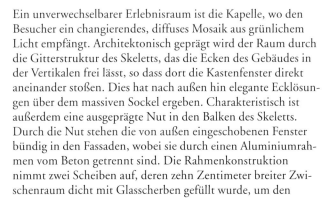

Lageplan
site plan

Ein unverwechselbarer Erlebnisraum ist die Kapelle, wo den
Besucher ein changierendes, diffuses Mosaik aus grünlichem
Licht empfängt. Architektonisch geprägt wird der Raum durch
die Gitterstruktur des Skeletts, das die Ecken des Gebäudes in
der Vertikalen frei lässt, so dass dort die Kastenfenster direkt
aneinander stoßen. Dies hat nach außen hin elegante Ecklösun-
gen über dem massiven Sockel ergeben. Charakteristisch ist
außerdem eine ausgeprägte Nut in den Balken des Skeletts.
Durch die Nut stehen die von außen eingeschobenen Fenster
bündig in den Fassaden, wobei sie durch einen Aluminiumrah-
men vom Beton getrennt sind. Die Rahmenkonstruktion
nimmt zwei Scheiben auf, deren zehn Zentimeter breiter Zwischenraum dicht mit Glasscherben gefüllt wurde, um den

nated body. And thirdly, the architects emphasise their choice of materials: 'The use of in-situ concrete, glass and aluminium invests the chapel with the ruggedness it needs to hold its own in the landscape of mountains and highway. The materiality of the concrete also corresponds to the location on the banks of the Reuss. The surfaces will gradually change over time, the patina will be a trace of exposure to the cardinal directions and the seasons'.

Chapel of World Religions

The path to the sanctuary leads first through a courtyard framed by a tall concrete wall with integrated benches, which provides a sound buffer from the traffic noise. This allows visitors to become attuned to the unique setting, catching glimpses, again and again, of the magnificent alpine landscape beyond the wall. The sensitive 'art for architecture' by Clara Saner and Selma Weber supports the ecumenical spirit of the chapel. Oversized rosaries and prayer beads, which were cast simultaneously with the wall in the shape of bas-relief, are suspended above the courtyard wall like forgotten ritual objects. The five 'petrified' objects symbolise Christianity, Islam, Buddhism, Hinduism and Judaism. The pieces are accompanied by a tablet inscribed with quotations from the books of the world religions.

The interior of the chapel is a unique experiential space, where the visitor is greeted by a changing, diffuse mosaic of greenish light. Architecturally, the space is characterised by the grid structure of the skeleton with exposed vertical edges so that the

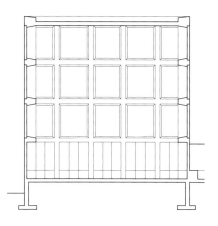

Schnitt Kapelle
section of chapel

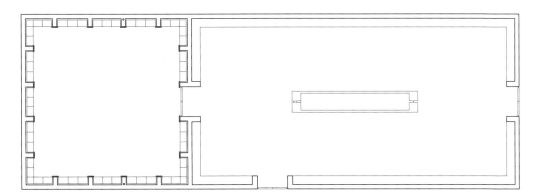

Grundriss
floor plan

windows join seamlessly at the corners. On the exterior, this has resulted in elegant corner solutions above the massive base. A pronounced joint in the beams of the skeleton is another distinctive feature: because of the joint, the windows — set into the walls from the outside — are flush with the façade level delineated by aluminium frames that separate them from the concrete walls. The frame holds two panes whose 10-centimeter-wide cavity is densely filled with glass shards to absorb the noise emanating from the highway. On the inside, the joint creates the impression that the glass surfaces are integrated directly into the skeleton, emphasising the lighting effect.

Locus of Silence

Otherwise, the tall sanctuary is nearly empty. The polished beech-panelled benches set into the walls and the showcase with an illuminated mountain crystal are the only indicators of the

Autobahnlärm zu schlucken. Nach innen hin sorgt die Nut
dafür, dass die Glasflächen direkt im Skelett zu sitzen scheinen,
was die Lichtwirkung verstärkt.

Ort der Stille

Ansonsten ist der hohe Andachtsraum nahezu leer. Lediglich
die mit poliertem Buchenholz verkleideten Sitzbänke in den
Wänden und die Vitrine mit einem beleuchteten Bergkristall
verweisen auf die sakrale Bestimmung des Ortes. Dem Besucher
sollen die Stille in Erinnerung bleiben und eine vom Licht er-
zeugte Atmosphäre, »die dem dichten Blätterdach in einem
Laubwald nahe kommt«. So ist es Guignard und Saner gelungen,
mit einfachen, aber intelligent eingesetzten Mitteln einen
Raum zu schaffen, der auch Nichtgläubige zur Besinnung ein-
lädt. Finanziert wurde diese konsequent moderne und zugleich
archaisch wirkende Kapelle durch Beiträge und Spenden von
Ämtern, Verbänden, Stiftungen, Firmen und Privatpersonen.

Guignard & Saner
Kapelle der Weltreligionen
chapel of World Religions
Gotthardpass / St Gotthard Pass, 1998

site's sacred function. The goal is to leave the visitor with a memory of silence and light, creating an ambience 'that resembles the dense canopy of leaves in a deciduous forest'. Guignard and Saner have intelligently employed simple means and succeeded in creating a space that invites even non-believers to contemplation. This rigorously modern and yet somehow archaic chapel was financed by contributions and donations from public sources, associations, foundations, as well as corporate and private donors.

Im Anhang sind die Ortsnamen
in der jeweiligen Landessprache
wiedergegeben.

In the appendices the place
names are quoted in the original
language.

Friedrich Achleitner
1930 in Schalchen, Oberösterreich, geboren. Architekturstudium bei Clemens Holzmeister an der Akademie der bildenden Künste in Wien, 1953 Diplom. Bis 1958 freier Architekt, seitdem freier Schriftsteller (Mitglied der ›wiener gruppe‹), Architekturkritiker und -publizist, Hochschullehrer, zuletzt Vorstand der Lehrkanzel für Geschichte und Theorie der Architektur an der Universität für angewandte Kunst in Wien. 1998 Emeritierung. Zahlreiche literarische Arbeiten und Publikationen zur Architektur, u.a. *Österreichische Architektur im 20. Jahrhundert* (1980–95, 4 Bände).

Fabrizio Brentini
Dr. phil., 1957 in Luzern geboren. 1977–82 und 1987–93 Studium der Theologie, Philosophie und Kunstgeschichte in Fribourg, Luzern und Zürich, 1994 Promotion. 1986–94 Präsident der Schweizerischen Lukasgesellschaft, in diesem Zusammenhang Organisation zahlreicher Tagungen und Ausstellungen zum Thema Kunst und Architektur im Kontext der Kirche. Lebt und arbeitet als Kunsthistoriker in Luzern. Zahlreiche Publikationen, u.a.: *Franz Bucher* (1993), *Bauen für die Kirche* (1994), *Hans-Peter von Ah* (1997), *Jo Achermann* (2000).

Marc Dubois
1950 im belgischen Ostende geboren. Architekturstudium am Hoger Architectuurinstituut Sint Lucas in Gent, Belgien, 1974 Diplom. Seit 1979 Professor an diesem Institut (WENK). Von 1986 bis 1994 Mitherausgeber der niederländischen Zeitschrift *ARCHIS*. Autor zahlreicher Publikationen und Mitherausgeber des flämischen Architektur-Jahrbuchs. Kurator mehrerer Architekturausstellungen, darunter über Architekten aus Flandern bei der Architektur-Biennale in Venedig 1991.

Albert Gerhards
Prof. Dr. theol., 1951 in Viersen geboren. Studien in Innsbruck, Rom und Trier. 1984–89 Professor für Liturgiewissenschaft an der Kath.-Theol. Fakultät der Universität Bochum. Seit 1989 in gleicher Position an der Universität Bonn, 1996–98 Dekan. 1985–98 Leiter der ›Arbeitsgruppe für Kirchliche Architektur und sakrale Kunst‹ (AKASK) der Liturgiekommission der Deutschen Bischofskonferenz. 1998–2002 Sprecher der Arbeitsgemeinschaft Katholischer Liturgiedozentinnen und -dozenten im deutschen Sprachgebiet. Zahlreiche Publikationen, besonders in den Bereichen Geschichte, Theologie und Praxis der Liturgie (Schwerpunkt: Eucharistisches Hochgebet, Judentum und Christentum), Ökumene, Kirchenmusik, Kirche und Kunst.

Winfried Nerdinger
Prof. Dr. phil., 1944 in Burgau geboren. Studium der Architektur und Kunstgeschichte, Promotion in Kunstgeschichte. 1980/81 Gastprofessur an der Harvard University. Professor für Architekturgeschichte und Direktor des Architekturmuseums der Technischen Universität München (seit Herbst 2002 mit eigenen Ausstellungsräumen in der Pinakothek der Moderne). Wissenschaftliche Leitung und Organisation zahlreicher Ausstellungen. Publikationen zur Kunst- und Architekturgeschichte des 18. bis 20. Jahrhunderts, zuletzt der Katalog zur Eröffnungsausstellung des Architekturmuseums in der Pinakothek der Moderne: *Exemplarisch. Konstruktion und Raum in der Architektur des 20. Jahrhunderts* (2002).

Riitta Nikula
Prof. Dr. phil., 1944 in Lahti, Finnland, geboren. Studium der Kunstgeschichte in Helsinki, Promotion 1981. 1982–88 Junior Research Fellow an der Finnischen Akademie. 1988–94 am Finnischen Architekturmuseum tätig, 1989–94 als stellvertretende Direktorin. Seit 1994 Professorin für Kunstgeschichte und Leiterin des Kunsthistorischen Instituts der Universität Helsinki. Zahlreiche Publikationen zur Kunstgeschichte sowie zu finnischer Architektur und Städtebau des 20. Jahrhunderts, u.a. Arbeiten über Armas Lindgren, Erik Bryggman und Alvar Aalto.

Wolfgang Pehnt
Prof. Dr. phil., 1931 in Kassel geboren. Architekturhistoriker und -kritiker. Studium der Germanistik, Kunstgeschichte und Philosophie, 1956 Promotion. Von 1957 bis 1963 Verlagslektor, anschließend bis 1995 leitender Kulturredakteur beim *Deutschlandfunk*. Lehrt seitdem Architekturgeschichte an der Ruhr-Universität Bochum. Lebt in Köln. Zahlreiche Veröffentlichungen zur Architektur des 19. und 20. Jahrhunderts, darunter Monografien über Rudolf Schwarz, Karljosef Schattner und Gottfried Böhm sowie das Standardwerk *Die Architektur des Expressionismus*.

Gabriele Schickel
Dr. phil., 1953 in Rosenheim geboren. Studium der Kunstgeschichte, Volkskunde und Archäologie in München. 1987–93 im Architekturmuseum der Technischen Universität München, 1993 an der Eidgenössischen Technischen Hochschule Zürich am Lehrstuhl für Geschichte des Städtebaus tätig. 1997 Lehrauftrag an der Hochschule für Technik in Stuttgart, Fachbereich Baugeschichte und Städtebau. 1999–2000 Bayerisches Nationalmuseum, München. Seitdem freie wissenschaftliche Autorin. Zahlreiche Aufsätze zur Architektur des 19. und 20. Jahrhunderts.

Horst Schwebel
Prof. Dr. Dr. h.c., 1940 in Frankfurt am Main geboren. Studium der Philosophie, Theologie und der Christlichen Archäologie in Frankfurt und Marburg. Seit 1980 Professor für Praktische Theologie an der Universität Marburg und Direktor des Instituts für Kirchenbau und kirchliche Kunst der Gegenwart. Publikationen zum Grenzbereich von Kunst und Theologie, zum Kirchenbau und zur Ikonographie der Religionen. 1997 Dr. theol. h.c. Universität Helsinki. Letzte Veröffentlichungen: *Die Kunst und das Christentum* (2002) und, gemeinsam mit Sigrid Glockzin-Bever, *Kirchen – Raum – Pädagogik* (2002).

Wolfgang Jean Stock
1948 in Aschaffenburg geboren. Studium der Neueren Geschichte, Politischen Wissenschaften und Soziologie in Frankfurt am Main und Erlangen. Nach wissenschaftlicher und journalistischer Tätigkeit von 1978 bis 1985 Direktor des Kunstvereins München. 1986–93 Architekturkritiker der *Süddeutschen Zeitung*, 1994–98 stv. Chefredakteur von *Baumeister*, Zeitschrift für Architektur. 1999 Chefredakteur der Zeitschrift *Der Architekt*. Seitdem freier Journalist und Buchautor in München. Veröffentlichungen zur Architektur, Stadtplanung, Denkmalpflege und Kunst im öffentlichen Raum. Mitherausgeber von *Architektur und Demokratie* ([2]1996).

Friedrich Achleitner
Born in 1930 in Schalchen, Upper Austria. He studied under Clemens Holzmeister at the Academy of Fine Arts in Vienna, gaining his degree in 1953. Achleitner worked as a freelance architect until 1958 when he became a freelance writer (member of the 'Vienna Group'), architecture critic and commentator, university lecturer and finally holds a chair in architecture history and theory at the University of Applied Arts in Vienna. He was made Emeritus Professor in 1998. He has written numerous works on architecture, including *Österreichische Architektur im 20. Jahrhundert* (1980–95, 4 vols.).

Fabrizio Brentini
Born in 1930 in Lucerne, Switzerland. Brentini studied theology, philosophy and art history in 1977–82 and 1987–93 in Fribourg, Lucerne and Zurich. He gained his doctorate in 1994. From 1986 to 1994 he was President of the Swiss Lukasgesellschaft and in this role he organised numerous conferences and exhibitions on the subject of art and architecture in a church context. He lives and works as an art historian in Lucerne. Among his many publications are: *Franz Bucher* (1993), *Bauen für die Kirche* (1994), *Hans-Peter von Ah* (1997), *Jo Achermann* (2000).

Marc Dubois
Born in 1950 in Ostend, Belgium, Dubois studied architecture at the Hoger Architectuurinstituut Sint Lucas in Ghent, gaining his degree in 1974. He has been Professor at this Institute (WENK) since 1979. From 1986 to 1994 he co-edited the Dutch journal *ARCHIS*. He is the author of numerous publications and co-editor of the Flemish architecture yearbook. He has curated many architectural exhibitions, among them on Flemish architects in the Venice architecture Biennale in 1991.

Albert Gerhards
Born in 1951 in Viersen, Germany. He studied at Innsbruck, Rome and Trier. From 1984 to 1989 he was Professor of Liturgical Studies at the Catholic Theological Faculty of the University of Bochum. Since 1989 he has held the same position at the University of Bonn, acting as Dean from 1996 to 1998. From 1985 to 1998 he led the Working Group on Church Architecture and Sacred Art (AKASK) of the liturgical commission of the German Bishops' Conference. Between 1998 and 2002 he was Spokesman for the Union of Catholic Liturgy Teachers in the German-speaking lands. He has published widely, particularly in the areas of history, theology and liturgical practice (with emphasis on eucharistic prayer, Judaism and Christianity), ecumenicism, church music, and the church and art.

Winfried Nerdinger
Born in Burgau, Germany, in 1944, he studied architecture and art history, receiving his doctorate in art history. In 1980/81 he was Visiting Professor at Harvard University. He is currently Professor of Architectural History and Director of the Architecture Museum of the Technical University in Munich (since autumn 2002 this is now housed in purpose-built rooms in the Pinakothek der Moderne). Nerdinger has conceived and organised numerous exhibitions. He has published on architectural and art history from the 18th to the 20th centuries, most recently the catalogue for the inaugural exhibition of the Architecture Museum in the Pinakothek der Moderne, *Exemplarisch. Konstruktion und Raum in der Architektur des 20. Jahrhunderts* (2002).

Riitta Nikula
Born in 1944 in Lahti, Finland. Nikula studied art history in Helsinki, gaining a doctorate in 1981. From 1982 to 1988 she was a Junior Research Fellow at the Finnish Academy, and from 1988 to 1994 she worked at the Finnish Architecture Museum, as Acting Director from 1989 to 1994. Since 1994 she has been Professor of Art History and Director of the Art History Institute of the University of Helsinki. She has published widely on art history, and on 20th-century Finnish architecture and urbanism. Her works include monographs on Armas Lindgren, Erik Bryggman and Alvar Aalto.

Wolfgang Pehnt
Born in 1931 in Kassel, Germany. He is an architectural historian and critic. He studied German, art history and philosophy, gaining his doctorate in 1956. From 1957 to 1963 he worked in publishing as an editor, culminating finally in 1995 as Head of Arts at German Radio. Since then he has taught architectural history at the Ruhr University in Bochum. He lives in Cologne. He has published many works on 19th- and 20th-century architecture, including monographs on Rudolf Schwarz, Karljosef Schattner and Gottfried Böhm, as well as the standard work, *Die Architektur des Expressionismus*.

Gabriele Schickel
Born in 1953 in Rosenheim, Germany, Schickel studied art history, folklore and archaeology in Munich. From 1987 to 1993 she worked at the Architecture Museum of the Technical University in Munich, and in 1993 she taught history of urbanism at the Technical University in Zurich. In 1997 Schickel lectured at the Technical University in Stuttgart in the areas of building and urbanism. From 1999 to 2000 she worked at the Bavarian National Museum in Munich, and since then has been a freelance technical author. She has written many essays on 19th- and 20th-century architecture.

Horst Schwebel
Born in 1940 in Frankfurt am Main, Germany. He studied philosophy, theology and the archaeology of Christianity in Frankfurt and Marburg. Since 1980 he has been Professor of Theological Practice at the University of Marburg and Director of the Institute of Church Architecture and Contemporary Church Art. He has published on the links between art and theology, on Church architecture and on the iconography of religion. In 1997 he was made a Doctor of Theology Honoris Causa at the University of Helsinki. His most recent publications are: *Die Kunst und das Christentum* (2002) and with Sigrid Glockzin-Bever, *Kirchen – Raum – Pädagogik* (2002).

Wolfgang Jean Stock
Born in 1948 in Aschaffenburg, Germany. He studied modern history, political science and sociology at Frankfurt am Main and Erlangen. After a period in academia and journalism Stock served as Director of the Kunstverein in Munich from 1978 to 1985. Between 1986 and 1993 he was architectural critic of the *Süddeutsche Zeitung*, and from 1994 to 1998 acting editor-in-chief of *Baumeister. Zeitschrift für Architektur*. In 1999 he became editor-in-chief of *Der Architekt*. Since then he has been a freelance journalist and author in Munich. He has published on architecture, city planning, preservation of historic monuments and public art. He is co-editor of *Architektur und Demokratie* (second edition, 1996).

u = unten / below; o = oben / above
r = rechts / right; l = links / left; M = Mitte / centre

Die nicht namentlich benannten
Fotos sind uns freundlicherweise von
Architekten, Diözesen, Pfarrämtern,
Universitäten und den Archiven der
Architekturmuseen zur Verfügung ge-
stellt worden.

Any photographs not listed here were
kindly supplied by the relevant architects, parish offices, universities and
architectural museums.

Impressum / Colophon

Die Deutsche Bibliothek verzeichnet diese Publikation in der Deutschen Nationalbibliografie; detaillierte bibliografische Daten sind im Internet über ‹http://dnb.ddb.de› abrufbar.

Die Deutsche Bibliothek lists this publication in the Deutsche Nationalbibliografie; detailed bibliographic data is available on the Internet at ‹http://dnb.ddb.de›

Library of Congress Control Number:
2002 11 3041

© Prestel Verlag, München / Munich ·
Berlin · London · New York 2002
2. durchgesehene Auflage /
2nd revised edition 2003

Prestel Verlag
Königinstraße 9
D-80539 München
Tel. (089) 38 17 09-0
Fax (089) 38 17 09-35
www.prestel.de

Prestel Publishing Ltd.
4 Bloomsbury Place
London
WC1A 2QA
Tel. (020) 7323 5004
Fax (020) 7636 8004

Prestel Publishing
175 Fifth Avenue, Suite 402
New York
NY 10010
Tel. (212) 995 2720
Fax (212) 995 2733

www.prestel.com

Prestel books are available worldwide. Please contact your nearest bookseller or any of the above addresses for information concerning your local distributor.

Lektorat / Editors:
Gabriele Ebbecke, Stella Sämann
Mitarbeit / Editorial Assistance:
Birgit Schmolke
Übersetzung Deutsch–Englisch
Translation German–English:
Jenny Marsh, Elizabeth Schwaiger
(Essays)
Übersetzung Englisch–Deutsch
Translation English–German
(Essays Dubois und / and Nikula):
Christiane Court
Bildrecherche / Picture research:
Beatrix Birken, Mechthild Otto,
Birgit Schmolke

ISBN 3-7913-2744-5

Visuelles Konzept und Gestaltung
Visual concept and design:
Schwaiger Winschermann, München
Elena und Walter Schwaiger, Alfred Kern
Systemtechnik / Technical support:
Thomas Schatzl
Neuzeichnung Pläne / Revised drawings:
Florian Lechner

Produktion / Production:
Matthias Hauer
Lithographie / Lithography:
Repro Ludwig, Zell am See
Druck / Printing: Sellier, Freising
Bindung / Binding:
Conzella, Pfarrkirchen

Gesetzt aus der / Set in:
agBuch BQ, Adobe Garamond

Gedruckt auf chlorfrei gebleichtem
Papier / Printed on acid-free paper
Printed in Germany

Umschlag-Vorderseite / Front jacket:
Vuoksenniska Kirche / Church,
Seite / page 232
Frontispiz / Frontispiece:
Pastoor van Ars Kirche / Church,
Seite / page 128